THE CAMBRIDGE COMPANI
LITERATURE AND SCIEN

In 1959, C. P. Snow lamented the presence of what he ʻ
the apparently unbridgeable chasm of understanding ..... knowledge between
modern literature and modern science. In recent decades, scholars have worked
diligently and often with great ingenuity to interrogate claims like Snow's that
represent twentieth and twenty-first-century literature and science as radically
alienated from each other. *The Cambridge Companion to Literature and Science*
offers a roadmap to developments that have contributed to the demonstration
and emergence of reciprocal connections between the two domains of inquiry.
Weaving together theory and empiricism, individual chapters explore major
figures – Shakespeare, Bacon, Emerson, Darwin, Henry James, William James,
Whitehead, Einstein, Empson, McClintock; major genres and modes of writing –
fiction, science fiction, non-fiction prose, poetry, dramatic works; and major
theories and movements – pragmatism, critical theory, science studies, cognitive
science, ecocriticism, cultural studies, affect theory, digital humanities, expanded
empiricisms. This book will be a key resource for scholars, graduate students,
and undergraduate students alike.

Steven Meyer is Associate Professor of English at Washington University in
St. Louis. He is the author of *Irresistible Dictation: Gertrude Stein and the
Correlations of Writing and Science* (2001). He has co-edited a special issue of
Configurations on the surge of interest in Whitehead's "process philosophy"
among practitioners of science studies and Literature and Science. He recently
served on the Executive Committee of the MLA Division on Literature and
Science (2011–16; chair, 2014–15). He has also been awarded fellowships by
Yale's Whitney Humanities Center, the Stanford Humanities Center, and
Rutger's Center for Cultural Analysis.

A complete list of books in the series is at the back of this book.

THE CAMBRIDGE
COMPANION TO
LITERATURE AND SCIENCE

EDITED BY
STEVEN MEYER
Washington University in St. Louis

CAMBRIDGE
UNIVERSITY PRESS

University Printing House, Cambridge CB2 8BS, United Kingdom

One Liberty Plaza, 20th Floor, New York, NY 10006, USA

477 Williamstown Road, Port Melbourne, VIC 3207, Australia

314–321, 3rd Floor, Plot 3, Splendor Forum, Jasola District Centre, New Delhi – 110025, India

79 Anson Road, #06–04/06, Singapore 079906

Cambridge University Press is part of the University of Cambridge.

It furthers the University's mission by disseminating knowledge in the pursuit of education, learning, and research at the highest international levels of excellence.

www.cambridge.org
Information on this title: www.cambridge.org/9781107079724
DOI: 10.1017/9781139942096

© Cambridge University Press 2018

First published 2018

Printed in the United States of America by Sheridan Books, Inc.

A catalogue record for this publication is available from the British Library.

Library of Congress Cataloging-in-Publication Data
NAMES: Meyer, Steven, 1959– editor.
TITLE: The Cambridge companion to literature and science / edited by Steven Meyer, Washington University, St Louis.
DESCRIPTION: New York : Cambridge University Press, 2017. | Series: Cambridge companions to literature | Includes bibliographical references and index.
IDENTIFIERS: LCCN 2017028550 | ISBN 9781107079724 (hardback) | ISBN 9781107439030 (paperback)
SUBJECTS: LCSH: Literature and science. | Literature and techology. | Science in literature. | Technology in literatuare. | Literature, Modern – History and criticism.
CLASSIFICATION: LCC PN55 .M48 2017 | DDC 809/.9336–dc23
LC record available at https://lccn.loc.gov/2017028550

ISBN 978-1-107-07972-4 Hardback
ISBN 978-1-107-43903-0 Paperback

And the triumph of empiricism is jeopardized by the surprising truth that our sense data are primarily symbols.

Susanne K. Langer, *Philosophy in a New Key*
[as cited in *Elaine's Book* by Jay Wright]

CONTENTS

CONTRIBUTORS

TIM ARMSTRONG is Head of the Department of English at Royal Holloway, University of London. His publications include *The Logic of Slavery: Debt, Technology and Pain in American Literature* (2012), *Modernism: A Cultural History* (2005), *Haunted Hardy: Poetry, History, Memory* (2000), and *Modernism, Technology and the Body* (1998). He edits the Edinburgh Critical Studies in Modernist Culture series. His current project, *Micromodernism*, is a study of modernist localism.

JAMES J. BONO is Associate Professor of History and Medicine at the University at Buffalo; past president of the Society for Literature, Science, and the Arts; and founding editor of *Configurations*. He is author of *The Word of God and the Languages of Man: Interpreting Nature in Early Modern Science and Medicine*, vol. 1 (1995), *Ficino to Descartes* (vol. 2, *England, 1640–1670*, forthcoming) and co-editor of *Ethical Issues in Health Care on the Frontiers of the Twenty-First Century* and *A Time for the Humanities: Futurity and the Limits of Autonomy* (2008). He has been a member of the Institute for Advanced Study, an Eccles Fellow at the Tanner Humanities Center, a recipient of several National Science Foundation grants, and a National Endowment for the Humanities Senior Fellow at the Folger Shakespeare Library. *Figuring Science: Metaphor, Narrative, and Scientific Practices* and *Imagining Nature: Technologies of the Literal, the Scientific Revolution, and Visual Cultures of Early Modern Science* are in progress.

MARY BAINE CAMPBELL is Professor Emerita of English, Comparative Literature, and Women's, Gender, and Sexuality Studies at Brandeis University. Scholarly books concerned with the junction of knowledge and imagination include *The Witness and the Other World: Exotic European Travel Writing, 400–1600* (1988 and 1992) and *Wonder and Science: Imagining Worlds in Early Modern Europe* (1999 and 2004, winner of the Modern Language Association's James Russell Lowell Prize). She has also published two volumes of poetry: *The World, the Flesh and Angels* (1988, winner of the Barnard New Women Poets Prize) and *Trouble* (2003). More recently she has been writing on the dream culture of the early modern Atlantic, especially in Old and New England and France.

T. HUGH CRAWFORD is Associate Professor of Science, Technology, and Culture Studies at the Georgia Institute of Technology. Former editor of *Configurations* and past president of the Society for Literature, Science and the Arts, he is author of *Modernism, Medicine, and William Carlos Williams* (1993) and is currently writing on philosophy, literature, and walking.

WAI CHEE DIMOCK has written on American literature of every period, from Anne Bradstreet to Star Trek. She argues for a broad conception of literature that embraces a variety of timeframes and brings together materials both high and low, and scales both local and global. Editor of *PMLA* and a film critic for the *Los Angeles Review of Books*, her essays have also appeared in *Critical Inquiry*, the *Chronicle of Higher Education*, the *New York Times*, and the *New Yorker*. She is now working on two book projects, *Weak Theory: Low-Bar Networks, Fuzzy Genres, Minimal Criticism* and *Low Epic: Recycled Forms and Nonhuman Life*.

ADAM FRANK'S essays on affect, media, and American literature have appeared in *ELH, Criticism, Critical Inquiry, Science in Context* and elsewhere. He is the author of *Transferential Poetics, from Poe to Warhol* (2015), the co-editor (with Eve Kosofsky Sedgwick) of *Shame and Its Sisters: A Silvan Tomkins Reader* (1995), and co-author (with Elizabeth Wilson) of *A Silvan Tomkins Handbook* (forthcoming). He has produced two full-length recorded audio-dramas, *Overpass! A Melodrama* (2007) and *Some Mad Scientists* (2010). Current research includes the *Radio Free Stein* project (www.radiofreestein.com). He is Professor in the Department of English and Co-chair of the Graduate Program in Science and Technology Studies at the University of British Columbia.

DEVIN GRIFFITHS is Assistant Professor in the English Department at the University of Southern California. His research examines the intersection of intellectual history, scientific literature, and the digital humanities, with emphasis on nineteenth-century British literature and science. Central to his work is the question of how literary form shapes our experience of time and natural systems. His book, *The Age of Analogy: Science and Literature between the Darwins* (2016), rethinks analogy in order to examine how historical novels furnished a relational understanding of history and helped to shape the disciplinary formations of both the life sciences and the humanities. He is working on two additional studies, *The Ecology of Form*, which adapts Darwinian theory to the study of literary forms, and *The Radical Catalogue*, which explores the science of order that organized nineteenth-century print and natural history collections and laid the foundation for modern information technologies.

TIM LENOIR is Distinguished Professor of Science and Technology Studies and of Cinema and Digital Media at University of Califorina, Davis. He has published several books and articles on the history of biomedical science from the nineteenth century to the present and on the roles of federal programs and university-industry collaborations in stimulating innovation in several areas of science, technology, and medicine. Lenoir has also published a number of recent studies on computational media and human technogenesis, including an extended essay, "Contemplating Singularity," an edited e-book, *Neurofutures* (2011), and essays in the area of game studies. With Luke Caldwell, Lenoir is co-author of *The Military Entertainment Complex* (2016).

STEVEN MEYER teaches intellectual history and modern and contemporary literature at Washington University in St. Louis. He is the author of *Irresistible Dictation: Gertrude Stein and the Correlations of Writing and Science* (2001) and co-editor with Elizabeth Wilson of the special issue of *Configurations* on "Whitehead Now" (2005). Currently he is completing *Robust Empiricisms: Jamesian Modernism between the Disciplines, 1878 to the Present*, a cross-disciplinary account of investigations in literature, literary criticism, philosophy, science studies, and the sciences – all within the robust empiricist lineage initiated by William James and Alfred North Whitehead and involving the development of techniques for eliciting something where, from the perspective of more traditional empiricisms, there appears to be nothing. He has published a half-dozen essays from this project, including "Of 'Experiential Togetherness': Toward a More Robust Empiricism" in *The Lure of Whitehead* (2014) and "Systematizing Emerson, Supplementing Whitehead: Reading Whitehead with Stengers" in *Process Studies* (2008).

REVIEL NETZ is Patrick Suppes Professor in Greek Mathematics and Astronomy and Professor of Classics at Stanford. He has published widely in Greek and premodern mathematics, and *The Shaping of Deduction in Greek Mathematics: A Study in Cognitive History* (1999) won the Runciman Prize for 2000. He is also the author of a projected three-volume translation and commentary of the works of Archimedes; the first, *The Two Books on the Sphere and the Cylinder*, appeared in 2004. With Nigel Wilson he is preparing an edition of the recently discovered Archimedes Palimpsest, and his popular account of the Archimedes Palimpsest Project, *The Archimedes Codex* (2007, co-authored with William Noel) was awarded the Neumann Prize. An interest in ecological history resulted in *Barbed Wire: An Ecology of Modernity* (2004), and together with his wife, the Israeli author Maya Arad, he has published a collection of essays on Israeli literature, *Positions of Stress* (2008).

KITT PRICE teaches modern and contemporary literature at Queen Mary University, London. kitt has published essays on William Empson's early metaphysical poetry, and a book inspired by Empson's reading of modern physics: *Loving Faster than Light: Romance and Readers in Einstein's Universe* (2012). Note to reviewers: kitt prefers to be referred to with gender-neutral pronouns (they / their / them).

ALAN RICHARDSON is Professor of English at Boston College. His books include *British Romanticism and the Science of the Mind* (2001) and *The Neural Sublime: Cognitive Theories and Romantic Texts* (2011). He is co-editor, with Francis Steen, of a special issue of *Poetics Today* on "Literature and the Cognitive Revolution" (2002) and, with Ellen Spolsky, of *The Work of Fiction: Cognition, Culture, and Complexity* (2004). His current research concerns literary and scientific conceptions of imagination from Romanticism to the present.

JOAN RICHARDSON is Distinguished Professor at The Graduate Center, City University of New York. Author of a two-volume critical biography of Wallace Stevens, she also co-edited *Wallace Stevens: Collected Poetry and Prose* (1997). Essays on Stevens, Emerson, Edwards, William James, Whitehead, and Cavell have appeared widely in journals and collections. *A Natural History of Pragmatism: The Fact of Feeling from Jonathan Edwards to Gertrude Stein*, published by Cambridge in 2007, was followed by *Pragmatism and American Experience* in 2014. In 2017 her *How to Live. What to Do: Thirteen Ways of Looking at Wallace Stevens* will be published. She has received several awards including a Woodrow Wilson Fellowship, a Senior Fellowship from the National Endowment for the Humanities, and a Guggenheim Fellowship for her current project, *Images, Shadows of Divine Things*, an experiment in secular spiritual autobiography. Her work examines the ways philosophy, natural history, and science intersect with literature.

HAUN SAUSSY is University Professor at the University of Chicago. His books include *The Problem of a Chinese Aesthetic* (1993), *Great Walls of Discourse and Other Adventures in Cultural China* (2001), *The Ethnography of Rhythm: Orality and its Technologies* (2016), *Translation as Citation: Zhuangzi Inside Out* (2017), and, as editor or co-editor, *Comparative Literature in an Age of Globalization* (2006), *Sinographies: Writing China* (2007), *Fenollosa/Pound, The Chinese Written Character as a Medium for Poetry: A Critical Edition* (2009), *Partner to the Poor: A Paul Farmer Reader* (2010), and *A Book to Burn and a Book to Keep Hidden: Selected Writings of Li Zhi* (2016).

ISABELLE STENGERS is Professor at the Free University of Brussels, and author and co-author of more than two dozen books. Single-author works (in translation) include *Power and Invention: Situating Science* (1997), *The Invention of Modern Science* (2000), *Cosmopolitics I and II* (2010/11), *Thinking with Whitehead* (2011), and *In Catastrophic Times: Resisting the Coming Barbarism* (2015). Jointly authored works include *Order Out of Chaos: Man's New Dialogue with Nature* (1984, with Nobel-Prize winner Ilya Prigogine), *A Critique of Psychoanalytic Reason: Hypnosis as a Scientific Problem from Lavoisier to Lacan* (1992, with Leon Chertok), and *Capitalist Sorcery: Breaking the Spell* (2011, with Philippe Pignarre).

Among other honors, she has received the 1993 Grand Prize in Philosophy from the Académie Française, the 2010 FNRS Ernest-John Solvay Scientific Prize in Human and Social Sciences, and, for *Cosmopolitics*, the 2013 Ludwick Fleck Prize from the Society for Social Studies of Science for the best book in science and technology studies.

Premodern

Fourth century BCE	first collection recorded of the Fables of Aesop (sixth century BCE)
c. third century BCE	assemblage of Sanskrit animal tales in the *Panchatantra*
c. 225 BCE	Archimedes, *On the Sphere and the Cylinder*
First century BCE	Lucretius, *De Rerum Natura* [*On the Nature of Things*]
Fourth century CE	Oribasius canonizes Galen's (first century CE) medical writings
Twelfth century CE	translation into Latin of al-Khwārizmī's ninth-century CE account of Hindu arithmetic with its positional decimal numeral system ("algorism" is a corruption of the Persian author's name, just as "algebra" is derived from the name of a key procedure in another influential treatise by al-Khwārizmī)

Early Modern

c. 1594	William Shakespeare, *A Midsummer Night's Dream*
1610–11	William Shakespeare, *The Tempest*
1620	Francis Bacon, *Novum Organon*
1627	Francis Bacon, *The New Atlantis*
1632–3	Galileo, *Dialogue on the Two Chief World Systems, Ptolemaic and Copernican*; trial and condemnation by the Catholic Inquisition
1665	founding of the Royal Society in London Robert Hooke, *Micrographia*

1667   Thomas Sprat, *History of the Royal Society*
1687   Isaac Newton, *Philosophiae Naturalis Principia Mathematica*
1690   John Locke, *An Essay Concerning Human Understanding*

Eighteenth and Nineteenth Centuries

1775   Sanskrit *Fables of Pilpay* translated into English
1778   Lavoisier isolates and names oxygen
1791–3/4   Wordsworth lives in revolutionary France; Lavoisier guillotined
1800–2   Wordsworth writes "Preface" to *Lyrical Ballads*
1810   Johann Wolfgang von Goethe, *Theory of Colors*
1836   Ralph Waldo Emerson, "Nature"
1840   William Whewell, *The Philosophy of the Inductive Sciences*
1841–4   Ralph Waldo Emerson, "The Method of Nature"; "Circles"; "Experience"
1854   Henry D. Thoreau, *Walden*
1859   Charles Darwin, *On the Origin of Species*
1862   Max Müller, *Lectures on the Science of Language*
1865–6   William James accompanies naturalist and creationist Louis Agassiz on expedition to Brazil
1869   Henry James Sr., *The Secret of Swedenborg: Being an Elucidation of His Doctrine of the Divine Natural Humanity*
1871   Charles Darwin, *The Descent of Man*
1881   Thomas Henry Huxley, *Science and Culture*
1882   Matthew Arnold, "Literature and Science"
1883   Wilhelm Dilthey, *Introduction to the Human Sciences*
1884   Henry James, "The Art of Fiction"
1890   William James, *The Principles of Psychology*
1894   Charles S. Peirce, "What Is a Sign?"
1895   Wilhelm Röntgen detects and names X-rays; H. G. Wells, *The Time Machine*

Twentieth Century

1904   William James, "The Experience of Activity"; "Does 'Consciousness' Exist?"; "A World of Pure Experience"
1905   Albert Einstein, "On the Electrodynamics of Moving Bodies" (on the special theory of relativity)

1907	William James, *Pragmatism: A New Name for Some Old Ways of Thinking*
1910	H. G. Wells, *The Sleeper Awakes*
1915	Albert Einstein, "The Field Equation of Gravitation" (on the general theory of relativity)
1916	Ferdinand de Saussure, *Course in General Linguistics*
1917–26	A separate School of English is established at Cambridge University
1919	Eddington leads expedition to Africa to witness solar eclipse and test Einstein's predictions for the bending of light around the Sun
1923–31	*Today & Tomorrow* book series at Kegan Paul
1923	J. B. S. Haldane, *Daedalus, or Science and the Future*
1924	I. A. Richards, *Principles of Literary Criticism*
1925	Alfred North Whitehead, *Science and the Modern World*
1926	I. A. Richards, *Science and Poetry*
1927	J. B. S. Haldane, *Possible Worlds and Other Essays*
1928	Arthur Eddington, *The Nature of the Physical World*
1928–9	William Empson, "Relativity" ["The World's End"]; "Letter I"; "The Ants"; "Camping Out"
1929	I. A. Richards, *Practical Criticism*; Alfred North Whitehead, *Process and Reality*
1929–30	H. G. Wells, Julian Huxley, and G. P. Wells, *The Science of Life: A Summary of Contemporary Knowledge about Life and Its Possibilities*
c. 1929–35	William Empson, "Doctrinal Point"
1931	John Hargrave, *The Imitation Man*
1936	Wallace Stevens, "The Irrational Element in Poetry"
1939	Establishment of the Division for Literature and Science, MLA
1942	Julian Huxley, *Evolution: The Modern Synthesis*
1946	Marjorie Hope Nicolson, *Newton Demands the Muse: Newton's Opticks and the 18th Century Poets*
1953	Watson and Crick establish structure of DNA
1956	Marjorie Hope Nicolson, *Science and Imagination*
1957	William Empson, "Donne the Space Man"
1959	C. P. Snow, *The Two Cultures and the Scientific Revolution*
1962	Thomas Kuhn, *The Structure of Scientific Revolutions*; Silvan S. Tomkins, *Affect Imagery Consciousness, vol. 1, The Positive Affects*; Wilfred Bion, *Learning from Experience*
1963	Aldous Huxley, *Literature and Science*

1987–2000   *Science and Literature* book series at University of Wisconsin Press

1987   Inaugural conference of the Society for Literature and Science; George Levine, "One Culture: Science and Literature"; Bruno Latour, *Science in Action*; Gilles Deleuze and Félix Guattari, *A Thousand Plateaus: Capitalism and Schizophrenia* [1980, in French]

1988   George Levine, *Darwin and the Novelists: Patterns of Science in Victorian Fiction*; Donna J. Haraway, "Situated Knowledges: The Science Question in Feminism and the Privilege of Partial Perspective"

1989   Donna J. Haraway, *Primate Visions: Gender, Race, and Nature in the World of Modern Science*

1990   Establishment of Center for Interdisciplinary Studies in Science and Cultural Theory at Duke University; Friedrich Kittler, *Discourse Networks 1800/1900*; Mary Jacobus, Evelyn Fox Keller, and Sally Shuttleworth, eds., *Body/Politics: Women and the Discourses of Science*

1991–2011   *Studies in Literature and Science* book series at University of Michigan Press

1991   Franciso J. Varela, Evan T. Thompson, and Eleanor Rosch, *The Embodied Mind: Cognitive Science and Human Experience*

1992   Léon Chertok and Isabelle Stengers, *A Critique of Psychoanalytic Reason: Hypnosis as a Scientific Problem from Lavoisier to Lacan* [1989, in French]; Andrew Pickering, ed., *Science as Practice and Culture*; Evelyn Fox Keller, *Secrets of Life, Secrets of Death: Essays on Language, Gender and Science*

1993   Joseph Rouse, "What Are Cultural Studies of Scientific Knowledge?"; George Levine, ed., *Realism and Representation: Essays on the Problem of Realism in Science, Literature and Culture* (including "Constrained Constructivism: Locating Scientific Inquiry in the Theater of Representation" by N. Katherine Hayles); Bruno Latour, *We Have Never Been Modern* [1991, in French]; Brian Rotman, *Signifying Nothing: The Semiotics of Zero*; Ellen Spolsky, *Gaps in Nature: Literary Interpretation and the Modular Mind*

1994–2008   *Writing Science* book series at Stanford University Press

1994–   C. J. Cherryh, *The Foreigner Universe*

1994   Hans Ulrich Gumbrecht and Karl Ludwig Pfeiffer, eds., *Materialities of Communication*; Susan Merrill Squier, *Babies in Bottles: Twentieth-Century Visions of Reproductive Technology*

1995   S. L. Pimm, G. J. Russell, J. L. Gittleman, and T. M. Brooks, "The Future of Biodiversity"; Edwin Hutchins, *Cognition in the Wild*; Ian Hacking, *Rewriting the Soul: Multiple Personality and the Sciences of Memory*; Andrew Pickering, *The Mangle of Practice: Time, Agency, and Science*; Eve Kosofsky Sedgwick and Adam Frank, "Shame in the Cybernetic Fold: Reading Silvan Tomkins"; Brian Massumi's "The Autonomy of Affect"; James J. Bono, "Locating Narratives: Science, Metaphor, Communities, and Epistemic Styles"

1996   *Social Text* publishes Alan Sokal's "Transgressing the Boundaries"; Gillian Beer, *Open Fields: Science in Cultural Encounter*; Peter Galison and David J. Stump, *The Disunity of Science: Boundaries, Contexts, and Power*; Niklas Luhmann, *Social Systems* [1984, in German]

1997   David Abram, *The Spell of the Sensuous: Perception and Language in a More-Than-Human World*; Hans-Jörg Rheinberger, *Toward a History of Epistemic Things: Synthesizing Proteins in the Test Tube*; Peter Galison, *Image and Logic: The Material Culture of Twentieth-Century Physics*

1998   Jan Golinski, *Making Natural Knowledge: Constructivism and the History of Science*; Timothy Lenoir, ed., *Inscribing Science: Scientific Texts and the Materiality of Communication*; Andy Clark and David J. Chalmers, "The Extended Mind"; Tim Armstrong, *Modernism, Technology and the Body*

1999   Mario Biagioli, ed., *The Science Studies Reader*; Bruno Latour, *Pandora's Hope: Essays on the Reality of Science Studies*; Geoffrey C. Bowker and Susan Leigh Star, *Sorting Things Out: Classification and Its Consequences*; Katharine Park, "Natural Particulars: Epistemology, Practice, and the Literature of Healing Springs"; Mary Campbell Baine, *Wonder and Science: Imagining Worlds in Early Modern Europe*; Reviel Netz, *The Shaping of Deduction in Greek Mathematics: A Study in Cognitive History*; N. Katherine Hayles, *How We Became Posthuman: Virtual Bodies in*

Cybernetics, Literature, and Informatics; Friedrich Kittler, *Gramophone Film Typewriter*; Jean Petitot, Francisco J. Varela, Bernard Pachoud, and Jean-Michel Roy, eds., *Naturalizing Phenomenology: Issues in Contemporary Phenomenology and Cognitive Science*

Twenty-First Century

2000–10   *Science and Cultural Theory* book series at Duke University Press

2000   Isabelle Stengers, *The Invention of Modern Science* [*Invention des sciences modernes*, 1993]; Brian Rotman, *Mathematics as Sign: Writing, Imagining, Counting*; Franco Moretti, "Conjectures on World Literature"; Mark Hansen, *Embodying Technesis: Technology Beyond Writing*

2001   James J. Bono, "Why Metaphor? Toward a Metaphorics of Scientific Practice"; Steven Meyer, *Irresistible Dictation: Gertrude Stein and the Correlations of Writing and Science*; Michael Whitworth, *Einstein's Wake: Relativity, Metaphor, and Modernist Literature*; Mary Thomas Crane, *Shakespeare's Brain: Reading with Cognitive Theory*; Alan Richardson, *British Romanticism and the Science of the Mind*

2002   Pamela Gossin, ed., *The Encyclopedia of Literature and Science*; Rodney Brooks, *Flesh and Machines: How Robots Will Change Us*; David A. Mindell, *Between Human and Machine: Feedback, Control and Computing before Cybernetics*; Brian Massumi, *Parables for the Virtual: Movement, Affect, Sensation*; Ellen Spolsky, "Darwin and Derrida: Cognitive Literary Theory as a Species of Post-Structuralism"

2003   Bruno Latour, "The Promises of Constructivism"; Andy Clark, "Magic Words: How Language Augments Human Computation"; Ursula Le Guin, *Changing Planes*; Laura Dassow Walls, *Emerson's Life in Science: The Culture of Truth*; Donna J. Haraway, *A Companion Species Manifesto: Dogs, People, and Significant Otherness*

2004   Bruno Latour, "Why Has Critique Run out of Steam? From Matters of Fact to Matters of Concern"; Alan Richardson, "Studies in Literature and Cognition: A Field Map"

2005   Bruno Latour, *Reassembling the Social: An Introduction to Actor-Network-Theory*; Isabelle Stengers, "The Cosmopolitical Proposal"; James J. Bono, "Perception,

STEVEN MEYER

Introduction

Over the past four decades, and in ongoing dialogue with science studies, the innovative interdisciplinary field of Literature and Science has become a dynamic platform for investigation into the many ways that the humanities and sciences share (1) a fundamentally pluralistic outlook; (2) common cultures, discourses, and practices; and (3) a commitment to expanding the range and capabilities of empiricist approaches. The fourteen essays in *The Cambridge Companion to Literature and Science* supply an integrated set of accounts of this multilevel undertaking through a rich portrayal of the interweaving of theory and practice in recent scholarship as well as of the historical expansion of empiricism to which Literature and Science itself contributes.

The *Companion* is designed, in the first instance, for undergraduates and graduate students in an academic setting where students increasingly major in the sciences, especially the life sciences, and often specialize earlier. Also nonscience majors are more likely to be exposed to introductory biology courses, which, it has been argued, are assuming the unifying role in the curriculum formerly played by core humanities courses.[1] The volume should appeal to the smart undergraduate in academics at any stage in their careers. Although humanities faculty are likely to be less familiar with the sciences than their students, in a world increasingly mediated by technoscience it may be expected that many will wish to know more about how the sciences and humanities inform one another, and so will want to grasp the essentials of this still emerging field. Much material in the *Companion* will be unfamiliar to most practicing scientists, yet because investigations of scientific practice occupy the central ground of the discipline, they may find themselves pleasantly engaged. Nonacademics are invited to join in the fun – this is your world too!

Because Literature and Science today is not what it was, it is probably not what you think it is. In the first place it both is and is not a branch of another interdiscipline, science studies or the sociology of science. Understood simply enough as a matter of "studying science" and consequently as being at once "unified (in terms of its object of study) and strongly disunified (in terms of its methodologies, research questions, and institutional locations)," science studies has offered one of the most exciting arenas for academic investigation over the past three decades.[2] Mario Biagioli goes on to emphasize a feature of science studies that accounts for a good deal of the ferment and excitement: "As science studies produces more empirical work, it further 'disunifies' itself methodologically while producing increasingly complex and 'disunified' pictures of science, *a double trend toward disunity that dissolves neither the field nor its subject matter*" (xiv). In the process an enormous range of hybrid approaches and subjects has developed, from feminist science studies to biosemiotics, from complexity theory to the medical humanities, from the ecosocial to the biocultural, from the digital humanities to innovation studies, from affective neuroscience to animal studies and posthumanism – each with a firm place under the science studies umbrella.

Biagioli is also careful to note in *The Science Studies Reader*, the landmark volume he edited, that "practitioners" of science studies are "dispersed over the widest range of departments and programs" and that these expressly include literature departments (xi). Yet it is no less noteworthy that none of the thirty-eight contributors to the *Reader* was actually located in such a department. (G. E. R. Lloyd might seem an exception as a member of the Faculty of Classics at Cambridge; still he held a Chair in Ancient Philosophy and Science.) More recently Biagioli has proposed that "the disciplinary boundaries of science studies ... include the history, sociology, philosophy and ethnography of science, technology and medicine, as well as studies of the relationship between science and literature, science and law, and science and visual studies."[3] No doubt from the perspective of science studies this is about right; all the same, Literature and Science is not quite so readily folded into science studies. For these are actually two discrete fields or interfields. Admittedly, there is a tremendous amount of overlap between them, but as the essays collected in the present volume demonstrate, an adequate sense of the complex imbrications of literature and science historically as well as of recent and ongoing work in Literature and Science cannot simply be conveyed by mapping Literature and Science onto science studies – certainly if the full richness and excitement of the field is to emerge.

The institutional history of Literature and Science, particularly as it has developed in the US, is a complicated enough story but two additional factors complicate it further. In the first place, the establishment in 1939 of what would become the Literature and Science Division of the Modern Language Association – basically taking the form of a subdiscipline of the history of science concerned chiefly with representations of science in literature and marking the advent of what may be termed first-wave Literature and Science – by no means provides the actual starting point of the story.[4] To take one prominent example, in *Science and the Modern World* (1925), the philosopher and mathematician Alfred North Whitehead had insisted on the need to interpret modern science in a manner that would take no less seriously the criticisms of traditional scientific conceptualization made by the British romantic poets William Wordsworth and Percy Bysshe Shelley than, somewhat less controversially, it would take the patently nontraditional aspects of scientific innovations of the past century or two. Whitehead's alternate conceptualization, discussed in the *Companion*'s final chapter, went against the grain of the positivist history of science that was already being institutionalized as he wrote.[5] As a result, his proposals regarding the imbrications of literature and science were rarely followed through until what may be termed second-wave Literature and Science developed much later in parallel with science studies. Therefore a strictly narrative account of the field's development won't do.

So that is the first complication. The second is that things don't necessarily look the same in England as they do in the US, let alone on the Continent and elsewhere.[6] One striking difference emerges when one compares the annual conferences of the leading US and British organizations devoted to Literature and Science: where the fecund triangulations described throughout the *Companion* dominate the Society for Literature, Science and the Arts in the US (as well as the society's biannual meetings abroad, under the aegis of the European Society for Literature, Science and the Arts), considerably more traditional research sets the tone for the British Society for Literature and Science. One consequence is that in a British context, "Literature and Science" may suggest a mix of first-wave work and of the initial phase of second-wave Literature and Science, while in the US second-wave Literature and Science is more likely itself to have already entered a new phase. In this respect the descriptions offered in the *Companion* of the robust practices characteristic of Literature and Science should be understood principally with US developments in mind, although these practices are by no means limited to any single national tradition.

As an academic field of study, then, Literature and Science has advanced in two waves, roughly covering the three and a half decades between 1945 and 1980 and an equal timespan since. In turn, each wave has unfolded in a pair of distinct phases. George S. Rousseau, in an important 1978 article on "the state of the field" in the US, observed that investigations of the relation between literature and science prior to 1950 were largely philological, a matter of "document[ing] scientific references in literature."[7] (There were of course exceptions, such as I. A. Richards's 1926 *Science and Poetry* and Edmund Wilson's 1931 *Axel's Castle*.)[8] As such they were increasingly challenged by a more recent constellation of what Rousseau somewhat idiosyncratically labeled "theorists" (584). This cohort of Literature and Science scholars sought to trace the history of scientific concepts within literary contexts as well as the influence of science on literature more generally. The new analytic field, largely the province of "intellectual historians with degrees in history and/or literature," could just as well have been labeled Science and Literature, and often was (584). It constituted the inaugural phase of first-wave Literature and Science.

In a discussion of Darwin scholarship in Chapter 3 of the *Companion*, Devin Griffiths divides Literature and Science into three waves rather than two. Appearances to the contrary, Griffiths's schema is equivalent to that proposed here, as his initial pair of waves corresponds to the two *phases* of first-wave Literature and Science. The first is largely limited, as Rousseau had proposed, to consideration of the influence of science on literature, whereas the subsequent one complicates this stance by emphasizing the influence of literature on science instead. By 1978, when Rousseau released his report, the field was in such disarray that the continued existence of the MLA's Literature and Science Division, which had flourished since the 1950s, was "very much in doubt" (589); yet some thirty-five years later, the same division possessed nearly 3,000 members (as of 2013). It is this reversal in fortune that the essays in the *Companion* exemplify while they also seek to account for it. *What happened in the interim is best understood as the displacement of one field, called Literature and Science, by another, also called Literature and Science*; and one striking consequence is that a disconnect has arisen between what individuals outside the field think Literature and Science is or should be – something resembling what it really was prior to 1980 – and what it now actually is.

According to Rousseau, the impending demise of first-wave Literature and Science was due largely to the entrance of structuralism onto the American scene. The effect of this "structuralist intrusion" was somewhat paradoxical, "typified" as it was by Michel Foucault, "all of whose books inherently deal with literature and science." (In Chapter 6 T. Hugh Crawford assesses Foucault's role in the field's transformation.) In any event, the subfield of intellectual history called Literature and Science was "render[ed] obsolete" insofar as its methodological premises came under withering attack even as the "impression ... that structuralists were finally turning literary criticism into a science" led to a backlash against prior associations of science and literary study (589). The subsequent emergence of a second wave of Literature and Science (Griffiths's "third"), no longer a subfield but an interfield, may accordingly be attributed to a pair of factors – the first hinted at by Rousseau, the second unacknowledged in his account.

The missing factor, by no means absent however from the intellectual climate of 1978, was the maturation of theory (in its more customary usage) from structuralist to poststructuralist manifestations. Like its sister discipline, science studies, second-wave Literature and Science has from its inception been a hotbed of theoretical application and testing. The particular disciplinary signature of this new Literature and Science was already suggested by Rousseau, albeit in the register of a possible future for a dying discipline. "There is no reason to disbelieve on logical or epistemological grounds," he proposed,

> that literature and science affect each other reciprocally. That is, that each influences the other in just about the same degree, although conceivably in different ways. It is also probably valid to assume, although it would be practically impossible to prove, that science shapes literature to the same degree that imaginative literature shapes science. [Yet] only the former has been studied in any depth ... The latter is an unexplored territory, probably the one in greatest need of cultivation right now and also the one requiring learning so vast that it is hard to imagine it in a single scholar (587–8).[9]

Another way to put this is that further development of first-wave Literature and Science, and of its second phase in particular, would require changes in the field that effectively caused it to morph into a different field – and the new field also unfolded in a pair of fairly distinct phases. Thus Darwin scholars like George Levine and Gillian Beer, who have tended to emphasize the "one culture" shared alike by scientists and literary figures, may usefully be contrasted with the broad pluralism Griffiths locates in more recent work, thereby exhibiting the alternately monocultural and pluralistic phases of second-wave Literature and Science.[10] Of course each phase possesses multiple distinguishing features, from the emphasis on discourse characteristic of so many phase-one investigations to the rigorous hybridization of theory and practice, and the treatment of *possibility* as an indispensable ontological category (discussed by Isabelle Stengers in Chapter 1), that identify so much recent work in Literature and Science as phase-two products. A nice coincidence links the second phase – by way of the two most junior contributors to the *Companion* – to Levine and Beer, among the most prominent first-phase figures in second-wave study of Victorian literature and science: Griffiths was Levine's last PhD student, and kitt price one of the last to work with Beer.

The Cambridge Companion to Literature and Science offers twenty-first-century readers a roadmap to the many robust developments that have contributed, at both the individual scholar and community-of-scholars levels, to the emergence of a great variety of approaches to the reciprocity between literature and science – the absence of which Rousseau lamented as a missed opportunity even as he hailed it as a largely unrealized possibility. Yet the reciprocity in question is also more than that. As has become clear, especially in the context of parallel developments in STS (science and technology studies), another moniker for science studies, second-wave Literature and Science, unlike its predecessor, isn't just concerned with literature and science or even literatures and sciences. One effect of the combination of an increasing range of theoretical approaches entertained within the humanities along with an emphasis on practice in science studies and a broad focus on multidirectional reciprocity throughout the academy has been a healthy expansion of the extent of such reciprocity within Literature and Science itself. No longer limited to literature and science as such, the field triangulates any number of foci in the arts, the non- or extra-literature humanities, and the social sciences.

That the resultant field of study retains the name Literature and Science is a matter of some contention, and therefore the designation remains actively in play. One reason for keeping the old name to designate new circumstances derives from that very resonance. Unlike first-wave Literature and Science, the repurposed name is packed with meaning, and the controversies it may provoke – for instance, regarding whether it unduly privileges literature over other arts and humanities – constitute part of its significance, even its allure. When the Society for Literature and Science rebranded itself a dozen years ago as the Society for Literature, Science and the Arts, the gain in clarity, given the strong presence of artists and art historians at the annual conferences, may have come at the expense of such phrasal undertones.[11]

Another reason for sticking with Literature and Science is that the new field emerged against the backdrop of the two-cultures paradigm – the essence of which, as C. P. Snow famously characterized it in his 1959 Rede lecture, "The Two Cultures and the Scientific Revolution," was that "literary intellectuals" and scientists represented opposite poles within a larger spectrum of specialists.[12] Although one may dispute Snow's opposition in many respects, it cannot be denied that in the context of increasingly specialized practices of inquiry, literature and science, speaking very broadly, do appear at considerable variance (to put it mildly). Snow himself came to regret the sharpness of the division, even proposing a third culture, sociological in nature, to bridge it.[13] In Britain his proposal was taken up, if not quite according to his specifications, with the emergence in the 1960s and 1970s of the sociology of scientific knowledge (SSK) at the Edinburgh Science Studies Unit. (This is discussed further in Chapter 8.)

It is in the present context that the distinction between science studies and second-wave Literature and Science is perhaps clearest. Historically, science studies is a successor discipline to Snow's two-cultures paradigm insofar as it developed in response to the project of a sociology of the sciences that Snow himself endorsed. Literature and Science, by contrast, represents a more frontal attack on Snow's initial premise, particularly in the form the field has taken since the 1970s. At the same time, the general position that integrates literature and science as well as the diverse approaches of second-wave Literature and Science long predates Snow's argument (although he pays it no heed). Interestingly, as Tim Armstrong demonstrates in Chapter 12, extended dialogue between fiction and the life sciences already characterized Cambridge University in the 1920s and 1930s – where Snow acquired a PhD in physics and subsequently conducted research in physical chemistry. (For a detailed account of concurrent exchanges at Cambridge between poetry and physics, see Chapter 5.)

One of the chief ambitions of the *Companion* is to present the lineaments of an alternate argument to Snow's as it may be traced in the development of a more expansive empiricism than has generally been assumed by traditional accounts of modern science. As Mary Baine Campbell demonstrates in Chapter 2, this development is already suggested in early modern literary practices that predated the consolidation of modern science in the mid-seventeenth century. (Both Chapters 1 and 2 include descriptions of Renaissance stances more closely aligned with expansive empiricist practices than rigidly empiricist ones.) And it fully comes into its own – see Chapters 3 and 4 – following Darwin's quite literally earth-shattering innovations in the mid-nineteenth century and the gradual ascent of the life sciences in the hierarchy of sciences. In this manner the more expressly historical section of the *Companion* (Part II, "Snapshots of the Past") addresses increasingly expansive empiricist practices as they were introduced into the modern sciences, including Einsteinian physics in Chapter 5 – as does the *Companion*'s final chapter, with its focus on the significance that Whitehead's highly original account of modern scientific development holds equally for second-wave Literature and Science and for science studies.

In sum, Literature and Science as the name for the discipline to which this volume serves as *Companion* conveys the strongest possible position against the radically conservative "two cultures" stance. From the perspective commonly associated with Snow (whether properly or not), literature and science stand at opposite ends of pretty much everything – unlike science and art, for instance – so their direct conjunction represents an especially sharp slap in the face. To the extent that literature and science do not actually represent thoroughly separate cultures (quite the contrary), practitioners of Literature and Science and adherents of the two-cultures paradigm, including successor formulations such as E. O. Wilson's single "consilient" culture, may well constitute a less navigable divide.[14] This holds true for the monocultural as well as the pluralistic phases of second-wave Literature and Science, both of which define themselves against the dual-culture model. If one work best represents the transition from first-wave to second-wave Literature and Science, it is probably Bruno Latour and Steve Woolgar's 1979 study *Laboratory Life: The Social Construction of Scientific Facts*.[15] Just why this is a key text for Literature and Science and not only for science studies will remain largely unelaborated here, other than to observe that it has partly to do with the challenge posed to claims for the new field's autonomy ("the idea," as Rousseau put it, "of [L]iterature and [S]cience practised as a separate field or discipline")[16], partly with the postpositivist[17] suspicion directed at the fact/value dichotomy (see Chapters 5 and 9 as well as the *Companion*'s concluding chapter), and partly with the attention displayed to the role of writing technologies in laboratory practices (see Chapter 7). Suffice to say, *that* it is a key text for both fields poses a decisive challenge to the two-cultures paradigm.

The many triangulations permitted within the generous embrace of Literature and Science – with theory in general, with particular theories, with science studies, with other disciplines in the humanities and/or social sciences and/or arts, between several literatures and science, or between one or more literatures and one or more sciences – are a source of continuing strength and interest for a tolerably new discipline that, as it advances into its fourth decade, shows no sign of letting up.*

Biography of a Latourian Field

I have just alluded to Bruno Latour's first book, *Laboratory Life*, coauthored with Steve Woolgar. Together with colleagues that include the Belgian philosopher Isabelle Stengers (a contributor to this volume) and the feminist technoscience theorist Donna Haraway, Latour proceeded to upend the still-new sociology of science that in the 1970s had begun to bridge gaps between the sciences and humanities with its emphasis – in the largely Foucauldian manner of phase-one second-wave phase-one Literature and Science – on social, cultural, and discursive factors. T. Hugh Crawford and James J. Bono (in Chapters 6 and 8, respectively) discuss Latour, Haraway and Stengers in the context of science studies, so I won't address Latour's STS work directly,

---

* The index to the *Companion* supplies a preliminary mapping across the entire volume and consequently a representative sampling of Literature and Science circa 2018. See the entries for empiricism, extended empiricisms, and experience, for example, or those for consequences, construction, practice(s), and pragmatism.

aside from observing in the first place that already in the 1979 collaborative volume, traces may be found of what Haun Saussy and Tim Lenoir in Chapter 7 speak of as *posthermeneutic* attention to *non*discursive aspects of writing practices. (In decades to come such attention would variously characterize the work of many practitioners of second-phase second-wave Literature and Science.) In addition, like Haraway and Stengers and the other contributors to this *Companion*, Latour has positioned his investigations from the start against the feature that the public probably most strongly identifies with science studies, despite its being more accurately associated specifically with cultural studies and the SSK school: "the motto," as Stengers puts it in Chapter 1, of "'only' a representation or construction." (Latour and Woolgar's own use of "social construction" has understandably caused a good deal of confusion, although they meant something quite different from what cultural critics might mean – consequently, in a new edition half a dozen years later, they removed "social" from the subtitle.)[18]

Within science studies, Latour's retooling of sociology as a discourse concerned with the emergence of surprising forms of togetherness rather than the more traditional focus on inhibiting or enabling effects of already established social cohorts and situations has had an enormous effect – especially when coupled with a second major innovation of extending the category of social being to apply not just to the usual human suspects but also to any moderately active *nonhuman* that gives evidence of functioning dynamically within some larger network of beings and becomings. As can be imagined, the combination of these two transformations makes an enormous difference in the sociological analyses that ensue, and science studies has been the beneficiary. In the present context, I want to address, ever so briefly, the related matter, not of Latourian science studies but of the appropriateness and even necessity of bringing the tools and practices of Literature and Science to bear on Latour's almost forty years of sociological inquiry. What can Literature and Science tell us about his work that other approaches, including those of science studies itself, are more likely to miss, or dismiss? I'd like to propose six areas of overlap of Latour and Literature and Science, although I will only discuss the first, more general, one here: (1) the expansion of empiricism in such a manner that it becomes readily available for literary scholarship despite the strong theoretical commitments of many scholars;[19] (2) the significance for Latour of the French philosopher of science Michel Serres;[20] (3) Latour's use of the structural semiotics of Algirdas Julien Greimas;[21] (4) his use of Whiteheadian metaphysics, initially to supplement Greimas;[22] (5) early studies by Latour of the French philosopher and poet, Charles Péguy;[23] and (6) a series of exchanges between Latour and the novelist Richard Powers.[24] Needless to say, elements of Latour's anthropology of science have proven of considerable use to literary scholars as well.[25]

One of Latour's better-known slogans derives from the title of his 1991 work of speculative philosophy, *We Have Never Been Modern.*[26] The modernity in question is described in terms that Latour draws from accounts of the development of the experimental sciences in the seventeenth century. (Some of these are quite familiar: dualisms of body and mind, for instance; or objectivity and subjectivity; or primary and secondary qualities – extension, say, by contrast with color.) In each case hybridization is forbidden, and it is this insistence on purity that makes the associated dualisms *modern.* When Latour proposes instead that we have never been modern, he means that the assertion of modernity, including the implicit contrast with something nonmodern – something chronologically prior (medieval, ancient) or developmentally (primitive, naive) – turns out to rely on practices that involve the very hybridity the claim of modernity had eschewed! Certainly, Latour's counterclaim would seem to run the risk of alienating a key cohort of Snow's "literary intellectuals" who might be expected to provide especially important evidence for him: namely, *early modernists,* as scholars of the sixteenth and seventeenth centuries like Mary Baine Campbell (Chapter 2) and James J. Bono (Chapter 8) call themselves: students of the early modern period.

How can you be an early modernist if the communities you study were never actually modern? In fact, it is relatively easy – insofar as the communities seem to have found it relatively easy to speak of themselves *as if* they were modern. In other words, they embraced the discourse of modernity regardless of how imprecise that discourse might prove to have been. Consequently, inquiry into the "anthropology of the moderns" remains a viable enterprise, perforce an exciting one, despite the early moderns having been no more modern than the early modernists themselves are![27] This still leaves open the possibility that they might have been modern *in a different way,* one more in tune perhaps with what Latour elsewhere calls "matters of concern" by contrast with "matters of fact" – in addition to raising the question of how they were able to pass themselves off as modern in the more usual sense (to themselves first of all).[28] In *We Have Never Been Modern* Latour proposed fairly speculative answers, and since then he has alternated between theoretical and empirical inquiry into the matter – leading some two decades later to the unabashedly philosophical *An Inquiry into Modes of Existence* (2013), which exhibits a process ontology supported by the empirical results of multiple case studies.

One way to rephrase Latour's slogan is *we have never been rigid empiricists.* Despite claiming to derive knowledge exclusively from sense experience – the traditional definition of empiricism – "modern" empiricists never actually succeeded in being the rigid empiricists they said they were.

Instead they were obliged to rely on something besides sense data as such to actually acquire their knowledge and even to account for the acquisition of knowledge. What makes this especially interesting for literary intellectuals is that, despite their sharp criticism of more rigid empiricists, Whitehead and Latour – like William James before them, with his "radical empiricism," and like Stengers – still insist on calling themselves empiricists.[29] ("Rigid empiricism" is Whitehead's phrase.)[30] Because they do this, it becomes possible, and even desirable, for literary scholars to conceive of their own investigations as involving a form of empiricism, expansive rather than rigid. The opposition between theory and empiricism long prevalent in the academy begins to lose its grip, and we can speak instead of more expansive practice-based empiricisms – such as Stengers's *ecology of practices* – and of empiricisms involving speculative, not just critical, thought.[31]

In "Why Has Critique Run Out of Steam?" – a 2004 essay published in *Critical Inquiry* – Latour made just these sorts of proposals, and for many literary intellectuals the essay's publication marked a turning point. (Latour's emphasis in works like this and even more notably in *Reassembling the Social* a year later, on how the investigation of processes of assemblage was displacing critique in science studies, closely lines up with a physics, metaphysics, and physiology of entanglement that possesses particular relevance for Literature and Science.)[32] It marked a turning point for Latour as well, in allowing him to embrace his literary intellectual side without having to sign over the speculative interests motivating so much of his work. No longer would literary intellectuals be required to pledge allegiance to exclusively critical practices on entering or leaving science studies. Latour himself had never done this – as when, in 1993, he published an important study of contemporary technoscience in the form of a novel, or "scientifiction," that he called *Aramis, or the Love of Technology*.[33] In Latour's case the new dispensation differed from the old one chiefly because he would have more company – at least that was the idea.

A Reader's Guide

As the preceding remarks on Latour suggest, Literature and Science involves the investigation of continuities and discontinuities among areas of inquiry broader than special disciplines as such. There are many sciences, many literatures, yet strictly speaking there are no discrete disciplines called science or literature. Literature and Science provides a space where the "disparate cultures" of science studies and comparative literature, among many other interdisciplines, may themselves meet.[34] One of the beauties of Literature and Science as the name for the current field, or interfield, lies in its exemplary resistance to disciplinary calcification. As I have already proposed, in order for inquiry within this area to achieve robust results, literature and science must be supplemented by additional disciplinary formations. An obvious route passes through science studies when one or another sociological approach is added to the mix (see especially Chapters 1, 6, 8, and 13). Alternate routes mix Literature and Science with history of science and intellectual history (Chapters 4 and 6–9), with self-consciously speculative literary practices (Chapters 1, 4, and 5), with theory, literary and "othery" (Chapters 6–9), with assorted disciplines in the humanities, social sciences, and arts (throughout the *Companion*). Of course, none of these are mutually exclusive, and in actual practice, the paths chosen differ chiefly in emphasis. To reiterate: the emphasis falls on triangulations of Literature and Science with science studies in Parts I and IV; on triangulations of Literature and Science with history of science in Part II; and on triangulations of Literature and Science with critical theory in Part III.

Consequently, this *Companion to Literature and Science* could never simply be about literature and science. It needs to provide a compelling account of how twenty-first-century literary studies and science studies have come to be so richly integrated with literature and science, and may become still more so. One way the *Companion* accomplishes this is by conceiving the organization of the volume as a coordinate space, with literature and literary studies along one axis, and science and science studies along the second. Part I combines literature and science studies; Part II, literature and science; Part III, literary studies and science studies; Part IV, literary studies and science. Each of the individual essays introduces a particular way of thinking about the relations between literature or literary studies and science or science studies. Obviously, there is considerable slippage among the categories in question in each quadrant, and the sharpness of the distinctions between sections is heuristic. Nevertheless the four-part structure remains useful, especially as it points to very real differences in emphasis among the various approaches to describing alternate aspects of Literature and Science, even as those grouped within any single quadrant share certain emphases. Furthermore, an additional pair of contrasts central to Literature and Science as well as to science studies (and not just to them) is mapped onto the same quadrants. In Parts I and II, present and future are contrasted with historical past; in Parts III and IV theory is contrasted with practice. Indeed, at a slightly more general level of analysis, the latter contrast undergirds the *Companion* as a whole, insofar as terms and approaches that might be thought to divide the institutional cultures of contemporary literary and scientific study between them – theory, on one hand, empiricism, on the other – ultimately ground Parts I and III, and II and IV, respectively.

Consequently, where the essays in Part II focus on key historical expansions of empiricism, those in Part IV describe a range of empiricisms of practice; by contrast, the essay in Part I is concerned directly with forms of speculation and speculative theory, and those in Part III with expansions of critical theory. Such interweaving of theory and empiricism, and of speculative and critical theory, is no less central to the configuration of present-day Literature and Science than it is to science studies.

A useful comparison may be drawn with *The Routledge Companion to Literature and Science*, published a half-dozen years ago.[35] This is a hefty volume, with more than forty contributors, and despite bringing together a remarkable amount of excellent work, it possesses one clear limitation by contrast with the *Cambridge Companion*. Because it is quite deliberately a collection of essays by diverse hands, the responsibility devolves on the reader to mix and match. Not only does this suggest the need for a more coherently organized work, it may be argued that the field requires such an approach. The Cambridge and Routledge Companions share the impression that Literature and Science "is by far the most eclectic and experimental of the (post)humanistic interdisciplines" (241). (Indeed, Literature and Science ups the ante regarding the "double trend toward disunity" that Biagioli identified in science studies.) Yet where the *Routledge Companion* chiefly offers instances of the pluralistic practices at the heart of the interdiscipline, the *Cambridge Companion* aims to provide an integrated understanding of this multilevel, even multicellular, collective inquiry – in order to establish a sufficiently robust sense of the lines of force crisscrossing a natively pluralistic field still very much in the making.

To conclude, then, here are brief overviews of the *Companion*'s four parts: Part I ("Glimpses of Present and Future: Literature and Science Studies") consists of just a single essay, by one of the major practitioners of twenty-first-century science studies. Isabelle Stengers's essay was initially supposed to be paired with a second, also on science fiction and science studies, by Donna Haraway; owing to a mix-up, however, a version of Haraway's essay appeared online, and it could not be included in the *Companion*. For Haraway, and it turns out for Stengers as well, "SF" – used in reference to works of science fiction they find indispensable for their own work in science studies –

> is that potent material-semiotic sign for the riches of speculative fabulation, speculative feminism, science fiction, speculative fiction, science fact, science fantasy – and, I suggest, string figures. In looping threads and relays of patterning, this SF practice is a model for worlding. Therefore, SF must also mean "so far," opening up what is yet-to-come in protean entangled times' pasts, presents, and futures.[36]

Stengers makes highly productive use of Haraway's multivalent concept in the opening chapter, and the complex temporal threads involved are picked up again in the volume's coda.

In his 1978 report, Rousseau had characterized science fiction as "the great anomaly."[37] Despite being "the most natural literary form to be scrutinized by the serious student of the field, [it] has rarely been given serious consideration by literary critics, nor has it engaged the critical energy of scientists who doubtlessly read it and enjoy it." Rousseau attributed the "curious place" of science fiction at the time to a pair of "political and sociological factors." One was the relative absence of science fiction writers in "prestigious academic posts" by contrast with "other types of authors." The second involved ongoing tensions between "the bona fide scientific professional community and authors of science fiction, who rarely are members of that community"; these "cross-accusations" concerned claims for the origin in works of science fiction of important scientific ideas as well as the accuracy of how science is portrayed in science fiction (588). Differences between first-wave and second-wave Literature and Science are nowhere clearer than with respect to their treatment of science fiction. Far from handling science fiction in an anomalous fashion, second-wave Literature and Science embraces it as a model area of inquiry for the interfield as a whole.

In "Science Fiction to Science Studies," Stengers examines how the reading of science fiction influenced her path-breaking studies of modern and contemporary science. In evaluating the contributions that individual works of science fiction have made and continue to make to her approach to the functional analysis of science, Stengers also addresses the exemplary role that science fiction has played, more broadly, in the development of science studies. In particular, science fiction resonates with the more speculative aspects of scientific inquiry inasmuch as these are understood as a necessary complement to strictly empiricist practices. It is recognition of this last (or first) fact that has led to the reframing of empiricism in the more expansive, constructivist terms already discussed, so central to second-wave Literature and Science as well as to science studies. The reframing of empiricism stands or falls depending on whether it does a better job at conveying the actual processes of "making knowledge" – that is what *constructivism*, discussed further in Chapter 8, means in the hands of figures like Stengers, Latour, and Haraway – than do accounts premised on more rigid, that is to say, deliberately more limited, empiricist notions.[38]

Despite the necessary selectivity of the topics addressed in the *Companion*, the volume still seeks to model the robust nature of the pluralistic interdiscipline of twenty-first-century Literature and Science as an ever-changing whole. On a different scale, Stengers's essay may serve as a baseline or tuning fork for measuring the other essays in the volume, especially with regard to the speculative and extended empiricist features they share with Stengers's richly constructivist practices. The chapters in Part II ("Snapshots of the Past: Literature and Science") offer a sample of how the history of science has been transformed in recent decades by developments in Literature and Science. In a sense, they represent the most traditional aspect of second-wave Literature and Science insofar as they focus on much the same sort of material as first-wave Literature and Science did or might have done. The difference is that first-wave Literature and Science is here reconfigured in terms of second-wave Literature and Science; second-wave Literature and Science thereby triangulates first-wave Literature and Science.

As mentioned above, the subjects of these chapters have been chosen to display several key expansions of empiricism.[39] Chapter 2 thus offers an overview of the challenges posed by Shakespearean practices to traditional understandings of empiricism between the seventeenth and nineteenth centuries; Chapters 3, 4, and 5 then present episodes in the expansion of empiricism in the context of developments in the life sciences in the nineteenth century as well as the Einsteinian response to such developments. Each chapter pairs figures conventionally viewed in either literary or scientific frameworks: Shakespeare and Bacon, Henry James and William James, Empson and Einstein. The exception is the chapter devoted to Darwin, which focuses on competing portrayals of Darwin and the difference these make for how one understands relations between literature and science.

Undoubtedly, a primary source of interest that second-wave Literature and Science provides for scholars of literature is the way it demonstrates the tremendous range of uses science studies may possess for literary studies – often productively collapsing differences between approaches to the sciences and humanities and in the process contributing to transformations in disciplinary organization. By contrast, a primary source of friction between science studies and those who greet such postpositivist investigations with skepticism and even hostility has been the introduction of "theory" into the discourse of the empirical sciences – and theory in this sense has typically been identified with literary theory. Part III ("In Theory: Literary Studies and Science Studies") addresses different aspects of these alternative responses. Chapter 6 offers an overview of the many varieties of theory utilized in science studies and second-wave Literature and Science, and subsequent chapters focus on theoretical approaches especially prominent in Literature and Science: in Chapter 7, media theory (including "technologies of writing" and "materialities of communication" broadly construed); in Chapter 8, cultural studies and the surprising forms cultural analysis has taken in second-wave Literature and Science and science studies; and in Chapter 9, renewed interest in the composition of subjectivity at the juncture of affect theory and science studies.

Several remarks by James J. Bono are especially germane where the forms of attention displayed and examined in Part IV ("In Practice: Literary Studies and Science") are concerned, although they also apply to the various approaches to second-wave Literature and Science taken up throughout the *Companion*. Half a dozen years ago, Bono observed of Literature and Science that it "is a robust field, one whose practitioners regularly work at and across the permeable boundaries it shares with history of science. Indeed, while the field continues to be populated by a growing number of literary scholars, its practitioners now include science studies scholars from a broad range of disciplines, including history of science."[40] Bono properly stressed the shared focus on practice: "Surely one major pertinent transformation has involved a recalibration of the analytic practices of, on the one hand, literary scholars interested in science and, on the other, select cohorts of science studies experts. In each case, such recalibration involved new and intensive attention to the practices of 'scientists' themselves" (556). If Bono puts *scientists* in scare quotes, this is not because he is denying that scientists actually are scientists but because he works primarily in the early modern period, which was centuries before the term emerged in the 1830s, expressly by analogy with *artist*, as Joan Richardson explains in Chapter 4. (Consequently Bono's scientists, like Mary Baine Campbell's in Chapter 2, are "scientists"; and Henry David Thoreau, writing in the 1840s and '50s when we encounter him in Chapter 10, is still learning to be a scientist and not just a naturalist.) Like science studies, second-wave Literature and Science aims to "understand the making of science – that is, the making of the different forms of knowledge of things and events in nature – through attentive focus on scientific practice(s) as performative" (557). Both inter-fields, Bono concludes, "explore science as a form of making that involves the convergence of things, material practices, and 'meaningful artifacts,' embracing a panoply of possibilities from metaphoric to narrative to visual to instrumental resources" (559). Chapters 10, 11, and 12 each focus on different aspects of the empiricisms of practice so central to second-wave Literature and Science in the contexts of ecology, cognitive science, and the life sciences, respectively; Chapter 13 then examines how such aspects operate together in inquiry regarding the changing relations of literature and science in the ancient world.

Finally, the coda to the *Companion* moves from what Reviel Netz in the penultimate chapter refers to as the long history of cognitive practices to nearer-term historical considerations in which echoes of the present, and of the development of an extended empiricism like that which characterizes the second phase of second-wave Literature and Science, may already be heard – presenting "an invitation," as Tim Lenoir and Haun Saussy propose at the close of their joint chapter, "for further work."

NOTES

1. See Scott F. Gilbert, "Bodies of Knowledge: Biology and the Intercultural University," in *Changing Life: Genomes Ecologies Bodies Commodities,* ed. Peter J. Taylor, Saul E. Halfon, and Paul N. Edwards (Minneapolis: University of Minnesota Press, 1997), 36–55.
2. Mario Biagioli, ed., *The Science Studies Reader* (New York: Routledge, 1999), xi.
3. Mario Biagioli, "Postdisciplinary Liasons: Science Studies and the Humanities," *Critical Inquiry* 35 (Summer 2009): 816–33, at 817.
4. Marjorie Hope Nicolson, "Resource Letter SL-1 on Science and Literature," *American Journal of Physics,* 33.3 (March 1965): 176. Also see Nicolson's "Two Voices: Science and Literature," *The Rockefeller Institute Review* 1.3 (June 1963): 1–11.
5. Herbert Feigl, "Positivism and Logical Empiricism," in *The New Encyclopaedia Britannica,* vol. 14 (1978), 877–83.
6. See, for example Bruno Latour and Geof Bowker, "A Booming Discipline Short of Discipline: (Social) Studies of Science in France," *Social Studies of Science* 17.4 (November 1987): 715–48.
7. G. S. Rousseau, "Literature and Science: The State of the Field," *Isis: A Journal of the History of Science Society* 69 (1978): 583–91, at 584. In 1991 Rousseau collected this essay along with four others addressing "the discourses of literature and science" and "literature and medicine" in *Enlightenment Borders: Pre- and Post-modern Discourses: Medical, Scientific* (Manchester: Manchester University Press, 1991). See also Stuart Peterfreund, "Literature – Relations to Science and Technology," in *The History of Science in the United States: An Encyclopedia,* ed. Marc Rothenberg (New York: Garland, 2001), 320–3.
8. I. A. Richards, *Poetries and Sciences: A Reissue of Science and Poetry (1926, 1935) with Commentary* (New York: Norton, 1970), and Edmund Wilson, *Axel's Castle: A Study in the Imaginative Literature of 1870–1930* (New York: Farrar, Straus and Giroux, 2004), esp. Chs. 1, 7, and 8. For second-wave Literature and Science that extends these studies, as well as related work by figures such as Whitehead and William Empson, see Angus Fletcher's astonishing trilogy: *A New Theory for American Poetry: Democracy, the Environment, and the Future of Imagination* (Cambridge: Harvard University Press, 2006); *Time, Space, and Motion in the Age of Shakespeare* (Cambridge: Harvard University Press, 2007); and *The Topological Imagination: Spheres, Edges, and Islands* (Cambridge: Harvard University Press, 2016).
9. Not wholly unexplored, however: see Elizabeth Sewell, *The Orphic Voice: Poetry and Natural History* (New Haven: Yale University Press, 1960) for a first-wave example.

10. See George Levine, ed., *One Culture: Essays in Science and Literature* (Madison: University of Wisconsin Press, 1987), and Gillian Beer, *Open Fields: Science in Cultural Encounter* (Oxford: Oxford University Press, 1996). The earliest of the essays collected in Beer's volume originally appeared in Levine's.

11. Regrettably, it has not been possible to include stand-alone chapters on the arts and art history in the *Companion*. In their place the following works may suggest the richness of these areas of inquiry: Linda Dalrymple Henderson, *Duchamp in Context: Science and Technology in the* Large Glass *and Related Works* (Princeton: Princeton University Press, 1998); James Elkins, *Six Stories from the End of Representation: Images in Painting, Photography, Astronomy, Microscopy, Particle Physics, and Quantum Mechanics* (Stanford: Stanford University Press, 2008); and Barbara Maria Stafford, *Echo Objects: The Cognitive Work of Images* (Chicago: University of Chicago Press, 2009). See also Stafford, ed., *A Field Guide to a New Meta-Field: Bridging the Humanities-Neuroscience Divide* (Chicago: University of Chicago Press, 2011).

12. C. P. Snow, *The Two Cultures* (Cambridge: Cambridge University Press, 1998), with introduction by Stefan Collini. See also F. R. Leavis, *Two Cultures? The Significance of C. P. Snow* (Cambridge: Cambridge University Press, 2013), also with an introduction by Collini; and Guy Ortolano, *The Two Cultures Controversy: Science, Literature and Cultural Politics in Postwar Britain* (Cambridge: Cambridge University Press, 2009).

13. For the long prehistory of Snow's turn to sociology, see Wolf Lepenies, *Between Literature and Science: The Rise of Sociology* (Cambridge: Cambridge University Press, 1988).

14. E. O. Wilson, *Consilience: The Unity of Knowledge* (New York: Alfred A. Knopf, 1998). For a counterargument to Wilson much more in tune with the robust empiricist approaches shared by many of the contributors to this *Companion* as well as their subjects, see Stephen Jay Gould's posthumously published *The Hedgehog, the Fox, and the Magister's Pox: Mending the Gap between Science and the Humanities* (New York: Harmony Books, 2003).

15. Bruno Latour and Steve Woolgar, *Laboratory Life: The Social Construction of Scientific Facts* (Los Angeles: Sage, 1979). This work is further discussed in Chapter 6 of the *Companion*.

16. Rousseau, *Enlightenment Borders*, 236.

17. For a richly historical discussion of postpositivism, see John H. Zammito, *A Nice Derangement of Epistemes: Post-Positivism in the Study of Science from Quine to Latour* (Chicago: University of Chicago Press, 2004).

18. Latour and Woolgar, *Laboratory Life: The Construction of Scientific Facts*, 2nd ed. (Princeton: Princeton University Press, 1986). See also Ian Hacking, *The Social Construction of What?* (Cambridge: Harvard University Press, 1999), and Barbara Herrnstein Smith, *Scandalous Knowledge: Science, Truth, and the Human* (Durham: Duke University Press, 2006).

19. Latour distinguishes between first and second empiricisms (roughly matching up with the contrast between traditionally rigid empiricisms and more expansive or robust ones) in his 2005 Spinoza Lectures, *What Is the Style of Matters of Concern?* (Assen NL: Van Gorcum, 2008), reprinted in abridged form in *The Lure of Whitehead*, ed. Nicholas Gaskill and A. J. Nocek (Minneapolis: University of Minnesota Press, 2014), 92–126.

20. Michel Serres, with Bruno Latour, *Conversations on Science, Culture, and Time* (Ann Arbor: University of Michigan Press, 1995); and Bruno Latour, "The Enlightenment without the Critique: A Word on Michel Serres' Philosophy," in *Contemporary French Philosophy*, ed. A. Phillips Griffiths (Cambridge: Cambridge University Press, 1987), 83–97. Two excellent essays on Serres are Ilya Prigogine and Isabelle Stengers, "Postface: Dynamics from Leibniz to Lucretius," in Michel Serres, *Hermes: Literature, Science, Philosophy*, ed. Josué V. Harari and David F. Bell (Baltimore: Johns Hopkins Press, 1982), 135–55; and Michael Shortland, "Michel Serres, passe-partout," *British Journal for the History of Science* 31 (1998): 335–53.

21. Madeleine Akrich and Bruno Latour, "A Summary of a Convenient Vocabulary for the Semiotics of Human and Nonhuman Assemblies," in *Shaping Technology/Building Society: Studies in Sociological Change*, ed. Wiebe E. Bijker and John Law (Cambridge: MIT Press, 1992), 259–64; and Latour, "Pasteur on Lactic Acid Yeast: A Partial Semiotic Analysis," *Configurations* 1.1 (Winter 1993): 129–45, where Latour famously remarks that "semiotics is the ethnomethodology of texts" (131). Also see Timothy Lenoir, "Was the Last Turn the Right Turn? The Semiotic Turn and A. J. Greimas," *Configurations* 2.1 (1994): 119–36.

22. Bruno Latour, "Do Scientific Objects Have a History? Pasteur and Whitehead in a Bath of Lactic Acid," *Common Knowledge* 5.1 (1996): 76–91.

23. Bruno Latour, "Charles Péguy: Time, Space, and *le Monde Moderne,*" *New Literary History* 46.1 (Winter 2015): 41–62. See also Henning Schmidgen, "The Materiality of Things? Bruno Latour, Charles Péguy and the History of Science," *History of the Human Sciences* 26.1 (2012): 3–28; and Schmidgen, "Exegesis and Ethnology," in *Bruno Latour in Pieces* (New York: Fordham University Press, 2015), 9–24; among other topics, Schmidgen discusses the significance for Latour of Gilles Deleuze's reading of Péguy in *Difference and Repetition* (New York: Columbia University Press, 1994).

24. Bruno Latour, "A Dialog with Richard Powers in Honor of HAL," *Common Knowledge* 7.1 (1998): 177–91, and Latour "Powers of the Facsimile: A Turing Test on Science and Literature," in *Intersections: Essays on Richard Powers*, ed. Stephen J. Burn and Peter Dempsey (Champaign IL: Dalkey Archive, 2008), 263–91.

25. See, for example, Susan Squier, "From Omega to Mr. Adam: The Importance of Literature for Feminist Science Studies," *Science, Technology, & Human Values* 24.1 (Winter 1999): 132–58; and Laura Dassow Walls, "From the Modern to the Ecological: Latour on Walden Pond," in *Ecocritical Theory: New European Approaches*, ed. Axel Goodbody and Kate Rigby (Charlottesville: University of Virginia Press, 2011), 98–110.

26. Bruno Latour, *We Have Never Been Modern* (Cambridge: Harvard University Press, 1993).

27. Bruno Latour, *An Inquiry into Modes of Existence: An Anthropology of the Moderns* (Cambridge: Harvard University Press, 2013). See also Bruno Latour, "Biography of an Inquiry: On a Book about Modes of Existence," *Social Studies of Science* 43.2 (2013): 287–301; John Tresch, "Another Turn after ANT: An Interview with Bruno Latour," *Social Studies of Science* 43.2 (2013):

302–13; and the accompanying website and platform for Latour's volume, modesofexistence.org.

28. Bruno Latour, "Why Has Critique Run Out of Steam? From Matters of Fact to Matters of Concern," *Critical Inquiry* 30.2 (Winter 2004): 225–48

29. William James, *Essays in Radical Empiricism* (Lincoln: University of Nebraska Press, 1996), including "Does 'Consciousness' Exist?" 1–38, and "A World of Pure Experience," 39–91, esp. 41–4.

30. Alfred North Whitehead, *Process and Reality*, corrected ed., ed. David Ray Griffin and Donald W. Sherburne (New York: Free Press, 1978), 4.

31. Isabelle Stengers, "Introductory Notes on an Ecology of Practices," *Cultural Studies Review* 11.1 (March 2005): 183–96. See also Stengers, *Cosmopolitics I and II* (Minneapolis: University of Minnesota Press, 2010–11); Thomas Lamarre, "Expanded Empiricism: Natsume Sōseki with William James," *Japan Forum* 20.1 (2008): 47–77; Didier Debaise, "The Emergence of a Speculative Empiricism: Whitehead Reading Bergson," in *Deleuze, Whitehead, Bergson: Rhizomatic Connections*, ed. Keith A. Robinson (Basingstoke: Palgrave Macmillan, 2009), 77–88; and Brian Massumi, "The Thinking-Feeling of What Happens: Putting the Radical Back in Empiricism," in *Semblance and Event: Activist Philosophy and the Occurrent Arts* (Cambridge: MIT Press, 2011), 39–86.

32. Bruno Latour, *Reassembling the Social: An Introduction to Actor-Network-Theory* (Oxford: Oxford University Press, 2005); Karen Barad, *Meeting the Universe Halfway: Quantum Physics and the Entanglement of Matter and Meaning* (Durham: Duke University Press, 2007); and Donna J. Haraway, *When Species Meet* (Minneapolis: University of Minnesota Press, 2008).

33. Bruno Latour, *Aramis, or the Love of Technology* (Cambridge: Harvard University Press, 1996). Also see Bruce Clarke, "Observing *Aramis, or the Love of Technology*: Objects and Projects in Gilbert Simondon and Bruno Latour," in *Neocybernetics and Narrative* (Minneapolis: University of Minnesota Press, 2014), 111–38.

34. Mary Louise Pratt, *Imperial Eyes: Travel Writing and Transculturation* (New York: Routledge, 1992), 4.

35. Bruce Clarke and Manuela Rossini, ed., *The Routledge Companion to Literature and Science* (New York: Routledge, 2011).

36. The URL for Haraway's essay (titled "SF: Science Fiction, Speculative Fabulation, String Figures, So Far") is http://adanewmedia.org/2013/11/issue3 -haraway/.

37. Rousseau, "Literature and Science," 588.

38. See James J. Bono, "Making Knowledge: History, Literature, and the Poetics of Science," *Isis* 101 (2010): 555–9.

39. Aside from several references in Chapter 11, the absence of any extended discussion of the eighteenth century testifies to the selectivity to which a volume like the present one is unavoidably subject. Excellent studies in the literature and science of the period include Jessica Rifkin, *Science in the Age of Sensibility: The Sentimental Empiricists of the French Enlightenment* (Chicago: University of Chicago Press, 2002); Sarah Rivett, *The Science of the Soul in Colonial New England* (Chapel Hill: University of North Carolina Press, 2011); and Courtney Weiss Smith's *Empiricist Devotions: Science, Religion, and Poetry in Early Eighteenth-Century England* (Charottesville: University of Virginia Press,

2016), on a "brand of meditative empiricism." Sarah Kareem's "Flimsy Materials, or What the Eighteenth Century Can Teach Us About Twenty-First Century Worlding" (*Critical Inquiry* 42 [Winter 2016], 374–94) offers an up-close account of travel on the eighteenth-century/twenty-first-century Express. For a broad overview of *medieval* literature and science (likewise limited here to a brief discussion in Chapter 13 and a passing mention in Chapter 2), see Arielle Saiber, "Middle Ages and Early Renaissance," in Clarke and Rossini, ed., *Routledge Companion*, 423–37.

40. Bono, "Making Knowledge," 556.

PART I

Glimpses of Present and Future
Literature and Science Studies

I

ISABELLE STENGERS

Science Fiction to Science Studies

Let us begin with an example, the account by science fiction writer Anne McCaffrey of how psy-talents eventually gained official recognition.[1] It would not be due to some scientific discovery, at last explaining the unexplainable, but as a consequence of what is probably the humblest among scientific events – the observation of a mere correlation. Molly, a nurse gifted with a "healing touch," realizes that a new electroencephalo-graph dubbed the Goosegg produces a sudden wild singular pattern at the very moment when she touches the injured Henry Darrow's forehead. Darrow is famous for his claimed precognitive talent, and he has just "seen" that he will marry Molly . . .

The correlation Molly has discovered will never be "scientifically explained" in the novel. But the Goosegg is gold for the gifted people who will use this correlation to identify genuine gifts reliably. They will no longer need to confront chicanery, suspicion, and derision. They will no longer have to submit to stupid tests, which are never sufficient to convince the skeptics anyway. Protected by the Goosegg from a hostile environment, an environment which infects even them with mistrust against would-be cheaters, they will be free to cultivate their gifts, to discover ways to enhance and stabilize them, and finally . . .

Science Fiction and the Activation of the Speculative Imagination

Both as a philosopher and as a reader science fiction, I have been involved in the social studies of science, or science studies. As a philosopher, after graduating with degrees in chemistry and philosophy, I learned my job working as a doctoral researcher in Ilya Prigogine's physical chemistry department at the Free University of Brussels.[2] I discovered the science studies field in the beginning of the eighties, and was both passionately interested and perplexed. My perplexity stemmed from the "deconstructive urge" of the new science studies specialists and the correlative "vigilante" character of the stories many came up with – debunking the scientists' claim to have produced "proof," instead of telling the many adventures involved in such claims and the way they create a pseudo-unity among scientific fields. My participation in the field of science studies has thus been motivated by a refusal of certain aspects of what was often termed a social constructivist approach, which, I felt, would provoke a scientist's legitimate anger.[3] It has furthermore been sustained by my experience as a science fiction reader, from which I learned that it is possible to fully affirm the "social" character of scientific practices without using such affirmation as a general critical weapon. The concepts of *practice, ecology of practices* and *cosmopolitics* which I have proposed[4] are meant to activate the speculative imagination – at once an appetite for what may be possible and resistance against the normalcy of what is considered self-evident.

McCaffrey's novel is a witness to the imaginative freedom of science fiction to ask questions that should in fact belong to mainstream social sciences. (I use "social sciences" as an inclusive category for all research fields, including science studies, which have to deal with the possibility that what they address is "concerned" with the questions of researchers in the field in question – in contrast with those sciences, such as physics, chemistry or astronomy, that may safely presuppose the "indifference" of the interrogated beings, which "react" in the terms of the proposed situation without being concerned with it. The latter are the "distant" or "remote" beings accessed under the mode REF in Bruno Latour's analysis of modes of existence.)[5] If the demand for "proof," the very soul of research experimental practices, produces admittedly nasty, polemical and destructive effects in other practical fields, why is it still generally dominant? Why is the debunking of errors, false perceptions and illusions the "normal" exercise in the social sciences? Why have they quasi-phobically avoided exploring the consequences of what they cannot but know – that in their field the questions are never simply "about" something but are always addressed "to" something or someone, and that the way one addresses a question is bound to become part and parcel of the addressee's "reality"?

In his *Cosmopolis*[6] Stephen Toulmin provides a perspective with which I will experiment in these pages: that what binds our many sciences to the authority associated with "science" is a "hidden agenda" which gave science a role in a "never again" "modern" commitment. According to Toulmin, modernity should not be characterized, in direct contrast with the medieval era, by its new sciences, its philosophical promotion of rationality, its dissociation from Church-dominated institutions. Instead, what distinguished modernity was the way it turned its back on what came in between, the shining, chaotic, speculative, violent, flourishing, tragic period known as the Renaissance: when a new tolerant humanism developed together with witch hunting; when a renewed scholarship escaped the instituted alliance between Christian theology and Aristotelian philosophy, while reason and magic forged strange, adventurous links; when printed books transformed the notion of an author, no longer an authority quoted to sustain an argument but a new kind of entrepreneur competing with others for the conquest of a literate "public"; and when religious wars tore Europe apart.

Toulmin challenges the usual historical perspective, dramatizing the discontinuities of a history that we may be tempted to turn into the implacable ascent of reason – from Plato disqualifying practical and opinion-based knowledges in the name of *logos* to the rise of science-based technology – with the obscurantist digression of the Age of Faith. His reading of the role of science in the service of intellectual, moral and public order concurs with Mary Midgley's sharp observation about scientists so often presenting science as a matter of salvation.[7] And with Bruno Latour's more recent claim that modernity is not reaching out toward a promised future, but rather running away from some monstrous past.[8] It may well be that social sciences were mobilized in order to diagnose, if not defeat, the power of the series of "monsters" that would personify what has become a ready-made role, that of reason's enemy. Among these monsters, we may point to the "credulity of the people" as displayed by the frightening popular success of the "charlatan" Mesmer and to the way communism was represented during the Cold War as making social conflict the ultimate truth of social relations.[9]

Toulmin goes further, however. He presents what has been dubbed the "counterculture" since the 1960s as a "second Renaissance" breaking the shackles of the modern, defensive ethos. Writing at the very end of the eighties, Toulmin certainly recognized that the decade just past "was a time for nostalgia rather than imagination," but he maintained an optimistic outlook. "The events of those years," he wrote, "still resonate in a dozen ways in the hearts and minds of those who were actively involved."[10]

I lived far away from the epicenter of those events, in a part of Europe that was only affected by rather secondary shock waves. I have more directly witnessed the way Toulmin's second Renaissance has become the new monster to escape – the "dream" was over, generalized economic war was the only reality. However, all along through the years my heart and mind have avoided despair thanks to resonances stemming from a backstairs source – neither secret nor hidden, just escaping the inquisitive gaze – that kept something of the second Renaissance alive. This is the particular kind of science fiction I will refer to as SF. (Science fiction – "sf," as it is commonly designated – is a continent. Some regions of it may have inspired Reagan's Strategic Defense Initiative; others ride on the contemporary experience of the shutting down of horizons, or feed the conviction that some technological fix will permit ongoing "progress," as this is defined today. I call the kind of science fiction which sustained me SF, a subset of the larger category, to pay a loving homage to Donna Haraway's fabulous play with this acronym: science fiction but also string figures, speculative fabulation, speculative feminism, science fantasy, scientific fact, so far ...)[11]

It was when reading Marion Zimmer Bradley's *The Mists of Avalon* (1983) that I first learned how the transformative, metamorphic efficacy of SF could directly concern me, not only touch "my" heart and mind but also that of the philosopher I had become.[12] The story is a retelling of the Arthurian legend as narrated by Morgaine (the sorceress Morgan Le Fay), who is here a priestess to the Celtic goddess at a time when the Christian church dedicated its growing theologico-political power to the eradication of the pagan creed. Bradley's novel is about the end of a world, but it is also about what we mean by truth. When the sacred isle of Avalon, now impossible to access, disappears in the mists, Morgaine knows that an epoch has ended, that the old rituals have lost their power. But she comes to understand that what has been destroyed is the Celtic access to the goddess, an access which could exist only so long as it was sustained. While the Christians who defeated her define their truth by its power to vanquish any rival, for Morgaine, the power of religions stems from the way they serve, and learn how to listen to, what none of them can appropriate. The goddess her religion honored has not been vanquished, she has "ingressed" (become an ingredient of) Christianity, right under the nose of male-chauvinist priests.

Bradley was an active protagonist in the second Renaissance's reinvention of feminism, and her novel was influential in the revival of neo-pagan cults, addressed to a goddess who is coming back. To me, as a philosopher, *The Mists of Avalon* marked the discovery of the possibility of a "constructivity" of truth – a noncritical concept that may be associated with what will be called below an art of consequences and that has accompanied my work ever since, for instance when thinking with the philosophers William James and Alfred North Whitehead.[13] In resisting philosophy as marked by the polemic power of truth against illusion, I learned to honor and carefully trust another kind of power gifted with what can be described as a bootstrapping efficacy, what social scientists usually debunk as the mother of all illusions. I understood that philosophy – as I had felt bound to practice it and as what Gilles Deleuze characterized as "the creation of concepts" – may be gifted with such an efficacy.[14] Philosophers perhaps "create" concepts, but they cannot appropriate them nor even define them: rather they are "created," or "animated," by the concepts they create and which in turn transform them, forcing them to a groping experimentation, not a discursive practice with chains of *thus*es and *then*s securing reason against illusion. Instead each *thus*, each *then*, and the ever-recurring *but*s serve as events that make thought zigzag.

Openly presenting myself as indebted to SF is not telling a private story. If we and our ideas are "of the world," together with so many other "critters," as Donna Haraway calls them, each having an agency of its own and a way of its own to have the world matter, it may well be that publically recognizing SF critters as part of our intellectual and affective ecology is a significant move. Strange Harawayan "string figures" may perhaps be woven among those thinkers who today loosen or break the injunction of modernity's hidden agenda – who dare to think with a world free from the stifling opposition between so-called sound science and mere fiction or speculation, a world that cannot be reduced to issues dealing with its capacity to validate the knowledge that sciences are able, or claim to be able, to extract from it.[15]

Let us be a bit more specific. SF not only survived the thrashing of Toulmin's second Renaissance, but it continued experimenting with questions about what we may become capable of. The point I wish to stress involves the verb "to experiment," which I will use instead of the usual one, "to experience." SF work can be, and indeed often is, evaluated by the ones who are concerned by, even engaged in, the questions it explores, and who *make* the experience, think with it and taste its effects. (Let us note that in twelfth-century French, the word *espermenter* existed, and that this may implicitly acknowledge there is no experimentation without hope [Fr. *espérer*].) Objections to the hierarchical flavor of Bradley's Celtic priesthood, for instance, have entailed the experimentation of new rituals by contemporary neo-pagan witches. Further, "experiment" obviously suggests a connection with scientific practices. Anthropologist Marilyn Strathern insists that it matters what ideas we use to think other ideas with.[16] I will use the idea of a thought experiment to complicate the idea that the sciences are as such part and parcel of "modernity's hidden agenda," an idea that implies that there can be no relation whatsoever between "scientific facts" and SF.

Maybe the most famous scientific thought experiment is Galileo's, which features a man perched on the mast of a boat moving on a river, who drops a stone (or in some versions an apple). "Where will the stone fall?" Galileo asks, and his fictional interlocutor, Simplicio, being a good Aristotelian, answers, "behind the mast, of course." "Wrong," triumphs Galileo, "it will fall at the very base of the mast!" With this "fact" Galileo has just allowed the earth to move around the sun without us experiencing it, thereby initiating the science we call physics not as a search for certainty against the vagaries of "belief," but as an adventure of consequential ideas. It is worth mentioning that René Descartes, the emblematic promoter of Toulmin's counter-Renaissance, never accepted Galilean physics, which scandalized his quest for a method warranting certainty against the wandering of ideas. It may therefore be said that right from the beginning, the Age of Reason (Descartes) and the Age of Science (Galileo) were at cross-purposes.

Are scientific facts (one signification of Haraway's SF) mere fictions claiming authority, or are they legitimate grounds for certainty? Such a polemical question is happily complicated by Galileo's stated "fact." In order to decide if his claim can be verified, not only should the boat move very very swiftly, but it would really be better to eliminate the correlatively swiftly moving air (so as to remove the effects of friction). A strange fact (SF!) indeed, it is the product of imagination rather than careful, repeated observation. All of physics's thought experiments happen in such fictive, rarefied environments from which anything that may blur the effect to be dramatized has been eliminated. But they are not "mere" fictions. They are consequential ones, the value of which depends on their consequences, on the possibility of actually enrolling what they address in the dramatization of hypotheses we call laboratory experimentation. "What if?" and "but then!" – such questions are the very soul of the experimental sciences, sciences that have populated our world with new entities and possibilities, from an Earth that can move without our knowing it to the atoms, molecules and microbes now coexisting with us, impacting our everyday lives in many controversial but incontrovertible ways. These are not discursive questions, submitting a situation to the power of reasoning; the way that what they address answers them remains a matter of suspense – and, when the suspense is over, it happens that the experimenters dance in the lab.

What if the social sciences had cultivated, like their experimental sisters, the art of the thought experiment? We know of such attempts in neuroethics or analytic philosophy, and they look more like exercises of flummoxing, of cornering thought than of unfolding the consequences of a daring hypothesis. Whatever the situation they invent, it first of all exhibits "subjects" deprived of the capacity to escape the net of discursive alternatives imposed upon them, of opening a door into the sky as Truman eventually does at the end of the show. One does not get out of Searle's Chinese room ... [17]

What is at stake here are not generalities like freedom or determinism but the nature of the rarefaction required to dramatize the consequences in question. Experimental sciences depend (or should depend, when they are not pseudo) on the possibility of framing what they address in the well-controlled environment we call laboratories without "impairing" the power of the addressee to put at risk the relevance of the question that is posed. But this is precisely what the "social sciences" cannot hope for – what they address cannot be presumed indifferent to the question. It cannot be postulated that the addressee will not produce its own interpretation of the question, that the answer arrived at can be disentangled from the way the addressee "worlds its world,"[18] from what matters for it, from the way it hears the question.

A hypothesis ("what if?") may then require a novel to fill it out, in the exploration of a world dense with its many entangled repercussions. For instance, when Ursula K. Le Guin explored the world of Earthsea, where, she hypothesized, magic and magicians exist, she did not try to determine the direct consequence of this hypothesis or to dramatize the possibility that beautiful girls may be turned into swans.[19] She addressed magic as a technique with its dangers, its rules of use, its ethics and the complicated way it connects people and their world. Correlatively, the "what if?" question did not aim to produce new "facts" claiming authority but instead resulted in a deliberate betrayal of modernity's hidden agenda: the crafting of a narrative that experimented with the pragmatic consistency of a different world, and positively proposed *not* to assimilate our world to "the world."

Le Guin named a collection of her SF short stories *Changing Planes*. Such phrasing may well be the signature of the daughter of an anthropologist, as she was. Contemporary anthropologists would certainly agree that immersing oneself in a different world, being willing to experience its manner of consistency and to experiment with the way it tests our certainties (to "decolonize thought," in Eduardo Viveiros de Castro's words)[20] indeed involves moving to a different plane. However, in her introduction to the collection Le Guin also plays with another meaning. "Changing planes" may be the dreary time spent between arrival and a delayed connecting flight:

> In this, probably its true aspect, the airport is not a prelude to travel, not a place of transition: it is a stop. A blockage. A constipation. The airport is where you can't go anywhere else. A nonplace in which time does not pass and there is no hope for any meaningful existence. A terminus: the end. The airport offers nothing to any human being except access to the interval between planes.[21]

A blockage. A constipation – no hope for meaningful existence. To me this characterization of the airport depicts the effects of the devastating opposition between a science that would "disenchant" the world and the soaring dreams of imagination that would re-enchant it. Contrary to futurology, or even anticipation, which is generally wide of the mark, SF is never wrong, just more or less interesting, because it is not about the future (or the past, or "another world") but about intervals, about what lurks in the interstices of the assigned signification of each moment as preparing for the next. It is about our own epoch's possibility of "changing planes," not by escaping the present but by suspending the continuity of self-answering problems (if-then), whatever their register (including the critical or demystifying ones), and exploring the virtual halo of the questions and speculations this particular epoch makes us capable of – the writer and her amateur audience, all experimenting with the metamorphic effect of an operation of dishabituation, that is, of the destabilization of the settled, authoritative distribution between the possible and the impossible, the acceptable and the unacceptable. (In French, I would probably have used *dépaysement*. Here I have chosen "dishabituation," the "restoration to full strength of a response that has become weakened by habituation,"[22] because it resonates with the opposition between imagination as a "strong response" to a problematic situation, and "imaginary" as something that never needs to be restored, rather endlessly diagnosed or attributed to others by social scientists, psychologists or critics – a "blockage" to use Le Guin's term. Dishabituation in this sense is similar to the Russian formalist concept of defamiliarization or *ostranenie*.) Our world does not need to be what it is, does not need to be thought and felt as it authoritatively demands to be. Another way, another composition of this world, is possible.

SF writers might then be understood as researchers, the authors of particular thought experiments that explore the questions their epoch is able to think and feel with, whatever the blocked, aggressive, constipated divides of the academic small world – with critical studies, for instance, mobilized to resist the "objectivist" sciences. They are certainly not able to bring reconciliation among the fighters, to bring peace where the science wars ruled, for instance, but the way they betray the respective versions of the hidden agenda those fighters have in common (as keepers of a truth besieged by illusions) might, if recognized, loosen the deadlock and irrigate the landscape with the blood of consequential ideas.

The Art of Consequences of SF Thought Experiments

Consider the famous theme of the "encounter" between worlds. Critical studies (mainly) are proud to debunk "our" representation of the others, to (justifiably) denounce the belief in the "objective" scientific, technical and rational superiority of the colonial powers and to cultivate a sense of guilt about the results of the "encounter." Yet they too often ignore that SF has explored many variants of this event which imply that, even if the critical lesson were learned, even if the incoming party was as "wise" as can be, catastrophic misunderstandings and surprises might still be on the menu. For instance, in *The Foreigner Universe* C. J. Cherryh dares to play with the explosive theme of the coexistence of two dangerously similar biological species.[23] The Atevi, on whose home world human colonists come to be stranded, look rather like humans (with an eighteenth-century technological development) and seem ready to learn, avid for technical novelties and extremely gifted for mathematics. Too late it will be discovered that humans, trusting in the possibility of friendship and cooperation, have unknowingly wreaked havoc on Atevi society, and a general war results. The point is that trust, friendship, love and cooperation are all untranslatable in the Atevi language. Instead what is passionately felt and socially structuring is the belonging to a clan. Atevi dramas do not play upon impossible loves but conflicts of loyalty. When peace is finally obtained, it is understood that any blending of the two species is too dangerous, although the Atevi still insist on sharing the technology brought by the humans. Only one human being, referred to as the *paidhi* and trained to bear affective solitude and avoid misinterpreting the relation he is required to entertain with the Atevi, will reside with them. (The others remain on an island.) His diplomatic task is to negotiate the process of technological transfer in a way that does not jeopardize the complicated fabric and ticklish values of the Atevi world.

This, at least, is the setting for the first volume of the series. It is a controversial setting indeed, since both humans and the Atevi are characterized in terms of gut-level, hardwired emotional compulsions. Is the need to love, trust or feel friendship really a "human" characteristic? Are not the Atevi a bit too close to an "orientalist" representation of the other? Is not the idea of biological wiring what gender studies denounce as "essentialism"? As a fiction writer, however, Cherryh needs the difference between humans and Atevi not to be a mere construct because the whole point of the series is to explore the consequences of this difference, namely, the slow, treacherous, deadly serious creation of a "middle ground" – with the weaving of relations that produce no leveling but a growing indeterminacy regarding what we call hardwired.[24] In order to tell how what first appear as incommensurable, invariant divergences may become transformative constraints, they have first to be accepted as such.

Cherryh's series develops as an adventure of diplomacy, the testing art of taking differences seriously without dreaming of an underlying unity or indulging in the abyss of incommensurability – not appropriate ways to behave when you are improvising in a political minefield. Treating this adventure as an *effectively* decolonial thought experiment, involving the construction of serious propositions, is not to deny that her work is a fiction, moreover a fiction written for a "popular" audience. But it should be added that it is written for a rather demanding connoisseur audience, an audience for whom the fact that "this is only a fiction" will not serve as an excuse.

From a science studies perspective, it is in fact striking how much the sf "fandom," with its conventions, prizes, magazines and now websites of all brands, resemble scientific communities, with ex-fans regularly becoming respected authors, often with the help and advice of confirmed ones. Science fiction thrives on the active interest, objections, cooperation and inspirational relays that characterize the very social fabric of the sciences when they escape the hidden agenda that makes them modern. I propose that this is much more than a contingent resemblance. I have already characterized thought experiments in the experimental sciences as not "only a fiction," but as consequential fictions, staging a hypothesis ("What if?") in the fictive rarefied world where its consequences would be dramatized ("but then!"). SF might well be answering the call for such an "art of consequences" in social sciences against the mutilation entailed by the model of "sound," "fact-based" science that dominates those fields. But in so doing, SF first and foremost asserts the very different meaning to be associated with "consequences" in the experimental and the social sciences respectively.[25] SF thought experiments are not *about* but *with*, not about "society" but with a public – a public who will abide neither the motto, *"only" a representation or construction*, nor any other operation depopulating the world. Academic social, fact-debunking, constructionism will not do for the amateurs if no character in a novel is promoting it, that is, if it plays no active, interesting part in the weaving of the novel. What the amateurs appreciate is the exploration of *effects*. What they taste is the crafted proposition of a world that is not rarefied in order to dramatize a particular hypothesis but is dense with the repercussions and consequences of this hypothesis – a world whose inhabitants live with the opportunities, problems, dilemmas, habits, hopes and fears the hypothesis makes possible but does not explain.

If we take SF seriously as a manner of thought experiment, the difference between mainstream social sciences and experimental sciences proves a matter of "changing planes." The point is no longer to criticize the first from the perspective of the second but to speculate: what would the impact of the social sciences have been *if* dishabituation, not demystification, had been the name of their game? Rather than accusing them, as I have often done, of having sold their adventurous, imaginative soul in order to gain the kind of authority from which their "older sisters" benefit, we may wonder about this very authority, that is, about what it requires from those who have to accept it.

Just who "accepts" this authority? Let us consider for instance the Higgs boson, which has now earned the precious title of a "really existing" experimental being. The authority associated with this title is not what specialized physicists "have to accept." Rather they rejoice at the high feat at last being achieved – the very costly and sophisticated "rendezvous" organized at CERN, where, "if it exists," the elusive boson would eventually have to show up, has been honored! As for myself, I am ready to trust those physicists when they authoritatively conclude that the suspense is over, because in this case I may trust that the people truly concerned in this suspense were gathered, active and in full array. I do not feel in the least excluded, as I would feel in having to accept an outside authority, because nobody is trying to formulate the difference which the fact that this boson "really exists" should make in my life. In the case of the threat posed by climate disorder, the situation is obviously different and the functioning of the Intergovernmental Panel on Climate Change (IPCC) is in itself a witness for the impact which this threatening "fact" is bound to make in innumerable lives, human and nonhuman. The specialists gathered by this institution know only too well that their assessments do not just concern the advancement of climate science but all inhabitants of the earth, and first of all the governments that should take them into account. This is why they have agreed that what may be claimed and what cannot must be determined under the punctilious supervision of representatives of these governments. As for how the peoples of this earth will be able to address the coming disorders, it is certainly not a matter of "accepting scientific authority." Climate science is mute about that. Instead it is a question which diffracts, or should diffract, across all our habits of thinking and imagining.[26]

The issue of authority is present, however, when scientists leave the "lab" – the techno-social rarefied milieu required by their operations and eventual achievements – in order to announce that at last they are able to define a scientific, rational, objective approach to a common concern, be it practical (synthetic life feeding the world) or existential (the possibility of an "augmented" human, even an immortal one). What is striking then is the habituation of the non-laboratory "milieu" with regard to those claims. The respect for the authority of the (rarefied) top over the (messy) bottom, the lack of an imaginative cultivation of the "What if?" and "But then!," affects even the (usually rather abstract, stereotyped) way this authority is contested. The mobilization against GMOs in Europe was an exception, and avoiding the repetition of what has been a nightmare for our policymakers has since become their priority.

Instead of criticizing the social sciences' sad mimicking of so-called sound sciences' authority, we may wonder what their impact might have been had they taken as their job to thwart any hasty judgments about or against the diverging voices which constitute the messy fabric of what we call a society, and to experiment with the means of making audible and articulate the consequences and repercussions that a "top" proposition may wish to ignore. Such social sciences, activating and empowering imagination against the standard opposition between "sound facts" and (unsound) values, would undoubtedly have been accused of mixing science with politics – that is, of unleashing the monster whose taming Toulmin associated with the Age of Reason. The enrollment of social sciences as a vector of the "disenchantment of the world" should not be separated from the "monstrous" consequences that would have followed had they conceived of dishabituation as being among their own specific achievements.

Let us finally turn toward our own epoch, when we face the prospect of being cursed by the children of our children for having placed our trust in the promises of progress associated with technoscience. It should first be remembered that Toulmin's second Renaissance was not a time of naive trust, rather one of anger and hope, sustained by unorthodox imaginative and experiential resources which must have felt frightening for those who relied on a taken-for-granted habituation regarding the settled order of progress. Yet today what seems settled is the prospect of a frightening future, challenging both hope and anger. Even denunciation becomes redundant – a bad fictional resource when a dominant theme of today's common imagination is already a vengeful Gaia punishing those who offended her. SF, as a thought experiment about the questions and speculations this particular epoch makes us capable of, is confronted, as we all are, with powerful myths that suddenly seem to acquire an awful veracity. More than ever, it takes imaginative means to resist the black hole attraction of tales of apocalypse.

That is why I have chosen to close with David Brin and his latest novel, *Existence* (2012), where he not only addresses this very situation but does it in a way that accords full importance to the unruly messiness of the world which the Age of Reason refused to acknowledge.[27]

Brin's midcentury world brims with the consequences of climate change and other ecological disasters, and also with conflicting ideas about how to save the planet. Here Brin confronts us with what we already "know": that there are billions of us on Earth, and even if our ideas about a liveable future convince millions, it will still be a tiny minority. In the future imagined by Brin, powerful groups actively promote different ideas with different, often dubious, means. In other words, no "moment of truth" has marked a turning point. Even so, everything has changed – nobody can envisage living without "ai [artificial intelligence] enhanced specs" permanently connecting its bearer with the web. In addition, one learns that the United States are no longer united and that, following a terrorist "awful day," an uneasy social peace has been obtained, involving the recognition of distinct "estates" – that of the very rich at the top, that of the billions of nobodies at the bottom, each with its rights and duties. Just about everything that we fear, denounce or wish for today is thriving, yet the question has not changed: does humankind have a future?

The thought experiment is about us, about our present imaginations of the future, about the tales of salvation we may secretly entertain, with providential heroes or saviors leading the masses into the light, be it through triumphant mastery or wise renunciation. As for Brin, he casts his lot with the precarious anomaly that started with the Renaissance: renunciation would require giving up a world whose achievement, whatever its crimes, is that billions now read and wonder, and feel it normal to contest, denounce, take diverging positions. It would require returning to the elitist shackles of authoritarian traditions which have been the norm throughout human history. Desperate chic won't do for Brin[28]: we have to remember that the true heroes of 9/11 were the passengers of United Airlines Flight 93, normal people who were able, when they understood what was happening, to act and make a difference. If there is a future, it will not be through strict order taming "the people," messy, chaotic, undependable as they may be. They, one way or another, must be trusted.

In Brin's novel, this trust is verified by the anonymous existence of "smart mobs" self-organizing on the web around a "hot" question, collecting data, cross-analyzing them, uncovering hidden correlations, efficiently feeding those who most urgently need their help. But what difference can they make in this anxious, unsettled world haunted by the question: Where are the others? Why the great silence? Why did nobody ever come (and, we hope, say hello)? This is the so-called Fermi paradox, which in the 1980s was coupled with the idea of self-replicating "Von Neumann" probes, able to multiply exponentially and thus to spread throughout our galaxy within a "short" timespan with regard to cosmological time, so that they "should" have reached the earth. The question has been sporadically discussed by scientists and is a staple of science fiction writers. Brin proposes that, in 2050, it has become a real concern. The point is no longer the rarity of intelligent species but the possibility that any technologically advanced civilization is doomed to make one of the many "big blunders" capable of destroying its world.

Because this is SF, a possible answer comes under the guise of the dreamed-for extraterrestrial offer: "Join us." Is it an offer or an enticing trap? I will not try to summarize the story, just emphasize the dishabituating character of the hypothesis it unfolds: ours is not only a messy world but a messy universe. What the hypothesis of Von Neumann probes had forgotten, among other things, is that a proliferation of self-replicating (ai) creatures may also mean

Darwinian evolution at its "worst," the selection of viral beings most gifted at invading their prey and turning them into a means for their own proliferation.

Existence could well be a dark novel – from now on humankind will unceasingly have to resist ever more clever "attacks" by "viruses" who learn how to overcome or turn our defenses, who learn "us." Nevertheless, SF is not about doom (an easy matter) but about what we might possibly become able to think and feel and imagine. If we have a small chance it is because the initial offer, to "join us," had evolved as it was selected for efficacy on (the usual) hierarchical societies where the addressee of the offer is well-determined: "masters" that will join up with others who have already gained virtual immortality at the price of destroying their own planet as a virus destroys a cell, turning it into a factory for the virus's replication and propagation. The offer was not meant for an unruly society, with billions listening, speculating about its meaning, strongly disagreeing about the answer to be given and learning what it implies. And years later in *Existence* diversity seems to have been embraced as our only robust, resilient defense. Now included in humankind are all sorts of ai creatures, autists recognized as a "different" people, "uplifted" dolphins,[29] robots from a previous wave of exploration, found stranded, lurking in the asteroid belt, even revived Neanderthals. No clever trick will seduce in one stroke all these divergent intelligences. It is ecology all the way down, although Brin leaves it to the reader to grasp that this is the real thread – that *Existence* is all about dishabituating us of the unspoken dreams of elitist monoculture.

Brin's speculative commitment to the future resounds at the end of the book: "We are still tottering along . . . uncovering failure modes, just in time. Sometimes gaining a little breathing room and confidence. At other times barely avoiding panic. Doing some repair. Staving off tyrants and demagogues. Coping with both would-be godmakers and fanatical nostalgia junkies. Gradually learning to benefit from our multiplicity."[30]

There is no need to choose between the neo-pagan goddess and Brin's thoroughly urbanized world, between the thoughtful, intriguing Hainish stories of Le Guin and the dark outrage of ecofeminist Sheri Tepper – whom I have no room to present here, but who, from book to book, at least since her *Gate to Women's Country* (1988), asks the same two questions: What happened to this species of ours? And/or is there an escape from the deadlock? There is no need to choose, because their multiple voices are engaged in worlding (to invoke again Haraway's concept), opening interstices in the block of certainties that seems to condemn us.

A single interstice has no power in itself, it is not a path for salvation, and it authorizes no claim. Interstices call for the plural. It is the messy multiplicity of interstices, of faults or fissures that, physicists have learned, "materialize" matter, render materials so different from the ideal, intelligible matter beloved of theory.[31] It may well be that the freedom physicists derive from their sense of entitlement is what science studies may bring to social sciences. This, at least was the lesson Bruno Latour has derived from the science wars and which I had already learned working with physicists. The attempt by critical theorists to explain away what matters for the people they address, replacing these people's reasons by their own theoretical interpretation is an abuse of power. When science studies could be understood as doing that, it unleashed the so-called science wars because scientists felt entitled to strike back. But what of all the others who seemed to accept being insulted? For Latour "the failure of science studies to provide an explanation of the natural sciences was a *felix culpa*: this original sin that could lead the social sciences to another settlement by rejuvenating the very meaning of those two words, social and science."[32]

Rejuvenation is no easy matter. It demands that we agree that society as such, or any other sociocultural generality, is not a source of explanation of scientific achievements (when they actually occur) and that the job of the sciences (in the plural) is not to oppose objectivity to socio-cultural interpretations. When physicists recognized the difference between matter and materials, what prompted them was not the objectification of the materials' properties but the attempt to provide a *relevant* characterization of these properties, an open venture, at once creative and critical, which demands that what we address be allowed to meddle and challenge business-as-usual explanatory framing.[33] In all cases rejuvenation means the activation of imagination, with the ever-recurrent dishabituating question: what might this situation, which I could easily understand in the terms of my definition, become capable of, in escaping this definition? SF is not "only a fiction" – it is one resource, among others, that sustains our capacity to escape, to "change planes," to experiment with the trust that things did not, and do not, have to be "that" way. How many are those among us who may gratefully acknowledge that they owe to SF the capacity of being "materials," gifted with the surprising property of not completely conforming to theory, and so capable of keeping alive, resonating in their hearts and minds, echoes of the second Renaissance that was?

NOTES

1. Anne McCaffrey, *To Ride Pegasus* (New York: Ballantine, 1973).
2. Starting in 1972, my immersion in Prigogine's working group was marked by his 1977 Nobel Prize in Chemistry, and our coauthoring of *La nouvelle alliance* in

1979; see Ilya Prigogine and Isabelle Stengers, *Order out of Chaos: Man's New Dialogue with Nature* (New York: Bantam, 1984).

3. The first chapter of my 1993 *Invention des sciences modernes* diagnosed the reason for this anger that was soon to explode in the guise of "the science wars"; see *The Invention of Modern Science* (Minneapolis: University of Minnesota Press, 2000). For a summary of this sad episode, see https://en.wikipedia.org/wiki/Science_wars/.

4. Isabelle Stengers, *Cosmopolitics I* (Minneapolis: University of Minnesota Press, 2010) and *Cosmopolitics II* (Minneapolis: University of Minnesota Press, 2011).

5. Bruno Latour, *An Inquiry into Modes of Existence: An Anthropology of the Moderns* (Cambridge: Harvard University Press, 2013).

6. Stephen Toulmin, *Cosmopolis: The Hidden Agenda of Modernity* (Chicago: University of Chicago Press, 1992).

7. Mary Midgley, *Science as Salvation* (London: Routledge, 1992).

8. Bruno Latour, "Steps toward the Writing of a Compositionist Manifesto," *New Literary History* 41 (2010): 471–90.

9. Robert Darnton, *Mesmerism and the End of the Enlightenment in France* (Cambridge: Harvard University Press, 1986).

10. Stephen Toulmin, *Cosmopolis*, 206.

11. See the Introduction to the present volume and also Donna Haraway, *Staying with the Trouble: Making Kin in the Chthulucene* (Durham: Duke University Press, 2016).

12. I am aware that Marion Zimmer Bradley's personal life is now the object of painful questions, but this does not cancel my debt toward her work.

13. "Ingress" in the previous paragraph is a technical term of Whitehead's. The term "interstice" that I will use later is also inspired by Whitehead. "Life," he wrote, "lurks in the interstices"; see Alfred North Whitehead, *Process and Reality*, corrected edition, ed. David Ray Griffin and Donald W. Sherburne (New York: Free Press, 1979), 105.

14. Gilles Deleuze and Felix Guattari, *What Is Philosophy?* (New York: Columbia University Press, 1994).

15. For a powerful call for the social sciences to move beyond the critical obsession with the "subject"/"object" contrast, see Bruno Latour, "Why Has Critique Run Out of Steam? From Matters of Fact to Matters of Concern," *Critical Inquiry*, Special issue on the Future of Critique, 30.2 (2004): 225–48. For studies that beautifully evade this obsession, see for instance David Abram, *The Spell of the Sensuous: Perception and Language in a More-Than-Human World* (New York: Vintage Books, 1997); or Anna Tsing, *The Mushroom at the End of the World: On the Possibility of Life in Capitalist Ruins* (Princeton: Princeton University Press, 2015) – and of course Donna Haraway's SF work.

16. Marilyn Strathern, *Reproducing the Future: Essays on Anthropology, Kinship and the New Reproductive Technologies* (Manchester: Manchester University Press, 1992), 10.

17. John Searle, "Minds, Brains and Programs," *Behavioral and Brain Sciences* 3 (1980): 417–57.

18. I derive this formula from Donna Haraway. See *Staying with the Trouble*.

19. Ursula K. Le Guin, *The Earthsea Trilogy* (New York: Bantam Books, 1975).

20. Eduardo Viveiros de Castro, *Cannibal Metaphysics* (Minneapolis: Univocal, 2014).
21. Ursula K. Le Guin, *Changing Planes* (Orlando: Harcourt, 2003), 2.
22. As defined in the *Merriam-Webster Medical Dictionary*: www.merriam-webster .com/medical/dishabituation.
23. This is the general title of the series. The nineteenth volume, *Emergence*, appeared in 2018, and the first volume, *Foreigner*, in 1994.
24. Richard White, *The Middle Ground: Indians, Empires, and the Republics in the Great Lakes Region, 1650–1815* (Cambridge: Cambridge University Press, 2011).
25. For an essay in such an art, see Philippe Pignarre and Isabelle Stengers, *Capitalist Sorcery: Breaking the Spell* (London: Palgrave Macmillan, 2011).
26. Among the numerous books published on the coming climate disorder and the kind of thought it demands, see Isabelle Stengers, *In Catastrophic Times: Resisting the Coming Barbarism* (London: Open Humanities Press and Meson Press, 2015, free access online). Also see Donna Haraway's *Staying with the Trouble* as well as Bruno Latour's 2013 Gifford Lectures, *Facing Gaia*. An augmented version of the lectures has now been published: *Facing Gaia: Eight Lectures on the New Climatic Regime* (Cambridge: Polity Press, 2017).
27. David Brin, *Existence* (New York: Tor Books, 2012).
28. For more on Brin's deliberate refusal to renounce the US can-do mentality, see www.davidbrin.com/realworld.html.
29. These dolphins, whose sentience has been enhanced (or "uplifted"), are all that remain of an otherwise forgotten project that was aborted under the pressure of animal rights organizations. It is also a nod to Brin's own "Uplift Universe" saga – beginning with *Sundiver* (New York: Bantam Books, 1980) – an alternative future where the same project has been brought to completion and where another kind of "first encounter" also means the discovery by humans that they live in a universe (again very dangerous) where uplifting is the rule.
30. David Brin, *Existence* (New York: Tor Science Fiction, 2013), 858–9.
31. See Isabelle Stengers, "Wondering about Materialism," in *The Speculative Turn: Continental Materialism and Realism*, ed. Levi Bryant, Nick Srnicek and Graham Harman (Melbourne: re.press, 2011), 368–80.
32. Bruno Latour, "When Things Strike Back: A Possible Contribution of Science Studies to the Social Sciences," *British Journal of Sociology* 51.1 (2000): 107–23, at 112.
33. See Martin Savransky, *The Adventure of Relevance: An Ethics of Social Inquiry* (London: Palgrave Macmillan, 2016).

PART II

Snapshots of the Past
Literature and Science

2

MARY BAINE CAMPBELL

Shakespeare and Modern Science

Poor Tom; that eats the swimming frog, the toad, the tadpole, the wall-newt and the water; that in the fury of his heart, when the foul fiend rages, eats cow-dung for sallets; swallows the old rat and the ditch-dog; drinks the green mantle of the standing pool...

> William Shakespeare, *King Lear*

And finally, I interpose everywhere admonitions and scruples and cautions, with a religious care to eject, repress, and as it were exorcise, every kind of phantom.

> Sir Francis Bacon, "The Great Instauration"

[The members of the Royal Society] have therefore been most rigorous in putting in execution, the only Remedy, that can be found for this *extravagance*: and that has been, a constant Resolution, to reject all the amplifications, digressions, and swellings of style: to return back to the primitive purity, and shortness, when men deliver'd so many *things*, almost in an equal number of *words*. They have exacted from all their members, a close, naked, natural way of speaking; positive expressions; clear senses; a native easiness: bringing all things as near the Mathematical plainness, as they can.

> Thomas Sprat, *History of the Royal Society*

No ideas but in things.

> William Carlos Williams, "A Sort of Song"

Anyone who professes English literature will eventually make the acquaintance of several persons (usually lawyers, like Bacon) who have cracked the code to reveal that Francis Bacon, Lord Verulam, is, as long suspected, the true author of Shakespeare's works, not a wandering player from Stratford with an eighth-grade education. Yet no country-bred actor has tried to convince me that Shakespeare was the author of Bacon's many works. Surely the logic should work both ways? If the masters of empirical evidence see the imaginary Father of Modern Science in the works of the imagined Father of Modern Literature, should the masters of Shakespearian line-reading not see a cornucopian Shakespeare in Bacon's extended figures, his metaphorical perseverations, his delicious projections for natural histories of "Touch," "of things Ignited," of "the Blue Expanse"?[1]

It may be time to take the lawyers up on their traditional insight, which has for so long come knocking and withstood so many dismissive e-mails that their very fidelity to the idea demands consideration. Bacon was taught to them as the Father of Modern Science, but they are drawn to him as their fellow lawyer, eventually Lord Chancellor of England. For what Alfred North Whitehead calls "rigid empiricism" bears little relation to much modern science, particularly of the past century, which could not seriously operate within its strictures (try to imagine Einstein or Barbara McClintock reconceiving time, space and DNA on lines laid down by positivism), nor could early modern natural philosophy. The construction and deployment of data in a criminal court case comes closer to rigid empiricism (perhaps the "speculative empiricism" of our theme in this collection would be unseemly in a case that could lead to death or prison). Do lawyers, perhaps, want to see their data as the stuff of poetry?[2]

Well, the law is not our brief. The lawyers can only inspire us to posit that Bacon and Shakespeare, whose lifetimes overlapped, who shared a city of 225,000 and whose names and influences persist half a millennium later, have something in common worth our attention, and that what we have come to call empiricism, at least in its expanded sense, is involved. For certainly we can agree with "sirbacon.org" and its ilk to some degree: both were interested in dreams, both were maestros of metaphor, wrote plays and observed something they might have called "Nature" closely and attentively; both were iconoclasts, making radical and novel demands on the imaginations of their fellow citizens. Both were awake to the literally overwhelming beauty of sense impressions (Bacon died in pursuit of the secret essence of cold), and the attractively sensationalist effect of the words that referred to them. Were both, then, proto-scientists?

There was no strictly modern science in the offing during their lifetimes, nor would the word "scientist" be coined for centuries. But it is an interesting experiment in anachronism, to seek in their works a thread that might lead to the rigid or positivist empiricism that framed nineteenth-century science and nineteenth-century empire in the first age of the "scientist," and another thread leading to the more expanded empiricisms of figures like Darwin and Einstein.[3] Perhaps the early moments of, in Stengers's words, "what came in between, the shining, chaotic, speculative, violent, flourishing, tragic period known as the Renaissance" could partially redeem that even more tragic century-plus of "race science," slavery, colonialism, botany, massacre and genocide.[4] I would like to see Bacon and Shakespeare as the queer parents of a line that led to the Blaschka "glass flowers" at Harvard (to which that modernist devotee of the biosphere Marianne Moore famously claimed that superior guests did not require to be taken), rather than to the labs of Dow Chemical.[5] The flowers are beautiful not only visually but in their palpable glass bodies, the slight muting and subtilizing of their colors by the frosted texture of the glass. And beautiful not only in visual and tactile ways but by virtue of their connectedness and relatedness: each is a member of a cornucopian taxonomy that was until recently on display – in glass cabinets – all at once. And beautiful not only in their conceptual relatedness but in their gigantism, an imaginary scale that shrinks the human viewer, and their radically inappropriate fragility, nothing like the tougher world of biological flesh. They are at once information-laden, visually accurate, palpable, gorgeous, expensive, symbolic, impermanent, and hyperbolic. They represent, parody and honor the natural life forms they mimic, and represent the nineteenth century's atomization of scientific "objects" at its most extreme. In so doing they make it beautiful, and unreal.[6]

This essay will begin by demonstrating links between, on one hand, an empirical persuasion and the novelty of Shakespeare's language, and on the other, Bacon's conflicted natural philosophy, conjoining the austere, detached empiricism of the epigraph from "The Great Instauration" with the polysemy and aesthetic appeal of his texts.[7] Not for nothing did Bishop Sprat, in his *History of the Royal Society* (1667) recommend the Royal Society's experiments to the attention of the poets (and not for nothing did they reject the invitation).[8] What is the nature of the turn that literary studies see in the "Age of Shakespeare," and the history of science in the "Scientific Revolution," if we are to see it as a single turn from the perspective of Literature and Science? (I am not the first to wonder. The last twenty exciting years for the history of science have seen considerable interest in bringing the issues of early modern natural philosophy, and recently the data and ethics of its natural history, to bear on the work of Shakespeare, early modern literature, and even more broadly, the corpus of European literature in the period.)[9] What new vision did Shakespeare and Bacon share (sort of), that could degenerate into positivism or sprout, perhaps, as the literary modes we are pleased, if deluded, to call "realism" and "naturalism"?[10]

From Shakespeare to Science

This title sketches a long route: 228 years passed between the death of Shakespeare and the birth of the Victorian "scientist." In Shakespeare's time, "science" was felt directly as an Anglicization of the Latin *scientia* (via the French *cience*): things that are known, or knowledge. It was capable of pluralization, as many kinds of things were known: optical things, legal things, agricultural things, historical things, philosophical things, military things, mathematical things, poetic things. Ways of gilding copper, annealing steel, glazing pottery, tanning leather, binding books, grinding lenses, poisoning kings, counterfeiting coins, painting on copper.[11] The poet, soldier and courtier Sir Phillip Sydney called poetry the "Queen of the Sciences."

Occasional uses of the word "science" in Shakespeare's lifetime might seem familiar to us: for instance William Vaughan's in his advice book on governance, *The Golden-groue*: "The name of science is taken more strictly for a habit gotten by demonstration separated from wisedome; in which last signification Naturall philosophy, & the Mathematickes are called Sciences."[12] That separation from wisdom seems key, and it was pursued self-consciously in the seventeenth century: in the study of "literature and science" we observe its design and success. But here are two of Shakespeare's usages from around the same time: "I do present you with a man of mine Cunning in Music, and the Mathematics, / To instruct her fully in those sciences" (*Taming of the Shrew*, II.1.56–7); "Plutus himself, / that knows the tinct and multiplying med'cine, / Hath not in natures mystery more science, / Then I have in this Ring" (*All's Well that Ends Well*, III.5.116–17).[13] The "sciences" these characters refer to are music, mathematics and alchemy, forms of knowledge heavily imbued with kinds of meaning and signification lost to us at the other end of the story that separates demonstration from wisdom, or even from analogy. All were linked to magic and the occult sciences, and to the extent in which the Shakespearean corpus is focally concerned with the "science" practiced in his time, the plays seem particularly interested in magic, or the limit cases of the demonstrable (dream, projective belief, theatrical illusion, etc.).[14]

This is not however to ignore the evidence the plays and poems supply of massive interest in sciences of lesser status and more strictly empirical ground. Like Virgil before him, Shakespeare seems to have been at least somewhat familiar with all trades, their gear and tackle and trim. Carla Mazzio surveys a wondrous corpus of mostly late nineteenth- and prewar twentieth-century books by scientists and physicians on the plethora of data in which Shakespeare evidences his knowledge of, for example, "properties of the so-called Ancient Planets ... that he could not have known without telescopic aid."[15] The present essay is concerned with Shakespeare's epistemological grappling with the invisible and indeterminate and with his extraordinary eye for what his contemporary Bacon would theorize as preferable objects of attention: natural "things." Apprehensible objects, objects we can attend to with our sharpened, eventually artificially extended senses. That "dive-dapper peering through a wave, / Who, being looked on, ducks as quickly in" ("Venus and

Adonis," 86–8), that "watery glass, / Decking with liquid pearl the bladed grass" (*Midsummer Night's Dream*, I.1.213–14), that "plaster, or some loam, or some rough-cast ... to signify wall" (*Midsummer Night's* Dream, III.1.43–4), or King Hamlet's poisoned father: "a most instant tetter barked about, / Most lazar-like, with vile and loathsome crust, / All [his] smooth body" (*Hamlet*, I.5.76–78).

Or years later, when the Royal Society had crystallized around Bacon's old grant applications, the eyeball of a gray drone-fly in Robert Hooke's *Micrographia*, the greatest part of whose head

> was nothing else but two large and *protuberant* bunches, or *prominent* parts, ABCDEA, the surface of each of which was all cover'd over, or shap'd into a multitude of small *Hemispheres*, plac'd in a *triagonal* order, that being the closest and most compacted, and in that order, rang'd over the whole surface of the eye in very lovely rows, between each of which, as in necessary, were left long and regular trenches, the bottoms of every of which, were perfectly intire and not at all perforated or drill'd through, which I most certainly was assured of, by the regularly reflected Image of certain Objects which I mov'd to and fro between the [decapitated!] head and the light.[16]

A play like *Hamlet* (or *The Tempest*) is obviously bound up as well with more abstract thinking, which unlike Williams (see epigraph), Bacon does not abjure, but requires it to emerge from natural "particulars."[17] The particulars of *Hamlet* are the kind that tempted thinkers raised on Aristotle, and all that that name meant for the scholars of the time, to veer into occult territory: ghosts were among the limit cases – with comets, magnetism, phosphorescence and the metamorphosis of caterpillars into butterflies – of an empirical science based on faith in the legibility of the sensible world.[18]

Consider, for instance, Bacon's Idols of the Tribe: for "humane sense is fa[l]sely affirm'd to be the measure of things. On the Contrary, all the conceptions both of sense and reason are taken from the Analogy of man, not the analogy of the Universe."[19] The ghost looks like my father because all I can see is human things. And "words are imposed according to the vulgar capacity; therefore a vitious and an improper imposition of words doth wonderfully mislead and clog the Understanding" – what Bacon terms the Idols of the Market. The manifestation of dead spirits when they die unshriven or unrevenged is a received idea: language has made it thinkable. Above all, the Idols of the Theatre, so-called "because all the kinds of Philosophy ... we look upon as so many Fables produced and acted so as to make a fictitious and s[c]enical [staged] world." This is what makes Hamlet vulnerable to error in a situation so close to his heart: "Humane

Understanding is inclinable of it self to suppose a greater order and equality in things than it finds," and

> [t]he Humane Understanding attracts all other things to give its suffrage and consent unto those things which once please it, either because they are received and believed, or else they delight ... But in case this delight and vanity were wanting, yet it is a proper and perpetual error in Humane Understanding to be rather moved and stirred up by affirmatives than by negatives, although in truth it ought to be indifferent to both.

It is easier to believe the apparition is the ghost of his father than that it is nothing, easier to believe his uncle and mother killed his father out of incestuous lust and ambition than to believe in a sequence of meaningless or overdetermined accidents.

What differentiates Hamlet from Horatio, Polonius, Gertrude and the rest of the company is that he wants to know, even more than he wants revenge or peace. And so, *pace* Bacon, he produces and observes a fictitious and scenic world, as an experiment, to bring the occult forces, or their "signatures" in blush and gasp, to the surface of the phenomenal couple in the sight of all – in the market and theater.[20] Suspicious of "wisdom," Polonius' stock in trade, Hamlet seeks demonstration. Which of course provides only more phenomena demanding more penetration, and there cannot be an end of it. For Bacon's science–no vulgar empiricism, and not so new or singular as his prose makes out–demands that its ultimate object be matter:[21] "The Humane intellect is by its own Nature carried on to abstracts, and those things that are unstable it fancies to be constant. But it is better to dissect Nature than to abstract her ... For that purpose we must rather examine matter, its schemes and transformations, its pure acts, and the Law of action and motion. For Forms are but the invention of men's brains" (6).

But Hamlet does not like matter. He wants it to melt, resolve into a dew – even the matter of spirits should do so – and yet that dew is matter too.[22] He likes nothing, absence, zero, vacancy, all of which "Nature" abhors and her Law forbids – as we still believe. The word "O," newly ambiguous with the importation of "o" from Arab mathematics, is uttered more in *Hamlet* than in any play but *Othello*. And Hamlet says "no" more than any character in Shakespeare. This hatred of matter on Hamlet's part is shocking: it measures the greatest imaginable despair. For even the dead are matter. (Is this what generates a ghost in place of the corpse of his father?)

For our purposes in this collection *Hamlet* gives us a Shakespeare who associates the speculative empiricism of his tragic hero with a theoretical and life-threatening rage against the material world, with the matter thereof, and all that shares material existence and the senses that alert us to it – however inaccurately. Hamlet, we might say, is an ideologue: he investigates in order to expose, and as Bacon warns of the Idols of the Theatre, he knows or believes before he begins. Unlike Paracelsian matter, he has "something within that *passeth* show," and so, it must be, do we all. It doesn't lead to skepticism, though – which would be unendurable in the moral economy of this royal family. It leads to honest impasse: rigid belief run up against the sealed lips of other bodies and their unreadable signatures.[23] To make these silences and illegibilities more natural, Shakespeare kills off everyone in the play, by mistake.[24]

So Many Things, Almost in an Equal Number of Words

But unlike a "scientist," unlike even Bacon or Descartes, Shakespeare is not committed to an epistemology, or locked into a single pursuit of truth. However investigative the marvelous new medium of public theater may be, however similar it is, as William West has shown, to the great "theatrums" of cosmography and medicine – those books purporting to show us the big and little worlds (from which the word for the building that houses its performances was taken) – a playwright is free to try on as many epistemologies as will engage an audience.[25]

Would *Hamlet* even have been accessible to Einstein or Bohr, except as a play about a young man's Oedipal complex – which begs the question of why that young man should be a prince, and all Denmark "rotten"? To get a feeling for Shakespeare's episteme let us look at another of the plays in which his characters stage a performance. They do this three times overtly in his corpus, toward the beginning, the middle and the end of his career, in *A Midsummer Night's Dream* (1595), *Hamlet* (1603) and, our chief interest in this section, *The Tempest* (1611). In each case he puts to the question, as Lord Chancellor Bacon might say, the obviousness of the material world. But the questions are different.

In the interests of space I will say little about my favorite play, *A Midsummer Night's Dream* (1595), which shares with Shakespeare's epyllion "Venus and Adonis" (1592–3) an inebriate delight in detailing the objects of the senses, or simply listing them, as part of the play's irony-saturated focus on the division of actuality into "dream" (not real) and "reality" (impossible).[26] But a word is in order regarding this early work, from Shakespeare: "Good monsieur," orders Bottom, temporarily beloved of the fairy queen, "kill me a red-hipped humble-bee on the top of a thistle; and, good monsieur, bring me the honey-bag ... [A]nd good monsieur, have a care the honey-bag break not; I would be loath to have you overflown with a honey-bag, signior" (*A Midsummer Night's Dream*, IV.1.12–13): it is as if

Shakespeare had tried out Hooke's microscope – and thought through what he saw in terms of touch as well as sight.[27] Or, for a famous example of the play's lists (all the characters but the tight-lipped war-bride Hippolyta love them), Oberon's "bank where the wild thyme blows, / Where oxlips and the nodding violet grows; / Quite over-canopied with luscious woodbine, /With sweet musk-roses, and with eglantine" (II.1.254–7). Or, to quote a fragment from one of many passages displaying the careful study of animal behavior (ethology!) in "Venus and Adonis," on a hunted hare:

> poor Wat, far off upon a hill,
> Stands on his hinder legs with list'ning ear
> To harken if his foes pursue him still.
> Anon their loud alarums he doth hear ...
> Then shalt thou see the dew-bedabbl'd wretch
> Turn and return, indenting with the way,
> Each envious briar his weary legs do scratch,
> Each shadow makes him stop, each murmur stay (697–706).[28]

Ethology is far in the future, but, serving the different interests of imaginative sympathy and erotic bathos, it is also in the past. And though this kind of sensual detail, nowhere to be found in medieval poetry (where Oberon's list of plant species might be "flowers red and white") or natural history (where the hare might signify lust, or be hermaphroditic, but not suffering briars to scratch his weary legs), has become the now-familiar calling card of "realism," it was a striking novelty in the sixteenth century. It must have stood out as a kind of commitment in these texts to a previously neglected matter, to *enargeia* in the new form of a plenum of material objects. It is precisely the opposite of Hamlet's "nothing" and the moving speechlessness of all his O's.

By the time *The Tempest* is first performed in 1611, usually considered Shakespeare's last play though he coauthored *The Two Noble Kinsmen* with John Fletcher three years later, the telescope and microscope have been invented, their use published, and Bacon's *Advancement of Learning* (1605) come out in English. And Shakespeare has turned his kaleidoscope one more time.[29] Neither comedy nor tragedy, *The Tempest* is a sad play, a high stakes investigation of Bacon's Idols of the Theatre that ends, as comedy must, in a marriage that resolves, as Renaissance theatrical marriages must, political tensions, cementing new alliances and sealing the tombs of unforgotten wrongs. It is also, as part of its complex sadness, beautiful. Its fairies, like those of *A Midsummer Night's Dream*, are close observers of the natural world, which is once again prominent in a play that features magical illusion, shape-shifting spiritual bodies, enchantment, theatrical performance, and such ambiguous phenomena as "St. Elmo's fire."[30] (Or is that Ariel's magical imitation of a "real" illusion? – "I flamed amazement: sometimes I'd divide / And burn in many places: on the topmast, / The yards and bowsprit would I flame distinctly, / Then meet and join" [I.ii.229–32]). But rather than the flatly comic contradiction between fairy reality and the day-lit reality of Athens, none of it dreamed, all of it equally true, we have on "this island," as everyone calls it, a series of interrogations, or what Bacon would call "vexations" in *The Advancement of Learning* – in a term borrowed from the lingo of judicial torture.[31]

Let us look at three passages in Acts II and III in which language fails, or rather succeeds in suggesting the slippage between the actual and our means of representation or even apperception. This is the pair of problems that both very different mentors of the period's epistemological transformation, Bacon and Descartes, attempt to confront, and to which the epigraph from Sprat's *History of the Royal Society* is so memorably oblivious. The first passage is Trinculo's famous description of Caliban, who has "fallen flat" (II.2.17) and covered himself with his cloak at Trinculo's approach:

> What have we here? A man or a fish? Dead or alive? A fish: he smells like a fish: a very ancient and fishlike smell: a kind of not-of-the-newest poor-John. A strange fish! Were I in England now – as once I was – and had but this fish painted, not a holiday fool there but would give a piece of silver: there wouldst this monster make a man: any strange beast there makes a man ... Legged like a man and his fins like arms! Warm, o'my troth! I do now let loose my opinion ... this is no fish but an islander that hath lately suffered by a thunderbolt. (II.2.24–36)

Trinculo creeps under Caliban's cloak as the storm picks up again. Enter Stephano, responding to Caliban's "Do not torment me: O!" (II.2.56):

> What's the matter? Have we devils here? Do you put tricks upon's with savages and men of Ind, ha? I have not scaped drowning to be afeard now of your four legs. (II.2.57–62)

Stephano remains confused by the sight of Caliban and Trinculo largely hidden under Caliban's cloak, but eventually pulls Trinculo out by the legs, asking:

> How came thou to be the siege of this moon-calf? Can he vent Trinculos? *Trinculo*: I took him to be killed with a thunder-stroke: but art thou not drowned, Stephano? ... I hid me under the dead moon-calf's gabardine. (II.2.105–11)

Then, when the clowns figure out there are three living and articulate persons in the scene, Caliban gets into action, proposing to worship them and then to be their slave, and perceptions of him change again. Offered worship Trinculo cries, "By this good light, this is a very shallow monster. I afeard of him? A very weak monster!" Offered a slave's subjection he responds, "I shall laugh myself to death at this puppy-headed monster" (II.2.143–4, 153–4).

The history of directors' attempts to figure forth Caliban is panoplied: he is the crux of the play for them. Decorous Ariel, with his lovely songs, is a cinch to dress and set in motion. But this great and furious poet, this moon-calf, dog-head, merman, monster, cannibal, prince, hag-seed, man, abhorrèd slave, demi-devil, bastard, thing of darkness: he cannot be compassed. Language fails before him, though he is the play's master of it, speaking in every register while Prospero is condemned to princely and scholarly pomposities and Ariel to loveliness.

Not that Caliban can't do loveliness. When the clowns are frighted by the tabor-playing of an invisible Ariel ("the picture of Nobody," III.2.133), Caliban soothes them with a sensory description of "the isle" that hovers deliciously between dream and invisibilia, imagining an island purged of power:

> Be not afeard: the isle is full of noises,
> Sounds and sweet airs, that give delight and hurt not:
> Sometimes a thousand twangling instruments
> Will hum about mine ears; and sometimes voices,
> That if I had waked after long sleep,
> Will make me sleep again, and then in dreaming,
> The clouds methought would open and show riches
> Ready to drop upon me, that when I waked
> I cried to dream again. (III.3.118–26)

Bacon was interested in noises and music too. There is a department of sounds in *The New Atlantis's* Salomon's House (where the stereo is already invented), and natural histories of them are projected at the end of *The New Organon*, unfinished at his death: "69. History of Hearing and Sounds"; 70. "History of Music"; 13. "History of Sounds above (if there are any) except Thunder."[32] (Thunder was covered in "5. History of Lightening, Thunderbolts, Thunder and Sheet-lightning.") Speaking as a writer, I find his "Catalogue of Particular Histories" the single most beautiful text of the period, in any language. It does not get more speculative than this, the projection of topics into the wild blue yonder of other imaginations, others' labor, guided by little but the interior and implicit logic of a list.[33]

As a prospectus for the work of lyric and philosophical poetry for the next five centuries – for "numbers," as verse was then termed – it is powerful, if rarely read. As a prospectus for the work of the modern sciences, in the immortal phrase of the dreamer and quantum physicist Wolfgang Pauli, "it isn't even wrong."[34]

One last case of description from *The Tempest*'s cast of mazed and deluded investigators. To Gonzalo's worried question after Ariel (as harpy) presents the situation's guilty backstory to the enchanted aristocrats, Alonso, King of Naples, responds as if he alone had heard – and heard it not in speech but in noise and music (of which Caliban had sweetly warned, "this isle is full"):

> O, it is monstrous, monstrous:
> Methought the billows spoke and told me of it,
> The winds did sing it to me, and the thunder –
> That deep and dreadful organ-pipe – pronounced
> The name of Prosper: it did bass my trespass.
> Therefore my son i'the ooze is bedded: and
> I'll seek him deeper than e'er plummet sounded
> And with him there lie mudded.   (III.3.107–14)

A poem of remarkable sounds itself, which ends by bass-ing its speaker's intended next trespass, in a suicidal vision familiar from Hamlet's. After the windy hiss of "s" and "ss," transposed by "z": ooze is bedded and deeper plummet sounded and mudded. Language reaches beneath sense, recalling us to its own existence in the oozy depths as material phenomenon, vulnerable to magical abuse and perhaps to study, in some far-future Salomon's House.

But the rhetorical mode is *descriptio* and it essays to represent an event just transpired: we in the audience have just seen Ariel, dressed as a harpy, harass the courtiers for their past faithlessness. Yet Gonzalo addresses Alonso as if he himself had missed it altogether, and Alonso narrates it as if Ariel's narrative had been the noise of the tempest's wind and waves, or music of their song and organ. Sebastian and Antonio seem to have heard something, but not the words of Ariel or of Alonso. The director has staged a storm in the background, or she has relegated it solely to Alonso's words as metaphor: it could go either way. The storm is magical as far as we know, put on by Prospero for a show intended to expose the faithless politicians' guilt, as a younger Hamlet does in his own play of usurpation. Hamlet gets a rise out of his murderous uncle, but never gets to hear what we do – Claudius's soliloquized confession – and must continue reading signatures, convincing himself with signs that his belief is true and justified: is "science." Prospero's show certainly evokes affect in Alonso, but nothing else is certain. For no one has seen or heard the same thing; even we canny playgoers cannot be sure whether the magical storm is palpable, seen by all, seen by anyone, or, in the variety of its reception, simply the playwright's wordless metaphor for varying internal states of guilt, anxiety and blindness.

I do not mean to suggest this scene as an emblem of or provocation to skepticism. We can know, or speculate intelligently on, what Shakespeare's characters think and feel, but little of the author's point of view. We cannot really talk about the relation of this dead writer to the science of his time, a time that saw transformations in understanding of the cosmos, the planet, matter, of our species and "species" itself. But we can draw a line around the possibilities limned by his corpus as a whole, and particularly by those plays in which controlling characters compose, stage or act in theatrical performances. We can say that the staging or staged concealment of visibilia and invisibilia, of matter as question rather than datum, repeatedly attracted the author of Shakespeare's plays as opportunity for dramatic excitement. That the author frequently demonstrated this staging as staging, the visible as constructed, variously perceived, impossible to determine by mere witness, the lanthorn as the moon; I, the man i'the moon; this thorn-bush, my thorn-bush; and this dog, my dog.[35]

We can say that this excitement did not excite Lord Verulam, who warned against it volubly.[36] Who itemized the stark beauties of a world still innocent of smokestacks, car horns and fluorescent lights, and wanted to understand them as deeply as possible, who did not use his slender talent as a writer of masques to penetrate their "mysteries," and who did not write the plays of Shakespeare.

Bacon too felt mystery, and saw darkness.

[T]he universe to the eye of the human understanding is framed like a labyrinth, presenting as it does on every side so many ambiguities of way, such deceitful resemblances of objects and signs, natures so irregular in their lines and so knotted and entangled. And then the way is still to be made by the uncertain light of the sense, sometimes shining out, sometimes clouded over, through the woods of experience and particulars; while those who offer themselves for guides are ... themselves also puzzled, and increase the number of errors and wanderers.[37]

But he can tell us the way out.

In circumstances so difficult neither the natural force of man's judgment nor even any accidental felicity offers any chance of success. No excellence of wit, no repetition of chance experiments, can overcome such difficulties as these.

Our steps must be guided by a clue, and the whole way from the very first perception of the senses must be laid out upon a sure plan.

The lawyer offered the clue and the plan, and young scientists and indeed young humanists are still advised to read him on how to think.

Shakespeare's experiments are recommended to make us weep.[38]

NOTES

1. See Bacon's "Catalogue of Particular Histories by Titles" at the end of the "Outline of a Natural and Experimental History" in Francis Bacon, *The New Organon*, ed. Lisa Jardine and Michael Silverthorne (Cambridge: Cambridge University Press, 2000), 233–8.

2. If so, they should read Muriel Rukeyser's modernist long poem on the Gauley Bridge silicon disaster, "Book of the Dead"; see Muriel Rukeyser, *U. S. 1* (New York: Macmillan, 1938), or any of the more recent collections of her work; and Mary L. Leader, *Legible Ashes: Muriel Rukeyser's "The Book of the Dead,"* Diss. (Ann Arbor: Brandeis University, 2000).

3. The *OED* gives 1833 as its earliest instance of the word, faintly pejorative.

4. See Isabelle Stengers's essay in the present collection.

5. Marianne Moore, "Silence," in *Observations* (New York: Dial Press, 1925), 82.

6. For critique of the positivist epistemology behind much scientific discourse and science education in the schools, even in the social sciences – and which excludes, for example, a pilot's knowledge of how to fly a plane! – see Mary Baine Campbell, Lorraine Daston, Arnold I. Davidson, John Forrester, and Simon Goldhill, "Enlightenment Now: Concluding Reflections on Knowledge and Belief," *Common Knowledge* 13.2–3 (2007), 429.

7. Francis Bacon, "The Great Renewal" (more usually referred to as "The Great Instauration"), in *The New Organon*, 1–24, at 22.

8. Thomas Sprat, *History of the Royal Society*, ed. Jackson I. Cope and Harold Whitmore Jones (St. Louis: Washington University, 1958).

9. For examples, see suggestions in "Further Reading." See a few foundational works in early modern science studies per se: Paolo Rossi, *Logic and the Art of Memory* (1983; Chicago: University of Chicago Press, 2000); Hans Blumenberg, *The Legitimacy of the Modern Age* (1966; Cambridge: MIT Press, 1983); Steven Shapin and Simon Schaffer, *Leviathan and the Air-Pump: Hobbes, Boyle and the Experimental Life* (Princeton: Princeton University Press, 1985); Katharine Park and Lorraine Daston, ed., *The Cambridge History of Science, vol. 3: Early Modern Science* (Cambridge, Cambridge University Press, 2006); Pamela Smith, *The Body of the Artisan: Art and Experience in the Scientific Revolution* (Chicago: University of Chicago Press, 2006).

10. Mary Thomas Crane disagrees with this trajectory in her intelligent, well-informed account of relations between English literature and Renaissance "science," *Losing Touch with Nature: Literature and the New Science in the Sixteenth Century* (Baltimore: Johns Hopkins University Press, 2014). I agree with her, as far as she goes in her introductory survey of the range of natures across which sixteenth-century sciences cast their attention. But, in the interest of arguments tied to different histories, the path may branch toward a different end.

11. Historians of early modern knowledge have been increasingly interested in these applied sciences in recent years, notably but not exclusively Pamela Smith, William Newman, Pamela Long, Katharine Park, Marie-Noëlle Bourguet and Bettina Wahrig. Among younger scholars I think of Alicia Rankin's work on poisons and the pharmacopeia, Elly Truitt's on automata, Daniel Margocsy's on fencing, street magic and the display of horses. Lorraine Daston's department of the Max-Planck Institute for the History of Science in Berlin has also been a matrix for younger scholars taking up anew a challenge faced by Robert Hooke's *Micrographia* in 1665 (London: Jo. Martyn & Ja. Allestry) and re-articulated by Daston and Park in their *Wonders and the Order of Nature* (New York: Zone Books, 1997): to interest themselves and others in low-rent substances and objects of the phenomenal world. (As for the physics of low-rent substances, I recommend François Dagognet's *Les Detritus, des déchets, et de l'abjet* [Le Plessis-Robinson: Institut Synthèlabo pour le progress de la connaissance, 1997].)

12. William Vaughan, *Golden-groue* (London: 1600) Part I, p. 65 (sig. M).

13. Neither play has a certain date of composition, but they are assumed to be 1593 and 1602 respectively. All quotations from Shakespeare in this chapter are taken from the volumes of the same title of the RSC series, edited by Jonathan Bate and Eric Rasmussen, and quoted by act, scene and line number, or for poems by title and line number. The play texts are based very closely on the First Folio for all works that appear there. The volumes have also appeared all together in Bate and Rasmussen, ed., *The RSC Shakespeare: William Shakespeare Complete Works* (New York: Modern Library, 2007).

14. See Chapter 1 of Crane, *Losing Touch with Nature*, on differences and similarities between the so-called occult sciences of the period, with their magnetic center in Ficino, and more traditionally phenomenological sciences tethered to the name of Aristotle.

15. Peter D. Usher, *Shakespeare and the Dawn of Modern Science* (Amherst, NY: Cambria Press, 2010), xxi. For Carla Mazzio's respectful brief survey of older works in Usher's vein, see her "Introduction: Shakespeare and Science, c. 1600," in "Shakespeare and Science," special issue of *South Central Review* 26:1–2 (Spring/Summer, 2009): 1–23, esp. 5–6. She includes, for example, Henry Nicholson Ellacombe, *The Plant-Lore and Garden-Craft of Shakespeare* (London: 1884) and Dugald S. Hancock, *Meteorology in Shakespeare* (Bognor Regis: 1936).

16. Robert Hooke, *Micrographia*, 175–9.

17. For an instance of this term in Bacon, see my quotation at the end of this essay from his "Great Renewal"; Katharine Park's article, cited in n. 21, includes an account of links (and differences) between early Renaissance interest in "particulars" and modern empirical concern with unifying particulars under what came to be called "laws." For the source of Williams's line see "A Sort of Song" in *The Collected Poems of William Carlos Williams*, ed. Christopher MacGowan (New York: New Directions, 1986), 317.

18. On the divying up of *problemata* between the "Aristotelian" and "occult" sciences in the period, see again Crane's admirably clear survey, informed in part by Lorraine Daston's enlightening essay, "Preternatural Philosophy," in *Biographies of Scientific Objects*, ed. Daston and Fernando Vidal (Chicago:

University of Chicago Press, 1999), 15–41. "Aristotle" was the name for an attitude toward natural knowledge more than that of a historical writer – many works attached to the name were written in late Antiquity or the middle ages, and the accumulated commentaries on all these works were as important as Aristotle's original texts (themselves lecture notes by his students). To grossly oversimplify the inventor of taxonomy, he stood for what my text calls "faith in the legibility of the sensible world." Well before the sixteenth century he became the official pagan philosopher of the Church, which defended the literal truth of his dicta as if they were dogma.

19. Francis Bacon, *The New Organon*, 41–2.

20. Paracelsians, supporters of a new chemical understanding of medical treatment and the doctrine of "resemblances" between microcosm and macrocosm, believed that although the truth about material objects and beings was not self-evidently apparent to the senses, there were nonetheless surface traces that could be read: this was the doctrine of "signatures." The first major Paracelsian text in England was Richard Bostocke's anti-Aristotelian *The Difference between the Auncient Phisicke ... and the Latter Phisicke* (London: G. Robinson for Robert Walley, 1585).

21. See, for example, Katharine Park, "Natural Particulars: Epistemology, Practice, and the Literature of Healing Springs," in *Natural Particulars: Nature and the Disciplines in Renaissance Europe*, ed. Anthony Grafton and Nancy G. Siraisi, (Cambridge: MIT Press, 1999), 347–67.

22. On the insubstantiality of air in *Hamlet*, see Carla Mazzio, "The History of Air: Hamlet and the Trouble with Instruments" in her special issue of *South Central Review* on "Shakespeare and Science": 153–96. It would be more convincing if she admitted that air was matter in Shakespeare's time, but the essay is very rich and suggestive still.

23. Most critics who read Hamlet for philosophical content consider Hamlet a plangent version of the early modern skeptic. On the other hand, a formal reading of Hamlet's soliloquies as participating in Augustine's original genre suggests a structurally necessary doubleness of perspective in the soliloquy that need not be read as skeptical: see Julia D. Staykova, "The Augustinian Soliloquies of an Early Modern Reader," *Literature and Theology*, 23.2 (June 2009): 121–41.

24. Ophelia's suicide is an exception.

25. Consider, for instance, Abraham Ortelius, *Theatrum Orbis Terrarum* (Antwerp, 1570), Jacques Besson, *Theatrum instrumentorum et machinarum* (Leiden, 1578), John Parkinson, *Theatrum botanicum: the theater of plants* (London, 1640); see William N. West, *Theatres and Encyclopedias in Early Modern Europe* (Cambridge: Cambridge University Press, 2002), 43–79.

26. The list was a favorite trope of the sixteenth and seventeenth centuries, gradually differentiating poetic or literary from "scientific" or ethnographic representation as it developed into the organized catalogue and eventually Linnaean taxonomies for natural philosophers, remaining a signature of cornucopian materialism for poets. Early Americanist William C. Spengemann refers often to the foundational significance for American literature of the lists featured in travel writing of the "Discovery" period; see *The Adventurous Muse: The Poetics of American Fiction, 1789–1900* (New Haven: Yale University Press, 1977), esp.

"The Poetics of Adventure," 6–67. On other lists, including catalogs of wonder cabinets, see Chapter 3 of my *Wonder and Science: Imagining Worlds in Early Modern Europe* (Ithaca and London: Cornell University Press, 1999), 78–85.

27. On the sense of touch and its consequential exclusion from knowledge in this period, see Elizabeth Harvey, ed., *Sensible Flesh: On Touch in Early Modern Culture* (Philadelphia: University of Pennsylvania Press, 2003), and her forthcoming monograph "Sensational Subjects: The Rhetoric of Touch in Early Modern England."

28. See William Shakespeare, "Venus and Adonis," in *The Sonnets and Other Poems*, ed. Jonathan Bate and Eric Rasmussen, The RSC Shakespeare (New York: Modern Library, 2007), 3–53.

29. It is worth noting that *The Two Noble Kinsmen* also includes a staged performance (as in *A Midsummer Night's Dream* and *Hamlet*), a daughter in love (as in *A Midsummer Night's Dream*, *Hamlet*, and *The Tempest*), and a mad scene, as we see in versions real and apparently assumed in *Hamlet*, and that it shares a temporal setting with *A Midsummer Night's Dream*: the moment before the ambiguous wedding of Theseus and his war bride Hippolyta. An anonymous version of *TNK*, performed in 1594, may have inspired *A Midsummer Night's Dream*.

30. St. Elmo's fire is a plasma created by lightning, especially on pointy objects like masts and crossbars or airplane nosecones. It causes the electrical field around such objects to glow and was often seen as a good omen: supernatural rather than preternatural. (On the other hand it was famously observed on the propellers in the plane that carried the bomb to Nagasaki.)

31. "Vexation" was a customary term for judicial torture at the time, a practice under Bacon's jurisdiction as Lord Chancellor of England. He liked to speak of "vexing" Nature to get at "her" "truths": for one of several metaphorical uses of the term see Bacon, *The Advancement of Learning*, ed. Michael Kiernan (Oxford: Clarendon Press, 2000), 65.

32. Francis Bacon, "Catalogue of Particular Histories by Titles," in *The New Organon*, 233–8. Bacon's *New Atlantis* famously includes a tour of his academic utopia's "Salomon's House," a prototype for what became the Royal Society some forty years after Bacon's death: "We have also sound-houses, where we practice and demonstrate all sounds, and their generation . . . " ("New Atlantis," in *The Great Instauration and New Atlantis*, ed. J. Weinberger [Arlington Heights: Michigan State University, 1980], 77).

33. The French "natural philosopher," as Bacon might have recognized him, Michel Serres comes to mind in this connection: *Les cinq sens*, written in alarm at the découpage of the body in our thought ("To abstract means to tear the body to pieces rather than merely to leave it behind: analysis"), re-drowns us in the delighted, vagabond empiricism of Bacon (though not Bacon's puritanical refusal of the delight he revels in), above all in his many lists. See Michel Serres, *The Five Senses: A Philosophy of Mingled Bodies* (London: Continuum, 2008) – for example, the passage that starts "It is the beginning of patience. And infinite exploration. We feel our way in the thicket of circumstances . . . as though we were choosing colours of wool in the night . . . " (26–7).

34. This famous line has been anecdotally attributed to the theoretical physicist Wolfgang Pauli since his friend Rudolf Peierls circulated a story containing it:

Peierls, "Wolfgang Ernst Pauli, 1900–1958," in *Biographical Memoirs of Fellows of the Royal Society* (1960), 174–94, at 186.

35. Shakespeare, *A Midsummer Night's Dream* 5.1.139–41. In these lines Starveling, who plays Moonshine in "Pyramus and Thisbee," the play-within-the-play performed by the "rude mechanicals," addresses the audience to reassure them.

36. In 1618 Bacon was elevated to the Peerage of England as Baron Verulam. For one of his stern warnings see the epigraph from "The Great Renewal."

37. Francis Bacon, "The Great Renewal," in *The New Organon*, 10.

38. My thanks to SarahGrace Gomez, Steven Meyer and William Price for excellent editing and copy-editing, and angelic patience in a process more fraught with "natural particulars" than anyone expected.

3

DEVIN GRIFFITHS

Darwin and Literature

Today everyone has an opinion about evolution, and most of us have heard of the theory of natural selection and of *On the Origin of Species*. But Darwin, arguably the most famous scientist of the nineteenth century, is much larger than any single work or idea. His many writings hold a profound influence over modern thinking on a vast range of subjects. Setting to one side the biological sciences, it is hard to point to a field in the humanities or social sciences in which Darwin's works have not played a key role, especially at present. Darwin is still very much alive.

For this reason, there are many ways to think about Darwin; why should we focus on his relation to literature? For some, his writing is an impediment to understanding his thought. A new "modern rendition" rewrites *On the Origin of Species*, distinguishing between his science and the language that express it, arguing that the *survival* of Darwin's most famous work requires modernizing its language, making it "more accessible to more people."[1] For others, the problem is that his writings have been *too* successful. In a recent collection of primary sources titled *Victorian Science and Literature*, the editors include selections from a huge range of writers under subject headings like "Before Darwin" and "The Developmental Hypothesis," but no excerpts from Darwin's own works.[2] The implication is that Darwin's numerous writings are so widely read, written about, and reprinted today (all of his printed works and most of his manuscripts can be accessed free online) that excerpts would be redundant. There is a secondary implication: that we must work against "Darwin-o-centrism" (as Paul White has put it) in order to restore a fuller vision of what the intersection between science and literature looked like in the nineteenth century.[3] While groundbreaking works like Gillian Beer's *Darwin's Plots* (1983) retain monumental status in their exploration of Darwin as a deeply imaginative writer, there is also a sense that the huge scale of Darwin studies continues to dwarf other important subjects – from the place of metaphor in "hard" sciences like astrophysics and thermodynamics, to the broad cultural impact of "pseudosciences" like mesmerism and phrenology. Darwin, the definitive subject for Literature and Science, is both endangered and overplayed, belated and belabored.

Yet there *is* something special about Darwin's science as it marshals imaginative language to drive scientific discovery. His writing ripples with energy, humor, and curiosity. Works like the *Journal of Researches* (a.k.a. "Voyage of the Beagle," 1839), *On the Origin of Species* (1859) and *The Descent of Man* (1871) grabbed the modern imagination and have never let it go. Take the closing lines of the *Origin*: "There is grandeur in this view of life, with its several powers, having been originally breathed into a few forms or into one; and that, whilst this planet has gone cycling on according to the fixed law of gravity, from so simple a beginning endless forms most beautiful and most wonderful have been, and are being, evolved." The elaborate sentence resonates with wonder, distilling the astonishing scope of Darwin's ideas into a string of deceptively simple statements. Life evolves from a simple beginning to the extraordinary richness of the living world around us. As humans, we play a part in that story. Darwin helps us to see our lives as a soaring improvisation over the determinate patterns of the physical world and its "fixed law of gravity." Darwin upends Newton's mechanical science, instigating a dynamic and Romantic scientific revolution. We are left with tantalizing questions. Did life start with one creature or several? Who or what was it that "breathed" that first spark of existence into life? Does Darwin think it was a benevolent god, or something less aware? Darwin insists we remember that there is grandeur, as well as uncertainty, in this view, because the beauty of nature emerges from a constant struggle to live against a continuous background of death and destruction. In a nutshell, all life is precious, because all life is very, very fortunate. Such writing continues to inspire wonder and anxiety, religious debate, and new ideas about the nature of the world around us and our place within it.

Darwin's descriptions of the natural world demonstrate his passion for literature and imaginative play. The Darwin family read voraciously, spending upward of four hours a day reading fiction *viva voce*, from historical novels by Walter Scott and Harriet Martineau to travel fiction by lesser-known writers like Katherine Ellen Spence and Jemima von Tautphoeus. Darwin's relation to literature continually evolved. He loved poetry early in life and carried a tattered copy of John Milton's *Paradise Lost* around the world during his Beagle voyage, yet in his later days, found Shakespeare nauseating. But he always loved novels, especially those with happy endings and pretty heroines. If Darwin's later dislike for poetry was unusual, his wide novel-reading was typical in the age of lending libraries and sensational "penny dreadfuls."

Darwin is the central figure of Literature and Science because his writing *was* his science. His works have a powerful literary investment, relying on audacious leaps of imagination and a deep emotional concern for the enchanting and destructive world his science disclosed. Writing is crucial to Darwin because his science is more descriptive than experimental. Though we tend to think of science as driven by experiments that use advanced technical instruments, from Galileo's telescope to Robert Boyle's vacuum pump, Darwin relied upon pencils and notebooks to record direct observations and then produce imaginative accounts of the history of the natural world.[4] Nineteenth-century descriptive science deployed literary protocols to imagine what might have happened in situations and historical periods inaccessible to traditional scientific experiment: drawing from genres like the travel narrative and the epic, engaging particular literary modes like the sublime and the picturesque, and marshaling literary and rhetorical figures like personification, metaphor, and analogy.

Literature and Science, insofar as it is a subfield of literary studies, is peculiarly suited to engage Darwin's work because so many of its central methodologies – the close analysis (including critique) of representation and figurative language; the material history of the networks that constitute print production; and, the study of how biases regarding sex, social and economic status, and the larger world shape one's worldview – are attuned to the importance of textual media in Darwin's environment. His writing has much to tell us about the place of literature in science, particularly in the nineteenth century, and the various modes of reading, writing, and publication that sustain the commerce between them. Moreover, Darwin was a major theorist of the place of beauty in nature and in society. Works like *On the Various Contrivances by Which British and Foreign Orchids Are Fertilised by Insects* (1862) and *The Expression of Emotion in Man and Animals* (1872) permanently changed how we understand the function of beauty, the nature of aesthetic engagement, and the contribution of aesthetics to human communication. Darwin's theories took literary form, but they have also changed what "literature" means, in ways we are still working to understand.

Darwin and Literary Studies

Darwin's dislike of poetry became notorious in his own day; so much so that it provoked the poet and social critic Matthew Arnold to point to Darwin's example in arguing that literary study (which then meant a classical education in both Greek and Latin) should be more valued than scientific training.[5] (Arnold overlooked the fact that Darwin had a pretty traditional, classics-laden education, first in boarding school and then at university.) Despite Arnold's criticism, later generations have found Darwin's writing to be alive with literary sensibility and imaginative engagement. As I have already suggested, language, and especially literary language, is crucial to Darwin's science because it often imagines events – the evolution of the first eye, the destruction of fossil records or "missing links" – that could not easily be verified by more traditional means. Darwin understood that this made his science look less empirical in practice, and was consequently sensitive to the close relation between scientific writing and literary form in his work. He believed his *Origin* showed that the "metaphorical" terms that scientists commonly used to describe natural relationships – including "affinity," "community of type," and "paternity" – were not metaphorical at all, because they had a "plain signification" in actual evolutionary relationships between species.[6] Yet he also defended the value of a strong metaphor like his own "natural selection," as intellectual shorthand almost "necessary for brevity" in scientific discussion.[7] In making this point, Darwin echoed nineteenth-century scientist and historian William Whewell, who observed that major scientific innovations were often marked by new metaphors, like "gravity" (originally a term for social attraction), that later became conventional terms within the scientific understanding they helped produce.[8] Despite the Royal Society's famous motto "nullius in verba" (nothing in words), Darwin showed that words do important work in scientific discovery. "Natural selection" – a hotly contested theory in Darwin's own time – made the metaphorical and personifying features of scientific writing newly visible and troubling.

In this way, Darwin called attention to the intersection between literature and science, and between figurative description and the interpretation of nature. This attention fueled a debate about the relation between science and the humanities which developed in series of essays with titles like "Science and Culture," and "Literature and Science," and in coordination with the longer development of semi-professional "Arts and Sciences" institutions, which tended to conjoin but also reinforce the division between the "sciences" (both theoretical and practical) and the "arts" (including here both the fine arts and literature).[9] It is important to remember that these discussions responded to changes in the professional landscape of both the sciences and the humanities, in the print marketplace, and in broader demographic shifts.[10] At the dawn of the nineteenth century there were very few successful writers in Britain and virtually no professional scientists, but by the close, various factors contributed to the formalization of both "Science" and "Literature" as not only distinct areas of interest, but distinct academic curricula with particular institutional organs and professional paths. By the twentieth century, the "Victorian initiators of the great debate" (as Aldous Huxley described them), and the popular understanding of Darwin as both model scientist and literary philistine, cemented a sensed division between the concerns and methodologies of the sciences and the humanities.[11] Literature and Science, as a field, is organized by the continuing effort to work across this conjunctive "and" as an important legacy of these nineteenth-century formulations.

It is in the context of this strong thesis of division that modern studies of Darwin's writing became so important. The "modern" or "neo-Darwinian" synthesis of natural selection and Mendelian genetics that emerged in the 1930s and 1940s enshrined Darwin as central to modern biological thought. This renewed interest in Darwin's theories, in turn, gave impulse to the first wave of Darwin studies, which showed that the impact of Darwin's thinking spread well beyond scientific circles. The historian Robert Maxwell Young deployed C. P. Snow's famous description of the division between the "two cultures" to argue that Darwin's metaphors work across the characteristic modern division between science and other cultural forms.[12] In addition to important studies in the history of science, Lionel Stevenson's *Darwin among the Poets* (1932), Leo Justin Henkin's *Darwinism in the English Novel* (1940), and A. Dwight Culler's "The Darwinian Revolution and Literary Form" (1968) explored the broad impact of Darwin's vision on the kinds of plots that novels could imagine and the forms of connection that poetry could express. They often followed Darwin's lead, examining how central metaphors, like selection, adaptation, and struggle, translated into a larger literary environment. This diffusion-based approach, studying Darwin's impact *on* literature, has a deep kinship with both the history of ideas and an earlier twentieth-century configuration of the history of science, imagining Darwin as a kind of conceptual wave generator whose scientific discoveries rippled out into ever wider fields of natural and social description. These accounts encouraged a fresh look at the literary implications of Darwin's science, and produced a subsequent surge of studies that took Darwin's writings as "literary" in their own right. Works like Stanley Edgar Hyman's *The Tangled Bank* (1962) encouraged readers to take a fresh look at the literary qualities of Darwin's science, and to treat Darwin's writings *as* literature.

The third wave of Darwin studies in Literature and Science – the wave we are still riding now – came as a range of scholars began to work back and forth across the divide between science and literature; showing *both* how Darwin's science impacted literary form *and* how that science was, in turn, shaped by the literary examples Darwin had to draw from. Particularly important were Beer's *Darwin's Plots* (1983), published the year following centennial commemorations of Darwin's death, and George Levine's many studies of Darwin, especially *Darwin and the Novelists* (1988). As Beer put it, in a statement that proved foundational for the field, "The traffic [between science and literature] was two-way. Because of the shared discourse not only *ideas* but metaphors, myths, and narrative patterns could move rapidly and freely to and from between scientists and non-scientists: though not without frequent creative misprision."[13] Levine considerably expands this point in his own work, which interprets Beer as moving the relation between science and literature beyond the problem of direct influence toward the question of how the framing assumption of culture can explain "intellectual convergence" in the ideas expressed by both novelists and scientists.[14] The immediate implication, as Levine noted, was that C. P. Snow was wrong and that in the nineteenth century (at least) there was in fact "one culture" within which both literature and science operated.[15] Certainly, there is a case to be made that nineteenth-century intellectual culture was less differentiated than today, given the important fact that scientists, writers, historians, and other thinkers were often writing and reviewed within the pages of the same omnibus quarterly periodicals, and that much scientific vocabulary remained relatively unspecialized, especially in Britain.[16]

The one-culture thesis is particularly powerful for Darwin studies, opening up, in one direction, a way of connecting Literature and Science to cultural critique and a consideration of larger imperial and economic contexts, as demonstrated in Edward Said's analyses of the "cultural integrity of empire"; and in the other, suggesting that scientists and authors labored together in creating new literary forms and scientific developments.[17] Yet, in aligning the monoculture with nationalism and the imperial project, the one-culture thesis makes it more difficult to account for differences at smaller and larger levels of scale. How, then, to attend to the often distinct publics of scientific and literary writers, or the larger cosmopolitan and transnational communities they inhabited? From the perspective of *one* culture, such distinctions are hard to recognize. Moreover, as Gowan Dawson observes, this seeming coherence overwrites real tensions and disagreements by generally assuming that the interplay is "invariably creative and positive for both science and literature."[18] In this spirit, if Beer and Levine helped formulate Literature and Science as the study of a single culture with a coherent set of aims and procedures, in the pages that follow I look to a subsequent differentiation in the ways literary scholars engage Darwin's work, and the markedly different directions these new methodologies point us toward.

Darwin and Cultural Studies: Race, Class, and Sexuality

Literature and Science can be understood as a cross-disciplinary field analogous to the history or sociology of science, with one foot planted in literary studies, and the other in the study of scientific history and practice. And like other cross-disciplinary programs of study, the "Darwin Industry" (as Michael Ruse has called it) has profited from critical attention to the social, political, and economic implications of Darwin's writings and their context. These have been explored recently in an excellent collection edited by Jeanette Eileen Jones and Patrick B. Sharpe.[19] Darwin's writings and theories were both shaped *by* and had a profound impact *on* so many different disciplines, worldviews, and social movements that a wider scope is required. We still live in a Darwinian world.

It is often noted that, in their reception, Darwin's theories were understood to naturalize social norms, even as his writings – particularly his discussions of race and sexuality in *The Descent of Man, and Selection in Relation to Sex* – made social forms contingent and unstable. *The Descent of Man* takes up a problem Darwin alludes to at the close of the *Origin*: where did humans come from? On the one hand, this begged the question of humanity's special position within nature as a "higher" species, an implication Darwin scrupulously tried to avoid in earlier works like *On the Origin of Species*. On the other, as Darwin and his co-theorist Alfred Russell Wallace understood it, the problem was not merely to imagine a "missing link" – a human ancestor continuous with apes – but more fundamentally, to address the fact that the theory of natural selection, because it was based in competition between individuals, could not explain the collaborative features of human society. For this reason, *The Descent* turns to alternative evolutionary forces, including the selective advantages of cooperation and social instincts. Foremost among these is sexual selection, which supervenes on natural selection and fosters traits and behaviors, like the peacock's tail, that do not directly help the individual survive.

Sexual selection makes aesthetic taste, understood as the subjective assignment of value to different perceived qualities, central to Darwin's thinking, as noted most recently by Barbara Larson, Sabine Flach, and other contributors to a recent collection.[20] Darwin observes, for instance, that the explorer Mungo Park was often "rallied" by Africans "on the whiteness of his skin and the prominence of his nose, both of which they considered as 'unsightly and unnatural conformations,'" evidence for how "widely the different races of man differ in their taste for the beautiful."[21] He further argued that variation between individuals, both physical and in their aesthetic standards, was the source of beauty itself: "if every one were cast in the same mould, there would be no such thing as beauty" (652). Beauty, in Darwin's view, is an engine of sexual selection and so foundational to modern society. In short, race, sexuality, and the social body are intimately interwoven in Darwin's eyes, constantly in flux and dependent upon the relative perspective of the observer – including the naturalist.

For Darwin, "race" was a general term, like "variety," that applied both to other natural organisms and to human groups, and he understood such groups to function in similar ways, particularly with respect to evolution and divergence. As he summarized this in the *Descent*: "Man is liable to numerous, slight, and diversified variations, which are induced by the same general causes, are governed and transmitted in accordance with the same general laws, as in the lower animals" (67). For this reason, he lengthily and explicitly took up contemporary debates over whether there were, in fact, distinct human races, whether those races represent distinct species, and whether they descended from one or several distinct ancestral groups. Though he took the side of the "monogenists," arguing that all humans shared a common ancestry, his more basic point, if one accepts the evolutionary view, was that "race" as well as "species" are fuzzy and somewhat arbitrary designations, ways to abstract across uneven degrees of apparent difference and among innumerable features.

Darwin's theory and his discussions of race had a complex influence depending on how his readers weighed the instability of racial categories, the eugenic analogy to domestication of species, Darwin's use of phrases like "favoured races," and his own relational sense of value. As George Stocking has detailed, Darwinian ideas were crucial to the debates between anthropologists and ethnographers over the status and implications of race theory, with important differences in how these debates played out in different national contexts, particularly in Britain and the United States.[22] And as applied to economic inequality, what we now term "social Darwinism" was an approach to social analysis and engineering that actually predated Darwin's *Origin*, drawn from Thomas Malthus's study of population and Herbert Spencer's sociology. But social Darwinism gained substantial support from Darwin's theories, particularly as adapted by Darwin's cousin, Francis Galton. As extensively explored by historian Mike Hawkins, social Darwinism argued that human society necessarily entailed a kind of economic and subsistence-level "survival of the fittest," and suggested that societies should be organized to benefit the more successful and weed out the less.[23] These troubling implications became more sinister as a subsequent generation of eugenic theorists, including Galton and Karl Pearson in England, Cesare Lombroso in Italy, Max Nordau in Germany, and Charles Davenport in the United States, suggested a more active technocratic approach to population engineering, especially by preventing certain groups of people from reproducing, a genealogy most recently detailed by André Pichot in connection with the German Third Reich.[24] In addition to the study of Darwin's impact on social engineering, more attention needs to be paid to the importance of British imperialism to the global network of naturalists and collectors that Darwin relied upon. Darwin's works are a rich archive for exploring the "green imperialism" that, in Richard Grove's account, characterized thinking about environments and species in the colonial world.[25] Darwin privately acknowledged the troubling connections between his own discussions of "favoured races" and the brutality of imperial expansion. While his writings were only one part of the nested justifications and ideologies understood to support race theory, eugenics, and imperial expansion, and his work can be read to reach radically different conclusions, his visibility as the founder of modern evolutionary theory, particularly as applied to human civilization, makes him central to these discussions.

Darwin's work demands attention because his evolutionary theories and analysis of race are implicated in some of the most damaging historical traumas of the modern era.[26] Yet the major challenge, as a question of literary history, is not only to analyze what later generations made of him, but to provide a fuller account of what Darwin actually wrote, both in terms of immediate implications, and as a site of engagement and resistance between conflicting discourses about the nature of human society and difference. Historians Janet Browne, Adrian Desmond and James Moore have provided a rich analysis of Darwin's thinking by examining how his social position and his family history shaped his research. For one, Darwin used his family wealth and connections to secure a scientific standing that other naturalists like Wallace and Huxley struggled to maintain.[27] And insofar as we might see some class bias in Darwin's analogies between the natural and social world (in his notebooks he speculates that economic classes might, in fact, be like natural classes), we can endorse Karl Marx's critical observation that "It is remarkable how among beasts and plants Darwin rediscovers his English society with its divisions of labor, competition, [and] opening of new markets."[28] In the *Descent*, for example, Darwin argued (somewhat defensively) that "the inheritance of property by itself is very far from an evil" and that "moderate accumulation of wealth [does not] interfere with the process of selection," while he also surmised that "wealth when very great tends to convert men into useless drones, [though fortunately] their number is never large, ... for we daily see rich men, who happen to be fools or profligate, squandering away their wealth" (160). Yet Darwin also argued consistently against the stability of division at any scale, especially the putatively stable divisions used to justify human bondage. His family's long-standing opposition to slavery influenced his critical descriptions of its function in the natural world – for instance, in the example of slave-taking ants – and made race an important and consistent problem in his work.[29]

Darwin's understanding of sex was similarly complicated, but for different reasons. His earliest studies of molluscs, along with a knowledge of floral morphology, had convinced him that there were, in fact, at least three sexes – male, female, and hermaphrodite – and that these sexes, rather than fixed, often shaded into each other. His grandfather, Erasmus Darwin (both a major poet and important evolutionary theorist in his own right), had underlined the complexity of plant sexuality, and Charles's work showed that this complexity extended to complex life in general. As his theory of sexual selection showed, evolution itself seemed to upend gender norms by empowering females as primary selective agents. Sex stood in a critical relation to both species and race and the traits that defined them. Hence, even though "pop-Darwinism," as defined by Martha McCaughey, often cites evolution to prove the unreformed and essential nature of sexual identity, Darwin's writings open up a radically less stable understanding of how sexuality and gender interact over time, with queer implications for natural and human ecologies (explored extensively in works by Elizabeth Grosz and Robert Azzarello).[30] The point is not that Darwin was liberal (whatever that might mean today). Like many of his contemporaries, he often assumed a scale of improvement both between races and among sexual behaviors. But he advocated a radical new sense of what terms like "sex" and "race" and "class" meant, understanding these terms as slippery signifiers rather than real categories, and upended deeply held assumptions about the nature of the social world. For this reason, the study of Darwin continues to shed fresh light on gender and sexuality studies and on critical race theory.

Darwin and the Book

Darwin's most important research tools were the pen and the printed word. The sheets of his manuscripts and notebooks afforded him imaginative space to envision what might have happened in times and in locations that could not be physically explored. Perhaps more important, private correspondence and print venues linked Darwin to scattered communities of scientists and enthusiasts, the professional and amateur associations that coordinated their work, and the innumerable scientific and lay accounts that provided a huge archive of theories and observations to draw upon. Darwin's place in this deeply collaborative science – the "collective empiricism" of the nineteenth century, to borrow a phrase from Lorraine Daston and Peter Galison – was secured by the codex and the written word.[31] His letters, manuscripts, and printed works detail the evolving career of a writer who quickly became expert in enlisting help, insight, and specimens from others, in navigating between distinct protocols of professional and social support, and in communicating his findings through numerous scientific and popular institutions, publishers, and print venues.

Much of Darwin's primary material has been edited and published in a series of ambitious editorial projects. Darwin Online (darwin-online.org .uk), edited by John Van Whye, is the most comprehensive single resource for Darwin's publications, including digital facsimiles and transcripts of virtually all of his printed works, extensive editorial introductions to materials, a variorum edition of the *Origin* (adapted in visualizations by Ben Fry and by Stefanie Posavec and Greg McInerny), as well as numerous manuscript sources, notably Darwin's travel logs and working notebooks, and the catalogue of the library aboard the *Beagle* during Darwin's voyage.[32] Another extraordinary resource, more than thirty years in the making, is the Darwin Correspondence Project, comprised of both the ongoing printing of a thirty-volume edition of all of Darwin's known correspondence, and a searchable online database (currently to 1869) with extensive editorial notes (darwinproject.ac.uk). In addition to these, there are many excellent biographies, guides, and companions to Darwin's works.[33]

In counterpoint to these modern editions of Darwin's writings, scholars have begun to look back to the original works, and the material practices that supported them, for fresh insight into Darwin's science. Among the earliest was Paul H. Barrett and Howard E. Gruber's *Darwin on Man* (1974), a careful analysis of Darwin's transmutation notebooks that studies how Darwin's thinking about evolution evolved on the page. There is still much work to be done to understand the way the contemporary print market and printing practices shaped Darwin's science. He was part of the last generation of British naturalists for whom the scientific monograph – rather than the scientific article – would serve as the primary vehicle for publishing major findings, and his writing is an important a part of that story.

Darwin and the Visual Imagination

We cannot see the world the same way after reading one of Darwin's works. He had a captivating imaginative vision, and a remarkable ability to evoke events that seemed unimaginable. Take his description of the *Catasetidæ*, which he calls the "most remarkable of Orchids":

> [Nature] has endowed these plants with, what must be called for want of
> a better term, sensitiveness, and with the remarkable power of forcibly ejecting

their pollinia [or pollen organs] to a distance. Hence, when certain definite points of the flower are touched by an insect, the pollinia are shot out like an arrow which is not barbed, but has a blunt and excessively adhesive point. The insect, disturbed by so sharp a blow, or after having eaten its fill, flies sooner or later to a female plant, and, whilst standing in the same position as it did when struck, the pollen-bearing end of the arrow is inserted into the stigmatic cavity, and a mass of pollen is left on its viscid surface. Thus, and thus alone, at least three species of the genus Catasetum are fertilised.[34]

With remarkable economy Darwin imagines the orchid as the Robin Hood of forest plants, using insects as couriers that deliver its pollen-tipped arrows from plant to plant. Such descriptions were supported by elaborate illustrations and diagrams that fleshed out his important arguments. The most famous is the branching "tree of life" diagram in the *Origin*, which has received a huge amount of attention from scientists, theorists of information science, and historians of science – virtually anyone who's ever been interested in Darwin.[35] Yet the *Origin* is unusual among Darwin's works, as Jonathan Smith has pointed out, because it contains only one (relatively abstract) illustration. The rest of Darwin's works are crammed with woodcuts, lithographs, engravings and sketches that fill the pages with the visual vocabulary of the new evolutionary science. Smith's *Charles Darwin and Victorian Visual Culture* (2006) gives an illuminating treatment of the illustrations in Darwin's many other works; both the technologies and artists that helped him visualize the natural world he encountered and the visual conventions that brought this vision to the page.[36] Darwin's imagination was profoundly visual, from conjuring what a coral reef looks like deep in the ocean, to previewing the giant Madagascar moth that could pollinate the island's enormous orchids. And, as made abundantly clear in a recent touring exhibition developed by the Fitzwilliam Museum and the Yale Center for British Art, Darwin was intimately engaged both with contemporary Victorian visual culture and with contemporary scientific illustration.[37]

Darwin's writings also had a lasting impact both on the popular representation of nature and on the practice of art itself. Darwin's worldwide influence registered in a range of different media. Contemporary periodicals teemed with illustrations that depicted various people, including Darwin, as half-ape hybrids, a "Monkeyana" that, in the analysis of Janet Browne, conditioned popular thinking about the status of evolutionary theory and its implications.[38] Darwin's theories also spawned a huge range of illustrations depicting the evolution of humanity, from Benjamin Waterhouse Hawkins's comparison of ape skeletons to man (1863, executed for "Darwin's Bulldog," Thomas Henry Huxley and his *Evidence as to Man's Place in Nature*), to Rudolph Franz Zallinger's massively-influential

"Road to Homo Sapiens" (1965) – muse to innumerable T-shirts, coffee mugs, and ad campaigns. At the other end of the artistic spectrum, Diana Donald and Jane Munro have made the case that Darwin moved important currents in the art world, especially through the keen interest of French Impressionists and Post-Impressionists like Edgar Degas, Claude Monet, and Paul Cézanne. If Darwin's imaginative idiom was recognizably Victorian, the modern visual vocabulary continues to display deep Darwinian influences.[39]

Literary Darwinism

Darwin was a tremendously flexible thinker, both in his curiosity about the natural world, and in the changing patterns he disclosed within it. His flexibility is reflected in the wide range of natural and human subjects he was willing to turn an evolutionary eye to, from the action of earthworms to the vagaries of human fashion. His eclectic concerns raise an exciting possibility: given the numerous arenas where Darwin's thinking has been helpful, what might he tell us about literature itself? Recently a group of literary scholars have taken up this difficult task, exploring Darwinian ideas for an account of how literature works and how it came to be. Because this "literary Darwinism" has generated substantial controversy (at least, in academic circles), it is worth taking some time to consider the challenges literary Darwinism faces and the promise it holds for future work.[40]

Literary Darwinists propose that there is a "timeless evolutionary logic" (as Jonathan Gottschall has put it) that explains both the impact that literature has on the human experience, and the kinds of plots, social models, and genres that literature employs.[41] Joseph Carroll has recently summarized this approach: "To qualify as Darwinist, a reading would have to bring all its particular observations into line with basic evolutionary principles: survival, reproduction, kinship (inclusive fitness), basic social dynamics, and the reproductive cycle that gives shape to human life and organizes the most intimate relations of family."[42] For Carroll, strong criticism must articulate the relationship between a reading of a work of literature and the fact of biological evolution. Carroll shares with other literary Darwinists the central premise, derived from evolutionary and cognitive psychology, that literature, like other cultural forms, is subject to a genetic psychology fixed by human evolutionary history.

Though several aspects of this approach raise significant problems (for instance, in positing universal categories for human experience) a key challenge for the literary Darwinists is that their thesis of a "timeless evolutionary logic" excludes changeful, contingent, historical time – that most important dimension for Darwin's thinking and for modern literary criticism. Nothing that evolves, whether a species, a psychology, or a social form like a novel, can be "timeless." (This includes Darwin's *own theories*; the mutability of Darwinian thinking can be seen in recent work that turns away from an exclusive focus on "inclusive fitness" and toward more ecumenical models of inheritance and selection, from epigenetics to group selection.)[43] In more recent work that recognizes the problem of a timeless construction of evolutionary history, literary Darwinism itself continues to evolve. Brian Boyd, for instance, has emphasized both the "plasticity" of the human mind, its dynamic interaction with culture, and the greater responsiveness of different selective events to historical change and social context.[44] As these insights are drawn from evolutionary psychology, a crucial source for literary Darwinists, and in order to distance this field from other historical versions of Darwinism, Boyd prefers the designation "evocriticism" to literary Darwinism (though perhaps "evopsychocriticism" would be most accurate).[45] Yet in treating evolution as a given for psychology, and psychology as a given for literature, literary Darwinists see no place for a criticism that overlooks putative evolutionary facts.

Good cross-disciplinary work, however, adapts methods without adopting conclusions. The procedures for generating consensus in any field are specialized, and the further apart these fields are, the further apart those procedures. This cuts to the core of the challenge of Literature and Science as a field. We are simply not equipped, as humanists, to evaluate the results of evolutionary science, any more than an evolutionary scientist knows how to evaluate the contribution of a *PMLA* article. (I say this as someone who has participated in evolutionary research.) Any result, within its own discipline, is uncertain and subject to revision. There's a reason that scientific papers set results apart from subsequent (and even more tentative) conclusions. But when either is delivered as a *fait accompli* in an extra-disciplinary context – whether a popular science article or a critical essay – they suddenly gain the apparent solidity of proven facts. Crammed with observations and specific theories drawn from anthropology, evolutionary biology, psychology, and especially ethology (the comparative study of animal behavior), literary Darwinism often seems a portmanteau of scientific findings. Such a strategy uses purported evolutionary facts, delivered as examples and anecdotes, to explain literary features. I have no problem with critical pluralism – we don't need to have a fully self-consistent theory to adapt tools and get at real problems – but our tools should bear a strong relationship to one another and to the purpose at hand, here, literary scholarship. And the value of the approach – the standard of proof – should not stand on the apparently settled nature of evidence drawn from other disciplines, but instead, on the ability to address central questions about literature that other scholars find both convincing and valuable.

For this reason, literary Darwinism should be *more* Darwinian, not less. It should be responsive to Darwin's vision of natural and social systems in constant flux, his sense of wide variation within any group, and especially, to his modest understanding that no one theory, especially natural selection, can explain everything. This requires adjusting Darwinian thinking to better suit literature as a social and historical form. A strong literary Darwinism needs to be something more than a footman to evolutionary biology and a scold to literary criticism.

Fortunately, I think that we already have strong examples to look to, and I will give one here: the innovative, and widely influential work of Franco Moretti. Though he is now best known for provocative work on the digital humanities and the status of "world literature," Moretti began as a student of literary form, and one of his most remarkable early studies, *Signs Taken for Wonders*, concludes with a proposal for a Darwinian theory of genre. One of the most valuable features of this brand of literary Darwinism – and something it shares with the theories of Freud and Marx, two figures often derided by evocritics – is that it provides a strong case for the relation between an individual literary work and a larger social and historical context. The problem with most literary Darwinism is that this larger context is *too* large – comprising the entirety of humanity and most of its prehistory. This doesn't provide the necessary granularity for an interest in, for example, the emergence of the historical novel in the early nineteenth-century.

Moretti, on the other hand, recognizes that Darwinian ideas, to get at the problem of genre, must be adapted to the peculiar timescales and rhythms of literary forms. So, in *The Way of the World* and then *Signs Taken for Wonders*, he argues that the revolutions of the late eighteenth century elevated the Bildungsroman over competing genres because it was able to address the social contradictions exposed by revolutionary events. Much of Moretti's later work, from the *Atlas of the European Novel* to the innovative visualizations of *Graphs, Maps, and Trees* can be understood as attempts to map factually how such genres evolve, and hence, to set literary Darwinism on a more sound historical and empirical footing. The Darwinian impulse of Moretti's ecological vision is evident in his influential "Conjectures on World Literature," where he observes that "trees" and "waves" model the global diffusion of the novel. Though Moretti does not characterize himself as a literary Darwinist, the wide influence of his work demonstrates the power of Darwinian thinking to address central concerns for the study of literature.[46]

Conclusion

There has never been a better time to study Darwin. Interest in his work is widespread, both among humanists and among scientists, among thinkers of every stripe and in the public at large. We now have unprecedented access to his manuscript and print writings – the majority of which, only a couple of decades ago, were accessible only to the privileged few. Darwin's importance to modern understanding demands that we work to set his contributions, and more importantly, his place as author, in better perspective. First and foremost, Darwin was a powerful writer. No work of natural science from the nineteenth century is read today as widely, and in as many languages, as *On the Origin of Species*. We still have a lot of work to do if we are to explain why this is so – why Darwin's writings so moved his peers and why they continue to shape how we think today.

NOTES

1. Daniel Duzdevich, *Darwin's* On the Origin of Species: *A Modern Rendition* (Indianapolis: Indiana University, 2014), xxv–xxvi.
2. See Gowan Dawson and Bernard V. Lightman, *Victorian Science and Literature* (London: Pickering & Chatto, 2011–2).
3. Paul White, "Introduction: Science, Literature, and the Darwin Legacy," *19: Interdisciplinary Studies in the Long Nineteenth Century* 11 (2010): 1–7, at 3. Online at www.19.bbk.ac.uk.
4. See Eileen Reeves, *Galileo's Glassworks* (Cambridge: Harvard University Press, 2008); and Steven Shapin and Simon Schaffer, *Leviathan and the Air-Pump* (Princeton: Princeton University Press, 1985). The definitive account of Darwin's life and methods is given in Janet Browne's two-part biography, *Voyaging* (Princeton: Princeton University Press, 1996) and *The Power of Place* (New York: Knopf, 2002).
5. See Matthew Arnold, "Literature and Science," *The Nineteenth Century* 19 (Aug. 1882): 216–30.
6. Charles Darwin, *On the Origin of Species* 1st ed. (London: Murray, 1859), 485.
7. Charles Darwin, *On the Origin of Species* 3rd ed. (London: Murray, 1861), 85.
8. See William Whewell, *The Philosophy of the Inductive Sciences, Founded upon Their History* (London: Parker, 1840).
9. See Thomas Henry Huxley, *Science and Culture* (London: Macmillan, 1881). See also Arnold's essay, cited above. For a history of the arts and sciences institutions, and the important interplay between their constitutive categories, see John Klancher's *Transfiguring the Arts and Sciences* (New York: Cambridge University, 2013).
10. Among them: the expanding territorial and economic hegemony of the British empire; the growing economic and political strength of the working and professional classes; the expansion of the voting franchise; the subsequent reform of public education, and the extension of that education to women; and a decline in

religious observance that was coordinated with the growth of civic and educational institutions.

11. Aldous Huxley, *Literature and Science* (Woodbridge, CT: Ox Bow Press, 1991), 3.

12. See Robert Maxwell Young, "Darwin's Metaphor: Does Nature Select?" *The Monist* 55.3 (July 1971): 442–503; and C. P. Snow, *The Two Cultures and the Scientific Revolution* (Cambridge: Cambridge University, 1959).

13. Gillian Beer, *Darwin's Plots: Evolutionary Narrative in Darwin, George Eliot and Nineteenth-Century Fiction* (Cambridge: Cambridge University Press, 2000), 5.

14. George Levine, *Darwin and the Novelists: Patterns of Science in Victorian Fiction* (Cambridge: Harvard University Press, 1988), 5.

15. See George Levine, "One Culture: Science and Literature" in *One Culture: Essays in Science and Literature*, ed. George Levine and Alan Rauch (Madison: University of Wisconsin, 1987).

16. For an excellent comparative study of the specialization of scientific writing in Britain, France, and Germany, see Alan Gross, Joseph Harmon, and Michael Reidy, *Communicating Science* (New York: Oxford University, 2002), esp. chapter 6.

17. See Edward Said, "The Cultural Integrity of Empire," in *Culture and Imperialism* (New York: Vintage, 1993), 97–100.

18. Gowan Dawson, *Darwin, Literature, and Victorian Respectability* (Cambridge: Cambridge University, 2007), 193.

19. See Jeanette Eileen Jones and Patrick B. Sharpe, eds., *Darwin in Atlantic Cultures: Evolutionary Visions of Race, Gender, and Sexuality* (New York: Routledge, 2010).

20. See Barbara Larson and Sabine Flach, eds., *Darwin and Theories of Aesthetics and Cultural History* (Burlington, VT: Ashgate, 2013).

21. Charles Darwin, *The Descent of Man* (Amherst, NY: Prometheus, 1998), 646, 648. Further references given parenthetically by page.

22. See George Stocking, *Victorian Anthropology* (New York: Free Press, 1987).

23. See Mike Hawkins, *Social Darwinism in European and American Thought: 1860–1945* (New York: Cambridge University, 1997).

24. André Pichot's *The Pure Society: From Darwin to Hitler* (London: Verso, 2009) is less useful as an analysis of Darwin's attitudes toward race (which it substantially distorts) than as a strong critical analysis of how Darwin's theories were taken up by later generations of eugenicists and social engineers.

25. See Richard Grove, *Green Imperialism* (Cambridge: Cambridge University, 1995).

26. Sweden practiced compulsory sterilization as late as 2012.

27. See Adrian Desmond and James Moore, *Darwin: The Life of a Tormented Evolutionist* (New York: Warner Books, 1991) and Janet Browne's biographies, cited above.

28. To Friedrich Engels, June 18, 1862. From Karl Marx and Frederick Engels, *Marx & Engels Collected Works* vol. 30 (London: Lawrence & Wishart, 1988), 249.

29. See Adrian Desmond and James Moore, *Darwin's Sacred Cause: How a Hatred of Slavery Shaped Darwin's Views on Human Evolution* (Boston: Houghton Mifflin, 2009).

30. See Martha McCaughey, *The Caveman Mystique: Pop-Darwinism and the Debate over Sex, Violence, and Science* (New York: Routledge, 2007); Elizabeth Grosz, *The Nick of Time* (Durham: Duke University, 2004); and Robert Azzarello, *Queer Environmentality* (Burlington, VT: Ashgate: 2012).

31. Lorraine Daston and Peter Galison, *Objectivity*. New York: Zone Books, 2007.

32. See Ben Fry: http://benfry.com/traces/; and Stefanie Posavec and Greg McInerny: www.stefanieposavec.co.uk/-everything-in-between/#/entangled-word-bank/. *Darwin Online* also includes an online edition of R. B. Freeman's very helpful *Charles Darwin: A Companion* (2007, 2nd ed.).

33. If you are interested in what Darwin read, the Biodiversity Heritage Library has begun assembling an wide-ranging online edition of works within Darwin's home library, which incorporates a comprehensive bibliography, the material from Mario A. Di Gregorio and N. W. Gill's impressive *Darwin's Marginalia* (New York: Routledge, 1990), and in many cases, digital facsimiles of that marginalia as well (biodiversitylibrary.org/collection/darwinlibrary). *The Works of Charles Darwin* (New York: New York University Press, 1987–9), edited by Paul H. Barrett and Richard Broke Freeman, remains the standard print edition. In addition to these, the monumental Morse Peckham variorum edition of the *Origin* is still in print, and both the Robert J. Richards and Michael Ruse *Cambridge Companion to the Origin of Species* (Cambridge: Cambridge University Press, 2009) and the third edition of Philip Appleman's *Darwin: Texts, Commentary* (New York: W. W. Norton, 2001), which excerpts his writings with extensive contemporary sources, provide helpful introductions and context.

34. Charles Darwin, *On the Various Contrivances by Which British and Foreign Orchids Are Fertilised by Insects*. London: John Murray, 1862, 212–3.

35. See Stephen Jay Gould, *The Structure of Evolutionary Theory* (Cambridge: Harvard University Press, 2002), 12–23, 228–36; for a review of alternative interpretations of the diagram, see Laura R. Franklin-Hall, "Trashing Life's Tree," *Biology and Philosophy* 25:4 (2010): 689–709.

36. Jonathan Smith, *Charles Darwin and Victorian Visual Culture* (Cambridge: Cambridge University Press, 2006).

37. See also my discussion of Darwin's illustrations and gilt cover for the *Orchids* in *The Age of Analogy: Science and Literature between the Darwins* (Baltimore: Johns Hopkins, 2016), chap. 5, "The Origin of Charles Darwin's Orchids," 211–57.

38. Janet Browne, "Darwin in Caricature: A Study in the Popularization and Dissemination of Evolution," *Proceedings of the American Philosophical Association* 145:4 (Dec. 2001): 496–509.

39. See Barbara Larson and Fae Brauer, eds., *The Art of Evolution: Darwin, Darwinisms, and Visual Culture* (Hanover: Dartmouth College Press, 2009); and Diana Donald and Jane Munro, eds., *Endless Forms: Charles Darwin, Natural Science, and the Visual Arts* (New Haven: Yale University Press, 2009).

40. For a primer on recent critical accounts of Literary Darwinism, see Jonathan Kramnick's "Against Literary Darwinism," *Critical Inquiry* 37 (Winter 2011): 315–47, and the numerous responses, including those by Carroll and Boyd, in the subsequent winter issue.

41. Jonathan Gottschall and David Sloane Wilson, "Introduction: Literature – a Last Frontier in Human Evolutionary Studies," in *The Literary Animal: Evolution and the Nature of Narrative*, eds., Gottschall and Wilson (Evanston: Northwestern University Press, 2005), xvii–xxvi, at xviii.

42. Joseph Carroll, "Three Scenarios for Literary Darwinism," *New Literary History* 41:1 (Winter 2010): 53–67.

43. See for instance the excellent discussions of different approaches to the "levels of selection" problem in Samir Okasha's *Evolution and the Levels of Selection* (New York: Oxford University, 2006).

44. Brian Boyd, *On the Origin of Stories* (Cambridge: Harvard University, 2010), 94–8.

45. Boyd, *Origin of Stories*, 384–92. For three foundational works for the development of evolutionary psychology, see Edward O. Wilson, *Sociobiology: The New Synthesis* (Cambridge: Harvard University Press, 1975), Donald Symons, *The Evolution of Human Sexuality* (New York: Oxford University Press, 1979), and Jerome Barkow, Leda Cosmides, and John Tooby, *The Adapted Mind: Evolutionary Psychology and the Generation of Culture* (New York: Oxford University Press, 1992). For a slightly dated summary of the debate over evolutionary psychology, see Linda Gannon, "A Critique of Evolutionary Psychology," *Psychology, Evolution, Gender* 4:2 (Dec. 2002): 173–218; for a more recent account, see J. C. Confer, J. A. Easton, D. S. Fleischman, C. D. Goetz, D. M. Lewis, C. Perilloux and D. M. Buss, "Evolutionary Psychology: Controversies, Questions, Prospects, and Limitations," *American Psychologist* 65.2 (2010): 110–26.

46. See Franco Moretti, *The Way of the World* (London: Verso, 1987); *Signs Taken for Wonders*, 2nd ed. (New York: Verso, 2005); *Atlas of the European Novel* (New York: Verso, 1998); *Graphs, Maps, Trees* (New York: Verso, 2005); and "Conjectures on World Literature," *New Left Review* 1 (January–February, 2000): 54–68.

4

JOAN RICHARDSON

William James, Henry James, and the Impact of Science

> [S]cience is nothing more but the finding of analogy, identity, in the most
> remote parts. The ambitious soul sits down before each refractory
> fact ... and goes on for ever to animate the last fibre of organization,
> the outskirts of nature, by insight.
>
> Ralph Waldo Emerson, "The American Scholar"

"Scientist" on the Analogy of "Artist"

William and Henry James were born almost at the same time as the term
"scientist": William in 1842, Henry in 1843, "scientist" just a bit earlier, in
1833, the word first coined by the geologist William Whewell, master of
Trinity College, Cambridge University and one of the mentors of Charles
Darwin. Whewell presented the term at the third annual meeting of the
British Association for the Advancement of Science "in response to Samuel
Taylor Coleridge's strongly expressed objection to men of science using the
term philosopher to describe themselves."[1] There was during this period no
general designation for the various researchers and experimentalists working
in the different areas developing ever more vigorously after the advances of
the seventeenth-century Scientific Revolution: geologists, mineralogists,
botanists, paleontologists, zoologists, chemists, naturalists, philologists,
physiologists, physicists, anatomists, etc., all practicing within the ever-
burgeoning field once neatly contained under the heading of "natural philosophy." As Melinda Baldwin has recently reminded us, the term was not
easily accepted, at least not in Britain. Sixty years after Whewell proposed it
at the meeting of the British Association, a debate triggered by
J. T. Carrington, editor of the popular science magazine *Science-Gossip*,
found the anti-Darwinist Duke of Argyll and Thomas Huxley, "Darwin's
bulldog," for once on the same side of an argument in denouncing the term.
Baldwin adds tellingly that "Debates over its acceptance or rejection were, in
the end, not just about the word itself: they were about what science was, and
what place its practitioners held in their society."[2]

Baldwin goes on to note that shortly after introducing the term at the 1833 meeting, "Whewell first put the word 'scientist' into print in an 1834 review of Mary Somerville's *On the Connexion of the Physical Sciences.*" Baldwin continues:

> Whewell's review argued that science was becoming fragmented, that chemists and mathematicians and physicists had less and less to do with one another. "A curious illustration of this result," he wrote, "may be observed in the want of any name by which we can designate the students of the material world collectively." He then proposed "scientist," an analogue to "artist," as the term that could provide linguistic unity to those studying the various branches of the sciences.

Interestingly, while most scientific researchers in Great Britain persisted in resisting the term – preferring "man of science" to parallel "man of letters," a widely admired designation – in America the response was quite the opposite. As Baldwin reports, "By the 1870s, 'scientist' had replaced 'man of science' in the United States," where the word specified an individual devoted to "pure" science as against someone who used scientific knowledge for commercial gain. "Scientist" became so broadly used in America that many British observers, including Alfred Russel Wallace, believed the term had come from the stepchild across the Atlantic. The British prejudice against "scientist" was maintained well into the twentieth century, as evidenced by a renewed debate in 1924 sponsored by the premier British science journal *Nature*, with those arguing against its use maintaining the attitude expressed by the naturalist E. Ray Lankester, that "'[s]cientist' has acquired – perhaps unjustly – the significance of a charlatan's device." It is not difficult to read the residues of paternalism and class privilege in this judgment, shared by a significant enough number of the British scientific community to keep the word from being used in the journal. This bias was reinforced by the Royal Society of London, the British Association for the Advancement of Science, the Royal Institution, and Cambridge University Press, all of which institutions continued as of 1924 to reject "scientist." It was only after the Second World War that *Nature* would use "scientist" as "the accepted British term for a person who pursued scientific research."[3]

The James Boys

The atmosphere in which William and Henry James were reared and educated was this one, in which the place of science in society was just beginning to be defined, well before its broadly fatal separation from the humanities that C. P. Snow marked in the mid-twentieth century as a split between "two cultures." This was an extended moment before the fall into the many varieties of intellectual and spiritual experience that occurred during the nineteenth century as a result of myriad factors: not only the ever-proliferating information generated by the seventeenth-century Scientific Revolution, but also the findings of the Higher Criticism as well as the ongoing discoveries of "new worlds" and languages triggering the great interest in language theory and philology, which itself would serve as a model for Charles Darwin's thinking about the branching of species. (Worth noting is that the, as it were, prelapsarian situation is preserved today in the designation of "Faculty of Arts and Sciences" at many institutions of higher education.) Within this nineteenth-century intellectual landscape, the newest science to emerge was psychology, notably in Germany and the United States. And it was in this milieu that Henry James Sr. rigorously enjoined his children, as his son Henry would recall to "Convert, convert, convert . . . to convert and convert . . . everything that should happen to us, every contact, every expression, every experience."[4] The central concern of the arts and sciences bearing on human experience in the nineteenth century was, understandably, given the disappearance of God as source and provider with the gradual emergence of evolution, the nature of consciousness. It is not surprising that William and Henry James would both have this subject become the "storm center" of their interest.[5]

It is also not surprising that both would attempt to bridge the gap between science and varieties of religious or spiritual experience. They were, after all, "natives of the James family" in whose New York City household there was "Mr. Emerson's Room," ready always to receive the honored visitor.[6] The "James boys," as Emerson referred to them in a letter, remarking on their exquisite facility with words, would follow the task Emerson set for himself and the next generations – in this echoing Emanuel Swedenborg, the eighteenth-century Swedish scientist, theologian, mystic known as "The Buddha of the North" – "to annul the adulterous divorce which the superstition of many ages has effected between the intellect and holiness."[7] The importance of Swedenborg for Henry James Sr., and through him to William and Henry, cannot be overstated, particularly in connection with bridging the gap between science and spiritual experience.[8] As Henry James Sr. wrote in *The Secret of Swedenborg: Being an Elucidation of His Doctrine of the Divine Natural Humanity* (1869):

> To arrive at the knowledge of the soul by the strictest methods of science had always been his hope and endeavor. He conceived that the body, being the fellow of the soul, was in some sort its continuation; and that if he could only

penetrate therefore to its purest forms or subtlest essences, he would be sure of touching at last the soul's true territory.[9]

We shall return to discuss this aspect of joining science to spiritual experience further on in connection with the results of the kind of education that William and Henry received following their father's direction.

William James would come to pursue scientific studies both in America–at the Lawrence Scientific School (where he began his lifelong friendship with fellow student Charles Sanders Peirce), finally completing a degree in medicine at the Harvard School of Medicine – and, earlier, abroad: in France, Switzerland (at the Geneva Academy, now University of Geneva), and Germany. While still a medical student, William spent almost a year in Brazil (April 1865 to February 1866) participating in the Thayer Expedition led by Louis Agassiz, collecting specimens for his zoological museum (now the Harvard Museum of Comparative Zoology). In contrast, Henry's exposure to science was tangential, his knowledge of the developments during his lifetime coming largely through his reading, in conversation, and from correspondents. In spite of this practical, external difference, the common interest of the brothers in the nature of consciousness underwrote their separate endeavors to such an extent that as they approached the ends of their careers, when Henry read the manuscript of William's soon-to-be-published *Pragmatism: A New Name for Some Old Ways of Thinking* (1907), in which scientific method was distilled and repurposed to address the Darwinian information in relation to thinking and using language, he wrote to William that he had come to realize from reading his lecture/chapters how much all his life he had himself "unconsciously pragmatized."[10] Rather than being a flip remark in their ongoing badinage, this observation reflected the seriousness with which Henry recognized the importance of how each of them had come to attend both to their inheritances from Emerson and Swedenborg as well as to "the Darwinian facts."[11] Indeed, in his very last work – about which there will be more to say just further along – William, as though echoing Henry's observation, remarked, "In the end philosophers may get into as close contact as realistic novelists with the facts of life."[12] William noted this within his greater delineation of the ambit and method of philosophy, as he understood it, under which "science" was subsumed in its generality and specificities, thereby implicitly recuperating the older heading of "natural philosophy" for all the different practices of inquiry.

It is also worth commenting in the context of science and Henry's manner of inquiry, that he could quite accurately be figured as having anticipated the practice of "fieldwork" instituted by the first "official" anthropologists.

As a participant observer in and of the societies in which he found himself "more truly and more strange,"[13] he described the habits and minds of "fictional" individuals drawn from "real" ones on either side of "the great ocean-stream" though seemingly using the same language: "One writes the novel, one paints the picture, of one's language and of one's time, and calling it modern English will not, alas!, make the difficult task any easier."[14] "Where, within them, gracious heaven, were we to look for so much as an approach to the social elements of habitat and climate, of birds of that note and plumage?" James asks rhetorically in the preface to *The Aspern Papers*.[15] In his late field report on *The American Scene* (1907), he called himself "the restless analyst" as he recorded the changes that had occurred in America and its society during his twenty-year absence (1884–1904). It was, as we recall, over the course of the nineteenth century, exactly during James's lifetime, that anthropology began to grow increasingly distinct from natural history, crystallizing into its modern form as a discipline around the turn of the century, when fieldwork began to be expected and integrated into ethnographic study. The emergence and development of the realist novel parallels roughly the emergence and development of anthropology. It is worth noting as well that Henry James's astute powers of observation came somewhat naturally to him as a child constantly moving back and forth across the Atlantic, here and there in Europe and America with his family's peregrinations. Henry James Sr. carefully heeded his admired friend Emerson: "People wish to be settled; only as far as they are unsettled is there any hope for them."[16] Following "the admirable and exquisite Emerson," James Sr. believed that his children should experience many different kinds of education and social settings to prepare them as fully as possible to enjoy freedom in all its senses. As Henry James the novelist described in 1879:

> Emerson expressed, before all things ... the value and importance of the individual, the duty of making the most of one's self, of living by one's own personal light and carrying out one's own disposition. He reflected with beautiful irony upon the exquisite impudence of those institutions which claim to have appropriated the truth and to dole it out, in proportionate morsels, in exchange for a subscription. He talked about the beauty and dignity of life, and about every one who is born into the world being born to the whole, having an interest and a stake in the whole.[17]

William James would echo "having an interest and a stake in the whole" as the call to action in *Pragmatism* and elsewhere, underscoring that "In the total game of life we stake our persons all the while" and emphasizing repeatedly throughout his work that the key to unlocking one's possibility of having a real stake in the game of life is to follow and cultivate one's interest.[18] "Interest" was also the spring of Henry James's development of character and plot in his fiction as he described variously in his prefaces to the New York Edition.

With his training in anatomy, physiology, chemistry, and medicine, and his ongoing research into the newly budding aspects of psychology – his scientific credentials, so to speak – William set himself the task of translating for a professional academic audience all he had gleaned concerning experience in the expanded sense he had begun to learn from Emerson, particularly as it is inextricably implicated in what Darwin uncovered about human descent from "a hairy quadruped, furnished with a tail and pointed ears, probably arboreal in its habits."[19] This translation constituted the burden of William James's life's work, from the publication of *The Principles of Psychology*, effectively begun in 1878 and completed in 1890, through to what he was working on in the weeks before he died, an "Introduction to Philosophy" with which he "hoped ... to round out [his] system"; this text was published posthumously as *Some Problems of Philosophy* in 1911.[20] (It is important to note in the context of James's ever-deepening interest in psychology and experimental psychology that this was the period when hypnotism and multiple personality, for example, became legitimate scientific subjects, which Sigmund Freud, born a generation later, would bring to the forefront of popular attention.)

While the seventeenth-century Scientific Revolution was the engine propelling research in all areas well into the nineteenth century, the movement from what had been examined and speculated about under what was known in the first half of the nineteenth century as "development theory" to what came to be known after Darwin's monumental contribution in 1859 as "evolution" shifted the investigative focus from mechanism toward organism and brought science to the center of the West's cultural stage, where it has remained ever since, and with the dust from the explosion caused by what I have termed "the Darwinian information" still not settled.[21] It is against this background that what William and Henry James understood by "experience," early on articulated for them, as noted above, through Emerson and his work, must be considered. Oliver Wendell Holmes was the first to remark that Emerson had come to realize what came to be called "evolution" even before Robert Chambers's anonymously published *Vestiges of the Natural History of Creation* in 1844. Holmes based his judgment not only on the content of Emerson's work but also, significantly, on his style. It happens that Emerson read almost the same scientific texts and news of various discoveries from the late eighteenth into the nineteenth century as Darwin, and just as Darwin over the course of his six revisions of *On the Origin of Species* attempted with each draft to rid his sentences and paragraphs of the idea of teleology, fixed design, Emerson from as early as his own anonymously published volume, *Nature*, in 1836 attempted to "reconceive reason" – to borrow Stanley Cavell's phrasing – to devise a new form of argument capable of accommodating the accumulating "squirming facts" concerning the chance appearance and nature of human experience on the planet.[22] After a visit to the Jardin des Plantes in Paris in 1833, after witnessing firsthand evidence of one species changing into another, confirming speculations about which he had read, he wrote in his journal:

> The universe is a more amazing puzzle than ever, as you glance along this bewildering series of animated forms – the hazy butterflies, the carved shells, the birds, beasts, fishes, insects, snakes, and the upheaving principle of life everywhere incipient, in the very rock aping organized forms. Not a form so grotesque, so savage, nor so beautiful but is an expression of some property inherent in man the observer, – an occult relation between the very scorpions and man. I feel the centipede in me, – cayman, carp, eagle, and fox. I am moved by strange sympathies; I say continually "I will be a naturalist."[23]

Truth Happens to an Idea

In what is arguably his most famous lecture/essay, "Experience" (1844), Emerson elaborates as powerfully as he ever would the expanded sense of "experience" needed to understand human habitation on the planet in light of the evolutionary findings he had already begun to realize when he expressed the wish to "be a naturalist" just over a decade earlier. "Our life is not so much threatened as our perception," he wrote in opening his essay, intent on aligning our "axis of vision" with what had been learned about nature and the human place in it so to transcend the "paltry empiricism" handed down most recently by David Hume.[24] Emerson realized that the combination of the New World event and the discoveries that would issue in the Darwinian information could not be contained in the philosophy inherited from another time and another place – eighteenth-century empiricism, with "facts" understood as specimens fixed in a mechanical order. Instead he offered that this order belonged to the mind of man and recuperated what he had announced earlier in "The Method of Nature," an address delivered in 1841: "So must we admire in man, the form of the formless, the concentration of the vast, the house of reason ... Oh rich and various Man! Thou palace of sight and sound, carrying in thy senses the morning and the night and the unfathomable galaxy; in thy brain, the geometry of the city of God."[25] Emerson deconstructed, as it were, the inherited history of the world as he recovered the root of the word "empiricism," revealing it to be what had been forgotten along the way: its use by the ancient Greeks to mean "experience" itself, *empeiria*, coming from *peira*, a word carrying an array of meanings – "trial, attempt, experiment, essay, endeavor, risk, scrutinize, entice, discipline, examine, go about, prove, tempt" – all linked "through the idea of piercing."[26] "Once, a fear pierced him ... "[27] The fact of feeling cannot be separated from experience, as William James would make explicit. And as Stanley Cavell pointed out in one of his brilliant, necessary essays arguing for Emerson's place in the pantheon of philosophers, the word "peril" also shares its root with "experience."[28] Emerson had gathered the loose edges of experience's meanings into his own attempt to redirect attention to the fact that "the imperfect is our paradise," not some state of "imperishable bliss" where "ripe fruit never falls," and that within this actuality there is always the difficulty of uncertainty:

> Man lives by pulses; our organic movements are such; and the chemical and ethereal agents are undulatory and alternate; and the mind goes antagonizing on, and never prospers but by fits. We thrive by casualties. Our chief experiences have been casual.[29]

Sixty-three years later William James would rephrase these ideas in *Pragmatism*: "our knowledge grows in spots" (559)[30]; "Everything that happens to us brings its own duration and extension, and both are vaguely surrounded by a marginal 'more' that runs into the duration and extension of the next thing that comes" (563–4); "all our theories are *instrumental*, are mental modes of *adaptation* to reality, rather than revelations or gnostic answers to some divinely instituted world enigma" (571, emphasis James's); "Truth *happens* to an idea. It *becomes* true, is *made* true by events. Its verity *is* in fact an event, a process" (574, emphasis James's); "Experience is in mutation, and our psychological ascertainments of truth are in mutation" (585). And Henry James, at different moments in his career would offer his own variants of lessons learned from "the divine Emerson"[31]: "the *situation* [in which a character finds himself, in this case Strether in *The Ambassadors*] clearly would spring from the play of wildness and the development of extremes"; "One could only go by probabilities"[32]; "What it would be really interesting, and I dare say admirably difficult, to go into would be the very history of this effect of experience; the history, in other words, of the growth of the immense array of terms, perceptional and expressional"[33]; from "The Art of Fiction," "A novel is a living thing, all one and continuous, like any other organism"; and, finally,

> Experience is never limited, and it is never complete; it is an immense sensibility, a kind of huge spider-web of the finest silken threads suspended in

the chamber of consciousness and catching every air-borne particle in its tissue. It is the very atmosphere of the mind; and when the mind is imaginative ... it takes to itself the faintest hints of life, it converts the very pulses of air into revelations.[34]

Emerson planted the seeds that "the James boys" would gather as fruit.

The combination of Henry James Sr.'s liberal ideas about education and experience with his devotion to Swedenborg and Emerson exposed William and Henry from early on to the fringes of thinking and precluded that they would find themselves limited by the rules of any system – science included. Their preparation also stimulated them to experiment and consistently entertain multiple points of view. A memory of Henry James about William at fifteen gives a vivid sense of their natural habitat, so to speak. Henry recalled his brother's "interest in the 'queer' or the incalculable effects of things" during the summer of 1857 when the family had moved from Paris to Boulogne-sur-Mer, where William received his first formal scientific training:

> he had been ... addicted to "experiments" and the consumption of chemicals, the transformation of mysterious liquids from glass to glass under exposure to lambent flame, the cultivation of stained fingers, the establishment and the transport, in our wanderings, of galvanic batteries, the administration to all he could persuade of electric shocks, the maintenance of marine animals in splashy aquaria, the practice of photography in the room I for a while shared with him at Boulogne, with every stern reality of big cumbrous camera, prolonged exposure, exposure mostly of myself, darkened development, also interminable, and ubiquitous brown blot. Then there had been also the constant, as I fearfully felt it, the finely speculative and boldly disinterested absorption of curious drugs ... There was apparently for him no possible effect whatever that mightn't be more or less rejoiced in as such – all exclusive of its relation to other things than merely knowing.[35]

Roughly during this same period, Henry was also experimenting: cultivating his fluency in French and all manner of literary subjects, trying his hand – as his brother did – at painting, studying engineering and then entering law school briefly. By 1863 – only twenty – he committed himself to try writing as a career, beginning with book reviews; within a year and a half, his first signed tale, "The Story of a Year" was published in *Atlantic Monthly* (March 1865). From then began the "thought-experiments" he would offer in each of his fictions as well as in his ongoing reviews, travel pieces, and essays. As William remarked of the stories and novels, the "personages ... reflect on themselves and give an acute critical scientific introspective classification of their own natures & states of mind" – indeed Henry James was "pragmatizing" as his characters often illustrated psychoanalysis *avant la lettre*.[36] The science of mind was offered for all to explore. Throughout his career, Henry James observed in the same way as a clinical observer the human animal grappling with experience now realized to be uncertain, ultimately unknowable, transient, without purpose except for what each creature devised in a world made of words.

Whether writing fiction or non-fiction, however, Henry James's "true subject" – as distinct from what Wallace Stevens called "the poetry of the subject" – was the relation of language to thinking about thinking.[37] This was, of course, William's true subject as well, though he remained on the descriptive, rather than the "creative," side of the imaginary fence that the brothers seemed to have constructed for themselves. (Although this is a specious distinction, it serves to point the obvious difference in their engagements with their respective language games.) They were both riding the crest of a wave of investigation into what F. Max Müller, the eminent nineteenth-century comparative philologist, called "the Science of Thought," underpinned as it was, and as he demonstrated, by "the Science of Language" (which he importantly designated "One of the Physical Sciences"). As he noted in opening his 1861 edition of course material that he had offered over the years at Oxford and had presented in abbreviated form as a series of lectures at the Royal Institution in London in 1860: "There is more in words than is dreamt of in our philosophy," and quoting from Francis Bacon's *Novum Organum* of 1620, continued,

> Men believe that their reason is lord over their words, but it happens, too, that words exercise a reciprocal and reactionary power over our intellect. Words, as a Tartar's bow, shoot back upon the understanding of the wisest, and mightily entangle and pervert the judgment.[38]

While Müller quarreled with Darwin's view concerning the evolution of language in humans, arguing for language being the feature separating the human from other animals, his contribution to the sciences of language and thought were foundational. Emerson corresponded with him, William James read him. Müller's investigations belonged to the spirit of the age. Bacon's words quoted above might well have served as William's rallying cry as he composed the lectures on "some old ways of thinking" that would later become the chapters of *Pragmatism*. This passage from "What Pragmatism Means," the second lecture/chapter, which lays out the core of his argument, offers a good illustration:

You know how men have always hankered after unlawful magic, and you know what a great part in magic *words* have always played ... [T]he universe has always appeared to the natural mind as a kind of enigma, of which the key must be sought in the shape of some illuminating or power-bringing word or name. That word names the universe's *principle*, and to possess it is after a fashion to possess the universe itself. "God," "Matter," "Reason," "the Absolute," "Energy," are so many solving names. You can rest when you have them. You are at the end of your metaphysical quest.

But if you follow the pragmatic method, you cannot look on any such word as closing your quest. You must bring out of each word its practical cash-value, set it at work within the stream of your experience. It appears less as a solution, then, than as a program for more work, and more particularly as an indication of the ways in which existing realities may be *changed*.

"Theories thus become instruments," William concluded, *"not answers to enigmas in which we can rest*. We don't lie back upon them, we move forward, and, on occasion, make nature over again by their aid. Pragmatism unstiffens all our theories, limbers them up and sets each one at work."[39]

Platforms for Action

Complementing his brother's insight into the power and danger of words, Henry James would abundantly illustrate in the thought-experiments that were his novels how, indeed, words become what William James and his fellow pragmatists called "platforms for action," the stages on which we act out our beliefs.[40] In doing this, exploring every nook and cranny of conception, misconception, deceit, guile, motive, intention, constituting his characters' thinking, Henry James anticipated by more than a century research findings of those working today in the forefront of cognitive science. Underpinning his realization after reading *Pragmatism* that he had himself "all his life ... unconsciously pragmatized" was what he had learned from playing his own language game. As Andy Clark, a leader in the field of contemporary cognitive science, observes, "profoundly, the practice of putting thoughts into words alters the nature of human experience." The description Clark gives of the manner of this alteration – in technical language, the operation of *second-order cognitive dynamics* – provides an explanation of pragmatism, properly understood, as a moral activity. It is this kind of activity Henry James recognized as his "unconsciously pragmatiz[ing]" in composing his complex linguistic universe.

Noting the complementary work of other noted researchers into language and thought, such as Jean-Pierre Changeux and Derek Bickerton, Clark offers,

By second-order cognitive dynamics I mean a cluster of powerful capacities involving self-evaluation, self-criticism and finely honed remedial responses. Examples would include: recognizing a flaw in our own plan or argument, and dedicating further cognitive efforts to fixing it; reflecting on the unreliability of our own initial judgements in certain types of situations and proceeding with special caution as a result; coming to see why we reached a particular conclusion by appreciating the logical transitions in our own thought; thinking about the conditions under which we think best and trying to bring them about. The list could be continued but the pattern should be clear. In all these cases, we are effectively thinking about our own cognitive profiles or about specific thoughts. This "thinking about thinking" is a good candidate for a distinctively human capacity – one not evidently shared by the other, non-language-using animals who share our planet. As such, it is natural to wonder whether this might be an entire species of thought which is not just reflected in, or extended by, our use of words but is directly dependent upon language for its very existence. Public language and the inner rehearsal of sentences, would, on this model, act like the aerial roots of the Mangrove tree – the words would serve as fixed points capable of attracting and positioning additional intellectual matter, creating the islands of second-order thought so characteristic of the cognitive landscape of *Homo Sapiens*.

Henry James's thought-experiments perform exactly the function Clark goes on to describe:

> It is easy to see, in broad outline how this might come about. For as soon as we formulate a thought in words (or on paper), it becomes an object for both ourselves and for others. As an object, it is the kind of thing we can have thoughts about. In creating the object, we need have no thought about thought – but once it is there, the opportunity immediately exists to attend to it as on object in its own right. The process of linguistic formulation thus creates the stable structure to which subsequent thinkings attach.[41]

Reading Henry's sentences stimulates the growth of new dendritic connections as we compose observation platforms from which we learn about what the novelist called the "terms of cognition" belonging to, constituting, our consciousness. What better illustration could there be of William's "radical empiricism": "Really, universally, relations stop nowhere ... "[42]

NOTES

1. Thony Christie, introduction to "The History of 'Scientist'" by Melinda Baldwin, *The Renaissance Mathematicus* (blog), July 10, 2014, https://thonyc.wordpress .com/2014/07/10/the-history-of-scientist. See also Melinda Baldwin's *Making Nature: The History of a Scientific Journal* (Chicago: University of Chicago Press, 2015), 4–8.

2. Baldwin, "The History of 'Scientist'" (blog entry).

3. Baldwin, "The History of 'Scientist'" (blog entry).

4. Henry James, *A Small Boy and Others* (1913), collected in *Autobiography*, ed. Frederick W. Dupee (Princeton: Princeton University Press, 1983), 133.

5. The term "storm center" belongs to William James, who in his 1904 lecture "The Experience of Activity" (collected in *Essays in Radical Empiricism* [New York: Dover 2003]: 81–99) proposed: "The body is the storm center, the origin of co-ordinates, the constant place of stress in all that experience-train. Everything circles round it, and is felt from its point of view. The word 'I,' then, is primarily a noun of position, just like 'this' and 'here'" (89).

6. Henry James, *Autobiography*, 359.

7. Emerson's reference to the brothers ("How well the James boys understand the use of language") cited in *The Correspondence of William James, vol. 1, William and Henry, 1861–1884*, ed. Ignas K. Skrupskelis and Elizabeth M. Berkeley (Charlottesville: University Press of Virginia, 1992), 131, n. 3; Ralph Waldo Emerson, "The Method of Nature" in *Essays and Lectures*, ed. Joel Porte (New York: The Library of America, 1983), 113–32, at 130.

8. In *Notes of a Son and Brother* (1914), Henry James observed that the one constant feature of the James family's peregrinations in Europe and America were his father's "faded ... anciently red" covered copies of the greater number of Swedenborg's works: "I recall them as inveterately part of our very luggage" (*Autobiography*, 332).

9. Published in Boston by Fields, Osgood, & Co. This citation is from the first edition (12).

10. "On October 17, 1907 Henry had written to William explaining the delay in writing to him about his *Pragmatism: A New Name for Some Old Ways of Thinking* (1907) by "the very fact of the spell itself (of interest & enthrallment) that the book cast upon me; I simply sank down, under it, into such depths of submission & assimilation that *any* reaction, very nearly, even that of acknowledgment, would have had almost the taint of dissent or escape. Then I was lost in the wonder of the extent to which all my life I have (like M. Jourdain) unconsciously pragmatized. You are immensely & universally *right*." From *Henry James: A Life in Letters*, ed. Philip Horne (New York: Penguin, 2014), 482.

11. William James, *Pragmatism: A New Name for Some Old Ways of Thinking: Popular Lectures on Philosophy*, collected in *Writings 1902–1910*, ed. Bruce Kuklick (New York: The Library of America, 1987), 535.

12. William James, "Philosophy and Its Critics," in *Some Problems of Philosophy* (Cambridge, MA: Harvard University Press, 1979), 9–20, at 19.

13. Wallace Stevens, "Tea at the Palaz of Hoon," in *Collected Poetry and Prose*, ed. Frank Kermode and Joan Richardson (New York: The Library of America, 1997), 51.

14. Henry James, "The Art of Fiction" (1884), collected in Henry James, *Literary Criticism: Essays on Literature, American Writers, English Writers*, ed. Leon Edel (New York: The Library of America, 1984), 44–65, at 56.

15. Collected in Henry James, *Literary Criticism: French Writers, Other European Writers, The Prefaces to the New York Edition*, ed. Leon Edel (New York: The Library of America, 1984), 1181.

16. Ralph Waldo Emerson, "Circles," in *Essays and Lectures*, 403–13, at 413.

17. Henry James, "Nathaniel Hawthorne," collected in *Literary Criticism: Essays on Literature*, 382. James framed Emerson in his biographical essay on Hawthorne, which first appeared in Macmillan's "English Men of Letters" series, as the "Transcendentalist, *par excellence*" (382 in Library of America edition). The phrase "the admirable and exquisite Emerson" is also from this piece.

18. William James, "The Sentiment of Rationality," in *The Will to Believe and Other Essays in Popular Philosophy* (New York: Dover, 1956 [1897]), 63–110, at 94.

19. Charles Darwin, *The Descent of Man, and Selection in Relation to Sex* (Princeton: Princeton University Press, 1981), 389.

20. Edited by his son Henry James Jr., Horace Kallen, and Ralph Barton Perry; published by Longmans, Green. Bruce Kuklick in his chronology to James's *Writings 1902–1910* quotes from James's instructions on July 26, 1910 his hope that the volume would "round out my system" (1349).

21. I coined and began using this term in *A Natural History of Pragmatism: The Fact of Feeling from Jonathan Edwards to Gertrude Stein* (Cambridge: Cambridge University Press, 2007).

22. The phrase "squirming facts" comes from a poem by Wallace Stevens entitled "Connoisseur of Chaos," in *Collected Poetry and Prose*, 195; Cavell notes Emerson's aspiration "to reconceive reason" in the Introduction to his *Emerson's Transcendental Etudes*, ed. David Justin Hodge (Stanford: Stanford University Press, 2003), 7.

23. Notebook entry of July 13, 1833, in *Journals of Ralph Waldo Emerson 1820–1872, vol. 3, 1833–1835*, ed. Edward Waldo Emerson and Waldo Emerson Forbes (Boston and New York: Houghton Mifflin Company, 1910), 163. For a full discussion of development theory and its background and becoming "evolution," see Dov Ospovat, *The Development of Darwin's Theory: Natural History, Natural Theology and Natural Selection, 1838–1859* (Cambridge: Cambridge University Press, 1995). For a discussion of the common reading of Emerson and Darwin and of Emerson's style, see my *Natural History of Pragmatism*. For a more specific discussion of Emerson's involvement with science, see Laura Dassow Walls, *Emerson's Life in Science: The Culture of Truth* (Ithaca and London: Cornell University Press, 2003).

24. "Our life is . . . " and "paltry empiricism" are taken from "Experience"; "axis of vision" from *Nature* (1836); both in *Essays and Lectures*, 471, 492, and 47 respectively.

25. Emerson, "The Method of Nature," in *Essays and Lectures*, 122.

26. Liddell & Scott's *Greek-English Lexicon*, 9th ed. (Oxford: Oxford University Press, 1977), 544. See also discussion in Joan Richardson, *Pragmatism and American Experience: An Introduction* (Cambridge: Cambridge University Press, 2014), 13–14.

27. "Once, a fear pierced him . . ." is a line from the eleventh "way" of Wallace Stevens's "Thirteen Ways of Looking at a Blackbird," in *Collected Poetry and Prose*, 76.

28. Cavell plays elaborately on this common root throughout "Finding as Founding: Taking Steps in Emerson's 'Experience,'" in *Emerson's Transcendental Etudes*, 110–40.

29. Indented passage from "Experience," in *Essays and Lectures*, 483; earlier quotations from Wallace Stevens are from "Poems of Our Climate" ("imperfect … ") and "Le Monocle de Mon Oncle" (the other two), in *Collected Poetry and Prose*, 179, 10 respectively.

30. William James, *Pragmatism*, in *Writings 1902–1910*.

31. William James thus referred to Emerson in a letter to Henry dated May 3,1903. See *The Correspondence of William James, vol. 3, William and Henry 1897–1910*, ed. Ignas K. Skrupskelis and Elizabeth M. Berkeley (Charlottesville: University Press of Virginia, 1994), 234.

32. These two quotations are from the preface to *The Ambassadors*, in Henry James, *Literary Criticism: French Writers*, 1310; the emphasis is James's.

33. Preface to *The Golden Bowl*, in Henry James, *Literary Criticism: French Writers*, 1332.

34. Collected in Henry James, *Literary Criticism: Essays on Literature*, 54, 52.

35. Henry James, *Notes of a Son and Brother* in *Autobiography*, 308.

36. From a letter William James wrote to Henry on December 12, 1875, commenting on the success of his first novel *Roderick Hudson*, collected in *The Correspondence of William James, vol. 1: William and Henry, 1861–1884*, ed. Ignas K. Skrupskelis and Elizabeth M. Berkeley (Charlottesville and London: University of Virginia Press, 1992), 247.

37. Wallace Stevens makes the distinction between "the true subject" and "the poetry of the subject" in "The Irrational Element in Poetry," delivered as a lecture at Harvard University in 1936, later published in his *Opus Posthumous*, ed. Samuel French Morse (New York: Alfred A. Knopf, 1957), 216–28, and in *Collected Poetry and Prose*, 781–92. Stevens offers, "In a poet who makes the true subject paramount and who merely embellishes it, the subject is constant and the development orderly. If the poetry of the subject is paramount, the true subject is not constant nor its development orderly. This is true in the case of Proust and Joyce, for example, in modern prose" (227).

38. Max Müller, *Lectures on The Science of Language* (1862: Project Gutenberg, 2010), viii, www.gutenberg.org/files/32856/32856-pdf.pdf?session_id=235785b0 c1afc5efd9a1f7688bd2642480e55f80. The Bacon passage is from Aphorism LIX of his text, translated variously from the Latin. The full title in English is *The New Organon, or True Directions Concerning the Interpretation of Nature*. Müller's quotation is not from the standard translation, which is by James Spedding, Robert Leslie Ellis, and Douglas Denon Heath in *The Works of Francis Bacon* (Vol. 8), published in Boston by Taggard and Thompson in 1863; it is likely that the translation here is Müller's.

39. William James, *Pragmatism*, 509–10, emphases James's.

40. The Scottish philosopher Alexander Bain (1818–1903), founder of *Mind*, the first British journal devoted to psychology and philosophy, was a leading proponent of applying the scientific method to psychology. His definition of "belief" as "a platform for action" was adopted and used profitably by Charles Sanders Peirce and William James in their elucidations of the way beliefs animate the method of pragmatism.

41. Andy Clark, "Magic Words: How Language Augments Human Computation," in *Language and Thought: Interdisciplinary Themes*, ed. Peter Carruthers and

Jill Boucher (Cambridge: Cambridge University Press, 2003), 162–83, at 179, 177.

42. "Terms of cognition" comes from the preface to *The Golden Bowl*; "Really, universally, relations stop nowhere," from the preface to *Roderick Hudson*; both in Henry James, *Literary Criticism: French Writers*, 1330, 1041 respectively. See the Introduction to the present volume for more on William James's radical empiricism.

5

KITT PRICE

Empson's Einstein
Science and Modern Reading

What happens when you fall in love in four-dimensional space-time? This urgent problem was shared by an astrophysicist and a poet who each resisted modern specialization by conflating the mathematical physics of Einsteinian relativity with human interests and values. Arthur Stanley Eddington (1882–1944) was professor of astronomy at the University of Cambridge and an early supporter of general relativity at a time when his colleagues were ill disposed toward continental metaphysics and especially anything connected with Germany. Eddington led a 1919 expedition to test Einstein's law of gravitation by measuring the deflection of starlight passing close to the sun on its way to terrestrial observers, and he produced expository writings and lectures giving scientific and wider public audiences access to the intense abstractions of special and general relativity. William Empson (1906–84) studied mathematics at Cambridge but invested more energy in theatrical and literary pursuits. He began work on an influential study of literary ambiguity before being dismissed in 1929 for the possession of contraceptives. Empson's intense, energetic and at times controversial readings of sixteenth- and seventeenth-century English poetry secured him a place in literary history, but his own production of metaphysical poetry for the Einstein age is founded on reading practices that treat the latest scientific problems and insights as having comparable cultural value to the literary canon. The present chapter follows the invitation implicit in the notes that accompanied Empson's poems, to read along with him some of the extra-literary sources that informed his poetic adventures in Einstein's universe.

A voracious consumer of popular science, Empson channeled romantic and ethical perplexities into metaphysical poems packed with entomology, botany, geometry, astrophysics, space travel, archaeology, and anthropology. While there is no evidence that Eddington and Empson ever met, it is clear that Empson took Eddington's expository writings to heart. A generation apart, the two men differed in values and lifestyle: Eddington

97

was a lifelong member of the Society of Friends, while Empson was equally committed to rejecting Christianity, which he described as "torture-worship."[1] A student newspaper compared the latest generation of Cambridge poets unfavorably to their scientific counterparts:

> the brilliant thinker in Natural Science, the future Thompson or Eddington, does not wear a distinctive dress, does not converse publicly in such a loud voice and with such an air of arrogance that it sickens the ordinary man, and though he may have ideas on humanity as advanced and as intellectual as a prominent aesthete, does not disregard the fact that his ideas may be wrong. He does not drink foul drinks with foreign names, for the sake of being drunk in Russian rather than tight on beer.[2]

In Cambridge in the 1920s, the astronomer in his forties and the poet in his early twenties had incompatible nocturnal interests. But the accommodation of ideas that may be wrong was an integral strategy to both Eddington's astrophysical calculations and Empson's poetic analogies.

Love in Einstein's Universe

Eddington's models for stellar energy enabled advances at a time when stellar structure was uncertain, pushing the variables to absurd extremes and working back toward plausible values until the model fit with observed behavior of stars. This brought him into conflict with the more conservative tradition of celestial mechanics, according to which proposals about stellar behavior should be based on deductions from known physical properties.[3] Modeling from absurdity has its poetic counterpart in the tradition of metaphysical conceit: the drawing of unlike things into sustained comparison, resulting in an argument for seduction on the basis of flea bites, for instance, or an eclipse of the sun caused by a person blinking. Empson admired this tradition, exemplified by John Donne, because its exponents "believe (though not all solemnly) that a love-affair is the fundamental means of understanding the world, or that the real purpose of building any system of knowledge is to understand love."[4] Empson remained committed to a radical reading of Donne throughout his life, identifying him as a contemporary of the space age in 1957: "Donne, then, from a fairly early age, was interested in getting to another planet much as the kids are nowadays; he brought the idea into practically all his best love-poems, with the sentiment which it still carries of adventurous freedom."[5] This was, Empson insisted, a freedom from church authorities, because it derived from the revolutionary claims of Galileo and Copernicus. Aged thirteen when the testing of Einstein's general relativity made world headlines, Empson grew up amid enthusiasm for the new cosmology of the early twentieth century, and his undergraduate love poems record a sustained humanistic engagement with relativity: an updating of Donne's approach for the Einstein era. But as an anecdote in Eddington's best-selling exposition of the new physics indicated, love could go more badly wrong in Einstein's universe.

The key challenge facing any expositor of relativity was how to convey the idea of time as a fourth dimension. Victorian debates about relativism, coupled with transcendental affiliations of the spatial fourth dimension, only made this harder.[6] As Einstein remarked in his own attempt at a popular explanation, "The non-mathematician is seized by a mysterious shuddering when he hears of 'four-dimensional' things, by a feeling not unlike that awakened by thoughts of the occult. And yet there is no more common-place statement than that the world in which we live is a four-dimensional space-time continuum."[7] Readers for whom the standard expository equipment of measuring rods and trains had not been enthralling might well have enjoyed Eddington's approach:

> Suppose that you are in love with a lady on Neptune and that she returns the sentiment. It will be some consolation for the melancholy separation if you can say to yourself at some – possibly pre-arranged – moment, "She is thinking of me now." Unfortunately a difficulty has arisen because we have had to abolish Now. There is no absolute Now, but only the various relative Nows differing according to the reckoning of different observers ... She will have to think of you continuously for eight hours on end in order to circumvent the ambiguity of "Now."[8]

Empson's adventurous lovers encounter a range of relativistic difficulties. A 1928 poem originally titled "Relativity" (subsequently published as "The World's End") opens with a promise that outlawed love may find sanctuary at the outer reaches of space: "Fly with me then to all's and the world's end ... What tyrant there our variance debars?"[9] But the curvature of space-time in four dimensions means there can be no escape: "The world's end is here." As a bisexual man who found himself hopelessly in love with a close friend who did not "return the sentiment," Empson found in the curvature of space-time a means to universalize the personal pain of "variance." In another poem from 1928, "Letter I," the first of six poems addressed to this friend, the speaker relishes "dark spaces between stars" for their gift of privacy and the capacity to "say what they think common-sense has seen."[10] But the modern properties of space make a prison out of privacy, as the speaker descends into a "non-Euclidean predicament" thanks to the intense curvature of space around a massive dense star, which leaves it cut off from the rest of the universe. Astrophysical conjectures about the final stages of stellar existence are compounded with non-Euclidean geometry, resulting in a conceit for love that cannot be articulated: "Flame far too hot not to seem utter cold / And hide a tumult never to be told."

Is it too much to ask that readers verse themselves in the latest physics and astronomy in order to access the logic that gives the poem's "predicament" its emotive force? "Letter I" functions as an allegory of specialization. Its opening invocation of Pascal's "eternal silence of the infinite spaces" establishes intimacy through accessible, shared reading matter, before moving into the popular craze of talking to Mars by wireless. It then plunges into a dense package of ancient religion and modern physics, a daring marriage based on the current reading of Empson and his interlocutor, a classics student. It is a sensual proposal in which the words from the two men's bookshelves, and their conversations about books, are spliced and intermingled, the speaker's passion amplified through its restraint in regular verse form and its voicing in the detached languages of physical and human sciences. The result of this coupling across the disciplines is a hyper-specialization that leaves the speaker unable to communicate, however. The poem's achievement is in its apparent failure, as readers must decide how far to read in its sources, how far they are willing to extend the act of "reading a poem" into an exercise of reconstructive companionship, exploring specific texts in astrophysics and classical anthropology. For Empson, science is literature: "a physicist like Einstein or Eddington is making superb uses of the imagination ... I have always found the world-picture of the scientists much more stimulating and usable than that of any 'literary influence.'"[11]

Sustained literary engagement with scientific world-pictures also functions as interjection in scientific debate. The condition arrived at in the poem's conclusion, where the fate of a white dwarf star is merged with extreme curvature of space-time, predicts the black holes that were named as such around thirty years after the poem's completion, in 1967.[12] Eddington refused to countenance the idea of a massive dense star being cut off from the rest of space, undermining the proposals of his junior colleague Subrahmanyan Chandrasekhar and holding back enquiry into these stellar freaks.[13] Empson, operating beyond the power wrangles of the Royal Astronomical Society, was free to explore this outlawed stellar fate using metaphysical conceit instead of mathematical modeling. His poem participates in another tradition that he admired in Donne and others: the predictive capacity of literary creations. H. G. Wells was the exemplar here, and Empson singled out the "babble machine" from *The Sleeper Awakes* (1910) as Wells's most impressive case.[14] The novel's protagonist is a man named Graham who falls asleep in 1897 and wakes in the year 2100 to a revolutionary dictatorship in Britain. The ruler Ostrog disseminates news and propaganda through trumpet devices, around which workers gather and murmur their disapproval. Encountering this very scene in May 1926 amid the General Strike, when newspaper printing was suspended and radio became the principal news outlet, Empson realized that Wells had "forecast not merely the invention of the machine and its subsequent political importance but also the way Englishmen would feel about it in its political use."[15] This celebration of Wells was never published. It was cut from drafts of an essay on Donne, in which Empson asserted that Donne's commitment to life on other worlds resulted in him having "forecast the theological quarrel about astronomy ... about a third of a century before the trial of Galileo."[16] Empson reckoned this a lesser achievement compared to the "majestic foresight" of Wells's babble machine, but he was arguing for the significance of each author's science fiction credentials, established through their interleaving of science or technology with human interests. The reason for cutting these remarks was not that Empson had reneged on his commitment to science fiction, but because they were bound up with an intemperate attack on T. S. Eliot, whose lack of enthusiasm for Martian theology Empson read as an affront to Donne's ethics as a lover.

The only one of Empson's relativistic poems to end happily is also the only one explicitly coded as heterosexual. Published in 1929, "Camping Out" begins with a woman cleaning her teeth into a lake, and pursues a comparison between flecks of toothpaste and the reflection of stars in the water. As surface tension causes the flecks to move apart from each other, the speaker imagines that the two of them are traveling faster than light, the stars rushing past. It is a conceit inspired by Wells, and the poem's misty scenario matches the Time Traveller's accelerated view of the sun, stars and moon as he voyages into the deep future in chapter three of *The Time Machine* (1895). The poem's argument hinges on a turn away from religious authority to human independence. The image of a Madonna who "through-assumes the skies / Whose vaults are opened to achieve the Lord" is replaced by space travelers whose extreme velocity ruptures the fabric of space-time:

> No, it is we soaring explore galaxies,
> Our bullet boat light's speed by thousands flies.
> Who moves so among stars their frame unties;
> See where they blur, and die, and are outsoared.[17]

As Empson explained in his note to the poem, "if any particle of matter got a speed greater than that of light it would have infinite mass and might be supposed to crumple up round itself the whole of space-time – 'a great enough ecstasy makes the common world unreal.'"[18] Composed before the melodramatic isolation of "Letter I," this poem finds the same concept of extreme curvature to be a more positive condition. As the "common world" blurs, the adventurers come into the freedom of their own reality. More ominous implications are only hinted at in the poet's gloss, amplified in a later explanation: "Camping out together makes the lovers feel especially free from settled society, as if in a space-ship, but to see the stars like this they would have to be moving faster than light, and on the Einstein theory this would crack up the whole of space."[19] In the poem, that invitation to "See" the universe disintegrate like a firework display is a confident, communicable claim to knowledge from above: God's creation becomes a beautiful yet fleeting show for divine, intergalactic lovers. But the strain in this achievement lingers in the image of a universe "cracking up."

Christ Relativized

Although Empson was vehemently anti-Christian, theological problems are integral to his thinking and his analogizing of contemporary sciences. The most salient of these problems, linking his poetry and his critical writings, is that of the Martian Jesus. As Empson explained in "Donne the Space Man,"

> to believe that there are rational creatures on other planets is very hard to reconcile with the belief that salvation is only through Christ; they and their descendants appear to have been excluded from salvation; by the very scheme of God, indefinitely and perhaps forever. One might suppose, to preserve God's justice, that Christ repeats his sacrifice in all worlds ... but this already denies uniqueness to Jesus, and must in some way qualify the identity of the man with the divine person.[20]

The claim of terrestrial beings to divinity, to a Christlike condition, runs through Empson's poetry and criticism. Space travel, and the resulting extraterrestrial incarnations, are all about coming home: "It becomes natural to envisage frequent partial or occasional incarnations on this earth." Empson's biographer John Haffenden explains that in his second critical book, *Some Versions of Pastoral* (1935), "Christ is relativized" through analyses of sacrificial, mock-heroic figures ranging from Milton's Satan to *Alice in Wonderland*.[21] The power of these figures is articulated in terms drawn from Empson's reading of James Frazer's influential works *The Golden Bough* (1890) and *The Scapegoat* (1913):

> A majority of historical cultures, as Frazer so massively demonstrates, have placed faith in the concept of the *pharmakos* ("medicine"), a figure – in the beginning, he was literally a genuine criminal – who is appointed to assume the

guilt and suffering of the community which is to be purged by his death. The paradox is that by taking upon himself the sins of his world, this oblation – the *pharmakos* – is empowered and deemed to be quasi-divine; he is invested with an aura and with *mana*. Thus the criminal turns out to be the cure: the ritual sacrifice of the paradigmatic victim begets rebirth. From being the locus of evil, the receptacle of blame, the scapegoat is transfigured into a beneficiary who regenerates the society by which he is sanctioned.[22]

Frazer's thinking was amplified and adapted by fellow Cambridge classical scholars Jane Harrison and Francis Cornford, and Empson was especially taken with Cornford's account of tribal ritual as a basis not only for subsequent religious practices but also for early scientific or natural philosophical knowledge.

In the midst of a discussion of metaphysical poetry in *Some Versions of Pastoral* Empson summarizes Cornford's use of the term *physis*, or lifeblood:

the primitive Greeks invented Nature by throwing out onto the universe the idea of a common life-blood: the living force that made natural events follow reasonable laws, and in particular made the crops grow, was identified with the blood which made the members of the tribe into a unity and which they shared with their totem. So the physicist is well connected by derivation to the physician, the "leech" who lets blood.[23]

The combination of Frazer's *pharmakos* with Cornford's *physis* shapes Empson's engagement with Einsteinian physics in "Letter I," as it spirals away from more popular, accessible ideas about space into the formulation of intense doubt and isolation:

> Only, have we space, common-sense in common,
> A tribe whose life-blood is our sacrament,
> Physics or metaphysics for your showman,
> For my physician in this banishment?
> Too non-Euclidean predicament.

The "showman" here is a tragic hero or scapegoat who makes society possible, the physician or *pharmakos* whose function vanishes here because there is no community and no social sanction. But who or what is to blame for this extreme "predicament"? To what extent does the poem's conceit amount to a critique of scientific rationalism?

Metaphysical Insolence

Empson's mentor at Cambridge, the pioneering literary critic I. A. Richards, gave grounds for concern about more recent developments along the trajectory from magic to science. In the past, Richards argued, emotional life had been supported by religious belief, but the scientific knowledge that had dispelled religious faith was not capable of fulfilling its supportive function: "Over whole tracts of natural emotional response we are to-day like a bed of dahlias whose sticks have been removed ... we still hunger after a basis in belief."[24] In *Science and Poetry* (1926), Richards proposed that the experience of poems could teach readers to cultivate self-supporting attitudes, drawing our conflicting impulses into a balanced state and helping us to develop an outlook that could be maintained independently of external authorities. Richards followed Matthew Arnold in viewing scientific progress as a threat to human values and suggesting that salvation lay in the correct experience of culture, but he differed in seeking the remedy through close involvement with scientific methodology. "I'm seeing some of the younger physicists and logicians tonight," he wrote to T. S. Eliot in 1929, adding that he was "reading Eddington ... with a renewed sense that Physics is reaching a point where its *methods* can be understood. I think they are the methods of *all* descriptive explanation, *psychological* as well as physical, only carried further and if so the general consequences as to the inherent limitations of descriptions are very important."[25] Richards was probably reading *The Nature of the Physical World* (1928), where Eddington described the basis of physical law as a system of interconnected metrical readings, a "Cyclic Method" that leaves the inner nature of the underlying phenomena untouched. "In the relativity theory," Eddington explained, "we accept this as full knowledge, the nature of an object in so far as it is ascertainable by scientific enquiry being the abstraction of its relations to all surrounding objects."[26] The great advance associated with Einstein's theory was the "development of a powerful mathematical calculus for dealing compendiously with an infinite scheme of pointer readings," known as tensor calculus. The demand for an accessible account of relativity was at odds with the self-referentiality of scientific method: "we study the linkage of pointer readings with pointer readings. The terms link together in endless cycle with the same inscrutable nature running through the whole."[27]

Empson responded to the same passage in a poem that did not emerge in print until 1935, though it was likely composed earlier. "Doctrinal Point" dwells on the security of closed systems in contrast to more problematic states of being. The first example given is botanical: magnolias, the poem argues, cannot make wrong choices and "know no act that will not make them fair."[28] Functioning as their own saviors, the flowers are "Free by predestination in the blood, / Saved by their own sap, shed for themselves." This is the positive counterpart to the non-Euclidean predicament in "Letter I": the magnolias represent a self-contained system that produces only beauty, in contrast to the dying star-lover who is closed off from his fellows in unspeakable pain. The poem then leaps from flowers to physical law:

> Professor Eddington with the same insolence
> Called all physics one tautology;
> If you describe things with the right tensors
> All law becomes the fact that they can be described with them;
> This is the Assumption of the description.
> The duality of choice becomes the singularity of existence;
> The effort of virtue the unconsciousness of foreknowledge.

Eddington is teased here for the "insolence" of declaring physical law to be encased in a self-referential "Cyclic Method." Perhaps Empson had been reading Bertrand Russell's *The Scientific Outlook* (1931), which bases its chapter on "Scientific Metaphysics" on *The Nature of the Physical World*, repeatedly referring to its author as "Professor Eddington." Russell expresses concern that "official physics is just a little bit too official in Eddington's hands," and hopes that "it will not be impossible to allow it a little more significance than it has in his interpretation."[29]

How might we read the tone of this charge against "Professor Eddington" in "Doctrinal Point"? Empson's choice of the word "insolence" might be taken as a criticism of scientific hubris, but in the context of his metaphysical endeavors it becomes a sign of envy, for insolence is precisely the quality of bravado that motivates a successful metaphysical conceit. In manuscript notes to "Doctrinal Point" Empson registered a lack of metaphysical nerve in his recent work, stating "my last two poems have been failures for lack of political or economic convictions." Surmising that Marvell with his coy mistress "didn't *believe* in tearing pleasures with rough strife," Empson noted that "a great appearance of decision, of knowing one's own mind, is part of the (dynamic end of) metaphysical poetry. If only as a means of riding the storm of this universal doubt".[30] Eddington is envied here for the "tautology" in his "Cyclic Method of Physics," which deals with the problem of conviction in a way that is not open to the speaker of the poem. In his account of the "infinite scheme of pointer readings" in physics, Eddington introduced a character inspired by mystery fiction, "Mr X."[31] The role of "Mr X" is to stand for the reader's common sense objection to the "endless cycle of physical terms," because we all have direct contact with the physical world through our senses. But physics cannot accommodate our experience:

> It looks upon Mr X – and more particularly the part of Mr X that *knows* – as a rather troublesome tenant who at a late stage of the world's history has come to inhabit a structure which inorganic Nature has by slow evolutionary progress contrived to build. And so it turns aside from the avenue leading to Mr X – and beyond – and closes up its cycle leaving him out in the cold.[32]

Empson's "Doctrinal Point" is written from the perspective of that "troublesome tenant," the human subject left out in the cold by natural phenomena and physical laws that cannot share their art. While physical law achieves its own "Assumption of the description," skipping bodily death and being swept directly into heaven like the Virgin Mary, "Mr X" and his fellow tenants of the sensory world face endless decisions and dilemmas.

Underlying the argument of "Doctrinal Point" is a greater insolence: for Empson, "X" was shorthand for "Christ," and the poem therefore uses Eddington as a foil against which to elaborate the sufferings of a "Mr Christ," the incarnate reader perhaps. Where Eddington saw the laws of physics leaving "Mr X" "out in the cold," the final stanza of "Doctrinal Point" introduces a vulnerable "we" in contrast to the flowers and the laws of physics. Those who "cannot know of care"

> have no gap to spare that they should share
> The rare calyx we stare at in despair.
> They have no other that they should compare.

Change "calyx" (the casing that protects a flower's developing petals) to "calculus," and the poem is making a joke about tensor calculus, the central technique of relativity theory that is accessible only to hyper-specialized mathematical physicists. The poem's concern extends beyond specialization to the state of knowledge that can "have no other": they do not encounter alternative modes of existence, and have no cause to view themselves from the outside. Eddington's stories humanize relativity into parables about moving beyond egocentricity and developing respect for others with differing viewpoints, in accordance with the Quaker values that had led him to champion a theory associated with German science during World War I. The speaker's emphasis on "despair" in "Doctrinal Point" reasserts the limits on how far theoretical abstraction can be placed in the service of human interests. Where Richards drew from Eddington a conviction that the methods of physics were "the methods of *all* descriptive explanation, *psychological* as well as physical," Empson's poems dwell in a state of despair that overspills the emerging limits of description.

A More Desperate Effort

Eddington carries the burden in "Doctrinal Point," but he was far from being solely responsible for "insolent" thinking from science, which extended beyond physics to include the biological sciences. Reviewing *The Life of the White Ant* (1927), Empson commended Maurice Maeterlinck for having "taken upon himself one of the artist's new, important, and honorable functions, that of digesting the discoveries of the scientists into an emotionally available form."[33] The book portrayed a "miserly, sordid and monotonous existence" for termites, walled in their underground city as "dismal prisoners who never saw and never will see the light of day."[34] Inspired by the ubiquitous H. G. Wells, Maeterlinck conjectured that "cities of insects . . . might almost serve as a caricature of ourselves, as a travesty of the earthly paradise to which most civilised peoples are tending."[35] Yet Empson felt that

> the work itself calls for a more desperate effort of imagination. It is no use, for instance, wondering whether it mustn't be horrid for the poor creatures to eat each other's dung, when in the workers the whole process of digestion is inverted; or whether it must not be very sad to be blind, when they are so perfectly sure of their world, and can communicate with such nicety. The life of a termite, as he interprets it, is one of vivid but unrelieved horror; capable creatures of wide initiative do not usually think of themselves like that. It is hard to suppose a termite would agree.[36]

The "more desperate effort" urged here is to move beyond basic anthropomorphism of termites to imagine the white ant's existence on its own terms. Here is a real "other" that the human reader "should compare": not dung-eating, sightless underground workers, but the "capable creatures of wide initiative" who are "perfectly sure of their world." There is still anthropomorphism here, in the supposition of a captious termite reader, and this is where Empson differs from other critics of whimsical or emotive popular science writing who reject all human analogies as misleading. Popular science and literature engaged with scientific approaches to the world were valuable precisely because they facilitate a sharper sense of where human experience transitions into the extra-human.

Reviewing a memoir of incarceration in a mental institution, Jane Hillyer's *Reluctantly Told* (1926), alongside a collection of short stories by Wyndham Lewis, Empson identified as central to each work the exhilaration of encounter with "people with strong, able, well-marked systems of habits, absurdly unlike one's own. It gives a sort of courage, and it makes you feel more competent, even to have imagined them."[37] Conceding that "it is not better in real life, that the lady should bite her warders than help on her pupils," Empson queried the pleasure afforded by Hillyer's memoir:

> there is no doubt, in the book one prefers a well-documented account of biting; and she writes so much better in the grimmer parts that we may take it she herself felt the same. It does not please, I think, as exotic; as a relief to undigested neuroses, or simply as unexplained: given a superficial knowledge of Freud it seems perfectly sensible ... We must fall back on that magic word "scientific" used by the doctor in his introduction; both these books, I think, gratify our strong and critical curiosity about alien modes of feeling, our need for the flying buttress of sympathy with systems other than our own.[38]

The supportive function of such insights comes from taking a "scientific" approach, producing a "well-documented" and "sensible" account of the phenomena. In these reviews articulating his core values, written as his earliest metaphysical poems were beginning to form, Empson diverges from Richards's diagnosis of modern emotional life: the function of "sympathy with systems other than our own" can be supplied by reading scientific and literary works alike in anthropological temper, and support for beliefs is not the special preserve of poetry.

Empson's "flying buttress" is the key to his divergence from his mentor's critical project. At the conclusion to *Practical Criticism* (1929), Richards rehearsed what had become a familiar argument in relation to mass culture and modern media technologies. "Our everyday reading and speech now handles scraps from a score of different cultures," he noted, adding that we also have to shift between "ideas and feelings that took their form in Shakespeare's time or Dr. Johnson's time to ideas and feelings of Edison's or Freud's time and back again."[39] Meaningful communication was now in jeopardy, with language use becoming blurred, crude and inaccurate. Literary criticism could offer a vital service here, by establishing "systematic training in multiple definition," helping people to develop more supple forms of thought, speech and writing.[40] "The mind that can shift its view-point and still keep its orientation, that can carry over into quite a new set of definitions the results gained through past experience in other frameworks, the mind that can rapidly and without strain or confusion perform the systematic transformations required by such a shift, is the mind of the future," Richards affirmed in 1929.[41] The language here reflects his long-standing interest in relativity, which brought a new approach to the "frame of reference" underlying all measurements in time and space and the "transformations" used to mediate between those frames. Special relativity addresses the effect of velocity on the measurement of time and distance, and the fact that observers with differing relative velocities will produce conflicting measurements. A new form of absolute measurement common to all observers, the space-time interval, is encapsulated in Hermann Minkowski's famous words: "Henceforth space by itself, and time by itself, are doomed to fade away into mere shadows, and only a kind of union of the two will preserve an independent reality."[42]

Eddington dramatized frames of reference through a story about scientists based in a spiral nebula moving at a thousand miles a second relative to the earth, who do not take their own velocity into account when making measurements because they are convinced that it is physicists on the earth who are moving at this high speed, and who therefore need to make the adjustments. There is, Eddington remarks, "so deep a cleavage between us that we cannot even use the same space."[43] Having introduced the new absolutes made possible by including time as a fourth dimension, Eddington instructs readers that the "egocentric outlook should now be abandoned, and all frames treated as on the same footing."[44] The parallels with modern communication were clear to Richards, as he invoked a long-established association between higher dimensions and enlightened thinking: "To the eye of an intelligence perfectly emancipated from words most of our discussions would appear like the manoeuvres of three dimensional beings who for some reason believed themselves to exist only in two dimensions."[45] Envisaging an "infinitely plastic mind" of the future, he suggested that "present critical activities would compare with those of such a mind much as the physical conceptions of an Aristotle compare with these of an Eddington. We are still far from a General Theory of Critical Relativity, but at least we are reaching the point of knowing how much we shall soon come to need one."[46] By 1929, he had found in the latest cosmology a more sustained metaphor through which to express his ideal of mental stability, which had a few years earlier been represented through technology: "The view that what we need in this tempestuous turmoil of change is a Rock to shelter under or cling to, rather than an efficient aeroplane in which to ride it," he had written in 1924, "is comprehensible but mistaken."[47]

Empson's "flying buttress" differs significantly from Richards' relativistic aeroplane. Both rely on distance: Richards conceives of "emancipation from words," accompanied by a mental plasticity that can transcend any given cultural framework. Surprisingly, Empson the space man opted for a more earthbound, architectural image: a flying buttress keeps the wall from collapsing not through direct contact but across a gap, over which the arch or flyer extends. Maeterlinck on the white ant, Cornford or Harrison on totemic ritual and Hillyer on psychiatry are all valuable because of the alien experiences they depict, providing a gap across which the reader's imagination may extend. Even Eddington, presenting a system with "no gap to spare," is helpful because he makes the need for sympathy more pressing by his insistence that "Mr X" is left out in the cold by physical law. In contrast, Richards's proposal for self-supporting beliefs developed by readers of poetry resembles the security of those who "have no other" in "Doctrinal Point." That poem's concluding couplet matches the repeated "air" rhymes with a visual plenitude of arches: the rainbow of God's promise, the earth's atmosphere, and underground tombs: "Their arch of promise the wide Heaviside layer / They rise above a vault into the air." The Heaviside layer stands in opposition to the prospects of Martian wireless communication that briefly made space a hopeful place in "Letter I." A layer of ionized gas, it reflects radio waves so that they follow the curvature of the earth, enabling signals to be received over long terrestrial distances. The poem's self-redeeming systems have no need of God's covenant to Noah, raising their own "arch of promise." Scientific rationalism is not to blame for leaving humanity without a blanket of belief. In dialogue with religious tropes, scientific discourse offers terms through which to articulate stark problems of intimacy and ethics. But the full range of human and physical sciences, in a continuum with the various facets of emotional life, also has the capacity to engage "curiosity about alien modes of feeling." Eliot observed of Empson in 1941, "I don't think that his tiresome metaphysicality ... is just 'cerebral' or due to a desire to impress with cleverness, but that it springs from a peculiarly twisted and tormented, but very painfully suffering, soul."[48] Alien curiosity offers flashes of stability amid the vertiginous doubt, isolation and despair driving Empson's ravenous conceits.

William Empson's science fiction poems, composed during the late 1920s and early 1930s in tandem with his first two books of criticism, extend an invitation to readers who are also curious about the human interests and values operating across entomology, botany, geometry, astrophysics, space travel, archaeology, and anthropology. The question remains: does the poems' dense packing result in literary black holes, their signals cut off from the rest of the reading universe by over-densely packed matter? Or do the poems perhaps offer training for Richards' mind of the future, maintaining its orientation while shifting across different viewpoints? No two reading experiences are the same, but I hope I have succeeded in convincing you, as a reader of the present volume, that while there are indeed aspects of both black hole and steady aeroplane experience to be had from these poems, they also abound with flying buttresses, reaching out at a multitude of angles in an ever-shifting architecture of textual and ethical inquiry.

NOTES

1. Quoted in John Haffenden, *William Empson: Among the Mandarins* (Oxford: Oxford University Press, 2005), 62.

2. "Mario" (pseudonym), "Songs for Sixpence," *Cambridge Gownsman and Undergraduette* (November 20, 1929): 22.

3. Matthew Stanley, *Practical Mystic: Religion, Science, and A.S. Eddington* (Chicago: University of Chicago Press, 2007), 53–72.

4. William Empson, *Essays on Renaissance Literature: Donne and the New Philosophy*, ed. John Haffenden (Cambridge: Cambridge University Press, 1993), 4.

5. Empson, "Donne the Space Man," in *Donne and the New Philosophy*, 78–128, 78.

6. See Christopher Herbert, *Victorian Relativity: Radical Thought and Scientific Discovery* (Chicago: University of Chicago Press, 2001); and Linda Dalrymple Henderson, *The Fourth Dimension and Non-Euclidean Geometry in Modern Art* (Cambridge: MIT Press, 2013, rev. ed.).

7. Albert Einstein, *Relativity: The Special and the General Theory*, trans. Robert W. Lawson (London: Routledge, 1960), 55.

8. Arthur Eddington, *The Nature of the Physical World* (Cambridge: Cambridge University Press, 1928), 49.

9. William Empson, *The Complete Poems*, ed. John Haffenden (Harmondsworth: Penguin, 2000), 13.

10. Empson, *Complete Poems*, 31. For extended discussion of "Letter I" and "The World's End," see Katy Price, "Talking to Mars: William Empson's Astronomy Love Poems," in *Loving Faster Than Light: Romance and Readers in Einstein's Universe* (Chicago: University of Chicago Press, 2012), 156–85.

11. Quoted in Haffenden, *Among the Mandarins*, 8.

12. Kip S. Thorne, *Black Holes and Time Warps: Einstein's Outrageous Legacy* (London: Picador, 1994), 256. When "Letter I" was first published in 1928, it was missing the final stanza with the dense massive star conceit; this appeared in 1935 republications of the poem.

13. Stanley, *Practical Mystic*, 71–2; Thorne, *Black Holes and Time Warps*, 140–63. Subrahmanyan Chandrasekhar (1910–95) studied at Madras and Cambridge before moving to the University of Chicago, where he was a professor from 1937 until his death. He was awarded the Nobel Prize for Physics in 1983 for his contribution to theoretical understanding of the structure and evolution of stars. See Kameshwar C. Wali, *Chandra: A Biography of S. Chandrasekhar* (Chicago: University of Chicago Press, 1991).

14. *The Sleeper Awakes* is a revised telling of the earlier *When the Sleeper Wakes* (1899).

15. MS Eng 1401, bMS 870 (folder 4), Empson Papers, Houghton Library, Harvard University. Material from William Empson manuscripts reproduced with kind permission of Curtis Brown Group Ltd., London, on behalf of the Estate of William Empson.

16. MS Eng 1401, bMS 870 (folder 5), Empson Papers.

17. Empson, *Complete Poems*, 29.

18. Empson, *Complete Poems*, 205.

19. Empson, *Complete Poems*, 205.
20. Empson, *Donne and the New Philosophy*, 79.
21. Haffenden, *Among the Mandarins*, 387.
22. Haffenden, *Among the Mandarins*, 385.
23. William Empson, *Some Versions of Pastoral* (Harmondsworth: Penguin, 1995), 67–8. Cornford defines the totem as "a whole class of objects," for example a species of animals (such as the kangaroo), to which the "totem-clan" has a special and exclusive relation; see Francis Cornford, *From Religion to Philosophy: A Study in the Origins of Western Speculation* (New York: Longmans, 1912), 56. Empson's paraphrase of Cornford, in which an "idea" is "thrown out onto the universe," connotes the bravado that he found integral to the metaphysical conceit.
24. I. A. Richards, *Science and Poetry* (London: Routledge, 1926), 63–4, 67.
25. I. A. Richards to T. S. Eliot, February–July 1929, *Selected Letters of I. A. Richards*, ed. John Constable (Oxford: Clarendon Press, 1990), 49.
26. Eddington, *Nature of the Physical World*, 257.
27. Eddington, *Nature of the Physical World*, 260.
28. Empson, *Complete Poems*, 59.
29. Bertrand Russell, *The Scientific Outlook* (London: Allen & Unwin, 1931), 92.
30. Unpublished typescript, Empson Papers, Houghton Library, Harvard University, bMS ENG 1044. For a fuller discussion see Katy Price, "Monogamy and the Next Step? Empson and the Future of Love in Einstein's Universe," in *Some Versions of Empson*, ed. Matthew Bevis (Oxford: Oxford University Press, 2007), 242–63. The reference is to Andrew Marvell's poem, "To His Coy Mistress."
31. Eddington, *Nature of the Physical World*, 257.
32. Eddington, *Nature of the Physical World*, 263.
33. William Empson, *Empson in Granta: The Book, Film & Theatre Reviews of William Empson, Originally Presented in the Cambridge Magazine* Granta, 1927–1929 (Langton Green: Foundling Press, 1993), 23. For a fuller reading of Empson's review of *The Life of the White Ant* in the context of his own 1928 poem, "The Ants," see Katy Price, "William Empson, Ants and Aliens," in *Science in Modern Poetry: New Directions*, ed. John Holmes (Liverpool: Liverpool University Press, 2012), 116–29.
34. Maurice Maeterlinck, *The Life of the White Ant*, trans. A. Sutro (London: Allen and Unwin, 1927), 107.
35. Maeterlinck, *Life of the White Ant*, 164.
36. Empson, *Empson in Granta*, 23–4.
37. Empson, *Empson in Granta*, 31–2.
38. Empson, *Empson in Granta*, 32.
39. I. A. Richards, *Practical Criticism* (London: Kegan Paul, 1929), 339.
40. Richards, *Practical Criticism*, 345.
41. Richards, *Practical Criticism*, 343.
42. H. Minkowski, "Space and Time," in A. Einstein, H. A. Lorentz, H. Weyl and H. Minkowski, *The Principle of Relativity* (London: Methuen, 1923), 73–91, at 75. Hermann Minkowski (1864–1909) introduced the four-dimensional space-time continuum to relativity, in crucial work that enabled the development from Einstein's special theory of 1905 to the general theory of 1915.

43. Eddington, *Nature of the Physical World*, 13.
44. Eddington, *Nature of the Physical World*, 61.
45. Richards, *Practical Criticism*, 345–6. In Edwin Abbott's *Flatland* (1884), the narrator, a two-dimensional Square, has a dialogue with a Sphere from three-dimensional space.
46. Richards, *Practical Criticism*, 347.
47. I. A. Richards, *Principles of Literary Criticism* (London: Kegan Paul, 1924), 57.
48. Quoted in Haffenden, *Among the Mandarins*, 9.

PART III

In Theory
Literary Studies and Science Studies

6

T. HUGH CRAWFORD

Science Studies and Literary Theory

In 1978, George Rousseau published a retrospective essay in *Isis* entitled "Literature and Science: the State of the Field." He charts work across the twentieth century, much of which was inspired by his mentor Marjorie Hope Nicholson, that helped define a field of study largely concerned with influence – how literature was influenced by or embodied the spirit of the sciences of its particular era.[1] Rousseau noted that in the 1970s the size of the field of Literature and Science – at least as measured by MLA participation – had taken a "sharp plunge."[2] In part, he blames the emergence of structuralism in the American academy, singling out Michel Foucault as the most significant or perhaps pernicious influence, but Foucault was also accompanied by a more broadly construed critical pluralism: "linguists, semioticians, phenomenologists, Marxists, Maoists, hermeneuticists, neo-hermeneuticists, psychological critics, neo-Freudians, neo-Jungians, formalists just begin to describe the rampant proliferation" (590).

Far from describing the state of a dying field, Rousseau's essay marks the moment when literary theory entered what had been a fairly traditional philological practice. Indeed, in the decades that followed, Rousseau played a key role in the assimilation of literary theory into science studies, particularly regarding Foucault but also through his work on the imbrications of literature and medicine. The chaos he describes was real. Most scholars are familiar with the impact "theory" had on the literary studies from the late seventies on, but the story of science studies takes a slightly different path. Put bluntly, science was seen as occupying a significantly different epistemological realm, so while theorists studying literature and culture might be able to pronounce confidently that everything is a text, that everything generally did not include the objects science enables us to know. Literary theory moved into science studies in fits and starts.

The year 1987 marked the first conference of the newly formed Society for Literature and Science (an organization now called the Society for Literature,

117

Science, and the Arts). Its conveners, Lance Schacterle and Steven Weininger, were trained in literature and science respectively, both teaching at Worcester Polytechnic Institute. Schacterle was a student of modern literature, and Weininger a chemist. The program of that conference did not differ significantly from the earlier state of the field as described by Rousseau. A vast majority of the papers concerned the influence of science on literary texts, and few of the abstracts name the usual suspects one would associate with 1980s literary theory. In the early years of the SLS, conference organizers tried hard to interest scientists in attending and presenting, so they discouraged what was then perceived as the overly abstruse language of high theory.

It took little more than a year to upset that strategy. The 1988 conference was still replete with traditional one-way influence arguments or interpretive strategies modeled on science (e.g. a number of papers using cybernetics as a critical framework), but along with this emerged a number of papers exploring language and metaphor in science proper. Although presenters continued to avoid high theoretical discourse, the thinkers who formed the basis for the new studies in Literature and Science were appearing: Jacques Lacan, Jacques Derrida, Gilles Deleuze, Michel Serres, and of increasing importance over the years, N. Katherine Hayles, Donna Haraway, and Bruno Latour. All three were keynote speakers at later conferences, and Hayles served a term as president of the organization.

Words

Evelyn Fox Keller was one of the keynote speakers in the second SLS convention. (The other was Nobel Prize-winning physicist Ilya Prigogine who, along with coauthor Isabelle Stengers, introduced complexity theory to a broad audience in *Order out of Chaos* [1984].) Trained in biology, Keller became a leader in what could be called first-wave feminist science studies, developing an approach focused primarily on language use. Her work, particularly in *Reflections on Gender and Science* (1985), examines metaphors and rhetorical strategies deployed in canonical scientific texts. Perhaps most memorable is her detailed discussion of Francis Bacon's depiction of nature as a woman to be alternately seduced or ravaged. Her work is characterized by an attention to gendered language and depended on the insights of structural linguistics: that language was, in itself, an epistemology, a position epitomized by what is sometimes called the Sapir-Whorf Hypothesis.[3] Keller's approach can be linked to a range of other critics in the 1980s examining scientific textuality (Ludmilla Jordanova, the early work of Hayles and Haraway) and, in relation to science studies, marks a significant intervention in the critique of science itself, something that makes Keller's position as a trained scientist that much more important.[4] The sociology of science at least since Robert K. Merton tended to treat science externally on either the micro or macro level – as affected and influenced by the dynamics of a lab or broad external economic/social pressures.[5] The textual critics took that a step further, arguing that language profoundly influenced scientists' epistemology and consequently the very framework through which their work was done.

The work of Thomas Kuhn helped articulate this strategy. Although not adopted directly by many literary theorists, his *Structure of Scientific Revolutions* (1962) argues that scientific "discoveries" or significant changes in scientific practice result from paradigmatic shifts – that scientific paradigms which include "law, theory, application, and instrumentation together" constitute a scientist's world view at any given point in history.[6] From the perspective of intellectual history, Kuhn's work is very much a part of the structuralist moment and has much in common with a theorist whose work is more mainstream literary theory (and who continues to exert influence on science studies across a number of registers): Michel Foucault. It is hard to overestimate the shadow he casts over literary theory as it informs science studies. His early work, which was received as part of structuralism, was initially grasped as furthering the importance of language in articulating (and hence influencing) scientific practice. From *The Birth of the Clinic* (1963) with its "To see is to say" motto, Foucault's work pursued discursive practices that gave birth to the scientific object and formulated scientific knowledge. That early work culminated in *The Order of Things* (1966), titled *Words and Things* in France, and *The Archaeology of Knowledge* (1969) – his dense meditation on method. The English translation of the latter text included as appendix his influential essay "The Discourse on Language" (1971), which complicated and extended Kuhn's notion of the paradigm, introducing into critical discourse such terms as "the fellowship of discourse" and "the will to knowledge." These were powerful tools for critics who were confronting the textual production of practicing scientists, enabling the unveiling (and occasional denouncing) of a range of social and cultural biases embedded in linguistic practice, defended by the closure of a fellowship of discourse, supported by a range of institutions structured around a will to knowledge, and showing that the vaunted objectivity of scientists was inflected by the discursive regimes they occupied.

The other major French philosopher who looms over this literary theoretical moment is, of course, Jacques Derrida. More than Foucault, Derrida was the poster child of literary theory in the eighties, and perhaps was the single reason the SLS continually asked its speakers to refrain from jargon.

In the 1980s, theorists of all persuasions reveled in the Derridean practice of neologism and typographic play, but one phrase taken very much to heart was the simple mistranslated comment, "there is nothing outside of the text." In *Of Grammatology* (1967), Derrida wrote "*il n'y pas de hors-texte*," which would more felicitously be translated "there is no outside-text," itself a startling and profound claim, but one without the broader ontological implications of the more trendy version.[7] (If there is nothing outside the text, then being is only accessible through language.) Derrida and Derrideans were not alone is this embrace of all things textual. Roland Barthes's semiology was influential, and, from a completely different tradition, Fredric Jameson's *Prison-House of Language* (1972) was also important. Although sometimes playful, all these thinkers were making serious contributions to philosophical, literary, and cultural understanding. Unfortunately, a caricatured version of their intense focus on textuality prompted vilification and a high degree of critical acrimony, a backlash that did a great disservice to serious students of science.

Even though many scholars developed insights into scientists by examining carefully the way they articulated their findings and strategies, many practicing scientists and technocrats felt threatened by any perceived effort to diminish the objectivity of their practices. Reducing the world to text and then deploying the critical tools sharpened by literary theory raised the ire of a number of practicing scientists who were, at the same time, facing decreasing funding from the governmental sources – although blaming a small cadre of literary theorists for macroeconomic policy decisions, particularly in the United States where philosophy is afforded minimal respect, seems absurd at best. Nevertheless, for readers who did not understand some of the fine-grained strategies of theoretical discourse, and particularly if those same theorists dared discuss the fine-grained texts of scientific theory, feathers were indeed ruffled. These tensions came to a head in 1996 when the journal *Social Text* published the infamous Sokal Hoax. Alan Sokal, a physicist at New York University, submitted an article entitled "Transgressing the Boundaries: Towards a Transformative Hermeneutics of Quantum Gravity," which he later acknowledged as nonsense and devoid of scientific rigor. That event was possibly inspired by such books as Gross and Levitt's *Higher Superstition* (1994) and was chronicled in Sokal's own *Beyond the Hoax* (2008), along with responses by science studies scholars such as Robert Markley, Stanley Aronowitz, and a densely argued defense of Derrida's mathematics by a mathematician and former student of Derrida, Arkady Plotnitsky.[8] The dustup, usually referred to as "the science wars," brought with it defensiveness, anger, a lot of mass media attention, and also a renewed call for rigor and understanding. One thing it also revealed was that analysis purely on the level of the text, while giving insight into many perhaps unconsciously held attitudes by the language's users, cannot make large claims about science itself.

The trajectory of the career of one figure whose work has exerted a strong influence over science studies is instructive in this regard. Initially trained in anthropology doing work on the Ivory Coast, Bruno Latour wrote a grant to do an anthropological study of a scientific laboratory, a novel idea but one that led to the small but important subfield of "laboratory studies" (an area that includes Sharon Traweek, Karin Knorr-Cetina, and Donald McKenzie).[9] Latour found himself at the Salk Institute in La Jolla, California, working as a participant-observer in Nobel Prize-winner Roger Guillemin's laboratory isolating brain peptides. The result, published as *Laboratory Life* (1979) with coauthor Steve Woolgar, is in many ways a classic anthropological study of a hitherto unstudied tribe. Careful reading of this text shows Latour's attention to the broad range of artifacts that go into the construction of a scientific fact – buildings, equipment, slaughterhouse brains, funding, scientists and technicians of many different stripes, and texts – lots and lots of texts.

One of the most important claims Latour was to make in his later discourse on method – *Science in Action* (1987) – is that a scientific fact depends not simply on its status as "truth," but more importantly on those who pick it up and carry on its trajectory. The same fate holds true for his first book, and what was picked up from *Laboratory Life* was the claim that scientific facts are constructed and not discovered – a claim he has had to continually explain, defend, and rearticulate across his career. And there is the lesser but still influential idea that a disproportionate amount of the time spent by scientists involved shuffling a lot of paper, at one point noting that his anthropologist observer "was able to portray laboratory activity as the organization of persuasion through literary inscription."[10] Latour and Woolgar offer a much more complex discussion in the rest of the book so it was by no means a justification for a science studies based primarily on textual interpretation. Nevertheless, *Laboratory Life* did call attention to Latour as a thinker and to questioning how his work fit into the increasingly large constellation of figures inhabiting the field of theory.

Bodies

In *Science in Action*, Latour introduces the term "technoscience" in an effort to show how science, no matter how purely practiced, is caught up in a broad range of technologies and that technological innovations are implicated in science. The idea of science studies usually carries with it, as related inquiry, technology studies. The concept of technoscience helps make problematic a purely textual approach, foregrounding as it does material mechanisms and, even more important, the bodies that use them. Parallel to a science studies informed by literary theory and focused on textual production, is one attempting to understand and theorize the body, initially and particularly the human body. Once again, Foucault's work figures large. Although early efforts to position Foucault tend to link him to a Structuralism derived primarily from structural linguistics, close attention to his texts finds them populated by bodies: mad (*Madness and Civilization* [1961]), diseased (*The Birth of the Clinic*), and criminal (*Discipline and Punish* [1975]). Although it is fair to describe his work as the history of institutions or bureaucracies, when you include the three-volume *History of Sexuality* (1976–1984), a retrospective reading is that his work is a history of the human body, the way it is constituted by scientific observation, but equally the way it is articulated by sociotechnical practices. Although this complex of critical strategies goes by many names, science studies seems to have settled on the terms derived from the introduction to the *History of Sexuality*: biopower and its attendant term biopolitics remains an important field of inquiry.

A key point where theorizing bodies becomes vital in science studies is for people asking how humans are constituted by biology, medicine, and literature. Fundamental to this was Elaine Scarry's *The Body in Pain* (1985), a book where bodies were problematized in novel fashion. Once again, gender provided a key point of interaction as a broad range of theorists begin to question the scientific construction of sex. Parallel but following a different trajectory was the study of the historical construction of race, led in part by the work of Sander Gilman.[11] The turn toward forms of embodiment energized a generation of people working in science studies as it drew together biology, medicine, history, and politics. Judith Butler importantly prompted a turn from bodies as objects to race and gender as something performed.[12] Though much of her influence has been in the discipline of performance studies, her reconstitution of bodies in action helped open the door for a broad range of analyses, particularly in film and media studies, where bodies could be regarded as biological and cultural, stable and fluid.

Within the field of science studies, the influence of Donna Haraway (the keynote speaker for the third SLS conference) has been profound. Trained as a biologist (Yale PhD), her early work (published as *Crystals, Fabrics, and Fields* [1976]) is very much part of the textual critique of science, exploring as it does metaphor in biology. But in 1985 she published her "Cyborg Manifesto," perhaps the most influential essay in late twentieth-century science studies. There she questions directly the efficacy of postmodern focus on textuality: "'Textualization' of everything in poststructuralist, postmodernist theory has been damned by Marxists and socialist feminists for its utopian disregard for the lived relations of domination that ground the 'play' of arbitrary reading."[13] Haraway's turn is both toward the body, but also the material and semiotic systems within which it functions. The figure of the cyborg does not stabilize the body; instead it blurs boundaries, both material and disciplinary. Although she characterizes it as post-gender, the "Manifesto" provides a perspective on gender by calling attention to boundaries and helping to understand how they are policed. Crucially, she distances herself from Foucault and what she sees as a less effective form of political theory, describing her cyborg as "not subject to Foucault's biopolitics: the cyborg simulates politics, a much more potent field of operation" (163). Where Foucault generally describes overpowering institutional structures that define the body and the biopolitical, Haraway celebrates the potency of her cyborg precisely because it refuses categorization, rejecting institutionalization, and works across all such attempted forms of capture. Speaking at least in part because of her scientific credentials, but also through her own Marxist feminist stance, Haraway launches a direct critique of Western science's complicity with the perpetuation of white male patriarchy's domination of the global (nonwhite nonmale) other. For her, the task is not to use a social constructionist argument to dismiss scientific claims of access to knowledge about the material world, but instead to show how all arguments are necessarily partial and situated, a point she makes in the oft-cited essay first published in 1988, "Situated Knowledges: The Science Question in Feminism and the Privilege of Partial Perspective."[14] There she asserts, "We need the power of modern critical theories of how meanings and bodies get made, not in order to deny meaning and bodies, but in order to live in meanings and bodies that have a chance for a future" (187).

Haraway, Butler, Foucault, and a myriad of other thinkers produced a materialist theoretical perspective for the scientific construction of bodies with meaning. At the same time focus began to shift to the specific technologies that enabled and authorized those bodies to exist. As a consequence there was an effort to articulate a non-naïve materialist or even realist critical position. It is of some consequence that in 1989, Rutgers University hosted a conference convened by eminent Darwin scholar George Levine called "Realism and Representation." Albeit in a humorous fashion, the attendees were invited to choose sides via T-shirts marking their allegiance. As it was a conference attended primarily by literary scholars, the representation shirts outnumbered those of the realists. The "realists" in attendance generally acknowledged a "real" world out there that governed and even determined meaning, while the "representationalists" generally located all meaning within representational (usually textual) systems. Needless to say, the conference did not settle the question, though a volume of essays published in 1993 edited by Levine articulated a broad range of responses.[15] What was obvious at that particular historical moment was dissatisfaction with positivist realism, but at the same time, a clear recognition existed that a pure representationalist or social constructionist model was also untenable. An increasingly complex and nuanced move toward a different ground has followed, one more rooted in materiality, less dependent upon the instability of the text.

One perspective presented at the Rutgers conference was the notion of a "constrained constructivism" offered up by N. Katherine Hayles. Initially trained in chemistry, Hayles went on to get her PhD in literature from the University of Rochester. Her early book, *The Cosmic Web* (1984), focuses on language and metaphor in literature and science, and her second book, *Chaos Bound* (1990) brought a clear-sighted understanding of complexity theory to literary studies. But *How We Became Posthuman* (1999) has probably had the strongest impact, responding as it does to the problem of materiality, bodies, and informatics in a way that moves beyond an overly simplistic realism/representation binary. Hayles addresses many of the same questions as Haraway – for example, the function of informatics – although not from a Marxist feminist perspective. Instead *How We Became Posthuman* is a historical examination of information theory and computation. In it Hayles describes in detail how the idea of code (biological and computational), as a bioinformatic system, traverses bodies, machines and information retrieval, and in 1999, therefore helps set the stage for the posthuman turn.

Things

The twenty-first century marks the beginning of the posthuman era. Often wrongly figured as an expression of humans' cyborg nature, the concept extends far beyond the simple recognition that human bodies are traversed, augmented, and supplemented by technological prostheses (ideas made popular not so much by Haraway as by science fiction). In *The Order of Things* Foucault already claims that

> [M]an is an invention of recent date. And one perhaps nearing its end. If those arrangements were to disappear as they appeared, if some event of which we can at the moment do no more than sense the possibility ... were to cause them

to crumble, as the ground of Classical thought did, at the end of the eighteenth century, then one can certainly wager that man would be erased, like a face drawn in the sand at the edge of the sea.[16]

Despite the apocalyptic tone, what Foucault describes is the end of modernity structured by and through a knowing liberal humanist subject. The posthuman is not (necessarily) the disappearance of a species nor its technological transcendence, but instead is the moment after humanism.

Latour's short but important work, *We Have Never Been Modern* (1991), extends this questioning of the modern liberal humanist subject, seeing it, like Foucault, as a never-quite-accomplished historical figure. Through his own study of science, Latour argues that the anthropological distinction between modern and primitive is both naïve and porous, and that the modern distinction between a knowing subject and natural object is belied by the proliferation of hybrids or quasi-objects/subjects in the lived world.[17] A key insight of Latour's regarding the idea of modernity was that the birth of the modern human subject was necessarily accompanied by the birth of the natural object. Posthumanism does not simply displace the knowing subject; it also creates room for an entirely different articulation of things – as active, vibrant, and having agency.

Early in his career, Latour and several colleagues (John Law, Michel Callon) worked out what they called actor-network theory (ANT), an attempt to articulate the agency of both human and nonhuman actors as they function within extended sociotechnical networks. As seems obvious, such a theory requires an expansive concept of agency, a move Latour has continually had to defend, even as recently as his 2005 Clarendon Lectures, *Reassembling the Social: An Introduction to Actor-Network-Theory*. Nevertheless, reconceptualizing agency by turning to the nonhuman has found support in several other philosophical strands – Bill Brown's "Thing Theory," some of the thinkers associated with object-oriented ontology (Graham Harman, Ian Bogost, Timothy Morton), as well as the more recent work of Jane Bennett, particularly her *Vibrant Matter* (2010).[18] More closely associated with science studies is the work of Karen Barad, a theoretical physicist who proposes a *"posthumanist performative* approach to under-standing technoscientific and other naturalcultural practices that specifically acknowledges and takes account of matter's dynamism."[19] She argues for "agential realism," which rearticulates the real as active agents: *"agency is a matter of intra-acting; it is an enactment, not something that someone or something has.* It cannot be designated as an attribute of subjects or objects (as they do not preexist as such)" (178). Barad is acknowledging that "the world kicks back," but that in and of itself does not constitute reality (215). Indeed, the thing to understand is the kick – the material agency of the world.

Another scientist concerned with how the world "kicks back" is Belgian philosopher Isabelle Stengers. Initially trained in chemistry, Stengers collaborated with Ilya Prigogine on several books (including the previously mentioned *Order out of Chaos*), as well as with others on histories of psychoanalysis and chemistry.[20] The early work with Prigogine explored the long ignored problem of the "arrow of time" (irreversibility) in science, bringing with it a new perspective on uncertainty in scientific practices. Her deep engagement with the investigations of Gilles Deleuze and his sometimes collaborator Félix Guattari lay the philosophical ground for a series of short books on the philosophy of science which were later collected and published in two English-language volumes as *Cosmopolitics I and II*.[21] Those books, along with several other collections, brought her to the attention of larger group of English-speaking science studies scholars.[22] Stengers's wide-ranging subjects include not just the history and philosophy of science but also political activity surrounding such issues as drug policy, environmental degradation, and genetically modified crops (on the latter, see in particular *In Catastrophic Times*). Central to her work and where she can be directly connected to her friend and collaborator Bruno Latour, is her attention to scientific practice – the complex dance of individual scientists with their technologies, colleagues, government policies, and the material objects they study. Her "Cosmopolitical Proposal" is a manifesto that asks everyone (scientists, policymakers, everyday people) to pay due attention to the broad "political ecology" of scientific practices and policies.[23] To this end she invokes Deleuze's figure of "the idiot," taken from Dostoevsky, to invite naïve questioning, slow processes down, and ultimately question those who claim the authority to speak for objects of nature and for other humans. It is what she calls in another essay a plea for "slow science," one that listens, trying to account for and engage the complexity produced by the competing voices of these many human and nonhuman actors.[24]

While the idea of nonhuman agency was washing away the face Foucault drew in the sand, research in cognitive science was also decentering human cognition and knowledge – the mainstay of modernity – by displacing it from the mind to the body and, in the case of theories of distributed cognition, onto a broad range of sociotechnological systems.[25] Part of this move is exemplified by Rodney Brooks's work on embodiment and artificial intelligence at the MIT robotics lab. Using what he called "subsumption architecture," Brooks developed a series of robots with very simple perceptor/effector affordances and let them wander about, bumping into their world.

Even without an overriding computer "brain" or some form of cognitive map, Brooks's robots began to demonstrate what to an outside observer seemed intelligent behavior. His work has had a profound impact on research in robotics and AI, and in science studies helped turn the focus away from minds thinking toward bodies interacting in the material world. In cognitive science, this move has been called "the affective turn." Of course, the role of emotions in the constitution of the human has long been recognized, but late twentieth-century research in affect as it relates to conscious thought began to provide a more complex understanding. Philosophically at least, Deleuze and Guattari loom over this perspective, and Brian Massumi, the translator of *A Thousand Plateaus* (1980) into English, has extended the implications of their work in his *Parables for the Virtual* (2002).[26] In neurobiology, Antonio Damasio explores the importance of the affective body in the production of human knowledge. His *A Feeling of What Happens* (1999) helped bring a noncognitive body back into science studies, and *Descartes' Error* (1994) sharpened the critique of mind/body dualism. Francisco Varela, whose work with Humberto Maturana on autopoiesis strongly influenced Deleuze and Guattari, also worked out models of affect, cognition, and ethical practice.[27]

In addition, Maturana and Varela's concept of autopoiesis was adapted to social systems by Niklas Luhmann, and his systems theory, along with that of Gregory Bateson and Heinz von Foerster, helped a number of scholars of Literature and Science, including Cary Wolfe and Bruce Clarke, begin to articulate the complexity of human/nonhuman systems on a global scale.[28] The twenty-first century is not only posthuman but now also the geological era of the Anthropocene. Precisely when this era commenced is a matter of debate, but the recognition that the earth as system is dynamic and mutable, that humans are but part of an incredibly large and diverse system of actants, and at the same time they are transforming the earth on a global scale, has led to this designation. Of course it is not without some irony that we have moved into a posthuman world at precisely the moment we name the geological era after our species.[29]

On a slightly less global scale, the posthuman turn in environmental science studies is best characterized by the emergence of animal studies, particularly in Wolfe's *What Is Posthumanism?* (2009).[30] The theorists framing much of the discussion amongst animal studies scholars include Derrida, whose classic *The Animal That Therefore I Am* (1997), along with Giorgio Agamben's *The Open* (2004), Emmanuel Levinas's varied writings on animals, and Haraway's *Companion Species Manifesto* (2003), delineate the stakes in understanding how important animals have always been in propping up the idea of the humanist subject, even as that very notion fades. Derrida and Agamben make explicit philosophy's debt to animals as the nonhuman other used to define human being. Agamben's amplification of Martin Heidegger's notion of the animal as being "poor in world" (in *The Four Fundamental Concepts of Metaphysics* [1929–30]) is perhaps the clearest example. Moving from Heideggarian Being, Deleuze and Guattari's notion of "becoming animal" has also informed animal studies as in, for example, Ron Broglio's reading of biopolitical art in *Surface Encounters* (2011). Although not as well established as animal studies, scholars are also turning to plant studies, using a similar posthuman perspective, with Michael Marder taking the philosophical lead. His *Plant-Thinking: A Philosophy of Vegetal Life* (2013) works out the implications of the plant-as-other through readings of Heidegger, Nietzsche, and Derrida.

In many ways, the introduction of the Anthropocene, coupled with a complex understanding of climate change – the dynamic stability of the earth as a whole, and the increasingly fragile habitat or *umwelt* that humans occupy – leverages yet another turn, nonhuman: conceptualizing of a world without humans, a question addressed most directly by science and media scholar Eugene Thacker, whose *In The Dust of This Planet* (2011) draws together medieval scholasticism, Dante's *The Inferno*, horror films, and Black Metal music to try to think the world without humans. This question was also addressed in a 2012 symposium convened by science and media scholar Richard Grusin at the Center for 21st Century Studies at the University of Wisconsin, Milwaukee. Called "The Nonhuman Turn," it included presentations by Bennett, Massumi, Erin Manning, Morton, and Bogost among others.[31] Together, these critiques set the stage for a theoretically informed science studies of the Anthropocene, armed with a clearly articulated posthuman position where actors are constituted by the positions they occupy in larger assemblages, one that sees the human species as both fragile and destructive and as part of a much larger fragile and destructive world. From that perspective, the very idea of subjects and objects seems almost quaint.

NOTES

1. See for example her *Newton Demands the Muse: Newton's Opticks and the 18th Century Poets* (Princeton, NJ: Princeton University Press, 1946), and *Science and Imagination* (Hamden, CT: Archon, 1976).
2. George Rousseau, "Literature and Science: the State of the Field," *Isis* 69 (1978): 583–91, at 589.
3. The idea behind what is referred to as the Sapir-Whorf (or the Whorfian) hypothesis is that language structures the possibilities of thought in a given culture.

4. See Ludmilla Jordanova, ed., *Languages of Nature: Critical Essays on Science and Literature* (New Brunswick: Rutgers University Press, 1986); N. Katherine Hayles, *The Cosmic Web: Scientific Field Models and Literary Strategies in the Twentieth Century* (Ithaca: Cornell University Press, 1984), and *Chaos Bound: Orderly Disorder in Contemporary Literature and Science* (Ithaca: Cornell University Press, 1990); Donna J. Haraway, *Crystals, Fabrics, and Fields: Metaphors of Organicism in Twentieth-Century Developmental Biology* (New Haven: Yale University Press, 1976), and *Primate Visions: Gender, Race, and Nature in the World of Modern Science* (New York: Routledge, 1989).

5. Most important was Robert K. Merton, *The Sociology of Science* (Chicago: University of Chicago Press, 1973).

6. Thomas S. Kuhn, *The Structure of Scientific Revolutions* (Chicago: University of Chicago Press, 2012), 10.

7. Jacques Derrida, *Of Grammatology* (Baltimore: Johns Hopkins University Press, 2016), 172.

8. See Robert Markley, "After the Science Wars: From Old Battles to New Directions in the Cultural Studies of Science," in *After the Disciplines: The Emergence of Cultural Studies*, ed. Michael Peters (New York: Praeger, 1999), 47–70; Stanley Aronowitz, *Science as Power: Discourse and Ideology in Modern Society* (Minneapolis: University of Minnesota Press, 1988); and Arkady Plotnitsky, "'But It Is Above All Not True': Derrida, Relativity, and the 'Science Wars,'" *Postmodern Culture* 7.2 (January 1997): https://muse.jhu.edu/article/27605/.

9. See Sharon Traweek, *Beamtimes and Lifetimes: The World of High Energy Physicists* (Cambridge: Harvard University Press, 1988); Karin Knorr-Cetina, *The Manufacture of Knowledge: An Essay on the Constructivist and Contextual Nature of Science* (Oxford: Pergamon Press, 1981); and Donald McKenzie, *Inventing Accuracy: A Historical Sociology of Nuclear Missile Guidance* (Cambridge: MIT Press, 1990).

10. Bruno Latour and Steve Woolgar, *Laboratory Life: The Construction of Scientific Facts* (Princeton: Princeton University Press, 1986), 88.

11. See Sander L. Gilman, *Difference and Pathology: Stereotypes of Sexuality, Race, and Madness* (Ithaca: Cornell University Press, 1985), and *Freud, Race, and Gender* (Princeton: Princeton University Press, 1993).

12. See in particular Judith Butler, *Bodies That Matter: On the Discursive Limits of "Sex"* (New York: Routledge, 1993).

13. Donna Haraway, "A Cyborg Manifesto: Science, Technology, and Socialist-Feminism in the Late Twentieth Century," in *Simians, Cyborgs, and Women: The Reinvention of Nature* (New York: Routledge, 1991), 149–81, at 152.

14. Haraway, *Simians, Cyborgs, and Women*, 183–201. The use of the term "construction" by many theorists in this period brings a host of problems and misunderstandings. Although it can be value-neutral, simply an acknowledgement that scientific knowledge is built up through theories, instrumentation, and material interactions, when the term is paired with the social as in "social construction," it can seem to imply that scientific facts are merely social and not also material and technical.

15. See George Levine, ed., *Realism and Representation: Essays on the Problem of Realism in Relation to Science, Literature, and Culture* (Madison: University of Wisconsin Press, 1993).

16. Michel Foucault, *The Order of Things: An Archaeology of the Human Sciences* (New York: Vintage, 1973), 378.

17. Quasi-object and quasi-subject are terms Latour adapted from Michel Serres.

18. See Bill Brown, "Objects, Others, and Us (The Refabrication of Things)," *Critical Inquiry* 36.2 (2010): 183–217; Graham Harman, *The Quadruple Object* (Alresford: Zero Books, 2011); Ian Bogost, *Alien Phenomenology, or What It's Like to Be a Thing* (Minneapolis: University of Minnesota Press, 2012); Timothy Morton, *Hyperobjects: Philosophy and Ecology after the End of the World* (Minneapolis: University of Minnesota Press, 2013); Jane Bennett, *Vibrant Matter: A Political Ecology of Things* (Durham: Duke University Press, 2010).

19. Karen Barad, *Meeting the Universe Halfway: Quantum Physics and the Entanglement of Matter and Meaning* (Durham: Duke University Press, 2007), 135.

20. See Ilya Prigogine and Isabelle Stengers, *Order out of Chaos: Man's New Dialogue with Nature* (New York: Bantam, 1984), and *The End of Certainty* (New York: Simon and Schuster, 1997); Léon Chertok and Isabelle Stengers, *A Critique of Psychoanalytic Reason: Hypnosis as a Scientific Problem from Lavoisier to Lacan* (Stanford: Stanford University Press, 1992); and Bernadette Bensaude-Vincent and Isabelle Stengers, *A History of Chemistry* (Cambridge: Harvard University Press, 1996).

21. See Isabelle Stengers, *Cosmopolitics I* (Minneapolis: University of Minnesota Press, 2010), and *Cosmopolitics II* (Minneapolis: University of Minnesota Press, 2011).

22. See Isabelle Stengers, *Power and Invention: Situating Science* (Minneapolis: University of Minnesota Press, 1997); *The Invention of Modern Science* (Minneapolis: University of Minnesota Press, 2000); and *In Catastrophic Times: Resisting the Coming Barbarism* (London: Open Humanities Press and meson press, 2015, free access online).

23. Isabelle Stengers, "The Cosmopolitical Proposal," in *Making Things Public: Atmospheres of Democracy*, ed. Bruno Latour and Peter Weibel (Cambridge: MIT Press, 2005), 994–1003.

24. Isabelle Stengers, "Another Science Is Possible! A Plea for Slow Science" (2011): http://we.vub.ac.be/aphy/sites/default/files/stengers2011_pleaslowscience.pdf/.

25. See, for example, Edwin Hutchins, *Cognition in the Wild* (Cambridge: MIT Press, 1995).

26. See Adam Frank's essay in this volume for an account of central features of the affective turn that do not derive from Deleuze and Guattari. Also see Gilles Deleuze, *Essays Critical and Clinical* (Minneapolis: University of Minnesota Press, 1997) for a sampling of essays by Deleuze on literary figures.

27. See Franciso J. Varela, Evan T. Thompson and Eleanor Rosch, *The Embodied Mind: Cognitive Science and Human Experience* (Cambridge: MIT Press, 1991); and Francisco J. Varela, *Ethical Know-How: Action, Wisdom, and Cognition* (Stanford: Stanford University Press, 1999); as well as Humberto R. Maturana

and Francisco J. Varela, *Autopoiesis and Cognition: The Realization of the Living* (Dordrecht: Reidel, 1980).

28. See Niklas Luhmann, *Social Systems* (Stanford: Stanford University Press, 1996); Gregory Bateson, *Mind and Nature: A Necessary Unity* (New York: Dutton, 1979); Heinz von Foerster, *Understanding Understanding: Essays on Cybernetics and Cognition* (New York: Springer, 2002); Cary Wolfe, *Animal Rites: American Culture, the Discourse of Species, and the Posthumanist Theory* (Chicago: University of Chicago Press, 2003), and *What Is Posthumanism?* (Minneapolis: University of Minnesota Press, 2010); Bruce Clarke, *Neocybernetics and Narrative* (Minneapolis: University of Minnesota Press, 2014), and *Earth, Life, and System: Evolution and Ecology on a Gaian Planet*, ed. Bruce Clarke (New York: Fordham University Press, 2015).

29. See Claire Colebrook, *Death of the PostHuman: Essays on Extinction, vol. 1* (Ann Arbor: Open Humanities Press with Michigan Publishing, 2014).

30. Also see Stacy Alaimo, *Bodily Natures: Science, Environment, and the Material Self* (Bloomington: Indiana University Press, 2010).

31. See Richard Grusin, ed., *The Nonhuman Turn* (Minneapolis: University of Minnesota Press, 2015).

7

HAUN SAUSSY AND TIM LENOIR

From Writing Science to Digital Humanities

Dirty Language

"Writing Science" is at once a book series (Stanford University Press, 1994–2008), a multiyear workshop, a moment in the study of the history of science, and a methodological orientation.[1]

The moment brought together research programs in several adjoining fields: a processual emphasis in media studies and the history of the book, given new energy by the recent rise to dominance of electronically mediated culture; an attention to instruments and laboratory-based ethnography in history of science; the systems-theory approach to sociology; and a material-deconstructive turn in literary studies.[2] "Writing" provided a common term of reference for these overlapping epistemic projects. This essay will follow the thread of writing through the body of work associated with this media-oriented approach to scientific activity.

One way into the common argument about inscription and materiality that guided the "Writing Science" project is to outline the differences with structuralism. Ferdinand de Saussure's semiology, for example, both depended on and subordinated writing in the ordinary, physical sense. "The important thing in the word," he proposed,

> is not the sound alone but the phonic differences that make it possible to distinguish this word from all others, for differences carry signification ... In addition, it is impossible for sound alone, a material element, to belong to language ... Since an identical state of affairs is observable in writing, another system of signs, we shall use writing to draw some comparisons that will to clarify the whole issue. In fact,
>
> – The signs used in writing are arbitrary ...
> – The value of letters is purely negative and differential. The same person can write T, for instance, in different ways:

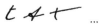

- Since the graphic sign is arbitrary, its form matters little or rather matters only within the limitations imposed by the system;
- The means by which the sign is produced is totally indifferent ... Whether I write the letters in black or white, in relief or incised, with a pen or a chisel, has no effect on their meaning.[3]

"Difference" and "indifference" are complexly intertwined here. Saussure wants to mark a difference between the differences that are semiologically relevant (the differences that make a difference: in writing, for example, the features that enable us to distinguish an L from an I and a T, and so forth) and the differences that are mere matters of execution, mere discrepancies among physical realizations of the sign. With this difference, he hopes to raise the study of language out of positivist inventorying and measuring. For the linguistics of Saussure's time was torn between philology (the study of texts as documents of the history of culture) and physiology (the registering, through experimental apparatus, of the muscular and auditory processes of speech).[4] Philology ran the risk of lapsing into prescientific appreciation of the "picturesque side" of a language.[5] Physiology, however, encumbered the study of language with apparatus – clocks, tuning forks, phonographs, tubes, plethysmographs, rotating cylinders, microphones, strobe lights.[6] It also cluttered scholarship with endless micro-measurements of pitch and duration, documenting the variants of a dialect, for example, by going from farm to farm and registering the speech of individuals.[7] It was uncertain about the boundaries that ought to separate the study of language from anatomy, psychology, acoustics, geography, national history, and the like. Positivist linguistics was condemned to an ever greater accumulation of detail together with an ever greater uncertainty as to its results, according to Saussure, because it failed to orient itself to the thing that made language work: the function, the code, the system of differences. His programmatic distinction between "langue" and "parole" ("language" and "speech," in the most familiar English translation) would dismiss the material realizations of speech in all their proliferating variety as belonging to the domain of "parole," while the domain of "langue" would be outlined by a minimal set of structuring differences. Not this T or that T or the word "rabbit" as pronounced by this or that individual on this or that occasion would be the cornerstone of semiology, but the immaterial distinction among ideal units of a communicative code. The individuality of those events would dissolve in the intersubjectivity of language.[8]

"Writing Science" reversed this emphasis. The "parole" of scientific research was to be foregrounded. The material traces left by instruments, lab protocols, experimental subjects, scholarly communication, and so forth were no longer artifacts to be discarded but the facts to be interrogated. Objects and contexts were to be accounted for as operators in historical acts of "parole": idiomatic, individual, open-ended utterances, answering other speech and anticipating an answer in yet further speech.[9] "Writing Science" continued the linguistic turn so prominent throughout the twentieth century.[10] But whereas structuralists and Kuhnians used the metaphor of language to reveal clean idealizations and epistemic breaks, the view of language and science as dirty, embodied, and contingent entailed a deeply, perhaps even radically, empirical style of narration among the "Writing Science" group.

Writing Apparatus

Thomas Kuhn's *Structure of Scientific Revolutions* is famous for its downgrading of a cumulative understanding of discovery. Although "normal science ... is a highly cumulative enterprise," "the view of science-as-cumulation is entangled with a dominant epistemology that takes knowledge to be a construction placed directly upon raw sense data by the mind."[11] History according to Kuhn takes discontinuous leaps: "The transition from a paradigm in crisis to a new one ... is far from a cumulative process, one achieved by an articulation or extension of the old paradigm. Rather it is a reconstitution of the field from new fundamentals" (84–5). "The normal-scientific tradition that emerges from a scientific revolution is not only incompatible but often actually incommensurable with that which has gone before" (103). Because the function of paradigms is less to reflect cognition than to organize it normatively, and because Kuhn does not admit a "hypothetical field of nature" that different investigators "saw differently," we must say, for example, that "after discovering oxygen Lavoisier worked in a different world" from his fellow scientists (109, 118). This world is defined in terms of language – for example, "oxygen" in Lavoisier's post-discovery discourse being now "incommensurable" with the words used under the former understanding of gases and combustion, the resulting "communication breakdown" requires pre- and post-oxygen chemists to become "translators" between each other's epistemologies (202–4).

Kuhn's account of scientific change as "paradigm shift" has become part of popular culture.[12] It goes – especially in popular rhetoric – with a differential valuation of the "normal" and "revolutionary" varieties of science. Normal science is "an immensely efficient instrument for solving the problems or puzzles that its paradigms define," but nothing more.[13]

Paradigm-shifting science breaks the instrumental relation. But sometimes, strangely, it is the instruments themselves that wreck instrumentality:

> The paradigms subscribed to by Roentgen and his contemporaries could not have been used to predict X-rays ... Though X-rays were not prohibited by established theory, they violated deeply entrenched expectations ... By the 1890s cathode ray equipment was widely deployed in numerous European laboratories. If Roentgen's apparatus had produced X-rays, then a number of other experimentalists must have for some time been producing these rays without knowing it. Perhaps those rays, which might well have other unacknowledged sources too, were implicated in behavior previously explained without reference to them. At the very least, several sorts of long familiar apparatus would in the future have to be shielded with lead. Previously completed work on normal projects would now have to be done again because earlier scientists had failed to recognize and control a relevant variable. X-rays, to be sure, opened up a new field and thus added to the potential domain of normal science. But they also ... changed fields that had already existed. In the process they denied previously paradigmatic types of instrumentation their right to that title (58–9).

The grammar of Kuhn's account is evocative. Not Roentgen, but X-rays themselves, "opened up a new field" and "denied" the previous paradigm-holders their title. Roentgen is presented as a mere onlooker and publicist for the work being done by his apparatus. In the future it and kindred sorts of apparatus will have to be "shielded with lead," lest in their inscriptive glee they continue to blot the results of scientific endeavor. For a scientific laboratory is a chain of inscribing mechanisms, some of which are human beings, and a struggle for control of the messages they write is the daily fare of "laboratory life." Ironically, even Kuhn, then, had his "Writing Science" moments.

Exteriority, Mediality, Corporeality

If there was anything like cohesion in the multidirectionality advocated by Gumbrecht, Pfeiffer, Godzich, Kittler, Lyotard and Luhmann in their anthology-manifesto *Materialities of Communication*, it was the act of taking distances from the habit of privileging meaning, of assuming that the job of the interpreter is always to recognize and reproduce meaning.[14] The new direction took inspiration from the philosophical deconstructions of Jacques Derrida. But the deconstructive move, powerful though it was, still provided safe harbor for various Marx- or Freud-inspired depth interpretations. The interpretational hangovers of (re)politicized versions of structuralism and poststructuralism still failed to understand their own position as effects of situations, media, and technologies of "communication." Communication here is not supposed to connote understanding, mutuality, or exchange as such. It unfolds as an open dynamic of means and effects. The point is to look for underlying determinants whose technological, material, procedural, and performative potentials have been all too easily swallowed up by the habits of interpretation.

Friedrich Kittler's two groundbreaking volumes, *Discourse Networks 1800/1900* and *Gramophone Film Typewriter*, are defining texts elaborating the "materialities of communication" program of Writing Science.[15] In his foreword to *Discourse Networks*, David Wellbery provides a brilliant overview of the presuppositions and key elements of posthermeneutic criticism. Hermeneutic theory conceives of interpretation as our stance in being: we cannot but interpret, we are what we are by virtue of acts of interpretation. Wellbery explains that posthermeneutic criticism, by contrast, presupposes poststructuralist thought as its operating system. In abandoning the language game and form of life defined by hermeneutic canons, "post-hermeneutic criticism, briefly, stops making sense" (xvi). Wellbery defines the three presuppositions of Kittler's posthermeneutic criticism as *exteriority, mediality,* and *corporeality*. According to the presupposition of exteriority, the notion of an internalized "humanist" core subject goes out the window, and language is treated as recalcitrant to internalization. In the presupposition of mediality Kittler generalizes the notion of a medium to apply it to all domains of cultural exchange. Mediality in any period is the general means of processing, storing, and transmitting data – in the nineteenth century, the book; in the early twentieth, book plus gramophone and film and typewriter. Finally, in his discussion of corporeality, Wellbery explains that the means of processing, storing, and transmission of our media serve as the link to the body. Indeed, the body – and in particular its nervous system – is itself a media apparatus, shaped and reshaped by the discourse networks to which it is joined. The concept of the body replaces the notion of the subject, and culture is the regimen that bodies pass through.

Systems of Inscription

The works selected for "Writing Science" adopt as their norm the scenario of Woolgar and Latour, in which a "strange tribe" of "compulsive and manic writers ... spend the greatest part of their day coding, marking, altering, correcting, reading, and writing," as inhabitants of a "system of literary inscription." Some members of the tribe may tend large and expensive machines that, whatever else they do, are in the nature of an "inscription device" that can "transform a material substance into a figure or diagram."[16]

No hierarchy among the "writers" and "devices" is to be taken for granted. Indeed, the relation between humans and machines is most often interactional, dialogical, divinatory. In this too it obeys a logic of writing rather than of speech. The spoken word is momentary, a point on a time-line. The verbal output of scientific research endures rather than being subordinated to the moment; it is planar rather than linear; it may have no definite emitter; it may be (imperfectly) erased or overwritten or reemerge long after its inscription to speak, as it were, from the grave (as befits an engraved trace). Hans-Jörg Rheinberger, in his own contribution to the "Writing Science" project, observes that

> The multiplicity of experimental systems endowed with their own times and, of course, their rationales, shifting and drifting in an open horizon, constitutes a historial ensemble. Such ensembles escape the strong notions of social history such as linear causation, retroaction, influence, dominance, and subordination. They also escape the notion of a purely contingent or stochastic process.[17]

The utility of an extended, "historial" conception of writing for understanding every phase of scientific work is made plainest in Brian Rotman's explorations of the graphic constitution of mathematics. The sign "zero," for instance, is as pure an instance of inscriptive meaning as can be found: not the sign "of" a referent, but a sign that performs the act of positing its referent, making it accessible to consciousness, on the one hand, but also to non-conscious algorithmic operations.[18] Proof of concept is important here: everyone will agree that physicists need scanning electron microscopes and that biologists need reagents; but that mathematics requires a technology (even so deceptively simple a one as marks on paper) brings the immaterial world of pure thought under the power of the artifact. Rotman considers mathematical proofs (especially those involving infinity) as self-experiments carried out through writing and involving two actors, Subject and Agent. The Subject must

> set up an imagined experience – a thought experiment – in which not he but his Agent, the skeleton diagram of himself, is required to perform the appropriate infinity of actions. By observing his Agent performing in his stead, by "reflective observation," the Subject becomes convinced . . . that were he to perform these actions the result would be as predicted.
>
> Now the Subject is involved in scribbling as well as thinking . . . [E]ach layer of the thought experiment . . . corresponds to some written activity, some manipulation of written signs performed by the Subject: so that, for example, in reading/writing an inclusive imperative the Subject modifies or brings into being a suitable facet of the Agent, and in reading/writing an exclusive imperative he requires this Agent to carry out the action in question, observes the

result, and then uses the outcome as the basis for a further bout of manipulating written signs.[19]

Self-awareness achieved through the manipulation of written signs that stand in, as Agent, for the Subject of scientific research: this perspective considers science to be not merely enmeshed in a web of after-the-fact communications, but to be, itself, a technology of communication, otherwise called thought.

To, From, and Beside Ourselves

The posthermeneutic framework outlined above has been central to the analysis of digital media and the prospects of a posthuman future implied by the direction of contemporary technoscience and our contemporary media regime. Rotman's work provides the crucial intervention in articulating the move from Writing Science to critical media studies inspired by material semiotics.

Since the completion of the Human Genome Project in the early 2000s the specter of a postbiological and posthuman future has haunted cultural studies of technoscience and other disciplines. Concern (and in some quarters enthusiasm) that contemporary technoscience is on a path leading beyond simple human biological improvements and prosthetic enhancements to a complete human makeover has been sustained by the exponential growth in power and capability of computer technology since the early 1990s. Also driving interest in such futuristic scenarios has been the increasing centrality of computational media to nearly every aspect of science, technology, medicine, society, and the arts. Taking stock of such developments and projecting them into the near future, Rodney Brooks asserts,

> We are on a path to changing our genome in profound ways. Not simple improvements toward ideal humans as is often feared. In reality, we will have the power to manipulate our own bodies in the way we currently manipulate the design of machines. We will have the keys to our own existence. There is no need to worry about mere robots taking over from us. We will be taking over from ourselves with manipulatable body plans and capabilities easily able to match that of any robot.[20]

Brooks's admonition that we are machines on a continuous path of coevolution with other machines prompts reflection on what we mean by "posthuman." If we are crossing to a new era of the posthuman, how did we get here? And how should we understand the process? What sorts of "selves" are imagined by Brooks and others as emerging out of this postbiological "human"?

In *Becoming Beside Ourselves*, Rotman addressed the impact of digitality on the self, subjectivity, and the body embedded in soon-to-be ubiquitous computing environments.[21] Already in the early 2000s the question of embodiment and the future of the human in networked digital environments had been the subject of numerous investigations.[22] In addition, a number of studies at that time explored the constitutive role of technology in shaping the human.[23] Rotman took a radically new approach to these critical issues in debates about posthumanity, putting the discussion on a coherent foundation for analysis based in semiotics and media theory.[24] For Rotman subjects are effects of media. Every medium projects a virtual user specific to it. This projected virtual user is a ghost effect: an abstract agency distinct from any particular embodied user, a variable capable of accommodating any particular user within the medium. While, unlike Stephen Wolfram and Edward Fredkin, he does not explicitly embrace cellular automata as the fundamental ontology of the universe, Rotman certainly is sympathetic to Deleuze and Guattari's understanding of the human body as an assemblage of mutating machines – a Body without Organs – rather than as a teleologically orchestrated organism with consciousness as the core of coherent subjectivity.[25]

Rotman's approach contrasts dramatically with those of other cultural theorists who have addressed the topic of the posthuman singularity and how, if at all, humanity will cross that divide. We speak about machines and discourses "co-constituting" one another, but in practice, we tend to favor discursive formations as preceding and to a certain extent breathing life into our machines. Exemplifying this style of approach are N. Katherine Hayles's numerous books (most impressively for the current context, *How We Became Posthuman* and *My Mother Was a Computer*). Hayles considers it possible that machines and humans may someday interpenetrate. But she rejects as highly problematic, and in any case not yet proven, that the universe is fundamentally digital, the notion that a Universal Computer generates reality, a claim that is important to the positions staked out by proponents of the posthuman singularity such as, in addition to Wolfram, Harold Morowitz, Ray Kurzweil, and Hans Moravec.[26] For the time being, Hayles insists, human consciousness and perception are essentially analog, and even the world of digital computation is sandwiched between analog inputs and outputs for human interpreters.[27] The way we will become posthuman, Hayles proposes, will be through interoperational feedback loops between our current mixed analog-digital reality and widening areas of digital processing. Metaphors, narratives and other interpretive linguistic modes we use in human sense-making of the world around us do the work of conditioning us to behave as if we and the world were digital. Language and ideological productions thus serve as kinds of virus vectors preparing the ground for the gradual shift in ontology. In the case of Wolfram and others, Hayles argues, the appropriation of computation as a cultural metaphor assumed to be physically true constitutes a framework in which new problems are constructed and judgments made. "On the global level," she explains in *My Mother Was a Computer*, "our narratives about virtual creatures can be considered devices that suture together the analog subjects we still are, as we move in the three-dimensional spaces in which our biological ancestors evolved, with the digital subjects we are becoming as we interact with virtual environments and digital technologies" (204). Narratives of the computational universe serve then as both means and metaphor.

Rotman moves beyond the notion of virtual creatures as rhetorical devices. In a brilliant synthesis of a large and wide-ranging body of empirical scientific research, he puts Guattari's cryptic and sketchily developed theses about "a-signifying semiological dimensions" of subjectification – "that function in parallel or independently of the fact that they produce and convey significations and denotations, and thus escape from strictly linguistic axiomatics" – on a solid foundation of what Rotman in turn calls "corporeal axiomatics."[28] Just what he means by "corporeal axiomatics" emerges from his analysis of gesture and prosody in relation to speech and written language, and the possibilities opened up by new digital systems of motion-capture for rendering gestures into discrete objects of awareness identifiable, portable, repeatable, and researchable, a new medium capable of doing for gestures what writing did for speech. The result of these new signifying systems and their imbrication with the existing semiological systems related to writing and speech would be to play on Deleuze and Guattari's notion once again, and to create a Body without Organs *of speech*: a new order of bodily signification and with it a new condition for being human.

One instance of this transformation already underway is described by Rotman as a replacement of serial or linear modes of organization by parallel ones. In nearly every venue of computing, from high-end processing of massive data sets such as the human genome and large-scale imaging projects such as geographic information system (GIS) maps, to routine gaming machines, computing is being performed by multiple machines working simultaneously in parallel on different parts of the job to be computed, or on multiple processors in the same machine. In addition, the computational affordances of cell phones, the pervasive technologies for multitasking such as instant messaging, manipulation of multiple avatars of the self in communally inhabited virtual worlds such as *World of Warcraft* and *Second Life*, and the engagement with a variety of forms of distributed agency, or blends of artificial and human agents in networked circuits: all these contribute, Rotman argues, to making the parallelist self radically different from the single, serial, alphabeticized psyche it is in the process of displacing.

Both crucial and symptomatic in this shift to parallelism is the centrality of visualization technology and the strategic influx of images into all forms of contemporary cognitive work. Everywhere pragmatic images, graphs, charts, tables, figures, maps, simulations, and other forms of visual artifact are permeating our reading and writing practices. These apparently innocuous information-bearing, instructional, explicatory and otherwise instrumentally-oriented images are, from Rotman's perspective, a (welcome) dimension of parallelism, prompting him to cite artist Helen Chadwick's dreamlike meditation, "What if dangerous fluids were to spill out, displacing logic, refuting a coherent narrative, into a landscape on the brink of I?"[29] Nothing better represents this "spillage of the Ego" as a prelude to the emergence of a para-self, Rotman urges, than the prevalence of the post-photographic digital image, and especially the GIS map. The post-photographic image "dissolves" the classic viewer rooted in Renaissance perspectivalism that privileged a self with a point of view outside the imaged object. An increasingly familiar example occurs in our obsession with GIS maps, such as the ones provided by Google Earth, with multiple separate graphic layers overlaying different kinds of information that can be viewed dynamically as a co-present assemblage of images and proactively navigated by the user. GIS maps of this sort enact the parallel experience of images that previously had to be viewed side-by-side, serially; in the process they reshape the fixity of the viewing subject and promote a dynamic viewing body that bypasses a perspectival mode of viewing. In terms of Rotman's thesis, this dissolution of seriality impinges directly on the subject and the construction of the self, resulting in a falling away from a one-dimensional, singular consciousness into parallel, distributed co-presence. Rotman summarizes this transition eloquently:

> Once, not so long ago, there was an absolute opposition of self and other: an "I," identical to itself, wholly present and as an autonomous, indivisible, interior psyche against an external, amorphous collectivity of third persons outside the skin. Now the I/me-unit is dissolving, the one who says or who writes "I" is no longer a singular integrated whole, but multiple: a shifting plurality of distributed I-parts, I-roles, I-functions, and I-presences. Now the "I" bleeds outward into the collective, and the collective introjects, insinuates and internalizes itself within the me. What was privately interior and individual is invaded by the public, the historical, the social. What was the outside world of events enters the individual soul in the mode of personal destiny.[30]

As we spend more time in electronically mediated environments, engaging with massively parallel distributed computing processes that are merging ever more seamlessly with the material processes and technological affordances of our everyday world, we are, in Rotman's terms, literally evolving, as distributed machinic multiples, para-selves beside ourselves.

Media Machines, Exteriority, and Intuition

The posthermeneutic ambitions of "Writing Science" turned around exposing the constitutive power of signifying machines, the exterior prelinguistic supplement conditioning the emergence of meaning-effects. However, as Mark Hansen discussed in *Embodying Technesis*, the program faltered dangerously on the problem of not fully embracing the machinic nature of signs, of continuously reducing technology to language, and not addressing the materiality of communicational media, the medium rather than the message being constitutive (to paraphrase Marshall McLuhan).[31] At the same time, embracing the full implications of the constitutive power and exteriority of media would set the program on a collision course with what Vivian Sobchack in her contribution to *Materialities of Communication* called the crisis of the lived body.

If the future path of electronic media as mapped out by Kittler, McLuhan, and André Leroi-Gourhan entailed the disappearance of the human in a disembodied digital cloud, a crucial task for media studies was "to get the body back in." "Unlike cinematic representation," Sobchack wrote, "electronic representation by its very structure phenomenologically denies the human body its fleshly presence and the world its dimension."[32] She continued:

> However significant and positive its values in some regards, the electronic trivializes the human body. Indeed at this historical moment in our particular society and culture, the lived-body is in crisis. Its struggle to assert its gravity, its differential existence and situation, it vulnerability and mortality, its vital and social investment in a concrete life-world inhabited by others is now marked in hysterical and hyperbolic responses to the disembodying effects of electronic representation . . . Devaluing the physically lived body and the concrete materiality of the world, electronic presence suggests that we are all in imminent danger of becoming merely ghosts in the machine (104).[33]

The task at hand, then, was to address the issue of whether "the body in code" as Hansen and Hayles described it in their works is in fact disembodied, or whether the phenomenal body of our lived conscious experience is compatible with a digitally mediated world. The groundwork for addressing these issues arose from a conjunction of advances in the cognitive and neurosciences and a revival of interest in phenomenology, particularly the phenomenology of Edmund Husserl and Maurice Merleau-Ponty.[34]

The Writing Science collective volume *Naturalizing Phenomenology* contributed to this development by advancing a merger of cognitive science with the phenomenology of Edmund Husserl. While Husserl explicitly rejected any scientific program aimed at naturalizing consciousness, the authors in this volume argue that current directions in the cognitive and neurosciences are in fact compatible with Husserl's phenomenology and the two can supplement one another in producing a more adequate theory of the mind.

The hallmark of consciousness in Husserl's scheme is intentionality (being-conscious-of-something as well as being-an-I). Intentionality takes two forms in Husserl: intuitive intentionality and symbolic intentionality. Jean-Michel Roy elaborates on the difference between intuitive and symbolic intentionality as follows: "in a symbolic intentional relation what is present to the subject is the substitute for an object, not the object itself. An intuitive intentional relation is direct, and in this sense it is a contact with the object itself, which is therefore present for the subject."[35] It is only in the sense that it is there itself, "in person" as Husserl likes to put it, that the object of the intuitive intentionality is grasped as being present.

This account illustrates that for Husserl perception is the intentional act of the conscious agent, and it illustrates further that the conscious agent is realized through its action in the world. Perception is not a static event but a dynamic process of enactive exteriorization. Husserl's treatment of visual perception is illustrative of how visual perceptions are assembled into a unified intentional object. The projection of images onto the retina are not what constitute the representation of an object. According to Husserl, certain types of motion are necessary for the constitution of three-dimensional space. More precisely, the correlations between ordered series of visual appearances and ordered series of kinesthetic circumstances when moving toward or away from an object or moving around it make possible "a new dimension, that makes a thing out of a picture, space out of the oculomotor field."[36]

Elisabeth Pacherie summarizes the main features of Husserl's theory of how objects are "given" in perceptual intuition:

> (1) it belongs to the essence of the mode of givenness of the object in perception that it be given as a series of profiles or appearances; (2) as a consequence, a certain temporal extension is constitutive of perception or, to put it otherwise, perception is essentially dynamic, and static content is a mere abstraction from

dynamic content; (3) only creatures endowed with a capacity for movement can enjoy perception of an objective three-dimensional world, and this perception is made possible by the functional dependence between series of visual appearances and series of kinesthetic circumstances (157).

Accounting for perception is the crossroads for the naturalization project, since, on the one hand, the whole project of a naturalization of the mental depends on the possibility of a naturalistic account of perceptual intentionality and since, on the other hand, perceptual experience is a paradigmatic illustration of the importance of the phenomenal and qualitative dimensions of mental life. The authors of *Naturalizing Phenomenology* point to examples of neurobiological research that synchronize with Husserl's phenomenological accounts of visual perception, such as David Marr's work on the different layers of neural process from retinal stimulation to constitution of the image in the brain providing the materiality of processes operative in Husserl's account.[37] Also, research has shown that the process of vision in primates is not a reconstruction of the image on the retina inside the brain by some inverse optics; instead, eye movements actively select an object by following points of interest for the organism. What counts as an object is also dependent on the proprioceptual data the organism actively provides, and movements of head and body provide such key information about depth that space cannot be seen as some neutral locus decoupled from bodily placement. Not only are these ideas important for the understanding of natural cognition, but because they can be implemented through computational means, they provide the key to far more effective designs in robotics.

The theme of dynamic exteriority in the constitution of the subject is extended further in Husserl's late works where he pushes constitutional analysis to investigate the processes of auto-constitution of the ego. Tim van Gelder and Francisco Varela point out that in Husserl's eyes the ego is not a mere static egological pole of intentional experiences. It also has a historical dimension in the sense that, through its continuous constitutional activity, it is progressively building up habits and properties, thereby making the present constitutions dependent on the past ones.[38] For Husserl and Merleau-Ponty, the body is not only an object in the world (a body) but also a medium whereby the world comes into being: an embodied experiencer.

Such an understanding of embodied cognition is not restricted to the philosophers in a particular genealogy stemming from Franz Brentano and subsequently from Husserl, Brentano's student. In *Irresistible Dictation: Gertrude Stein and the Correlations of Writing and Science*, Steven Meyer explores the subtle interrelationships between the psychology of William James and the verbal art of Gertrude Stein (who conducted experiments on automatic writing and "secondary personality" in the Harvard Psychological Laboratory in the mid-1890s).[39] Meyer argues that Stein, working in parallel with her close friend the philosopher and mathematician Alfred North Whitehead in James's own "radical empiricist" tradition, translated and ultimately transformed James's psychological theories by enfolding the neuroscience and biology of her day in a material semiotics that merged writing and neurology as two deeply interpenetrating aspects of consciousness. She thus replaced, Meyer contends, James's notions of "consciousness" with "writing," and in effect rewrote James's theory of consciousness as a theory of writing – even as like him she treated cognition not as the work of an abstract logic machine but as a function of organic mechanisms imbued with emotion and affect.[40] Indeed, in her development between 1912 and 1932 and already in her enigmatic work *The Making of Americans*, completed in 1911, Stein rejected all forms of consciousness that are not themselves forms of writing.[41] Meyer sees Stein's line of thinking, enacted in her avant-garde poetics, as meshing with the work of contemporary neuro- and cognitive scientists such as Varela who approach the idea of cognition as emerging from the meaningful couplings of situated, embodied-enactive agents with their surroundings; and with the work of Damasio on the role of emotion in cognition. (There is as well a resemblance with Clark and Chalmers's work on distributed cognition and extended minds.[42]) Through Stein, Meyer forges a new relationship between literature and science in which their differences are erased or overcome by their common basis in an active writing.

The Machine in the Ghost in the Machine

Popular representations of electronic media cast them as ghostly, disembodied, omnipresent, angelic virtualities. The half-pound of dried cellulose pulp formerly lobbed onto the porch by a boy on a bicycle has for many readers of the daily paper become an arrangement of pixels on a screen, summoned up and whisked away by minimal gestures. Going to the cinema or to a rave can be a matter of clicking three or four times on a download site or a multiuser domain. This is often taken to be a dematerialization of the object and of the self. Certainly some of the properties of the three-dimensional objects whose production and circulation have occupied most of human economic history (objects such as bushels of wheat, railroad cars, Old Master paintings) evaporate from their counterparts in digital commerce. But it would be an error to conclude that electronic objects lack materiality. Rather, they have a different materiality, contingent on different but no less material underpinnings. It is urgent to come to understand the materiality of the virtual in a time when many of the most visible human concerns are digitally mediated. Like cinema, court poetry or fireworks, digital media require a media-specific analysis (MSA), in Katherine Hayles's phrase, an analysis that recognizes that "texts must always be embodied to exist in the world." It is no less true of a Jane Austen novel (take whichever printing you prefer) than of a hypertext labyrinth or a Karen Finley performance piece that its

> materiality ... emerges from interactions between physical properties and a work's artistic strategies. For this reason, materiality cannot be specified in advance, as if it preexisted the specificity of the work. An emergent property, materiality depends on how the work mobilizes its resources as a physical artifact as well as on the user's interactions with the work and the interpretive strategies she develops.[43]

Users today can interact with *Pride and Prejudice* in ways that a contemporary of Austen could hardly have imagined. They can distill the electronic text into a word cloud; reorder its paragraphs; rename the characters (Mr. Darcy, you are henceforth Spongebob); map its every word onto a historical dataset containing hundreds of thousands of English-language texts; even subject it to automatic, if unreliable, translation into two dozen languages. In such acts of transformation the book may have lost its fixed verbal properties (along with the pages and the binding), but become material for a new project. The program of the OuLiPo group, ventriloquized by the critic Roland Barthes as a transformation of "works" into "texts," is within everyone's reach.[44] The digital text, because it is so readily manipulated, lends itself to "a serial movement of dislocations, overlappings, and variations. The logic that governs the Text is not comprehensive (seeking to define 'what the work means') but metonymic; and the activity of associations, contiguities, and cross-references coincides with a liberation of symbolic energy."[45] The wildest speculations of the high tide of literary theory, then, are turned into common sense and child's play by the recoding of the same words into a new medium. It may seem that the crystal of the artwork is being dissolved into the sea of language-in-general; but the view of the artwork that brings it into relation to the largest available collection of signs does as much to reveal its "autopoietics," the way it marks itself off from its environment.[46] (No text is an island.) Digital exploitations of a newly liberated text (liberated, that is, from the linear sequence of words on the page and from the norms of reading grounded in the norms of work and author) reveal, as a media-specific analysis should do, the new properties that differentiate the paper and electronic versions of a canonical novel.

The digital humanities (DH) are (or can be) a media-specific analysis of a new object: large samplings of text available for algorithmic search. This object is not the same thing as the "literature" understood in a previous age of literacy, any more than "oxygen" was the same thing as "dephlogisticated air." The first computerized text database was a concordance to the complete works of Saint Thomas Aquinas, begun by Father Roberto Busa in 1949 with the help of the IBM Labs.[47] The choice of author was pragmatic: an undeniably important thinker, whose immense and systematic corpus of work almost nobody has read through. But this encounter – the emergence of the digital humanities from theology – can also be seen as a recapitulation of history, for the term "humanities" (*studia humanitatis*) originated in the Renaissance as an answer to the then more prestigious discipline of divinity.[48] And indeed, Aquinas offers an encyclopedic treatment of what can be said about an immortal, immaterial, omniscient being identified with reason itself: what better subject for a publication-form with practically infinite volume and instantaneous search capacities? Verily, verily, for as it is written, "the 'content' of any [new] medium is always another [older] medium."[49]

What is new about the digital humanities? Busa and IBM's remediation connected a work from the manuscript age with the devices of the incipient digital age, using print only as a delivery mechanism for the results.[50] Early DH projects used the facility afforded by computers to do what humans shuffling index cards had been doing for centuries: concordances, lexica, tables of variants, bibliographies, chronologies. Computer-assisted researchers might also attempt to use new tools in cracking familiar problems, such as the authorship of Paul's letters or Shakespeare's plays. But stylometrics is hardly new, and its assumptions about authorial identity distinctly old-fashioned.[51] DH began to depart from these models when the availability of large datasets of human-generated text prompted researchers to exploit these in ways that went beyond unaided human imagining. Linguists, for example, rather than use the datasets as a control for manually constructed hypotheses about (for example) grammatical rules, let loose machine-learning algorithms on the data and waited to see the results.[52] Scholars of literature at first considered computers a labor-saving device capable of extracting the similarities among ten thousand novels that nobody had time to read – "the great unread," in Margaret Cohen's phrase.[53] But those with more training in statistics and computer science saw a different potential for research – for a form of research, however, that blends more readily with the work of linguists and sociologists than with the traditional work of the English department. The innovation would be providing quantifiable judgments on aspects of literature. But which aspects? One might, for example, use vocabulary lemmata and frequency of usage to assess the similarity between two works, or between two bodies of work. Or one might map a trend over time (the degrees of prevalence of "emotional" language in nineteenth-century fiction and oratory, contrasted). But the thought-experiment is best served by imagining a software automaton seeking regularities of any kind in the corpus presented it. A robot devising plans for reading texts originally written by humans, and emitting reports on its reading for humans or other robots to read, without human interests being in control, may look like a supremely misguided adventure to anyone with a traditional sense of the distinction between the sciences and the humanities as hinging on the presence of the human subject. One study concludes that "automated methods for assessing topic interpretability are negatively correlated with human evaluations of interpretability. In other words, though the machine does a very good job in identifying the topics latent in a corpus, the machine does a comparatively poor job when it comes to auto-identifying which of the harvested topics are the most interpretable by human beings."[54] This is not necessarily an unfavorable judgment on the machines. Were they designed to replicate human topic-modeling, their performance would be discouraging; but the discrepancy between responses of the human and machine populations is itself of interest and should spur further research into both kinds of readers. But the more a DH experiment relies on assumptions and categories that derive from the history of the objects under study, the less it has to tell us about the humanities that is new. The digital medium should rather permit those assumptions to be called into question.

Machine learning applied to human-generated data is unquestionably science of a kind – which is not to say that it is therefore truer, more reliable or more valuable than humanistic research. It simply represents an application of computer science to a new body of information: Tamil poetry, say, rather than the surface of Mars. And speaking of Martians, the experiment with machine learning would give us the closest approximation yet possible to an extraterrestrial's view of a significant realm of human feeling. The machine-readable text, already a fact of life for some seventy years now, necessitates new thinking about what "machine reading" could be. The prestige and authority of computers and numeration in our society, however, predetermines the popular understanding of machine reading as telling the truth (finally!) about literature by suspending subjectivity, art and enjoyment.[55]

The choice does not have to be so stark. Moreover, the mathematics behind DH need not be Platonic, generating self-evident, universally binding truths.

They can be (as Rotman has suggested about mathematics broadly) contingent, positional, corporeal, attuned to their media-specificity, "nomadic."[56]

Wilhelm Dilthey's 1883 distinction between the sciences of the spirit (*Geisteswissenschaften*), which are based on interpretation, and the sciences of nature, aiming at explanation, carved out a space for the humanities in a German university that he saw as increasingly tilted toward reproducible results and technological applications.[57] Where natural sciences pointed toward determinism and objective laws, human sciences made sense only on the assumption that people confronted open-ended situations as free agents. We "understand" the people of the past by putting ourselves in their shoes. For Dilthey, the great champion of hermeneutics, the humanities were thus an ethical position as well as a career. Already, however, in Dilthey's time the methods of natural-science research were grappling with the data of the humanities in ways that could not be called interpretive. The announcement by the Neogrammarians that "sound changes are without exception" sidestepped any attempt to draw motive or meaning from changes in pronunciation.[58] Experimental psychology proposed laws, ratios and explanatory mechanisms relating sensation and thought. Even Sigmund Freud, who today has his dwelling among the literary humanists, saw the task of psychoanalysis as explaining thought and behavior by reference to general causative mechanisms, not simply interpreting them in function of the individual case. Thus when, a century after Dilthey's epochal distinction, a new model for the humanities designated itself as "posthermeneutic," it was looping back into a history of science and technology that the material mediations of "Writing Science" have often foregrounded.

If the digital humanities promise a posthermeneutic science of literature, they are not quite there yet. The questions they ask often arise from a consensual or conventional judgment previously accepted by human readers, and the point of testing the data is to validate or invalidate the judgment.[59] One can always query if the question was the right one to ask, or if the algorithms correctly coded for the phenomenon to be studied. But experiments with autonomously generated data patterns are certainly posthuman. They offer a new way of analyzing the traditional humanities canon and a new object for the humanities. To get the full effect of this novelty, however, future experiments pursuing interactions between humanities and sciences should be reflexive, embodied, alert to contingency – they should do, in short, what "Writing Science" has attempted to do for the history of science. We present the open, unachieved frame here as an invitation for further work.

NOTES

1. For the series description, with links to the three dozen titles it ultimately included, see www.sup.org/books/series/?series=Writing%20Science.

2. For examples of each of these trends, see respectively Andrew Piper, *Book Was There: Reading in Electronic Times* (Chicago: University of Chicago Press, 2012); Bruno Latour and Steve Woolgar, *Laboratory Life: The Social Construction of Scientific Facts* (Beverly Hills: Sage, 1979; 2nd ed., 1986); Niklas Luhmann, *Social Systems* (Stanford: Stanford University Press, 1995); Friedrich Kittler, *Discourse Networks 1800/1900* (Stanford: Stanford University Press, 1990).

3. Ferdinand de Saussure, *Course in General Linguistics*, trans. Wade Baskin, eds. Perry Meisel and Haun Saussy (New York: Columbia University Press, 2012), 118–20 (translation modified); Ferdinand de Saussure, *Cours de linguistique générale*, ed. Tullio de Mauro (Paris: Payot, 1972), 163–6. "Semiology" (a discipline first defined by Saussure) is the formal study of sign systems.

4. On linguistics versus philology, see Saussure, *Cours*, ed. de Mauro, 410–11.

5. For this phrase, see Saussure's letter (written in an embittered mood) to Antoine Meillet of January 4, 1894, cited in Saussure, *Cours*, ed. de Mauro, 355.

6. On the development of physiological apparatus for the analysis of language, see Robert Brain, *The Pulse of Modernism: Physiological Aesthetics in Fin-de-Siècle Europe* (Seattle: University of Washington Press, 2015) and Haun Saussy, *The Ethnography of Rhythm* (New York: Fordham University Press, 2016).

7. See for example Pierre Jean Rousselot, *Les modifications phonétiques du langage, étudiées dans le patois d'une famille de Cellefrouin (Charente)* (Paris: Welter, 1891). Robert Brain discusses Rousselot's work in "Standards and Semiotics," in *Inscribing Science: Scientific Texts and the Materiality of Communication*, ed. Timothy Lenoir (Stanford: Stanford University Press, 1998), 249–84, at 270–7.

8. For an analogous move from the individual, contingent event of the sign to its categorical place in a structure, see Edmund Husserl, *Cartesian Meditations*, trans. Dorion Cairns (The Hague: Nijhoff, 1960), 70–2. Husserl will be discussed in some detail later in our essay.

9. To be fair, Saussure also delineated the domain of "parole," though his linguistics treated it as secondary. See Saussure, *Cours*, ed. de Mauro, 30–9. Mikhail Bakhtin's idea of the "answering word," introduced into models of scientific debate, would likewise recenter attention on the "parole" of specific interventions rather than on the "langue" of models and paradigms. See Bakhtin, *The Dialogic Imagination: Four Essays*, trans. Caryl Emerson (Austin: University of Texas Press, 1981), 280–1.

10. See Donald R. Kelley, "Linguistic Turn," in *New Dictionary of the History of Ideas*, vol. 3, ed. Maryanne Cline Horowitz (Detroit: Thomson Gale, 2005), 1290–2.

11. Thomas S. Kuhn, *The Structure of Scientific Revolutions* (Chicago: University of Chicago Press, 1962), 52, 96.

12. See Andrew Abbott, "*Structure* as Cited, *Structure* as Read," in *Kuhn's "Structure of Scientific Revolutions" at Fifty: Reflections on a Science Classic*, eds. Robert J. Richards and Lorraine Daston (Chicago: University of Chicago Press, 2016), 167–81.

13. Kuhn, *Structure of Scientific Revolutions*, 166 (our emphasis).
14. K. Ludwig Pfeiffer, "Materialities of Communication," in *Materialities of Communication*, eds. Hans Ulrich Gumbrecht and Karl Ludwig Pfeiffer (Stanford: Stanford University Press, 1994; original publication in German, 1988), 1–12, at 3. Also in *Materialities of Communication*, see Hans Ulrich Gumbrecht, "A Farewell to Interpretation," 389–402; Wlad Godzich, "Language, Images, and the Postmodern Predicament," 355–70; Friedrich Kittler, "Unconditional Surrender," 319–34; Jean-François Lyotard, "Can Thought Go on without a Body?," 286–300; and Niklas Luhmann, "*How Can the Mind Participate in Communication*," 371–87.
15. See Kittler, *Discourse Networks* and his *Gramophone Film Typewriter* (Stanford: Stanford University Press, 1999). Kittler's discourse network refers to the material structure prior to questions of meaning – in other words, constraints that select an array of marks from all possible writing constellations, paths and media of transmission, mechanisms of memory.
16. Latour and Woolgar, *Laboratory Life*, 48, 52, 51.
17. Hans-Jörg Rheinberger, *Toward a History of Epistemic Things: Synthesizing Proteins in the Test Tube* (Stanford: Stanford University Press, 1997), 181. For more on the Derridean contrast between historicity and historiality, see Hans-Jörg Rheinberger, "Experimental Systems: Historiality, Narration, and Deconstruction," *Science in Context* 7.1 (1994), 65–81.
18. See Brian Rotman, *Signifying Nothing: The Semiotics of Zero* (Stanford: Stanford University Press, 1993).
19. Brian Rotman, *Mathematics as Sign: Writing, Imagining, Counting* (Stanford: Stanford University Press, 2000), 17. On "inclusive" and "exclusive" imperatives, see Rotman, *Ad Infinitum: Taking God Out of Mathematics and Putting the Body Back In* (Stanford: Stanford University Press, 1993), 71–2. An inclusive imperative is a command to think that is addressed to both the mathematician and the non-mathematician, whereas an exclusive imperative – for example, *integrate the function* f(x) – "assumes that a shared world, that of the calculus, has already been instituted and asks for a specific action relevant to this world."
20. Rodney Brooks, *Flesh and Machines: How Robots Will Change Us* (New York: Pantheon, 2002), 236.
21. See Brian Rotman, *Becoming Beside Ourselves: The Alphabet, Ghosts, and Distributed Human Being* (Durham: Duke University Press, 2008).
22. See N. Katherine Hayles, *How We Became Posthuman: Virtual Bodies in Cybernetics, Literature, and Informatics* (Chicago: University of Chicago Press, 1999), and *My Mother Was a Computer: Digital Subjects and Literary Texts* (Chicago: University of Chicago Press, 2005), as well as Mark Hansen, *Embodying Technesis: Technology Beyond Writing* (Ann Arbor: University of Michigan Press, 2000), and *New Philosophy for New Media* (Cambridge, MA: MIT Press, 2004). For positions close to those developed by Rotman, see Hansen, *Bodies in Code: Interfaces with Digital Media* (New York: Routledge, 2006).
23. In addition to Mark Hansen's *Embodying Technesis*, cited above, see especially Gilbert Simondon, *L'individu et sa genèse physico-biologique: l'individuation à la lumière des notions de forme et d'information* (Paris: PUF, 1964), André Leroi-Gourhan, *Gesture and Speech* (original publication 1964–65; Cambridge: MIT

Press, 1993), and Bernhard Stiegler, *Technics and Time, 1: The Fault of Epimetheus* (Stanford: Stanford University Press, 1998).

24. Rotman builds here on his earlier semiotic approach to mathematics. For aspects of the semiotics of the US philosopher and logician Charles Sanders Peirce relevant to Rotman's work and to media studies, see Charles S. Peirce, "What Is a Sign?" (1894) in *The Essential Peirce: Selected Philosophical Writings, Volume 2 (1893–1913)*, ed. the Peirce Edition Project (Bloomington: Indiana University Press, 1998), 4–10. In the same volume also see "Excerpts from Letters to Lady Welby (1906–08)," 477–91, and "Excerpts from Letters to William James (1909)," 492–502. For an overview of the logical underpinning of Peirce's philosophical project, see his early essay, "On a New List of Categories" (1867) in *The Essential Peirce: Selected Philosophical Writings, Volume 1 (1867–1983)*, eds. Nathan Houser and Christian Kloesel (Bloomington: Indiana University Press, 1992), 1–10. An excellent discussion of Peircean semiotics may be found online – see Albert Atkin, "Peirce's Theory of Signs," *The Stanford Encyclopedia of Philosophy* (Summer 2013 Edition), ed. Edward N. Zalta: http://plato.stanford .edu/archives/sum2013/entries/peirce-semiotics/.

25. Stephen Wolfram, *A New Kind of Science* (New York: Wolfram Media, 2002); Edward Fredkin, *Introduction to Digital Philosophy* (2001), www.digitalphilosophy.org. Deleuze and Guattari develop the notion of the Body without Organs (BwO) in Gilles Deleuze and Félix Guattari, "November 28, 1947: How to Make Yourself a Body without Organs," in *A Thousand Plateaus: Capitalism and Schizophrenia* (Minneapolis: University of Minneapolis Press, 1987), 149–66. (The phrase is adapted from a 1947 radio play by Antonin Artaud; see Artaud, "To Have Done with the Judgment of God," in *Selected Writings*, ed. Susan Sontag [Berkeley: University of California Press, 1976], 555–71, at 571.) BwO is used by Deleuze and Guattari in an extended sense to describe an undifferentiated, unhierarchical realm that lies deeper than the world of appearances. It is the body seen from the viewpoint of its possibilities. For Deleuze and Guattari, every actual body has a limited set of traits, habits, movements, affects, etc. But every actual body also has a virtual dimension: a vast reservoir of potential traits, connections, affects, movements, etc. This collection of potentials is what Deleuze calls the BwO. In this sense, they even speak of a BwO of "the Earth" (*A Thousand Plateaus*, 40). For discussions of the Body without Organs see Bernadette Wegenstein, *Getting under the Skin: Body and Media Theory* (Cambridge: MIT Press, 2006), 117–18 and 120–1; and Brian Massumi, *A User's Guide to Capitalism and Schizophrenia: Deviations from Deleuze and Guattari* (Cambridge: MIT Press, 1992), 70–1.

26. Harold Morowitz, *The Emergence of Everything: How the World Became Complex* (New York: Oxford University Press, 2002); Ray Kurzweil, *The Age of Spiritual Machines: When Computers Exceed Human Intelligence* (Oxford: Oxford University Press, 2000); Hans Moravec, *Mind Children: The Future of Robot and Human Intelligence* (Cambridge: Harvard University Press, 1990).

27. See especially Hayles, *My Mother Was a Computer*, 206–13.

28. Félix Guattari, *Chaosmosis: An Ethico-Aesthetic Paradigm* (Bloomington: Indiana University Press, 1995), 4.

29. Rotman, *Becoming Beside Ourselves*, 99–100.

30. Rotman, *Becoming Beside Ourselves*, 100.

31. Hansen, *Embodying Technesis*, 225–7.
32. Vivian Sobchack, "The Scene of the Screen: Envisioning Cinematic and Electronic 'Presence,'" in *Materialities of Communication*, eds. Gumbrecht and Pfeiffer, 83–106, at 103.
33. Sobchack alludes here to Gilbert Ryle's well-known characterization of Cartesian mind-body dualism as adhering to "the myth of the ghost in the machine" (*The Concept of Mind* [New York: Barnes & Noble, 1949], 63).
34. Edmund Husserl, the author of *Cartesian Meditations* and *The Crisis of European Sciences*, originated modern phenomenology as the study of "intentional objects" in the "life-world," distinguishing these from a purported external world; see *Cartesian Meditations* (Dordrecht: Kluwer, 1960) and *The Crisis of European Sciences and Transcendental Philosophy* (Evanston: Northwestern University Press, 1970). His most famous student was Martin Heidegger. Maurice Merleau-Ponty further specified the horizon of phenomenology as the description of embodied experience: see Merleau-Ponty, *The Phenomenology of Perception* (New York: Routledge, 2012) and "Beyond the Gap: An Introduction to Naturalizing Phenomenology," in *Naturalizing Phenomenology: Issues in Contemporary Phenomenology and Cognitive Science*, eds. Jean Petitot, Francisco J. Varela, Bernard Pachoud, and Jean-Michel Roy (Stanford: Stanford University Press, 1999), 53.
35. Jean-Michel Roy, "Saving Intentional Phenomena: Intentionality, Representation, and Symbol," in *Naturalizing Phenomenology*, ed. Petitot et al., 111–47, at 134.
36. Edmund Husserl, *Ding und Raum* (1907), cited in Elisabeth Pacherie, "*Leibhaftigkeit* and Representatonal Theories of Perception," in *Naturalizing Phenomenology*, ed. Petitot et al., 148–60, at 157.
37. See David Marr, *Vision: A Computational Investigation into the Human Representation and Processing of Visual Information* (Cambridge: MIT Press, 2010).
38. Tim van Gelder, "Wooden Iron? Husserlian Phenomenology Meets Cognitive Science," *Naturalizing Phenomenology*, ed. Petitot et al., 245–65; Francisco J. Varela, "The Specious Present: A Neurophenomenology of Time Consciousness," *Naturalizing Phenomenology*, ed. Petitot et al., 266–314.
39. The resemblance between Husserl and James is hardly surprising, given the importance that James's 1890 masterpiece, *The Principles of Psychology*, possessed for Husserl; Dermot Moran thus observes that Husserl's "copy of James's *Principles* ... is closely annotated, especially chapters in volume 1 such as 'The Stream of Thought,' 'Attention' and 'The Perception of Space'" (*Edmund Husserl: Founder of Phenomenology* [Cambridge: Polity, 2005], 20). Also see Max Herzog, "William James and the Development of Phenomenological Psychology in Europe," *History of the Human Sciences* 8.1 (1995): 29–46, esp. 30–3.
40. Steven Meyer, *Irresistible Dictation: Gertrude Stein and the Correlations of Writing and Science* (Stanford: Stanford University Press, 2001), 128. "Organic mechanism" is a phrase used by Whitehead in his 1925 Lowell Lectures, published as *Science and the Modern World*.
41. On the central role played by Stein's Jamesian experiments in the subsequent development of the US novel, see Steven Meyer, "The Scientific Imagination of

U.S. Modernist Fiction," in *The Cambridge Companion to the American Modernist Novel*, ed. Joshua L. Miller (Cambridge: Cambridge University Press, 2015), 137–56.

42. See Francisco J. Varela, Eleanor Rosch and Evan Thompson, *The Embodied Mind: Cognitive Science and Human Experience* (Cambridge: MIT Press, 1991); Antonio Damasio, *The Feeling of What Happens: Body, Emotion and the Making of Consciousness* (New York: Harcourt Brace, 1999); Andy Clark and David J. Chalmers, "The Extended Mind," *Analysis* 58.1 (January 1998): 7–19.

43. N. Katherine Hayles, *Writing Machines* (Cambridge: MIT Press, 2002), 32–3. See also N. Katherine Hayles and Jessica Pressman, *Comparative Textual Media: Transforming the Humanities in the Postprint Era* (Minneapolis: University of Minnesota Press, 2013).

44. OuLiPo (the "Opener of Potential Literature"), a group founded in Paris in the 1960s, sought to expand the resources of creative writing by exploiting mathematical transformations and letter games. See OuLiPo [collective author], *La littérature potentielle* (Paris: Gallimard, 1973) and Warren F. Motte, *Oulipo: A Primer of Potential Literature* (Normal, IL: Dalkey Archive, 1998).

45. Roland Barthes, "From Work to Text," in Josué V. Harari, ed., *Textual Strategies: Perspectives in Poststructuralist Criticism* (Ithaca, NY: Cornell University Press, 1979), 73–81.

46. On this perspective, see Humberto R. Maturana and Francisco J. Varela, *Autopoiesis and Cognition: The Realization of the Living* (Boston: Reidel, 1980), and Jerome McGann, *The Textual Condition* (Princeton: Princeton University Press, 1991).

47. Susan Hockey, "The History of Humanities Computing," in *A Companion to Digital Humanities*, eds. Susan Schreibman, Ray Siemens, John Unsworth (Oxford: Blackwell, 2004), 3–19; available at www.digitalhumanities.org/companion/.

48. See Rens Bod, *A New History of the Humanities: The Search for Principles and Patterns from Antiquity to the Present* (New York: Oxford University Press, 2013), 145.

49. Marshall McLuhan, *Understanding Media: The Extensions of Man*, ed. Terrence Gordon (Corte Madera, Calif.: Gingko Press, 2003), 19.

50. Robertus Busa, ed., *Index Thomisticus* (49 volumes; Stuttgart: Frommann, 1974–1980): www.corpushomisticum.org. See also Jay David Bolter and Richard Grusin, *Remediation: Understanding New Media* (Cambridge: MIT Press, 1999).

51. See Mikhail B. Malyutov, "Authorship Attribution of Texts: A Review," in *General Theory of Information Transfer and Combinatorics*, eds. Rudolf Ahlswede, Lars Bäumer, Ning Cai, Harout Aydinian, Vladimir Blinovsky, Christian Deppe and Haik Mashurian (Berlin: Springer, 2006), 362–80.

52. See John Goldsmith, "Unsupervised Learning of the Morphology of a Natural Language," *Computational Linguistics* 27 (2001): 153–98.

53. Margaret Cohen, *The Sentimental Education of the Novel* (Princeton: Princeton University Press, 1999), 23.

54. Matthew L. Jockers, *Macroanalysis: Digital Methods and Literary History* (Urbana: University of Illinois Press, 2014), 128. Jockers was responsible for

much of the actual statistical research reported by the Stanford Literary Lab ("a research collective that applies computational criticism, in all its forms, to the study of literature"; see https://litlab.stanford.edu).

55. Joshua Rothman, "An Attempt to Discover the Laws of Literature," *The New Yorker*, March 20, 2014. See also, for a critical attitude to such authority, Hoyt Long and Richard Jean So, "Literary Pattern Recognition: Modernism between Close Reading and Machine Learning," *Critical Inquiry* 42 (2016): 235–67.

56. Brian Rotman, *Mathematics as Sign*, 143–53. For ethnographies of actual nomadic mathematics, see Edwin Hutchins, *Cognition in the Wild* (Cambridge: MIT Press, 1995) and David A. Mindell, *Between Human and Machine: Feedback, Control and Computing Before Cybernetics* (Baltimore: Johns Hopkins University Press, 2002).

57. Wilhelm Dilthey, *Introduction to the Human Sciences*, vol. 1 of *Selected Works*, eds. Rudolf Makkreel and Frithjof Rodi (Princeton: Princeton University Press, 1989).

58. The Neogrammarians, who had arisen in Germany in the 1870s "in staunch opposition to the metaphysical and biological approaches to language then current[,] insisted upon the absolute autonomy of phonology from syntax and semantics, with phonology having the most important position ... Although Saussure had a background in the historical study of language[,] he was unusually critical of [N]eogrammarian philology, which he accused of being overly absorbed in diachrony" or "issues of the evolution of languages" (Victor H. Mair, "Language and Linguistics," in *New Dictionary of the History of Ideas*, vol. 3, Maryanne Cline Horowitz, ed., 1225–6).

59. Richard Jean So and Andrew Piper, "How Has the MFA Changed the Contemporary Novel?" *The Atlantic*, March 6, 2016: www.theatlantic.com /entertainment/archive/2016/03/mfa-creative-writing/462483/.

8

JAMES J. BONO

Science Studies as Cultural Studies

The "cultural turn" has left its mark on the interpretive disciplines.[1] As one such instance, the emergence of science studies as a disciplinary formation since the 1980s owed much to attempts to trace the borders surrounding science, the social, and the cultural and to delineate the traffic among them. Of course, such metaphors are fraught with implications; they invite competing narrative interpretations of such foundational categories. At stake is precisely how they are to be thought together, and thought differently. One way of approaching science studies as cultural studies is to take each of the two terms as unproblematic – as established disciplinary methodologies – and simply survey how, for example, preoccupation with class, gender, racial, and/or power analyses have been transferred to the study of science and hence translated into exemplary studies of the impact of the "cultural" on "science." This essay will take as its charge a different task.

What is at stake in thinking of "science" and the "cultural" together? What long-standing assumptions can such analysis reveal, and how might that matter to the work of science studies? What we ought to place at the center of such analysis, I argue, are notions of practice and of science as practice. Of course, numerous scholars from diverse disciplines have written much in the past twenty-five years about science as practice and science as culture.[2] Rather than engage such arguments exhaustively, I intend to focus on the significance of thinking of "science" and the "cultural" in conjunction with a more recent turn, and to argue for the importance of this later turn to science studies: the turn to the ontological.[3] First, however, let me note a few key points and suggest something of the texture surrounding discussions of the cultural studies of science since the late 1980s.

Cultural Studies of Science

In the inaugural issue of *Configurations: A Journal of Literature, Science, and Technology*, philosopher Joseph Rouse argued forcefully for the importance of a body of new work that he collectively labeled "Cultural Studies of Science."[4] While granting their heterogeneous – even disparate – nature as the work of very different scholars with a multiplicity of individual approaches and commitments, nonetheless, for Rouse this loose collectivity of work lent itself to redescription as a patterned, if pragmatically constructed, constellation signaling something new in the firmament of academic science studies. Such work exhibited resistance to prevailing orthodoxies that Rouse saw fueling the so-called social construction of scientific knowledge. Put more positively, "cultural studies of science" – however heterogeneous as a collectivity – exhibited a number of promising working beliefs and practices that marked the cutting edge of an emergent discipline, science studies. These orienting beliefs and practices are worth enumerating here; according to Rouse, they include: (1) the "heterogeneity of science" – that science is both historically and culturally "variant," and therefore neither a "single kind" of knowledge, nor characterized by a single essential "aim" or form; (2) the "plasticity" of scientific practices, which resist the imposition of "social categories of explanation" especially when the latter are figured as separate from the process of articulating meanings inherent to a particular modality of knowledge production; (3) aligned with the above, the "local, material, and discursive character of scientific practice" embedded in the skills, protocols, instruments, and material objects of specific scientific complexes; (4) contra Kuhn, the "openness of scientific work" – scientific work as the work of translation with its "constant traffic across … boundaries" as championed by Bruno Latour, and others; and (5) science as inherently interpretive and performative activity.[5] The latter gloss on Rouse points to an important feature of characterizing, as I do, science as itself "cultural *poiesis*": what matters to science, following Latour, are "matters of concern" rather than "matters of fact"; or, following Alfred North Whitehead, "interest" rather than truth![6]

Rouse's essay intervenes in ongoing discussions of science and culture as captured, for example, in the formative collection of essays edited by Andrew Pickering, *Science as Practice and Culture*.[7] Pickering's collection brought together, among others, proponents of the sociology of scientific knowledge (SSK) and the ethnographic approaches associated with the likes of Latour and his sometime collaborator, Michel Callon, both closely identified with "actor-network" theory.[8] Rouse proved critical of an approach he and others associated with SSK[9]: a tendency to privilege the social as foundational to explanations of the formation of scientific knowledge. Hence, the identification of the so-called Strong Program in SSK with the social construction of science. Famously, Bruno Latour and Steve Wolgar dropped the word, "social," from the subtitle of their pathbreaking book, *Laboratory Life: The Social Construction of Scientific Facts* (first published in 1979), with the publication of the second edition in 1986.[10] For Latour and Woolgar, the term, "social," had lost its usefulness precisely because it could not – nor should – be disentangled from realms typically figured as distinct, such as another "foundational" category, that of "nature" or the "natural." The key move was to refuse such "a binary opposition" (281). Indeed, Latour would go on in later publications to articulate a vision of science studies built upon explicit embrace of such a refusal coupled with recognition of the centrality of that very binary to the formation of "modernity" and of the notion of "science" itself. The mythos of the separation of nature and culture (or society) was, for Latour, midwife to "The Modern Constitution" accompanying the birth of modern science in the seventeenth century.[11] While denying the binarism of this opposition, Latour acknowledges "the effectiveness of the separation" – what he describes as the "modern divide between the natural world and the social world" (13) – in propelling the growth and authority of science and scientists in the modern world. Ironically, the authority-generating force of this mythic birth of modern science was belied by close examination of the repressed history of that birth, which, in the example of Robert Boyle, turned upon the entangled operation of nature-culture in the very practices that gave rise to the scientific and sociopolitical "orders" in the seventeenth century.[12] This originary contamination of the natural by the social – and of the social by the natural – was neither accidental, nor avoidable, but, rather, a feature of lived historical experience itself. For despite our deeply rooted belief in the purity of such categories – and of the separations that it entailed of "human beings" and "nonhumans" – Latour insists that we have always operated in and experienced our world as a world of "hybrids": entities that are always already inextricably "natural" and "cultural" and "social" (10–11)! As a consequence, for Latour, "we have never been modern." Later still, Latour would critically deconstruct the very notion of "social construction," while offering an alternative "constructivist" analysis of science. (I discuss this in the next section.)

Returning for now to Pickering, in the introductory chapter to *Science as Practice and Culture*, he notes the parallelism between the traditional claims of science to its authority and the claims of SSK to explain scientific knowledge as the product of the social – of social contexts and constructions.[13] As he remarks, the problem for SSK with "traditional accounts" of science is that they "see scientific knowledge as largely given by the world itself, independently of the human scientists that function as nature's mouthpiece" (20). In such accounts, then, science is a product of nature and *not* of culture – much as Galileo in the seventeenth century purported to read the Book of Nature directly, without the mediation of mere human interpretation, thus uncovering a "science" scripted by nature itself.[14] While Latour and Callon agree with this characterization of traditional accounts of science – indeed, according to Pickering, concluding that such understandings have "situated their accounts of science at the 'nature' end of the spectrum – scientific knowledge is dictated by nature" – they view SSK, instead, as making "the radical move" of situating "itself at the other extreme: scientific knowledge is dictated by society" (21). Radical though that move seemed at the time, the point for Latour and Callon is, by contrast, "that the actor-network approach rejects the very concept of the nature-society spectrum." Further, in a point salient to this essay, they instead "begin from the idea ... that nature and society are intimately entangled in scientific and technological practice. Practice is where nature and society and the space between them are continually made, unmade, and remade." In attacking this "Kantian 'Great Divide' between nature and society" – implicitly between nature and culture, as Latour elsewhere adds[15] – Callon and Latour challenge the very assumptions that, in their view, underpins SSK's "appealing to the social as an explanatory principle": namely, the existence, authority, and stability of "the premise of the Great Divide between nature and society on which the authority of the natural scientists rests" (21). Challenging the very stability and givenness of the "social" or the "cultural," in their view and in the view adopted by this essay, lies at the heart of science studies and its complication of the very notion and status of authority.[16]

Rouse's advocacy for "cultural studies of science" builds upon such undoing of the nature-society and nature-culture binarisms. Nonetheless, in his important article, "Cultural History of Science: An Overview with Reflections," Peter Dear criticizes Rouse's advocacy precisely based on a reading of Rouse as unmooring the cultural from the social.[17] Dear identifies a "central problem" endemic to most claims for a cultural history of science, one that arises from the fact that "at its most fundamental, 'culture' is a concept that simply designates whatever *is not* nature" (151). Whatever Rouse's position, we've seen that such a characterization of culture, while fundamental to Latour's modern Constitution of "nature" and "culture" as separate realms, is by no means the only basis of analytic practices available to a "culturally" oriented science studies, let alone a universally accepted category. Dear himself acknowledges such alternatives, discussing Latour in particular as an exemplar of one such alternative (153). Furthermore, in place of the cultural history of science rubric, Dear insists upon a "different term": what he calls "'sociocultural' history of science" (154). For Dear, this designation serves to re-moor – to locate – the cultural dimension of science within its proper, local social situations; as he puts it in reference to one example of such historical work, "symbols do not float free of the society that displays them" (155).[18] Put thusly, one can hardly disagree with Dear: science, the social, and the cultural are not readily separated nor separable. The task of the historian of science – more broadly, of science studies generally – certainly ought to embrace rigorous and nuanced dissection of the entanglements inherent in the making of scientific knowledge through the repertoire of practices – the toolkit of techniques, *technē* – available to and devised by those who robustly experience, engage, and reflect on a world of encountered agencies.[19] If this is what Dear has in mind, there are no grounds for dispute. Certainly, his concluding remarks can be read in this way; yet, one can also wonder if there's more at stake in those remarks than may initially meet the eye:

> The past becomes a virtual present when its moorings in the specificities of another time and place (literal or figurative) are lost. In the historical study of culture, including that of science, losing sight of the constituting social world results in the study of chimeras: Cultural meanings that are not also social meanings are exactly like colors that are not colors *of* anything – they are properties without a subject. Culture is real: but it is not a thing. It is a property of its society, not a social epiphenomenon but what an Aristotelian would call an essential (i.e., constitutive) property. (165–166)

Insofar as these "moorings" may be identified with a "constituting social world" figured as itself independent and foundational, this characterization could, alternatively, be read as reintroducing the very binary that the account of scientific practice championed by Latour and others refuse as out of order. Is this move implicit in Dear's defense of the SSK (157)? If so, such a move would weaken, if not undermine, any robust appreciation of the world of experience as a thoroughly entangled world where the natural, cultural, social, human, and nonhuman are always encountered as inseparable, inter-dependent, and mutually constitutive.

Lest it appear that the contestation of such foundational binaries within science studies was something new with Latour and his collaborators, we should note not only (one of) its roots in deconstruction, but also the vigorous championing of alternative perspectives independent of such arbi-trary dichotomies found especially in feminist science studies. Here, without question, we find the most thoroughgoing critiques and contestations in the work of Donna Haraway. From her *Crystals, Fabrics, and Fields: Metaphors of Organicism in Twentieth-Century Developmental Biology* to *Primate Visions: Gender, Race, and Nature in the World of Modern Science,* and beyond, Haraway has relentlessly dissected the work that such binary oppositions have performed in various arenas of modern science, championing a science studies that details the simultaneous making of science-culture-society and the biopolitical.[20] In her transformative contribution to such contestations of the nature-culture and nature-society divides, "A Cyborg Manifesto," Haraway exposes the roots of such binaries in the multiple and multiplying "origin stories" that weave their way throughout the fabric of the West with its entangled histories of Judeo-Christian and secular-political mythologies. Such histories have consequential effects, not least for technologies of dominance and control: desires born in the Garden of Eden affecting and infecting a nostalgia for lost Adamic dominion as driving variously gendered fantasies of nature and society including our own information/informatics visions of a cyborg world.[21]

Practice and the Turn to Ontology

Much important work in science studies has analyzed the importance of discursive practices in the sciences such as the framing of boundaries and consequent strategies for working between, across, and against such conceptual, linguistic, and disciplinary divides in the production of scientific knowledge and the making of phenomena; or, as another example, the structuring effects and implications of various schemes for categorizing and parsing the world of objects and events.[22] Space does not permit exploration of these formative practices with their exemplifications of the inseparability of the social, cultural, scientific, and technological. Instead, the remainder of this chapter will explore what I see as key to understanding this vision of inseparability in connection with science and science studies: namely, the focus on practice and the turn to the ontological as marking the cultures of science.

By contrast, much traditional history of science operated, at least implicitly, on the assumption that science could best be characterized as a modality (and achievement) of thinking.[23] While the limits of such an assumption have become obvious since the publication of Thomas S. Kuhn's classic work, *The Structure of Scientific Revolutions,* it is worth noting that the subsequent turn to science as practice should not, and indeed does not, entail a binary opposition between thinking and practice. The thought-practice dichotomy is both false and, worse still, misleading, since thinking operates with and through its own tools and the practices associated with and generated by them.[24] If a focus on science as simply conceptual tended to privilege approaches to science studies and the history of science that placed epistemological considerations at the center of analysis, by contrast the turn toward practice – with the recognition it should bring that thought itself depends upon and operates with various material or materializable instruments – points toward the primacy of ontology. Practice, that is, operates by eliciting (and selecting from) the entangledness of things: a world of entangled agencies, networks, operations, and *relations*! Further still, such recognition changes the very way in which we ought to understand the "construction" of science: from "social construction" to what I have called science as *poiesis*, as *technē* – science as itself a process of making.

Here we must be careful, following Bruno Latour, to respect the precise force of "constructivism," the limits of human ingenuity, and the entangled operations of nonhuman agencies:

> Learning how to become responsive to the unexpected qualities and virtualities of materials is how engineers will account for the chance encounter with practical solutions: they will never think of describing themselves as little kids molding reality at will. If there is one thing toward which "making" does not lead, it is to the concept of a *human* actor *fully* in *command*. This is the great paradox of the use of the word construction: it is used by critical sociology to show that things are not simply and naturally *there*, that they are the products of some human or social ingenuity, but as soon as the metaphor of "making," "creating," or "constructing" barely begins to shine, then the maker, the creator, the constructor has to share its agency with a sea of actants over which they have neither control nor mastery. What is interesting in constructivism is exactly the opposite of what it first seems to imply: there is no maker, no master, no creator that could be said to dominate materials . . . [25]

It is precisely neither mastery, nor domination, that constructivism portends. Rather, it is attending to constructivism as process – to the process of making things "shine" forth as agents in an entangled world inhabited by a multiplicity of mutually intersecting human and nonhuman actants – that points to the real promises of constructivism. In such a world, the practices, tools, instruments, and strategies deployed by human actors forge ever changing connections – relations – to things, to things that are made, things that act and interact. Science as practice – as *poiesis* and making – entails attending to the ontological.

For far too long, science studies has been conditioned to attend, instead, to the epistemological without linking such analyses deriving from epistemological considerations robustly to questions of ontology: to "things," events, relations. The near exclusivity of such analytic perspectives have come at a great cost, as they have enforced in their very silence a blindness to the experience and implications of entangled ontologies operating in the world, while raising, instead, to the forefront the drama of human orchestration of the theater of things. Nowhere is this more evident than in the metaphorics of epistemological breaks, or ruptures, inhabiting (and inhibiting) the literature of science studies since the 1960s. I would argue that the turn to practice in science studies ultimately serves to undermine the dominance of epistemology, the metaphorics of ruptures, and the lingering desire to privilege either nature or the social in accounting for the work of science. This insistence on resistance to epistemological breaks or ruptures might strike some as a provocation. So, let me be clear. One possible provocation, for some, might consist in seeming to set up a hard and fast dichotomy: either science operates through a historical succession of conceptual breaks and ruptures, or, on the contrary, we come to understand science as practice. Breaks versus practice. One famous example serves to dispel this (unintended) inference exposing it as yet another false dichotomy. The example I have in mind is Thomas Kuhn's *The Structure of Scientific Revolutions*.[26] Kuhn's "paradigms" saddled an emergent science studies of the 1960s and 1970s with a model of scientific change as abrupt, totalizing, and gestalt-like paradigm change – his infamous scientific revolutions as wholesale paradigm changes. Nonetheless, as Joseph Rouse correctly insisted in 1998, Kuhn's book also represented a less well-remembered – yet, for Rouse and for me, a far more important – "turn to practice."[27] Clearly, then, the real – and for me the intended – provocation my essay represents lies elsewhere: namely, in an account of scientific practices that does not entail Kuhnian breaks as the engine of change.

Nevertheless, despite this criticism, I do not dismiss out of hand all talk of breaks or ruptures. Retrospectively, one can certainly describe changes in scientific thinking and practice whose effects are not simply the result of steady and undramatic accretion of new bits of information or pieces of a puzzle. These are changes that, by contrast, appear so fundamental or so unexpected as to seemingly transform the very nature of the game that doing a particular kind of science entails. Examples abound in the history of science: from Aristotelian to mechanistic or Newtonian worldviews; from pre- to post-Darwinian evolutionary biology; from Newtonian to Einsteinian physics; from classical to tectonic-plate geology. While the *result* of scientific change can evoke figurations of a break, rupture, or an impassable divide, a question remains: is *change itself* best figured as a break or rupture? To attempt an answer to such a basic question, I would argue that one must first examine how scientific practices operate within science in ways that produce scientific change, while simultaneously exemplifying the inseparability of nature-culture-society in the very same practices that both produce and are the products of science. As a radical replacement for mere accretion and puzzle-solving, Kuhn himself invokes paradigm shifts – gestalt-like shifts of model cognitive and experimental practices – as engines of scientific change. Alternatively, I am inclined to view scientific practices as constantly subject to reworking, reimagining, retranscription in processes akin to what Andy Pickering calls "tinkering" in his book, *The Mangle of Practice*, and akin as well to Hans-Jörg Rheinberger's account of experimental systems in his book, *A History of Epistemic Things*. Both the mangle of practice and epistemic things display nature-culture-society as mutually constitutive in the making of different kinds of scientific knowledge.

(The case study at the heart of Rheinberger's book focuses, for example, "on the construction of an in vitro system of protein biosynthesis and the laboratory emergence of what molecular biologists today call *transfer RNA*."[28] My own historical work on early modern science argues that attempts to understand the "Book of Nature" depended upon reimagining and reworking a range of established and newly emergent practices – anatomical practices; mapping, diagramming, and modeling practices; visual technologies; the production of tables, lists, and practices for storing, organizing, and retrieving information; practices associating with the uses of instruments; classifying and categorizing practices; among others. Such reimagining and reworking of material and meaning-making practices help us account for the different understandings of, for example, the heart and the pulse in the work of William Harvey in comparison to earlier anatomists, or of the movement of bodies in Galileo. Such practices, in turn, often arise out of reimagining and reworking metaphors foundational to the work of the sciences – for example, nature as a book; disease as imbalance, or as warfare; the brain as a computer – that continue to give us purchase on natural phenomena over long periods of time and across numerous wholesale changes in scientific theories.)

A problem with Kuhnian breaks – his paradigm shifts – is that Kuhn himself inscribes scientific practices within a totalizing narrative of conversion: one that ascribes the origin of practices and paradigms not to material or semiotic reworking of an available repertoire of practices, but starkly and simply to a radically new way of seeing. The key element here is Kuhn's insistence in *Structure* on revolutionary change – hence, also, on revolutionary practices – as rooted in *seeing*, and *not* in any species of reinterpretation, reworking, or retranscription of prior practices.[29] Like those who would assert the stability of observations – of seeing – whom he rightfully criticizes, Kuhn nonetheless accepts the premise that "interpretation" is a process that occurs *after* observation/seeing. By accepting this premise, he has no alternative but to root change in science in sudden perceptual shifts in seeing. Yet, it can be argued that how we see depends upon how we orient ourselves to the world of fluxes and flows – the phenomenal flow of experience – through what Whitehead would call "lures for feelings," or (as another, related, alternative) what I have called "performative metaphors." Such ways of orienting toward the world are also forms of making – of *poiesis* – that point to interpretation as prior to seeing, rather than simply and exclusively operating on that which is given in observation.

The seductive capacity of Kuhn's narrative in *Structure* threatens to blind us to what we might call forms of material-semiotic engagement with the flow and flux of entangled "things," relations, and processes in our experience of nature. (Semiotics is the study of signs and sign systems as they pertain to the making of meaning and production of meaningful communication. Science utilizes various sign-systems, including linguistic signs, to construct representations of natural phenomena and frame scientific explanations, and within science studies the relationship between representation and things, between language and things, between the semiotic and the material, has been a subject of considerable debate and inquiry. Indeed, the nature-culture dichotomy has often presupposed language-things and semiotic-material dichotomies.)[30] Without ascribing what I am about to suggest to Kuhn himself, such a totalizing narrative of conversion, and such an aversion to fine-grained analysis of the complexity of material-semiotic practices on the cusp of significant scientific changes within the history of science, threatens to collapse into repetition of formulaic patterns of heroic, even romanticized, models of Eureka-like discovery.

As an example, let me note in passing Richard Rorty's consideration of models of change in his *Contingency, Irony, and Solidarity*, where he speaks specifically of scientific change as *redescriptions of the world*.[31] In itself, concern with redescription is promising. Yet, for Rorty, emphasis falls less on "redescription" as a process – less, that is, on the interwoven, text-like, and contested terrain of the conceptual, material, and linguistic work involved in refashioning scientific practices that result in producing alternative descriptions – than on "redescription" as a radically different modality of change. In Rorty's vision, change is not about an extended and extensive process. Rather, select vocabularies get "in the way of each other" and a new vocabulary is then *invented* "to replace both." Thus, he claims, "revolutionary achievements ... typically occur when somebody realizes that two or more of our vocabularies are interfering with each other, and proceeds to invent a new vocabulary to replace both" (12). Rorty likens the agent of such change to the figure of the "poet" whose language-making invents new or alternative "tools." Yet, oddly enough, this description of metaphor, vocabularies, and the metaphorics of change comes perilously close to admitting no choice, *no intrinsic contest*, in the making of the new: to obscuring the textured, agonistic *work* of metaphor by eliding the arduous process of producing new vocabularies. It risks reauthorizing the view that, like genius, metaphor cannot be fathomed: that new vocabularies are simply *imposed* by creative human genius. In their insistence on the priority of seeing and/or of change-as-conversion, Kuhn and Rorty draw us dangerously close – despite disclaimers they would undoubtedly insist upon[32] – to a vision of science as hegemonically asserting the discovery of a "universal neutral key" that Isabelle Stengers has so witheringly criticized and warned against.

I'll return to Stengers presently. First, however, let me consider Gaston Bachelard, who is often cited in conjunction with Michel Foucault and Kuhn for his notion of an "epistemological break."[33] This association is something of a mischaracterization, since the "break" he points toward has less to do with an account of scientific change than it does with distinguishing science from a notion of "common sense." (According to Hans-Jörg Rheinberger, for instance, "The epistemological rupture serves to mark the transition from everyday knowledge to the act of scientific thinking.")[34] Far more interesting is Bachelard's view of science as a process and specifically of the role of scientific practices as captured in his rich notion of "phenomenotechnique." For Bachelard, scientific thinking, reason, and rationality cannot – indeed, should never – be separated from the techniques and material practices so inextricably associated with the production of scientific knowledge. All scientific knowledge then is specific and localized: as such, it is responsive both to the entanglement of "things" and to the humanly produced – the "social" – means constructed as instruments for disentangling them. To be clear, Bachelard's invocation of the social is not in service of postulating the kind of nature-society divide later criticized by Latour. His reference to the "social" points, instead, to "scientific activity" and knowledge production as a "collective enterprise," as Rheinberger remarks.[35]

"When the object under study," Bachelard writes in *Le nouvel esprit scientifique* first published in 1934, "takes the form of a complex system of relations, then it can only be apprehended by adopting an appropriate variety of methods. Objectivity cannot be separated from the social aspect of proof."[36] For Bachelard, the social with its entailment of codes, protocols, and selectivity of relations to be pursued, interrogated, and mapped opens up such objects and their relations to scrutiny and contestation. Such highly situated and constructed openings onto the world – a world populated by the flux of entangled things – strikes me as far removed from the totalizing effect of the sudden gestalt-like break or rupture characterizing postwar science studies in the immediate wake of Kuhn. Indeed, Bachelard places the making of scientific knowledge squarely within the terrain of contestation and construction:

> Scientific observation is always polemical; it either confirms or denies a prior thesis, a preexisting model, an observational protocol. It shows as it demonstrates; it establishes a hierarchy of appearances; it transcends the immediate; it reconstructs first its own models and then reality. And once the step is taken from observation to experimentation, the polemical character of knowledge stands out even more sharply. Now phenomena must be selected, filtered, purified, shaped by instruments; indeed, it may well be the instruments that produce the phenomenon in the first place. And instruments are nothing but theories materialized. The phenomena they produce bear the stamp of theory throughout.

"A truly scientific phenomenology," Bachelard concludes, "is therefore essentially a phenomenotechnology. Its purpose is to amplify what is revealed beyond appearance. It takes its instruction from construction."[37]

As Rheinberger notes, Bachelard's "technophenomena" generated by the sciences are at once "material and discursive."[38] Bachelard's understanding of science, however, is of a set of differential practices that are far removed from any universalizing and abstract characterization of "science." Indeed, it is the multiplicity of the sciences and of their practices or techniques that led him to insist upon a fine-grained analysis of what Rheinberger calls the "details of their diverse technical realizations" (316) and to characterize Bachelard's approach to the study of scientific knowledge as a "process epistemology": an "epistemology of emergence" (318)! The detailed, minute construction of knowledge in the sciences constitutes a process of "realization," rather than a simple story of discovery – whether slow and accretive or sudden and gestalt-like. As Rheinberger again notes, quoting Bachelard directly, "Science *realizes* its objects without ever finding them readymade. Phenomenotechnology *extends* phenomenology. A concept has become scientific according to the proportion to which it has become technical, to which it is accompanied by a technique of realization" (320–1).

Thinking under the Constraint of Creativity

With Bachelard's phenomenotechnology and characterization of science as process with its specificity and plurality of techniques and practices, we enter territory that bears comparison to the Whitehead-inspired work of Isabelle Stengers and that, additionally, signals the importance of resistance to epistemological breaks conceived as engines of scientific change. For Stengers, the "'cosmopolitical' proposal" she offers us "has meaning only in concrete situations where practitioners operate."[39] Like Bachelard, then, Stengers would have us in science studies enter an arena in which questions of theory are not separated from practice, most especially in service of "issues of authority." As we saw earlier in Latour and others who resist the implication found in SSK of science as grounded in and by "authorities," Stengers – building on Whitehead – questions the notion of authorities as well. Indeed, she looks instead to a "political ecology" inhabited by those who have "learned to laugh not at theories but at the authority associated with them" (994). In place of professionals who seek affirmation of their privileged perspectives on the world – who elevate and enshrine the authority of particular theories or theoretical perspectives – Stengers urges adoption of Gilles Deleuze's figure of "the idiot": that is, the "one who always slows the others down, who resists the consensual way" – dare we say, the paradigmatic way (994)! Pressing this cautionary political ecology further, she acknowledges that as students of nature "[w]e know," and furthermore that "knowledge is there, but," she insists, "the idiot demands that we slow down, that we don't consider ourselves authorized to believe we possess the meaning of what we know." In sum, Stengers insists that in the face of all the enticements to extend the reach of our theory-practices, we must instead work hard "to slow down the construction of this common world, to create a space of hesitation." Stengers's cosmopolitics[40] urges us, then, to embrace the "unknown constituted by ... multiple, divergent worlds," which, she adds, is "opposed to the temptation of a peace intended to be final, ecumenical" (995). Most of all, Stengers's cosmopolitical proposal, her embrace of the idiot and prescription to inhabit the space of hesitation, serves to counter and contain the "danger of reproducing" the all too familiar and seductive move that tempts all scientists – that threatens to mold them into mere self-affirming "professionals": namely, the common pitfall of "transforming a type of practice of which we are particularly proud into a universal neutral key, valid for all" (995).

This is a transformation, a *conversion*, if you will, that enacts and entails what Michel de Certeau points to – in the very different context of analyzing tactics of power and resistance characterizing early modern Iberian colonial domination in South America – as acts of forgetting constitutive of claims to authority asserted by those in power.[41] Such forgetting serves to "[camouflage] the conditions of the production of discourse and its object" whether that object is the subjugated indigenous American (44), or – as in the case of science studies – the established truths of a purportedly "timeless," universal scientific knowledge. In the case of Stengers's professionals and their presumptive claims to the mantle of authority, such slippage from localized practices to a "universal neutral key" masks the true, historical, and messy origins of all presumptively universal scientific theories as *ways of seeing*. Within such messy historical "origins," we find the conjunction – the mutual making – of nature-culture-society in the construction of science.

In her magisterial work, *Cosmopolitics*,[42] Isabelle Stengers attends carefully and in minute detail to the power and regional specificity of scientific practices, and thus to an understanding of scientific knowledge rooted in such practices in a manner that resists any notion of sudden and heroic breaks as the engine of change. The conjunction of localized but nonetheless powerful and productive practices with resistance to formulations of scientific change that fetishize creativity as an independent force wielded by exceptional individuals – hence, also, of the "social" as "dictating" science – reminds me of Stengers's own reflections upon Whitehead and "Thinking under the Constraint of Creativity" as pivotal to the latter's philosophy of organism.[43] In her analysis of Whitehead's account of the interplay between "reasons" that are gathered together in the becoming of his basic ontological units – which he terms actual occasions – and the "decisions" enacted in the making of such occasions, Stengers tellingly focuses upon precisely the constraint of creativity. The very way in which the many (the flux of entangled "things" and relations) become the one in the making of an actual occasion rests upon the means through which the many are gathered or held together (as the data that make up the one) in a highly specific configuration. According to Whitehead, the reasons that explain this actual entity – and, by implication, the society, enduring object, or organism it extends – are the result of a decision that "exemplifies creativity" (263). Even as the novel configuration gathers its reasons from the already-existing many, it depends upon the "subjective decision" of the emergent – the new – actual occasion in order to do so. (It is important to note that when Whitehead speaks of "subjects" and "subjectivity" he understands something quite radically different from concepts commonly found in Western philosophical traditions. The latter typically conceive of subjects as individual substances separate from other individual things, fully constituted in themselves, and encountering a world of already constituted objects. As Whitehead pithily observes, "The philosophies of substance presuppose a subject which then encounters a datum, and then reacts to the datum. The philosophy of organism presupposes a datum which is met with feelings, and progressively attains the unity of a subject. But with this doctrine, 'superject' would be a better term than subject.")[44]

Thinking under the constraint of creativity means that any reason has its limits; it cannot leap to "claim to be indubitable." All this is a consequence of holding fast to Whitehead's ontological principle, which "will demand reasons" for that which flows into the world, while also, in Stengers's riveting words, "forbidding that the slightest authority be conferred on reasons" (264). The forbidding of authority speaks volumes about the constraints of creativity, and testifies to at least some implications of Whitehead's thought for science studies. According to Stengers, for Whitehead, creativity is about the world, about what he calls "organism," about "what Deleuze and Guattari call the 'plane of immanence'" (268). It is *not* about the "adventure of creators," about those who purport to create a universal key "in the heroic mode" (272). As Stengers forcefully concludes, "When Whitehead makes creativity the ultimate, therefore, he does not particularly celebrate creators. Thinking under the constraint of creativity has nothing to do with a heroic adventure, and creativity demands nothing" (273).

This goes to the heart of Whitehead's project, his very different "adventure of a speculative cosmology," as well as to its implications for science studies and the conjoining of nature-culture-society as inseparables (274). That project recognized, as I've stressed elsewhere, that "we cannot think without abstraction." Yet, central to the Whiteheadian project, as Stengers notes, is simultaneously the insistence that "it is important to revise our modes of abstraction," and thus "not to abstract creators from the equipment on which they cannot help but rely" (274)!

The Whiteheadian prohibitions on conferring authority on reasons, on the one hand, and on celebrating the isolated, heroic, even romantic creator, on the other, should serve as bald, yet also bracing, reminder of the pitfalls that await those of us engaged in science studies. Equally important, however, is the antidote Whitehead (and, at least in part, Bachelard) prescribes for us: to attend carefully to our modes of abstraction and, especially, to the equipment – the tools, practices, and *technē* – used to study nature and thus produce the very knowledge that is the object of our interest. While Whitehead challenges us to revise our modes of abstraction and thus rethink – and "transform" – "our habits," his prescription is the very opposite of the seriousness of those "professionals" who Stengers tells us "are bereft of humor" (274). The Whiteheadian adventure of ideas is an open and playful response to the creativity exhibited concretely in the world of experience.[45] It is, I argue, opposed to the hubris of universalizing abstractions, to the hegemonic move of granting license to the imperial expansion of successful yet localized practices, to breaks – ruptures – figured as engines of change that simply conceal the local, entangled dynamics of change, and to reifying society or nature or culture as independently dictating "science" for us. Such an ontologically grounded understanding of science as practice may, then, open for us ways of thinking and practicing science studies as cultural studies.[46]

NOTES

1. See the following noteworthy volumes from the late 1980s that mark, and elucidate, this cultural turn: Lynn Hunt, ed., *The New Cultural History* (Berkeley: University of California Press, 1989); and Roger Chartier, *Cultural History: Between Practices and Representations* (Ithaca: Cornell University Press, 1988).

2. A number of these scholars are cited in the notes, below. Additionally, let me mention Mario Biagioli, Jed Buchwald, Raz Chen-Morris, Adele Clarke, Lorraine Daston, Paula Findlen, Joan Fujimura, Ofer Gal, David Gooding, Nicholas Jardine, Hannah Landecker, Timothy Lenoir, Michael Lynch, Trevor Pinch, Lissa Roberts, Simon Schaffer, James Secord, Steven Shapin, Pamela Smith, Emma Spary, and Richard Yeo, among many others.

3. See, for example, James J. Bono, "Perception, Living Matter, Cognitive Systems, Immune Networks: A Whiteheadian Future for Science Studies," *Configurations* 13 (2005): 135–81, esp. 136. More recently, the notion of an ontological turn has been picked-up by mainstream historians: Greg Anderson, "Retrieving the Lost Worlds of the Past: The Case for an Ontological Turn," *American Historical Review* 120 (2015): 787–810.

4. Joseph Rouse, "What Are Cultural Studies of Scientific Knowledge," *Configurations* 1 (1993): 1–22. Rouse's article was, indeed, the very first in this inaugural issue.

5. Rouse, "Cultural Studies of Scientific Knowledge," 7–8, 9–10, 11–12, 12–13, and 18.

6. Bruno Latour, "Why Has Critique Run Out of Steam? From Matters of Fact to Matters of Concern," *Critical Inquiry* 30 (2004): 225–48. Whitehead declares, "But in the real world it is more important that a proposition be interesting than that it be true. The importance of truth is, that it adds to interest" (Alfred North Whitehead, *Process and Reality: An Essay in Cosmology*, corrected edition, ed. David Ray Griffin and Donald W. Sherburne [New York: The Free Press, 1978], 259). For science as *poiesis* and an emphasis on science studies as positive rather than negative critique, as embracing the positivity of making, see Bono, "A Whiteheadian Future," 178, 169–170.

7. Andrew Pickering, ed., *Science as Practice and Culture* (Chicago: University of Chicago Press, 1992).

8. For an overview and introduction, see Bruno Latour, *Reassembling the Social: An Introduction to Actor-Network-Theory* (New York: Oxford University Press, 2005). Also see the introduction to the present volume.

9. Some foundational figures in SSK include Barry Barnes, *Scientific Knowledge and Sociological Theory* (London: Routledge and Kegan Paul, 1974), and *Interests and the Growth of Knowledge* (London: Routledge and Kegan Paul, 1977); David Bloor, *Knowledge and Social Imagery* (Chicago: University of Chicago Press, 1976); Harry Collins, *Changing Order: Replication and Induction in Scientific Practice* (Beverly Hills: Sage Publications, 1985); Karin Knorr-Cetina, *The Manufacture of Knowledge: An Essay on the Constructivist and Contextual Nature of Science* (Oxford: Pergamon Press, 1981); Michael Mulkay, *Science and the Sociology of Knowledge* (London: Allen and Unwin, 1979).

10. Bruno Latour and Steve Woolgar, *Laboratory Life* (Beverly Hills: Sage Publications, 1979; 2nd ed., Princeton: Princeton University Press, 1986).

11. Bruno Latour, *We Have Never Been Modern* (Cambridge: Harvard University Press, 1993).

12. Latour himself relies upon the now classic revisionist work by Steven Shapin and Simon Schaffer, *Leviathan and the Air-Pump: Hobbes, Boyle, and the Experimental Life* (Princeton: Princeton University Press, 1985). Robert Boyle (1627–91), of course, was a key figure in the so-called Scientific Revolution of the seventeenth century and member of the early Royal Society of London. On Boyle, see: Michael Hunter, *Boyle: Between God and Science* (New Haven: Yale University Press, 2009).

13. Andrew Pickering, "From Science as Knowledge to Science as Practice," in *Science as Practice and Culture*, 1–26.

14. See James J. Bono, *The Word of God and the Languages of Man: Interpreting Nature in Early Modern Science and Medicine, vol. 1, Ficino to Descartes* (Madison: University of Wisconsin Press, 1995), esp. "Galileo, Mathematics, and the Language of Nature: De-inscribing God's Book of Nature," 193–8.

15. For example, in Latour, *We Have Never Been Modern.*

16. For an approach to science studies consonant with such view, see Bono, "A Whiteheadian Future."

17. Peter Dear, "Cultural History of Science: An Overview with Reflections," *Science, Technology, and Human Values* 20 (1995): 150–70. See also Peter Dear and Sheila Jasanoff, "Dismantling Boundaries in Science and Technology Studies," *Isis* 101 (2010): 759–74.

18. For an approach arguing for the importance of the situated nature of scientific representations that ground them in specific social locations, see James J. Bono, "Locating Narratives: Science, Metaphor, Communities, and Epistemic Styles," in *Grenzüberschreitungen in der Wissenschaft: Crossing Boundaries in Science*, ed. Peter Weingart (Baden-Baden: Nomos Verlagsgesellschaft, 1995), 119–51.

19. On science studies, practices, and an emphasis on "agencies" rather than "representations" as fundamental to science, see Andrew Pickering, *The Mangle of Practice: Time, Agency, and Science* (Chicago: University of Chicago Press, 1995). Hans-Jörg Rheinberger, *Toward a History of Epistemic Things: Synthesizing Proteins in the Test Tube* (Stanford: Stanford University Press, 1997), provides a remarkably rich and sophisticated analysis of practice and the making of science, one that articulates the role and importance of representation in encountering, displaying, and dissecting agencies in scientific worldmaking. For an approach compatible with Rheinberger's, see Bono, "A Whiteheadian Future."

20. Donna J. Haraway, *Crystals, Fabrics, and Fields: Metaphors of Organicism in Twentieth-Century Developmental Biology* (New Haven: Yale University Press, 1976) [reprinted as *Crystals, Fabrics, and Fields: Metaphors that Shape Embryos* (Berkeley, Calif.: North Atlantic Books, 2004)] and *Primate Visions: Gender, Race, and Nature in the World of Modern Science* (New York: Routledge, 1989). Biopolitics has become a major area of research, discussion, and contestation within science studies and cultural studies spurred, in part, by the earlier work of Michel Foucault. See now Timothy Campbell and Adam Sitze, eds., *Biopolitics: A Reader* (Durham: Duke University Press, 2013).

21. Donna J. Haraway, "Manifesto for Cyborgs: Science, Technology, and Socialist Feminism in the 1980s," *Socialist Review* 80 (1985): 65–108, revised and

republished as "A Cyborg Manifesto: Science, Technology, and Socialist-Feminism in the late Twentieth Century," in her *Simians, Cyborgs, and Women: The Reinvention of Nature* (New York: Routledge, 1991), 149–81 and 243–8.

22. See, for example: Peter Galison, *Image and Logic: The Material Culture of Twentieth-Century Physics* (Chicago: University of Chicago Press, 1997); Peter Galison and David J. Stump, *The Disunity of Science: Boundaries, Contexts, and Power* (Stanford: Stanford University Press, 1996); Mario Biagioli, ed., *The Science Studies Reader* (New York: Routledge, 1999); and Geoffrey C. Bowker and Susan Leigh Star, *Sorting Things Out: Classification and Its Consequences* (Cambridge: MIT Press, 1999).

23. See Jan Golinski, *Making Natural Knowledge: Constructivism and the History of Science* (Cambridge: Cambridge University Press, 1998) for a thorough survey and discussion of the sea-changes occurring in the history of science – subsequently, in science studies – as a result of the turns to the social and to practice after the work of Thomas Kuhn. On page 9, Golinski refers to the "assumption that science was best regarded as a body of ideas," noting, however, that "As constructivist inquiry has unfolded ... analysts have increasingly tended toward an alternative view of science as a cluster of practices."

24. See the works by Bono, Pickering, and Rheinberger cited above (n. 19) as well as James J. Bono, "Why Metaphor? Toward a Metaphorics of Scientific Practice," in *Science Studies: Probing the Dynamics of Scientific Knowledge*, ed. Sabine Maasen and Matthias Winterhager (Bielefeld: Transcript, 2001), 215–34.

25. Bruno Latour, "The Promises of Constructivism," in *Chasing Technoscience: Matrix for Materiality*, ed. Don Ihde and Evan Selinger (Bloomington: Indiana University Press, 2003), 27–46; 31–2. In referring to "critical sociology," Latour has in mind practices like those of SSK discussed earlier.

26. Thomas S. Kuhn, *The Structure of Scientific Revolutions*, 2nd ed., enlarged (Chicago: University of Chicago Press, 1970).

27. Joseph Rouse, "Kuhn and Scientific Practices," *Configurations* 6 (1998): 33–50, part of a Special Issue on Thomas S. Kuhn edited by Nancy J. Nersessian.

28. Rheinberger, *History of Epistemic Things*, 6.

29. See especially the crucial passages in Kuhn, *Structure*, 120–3.

30. For Latour and others such dichotomies may be regarded as a consequence of the aforementioned "modern Constitution" of the seventeenth century. By insisting, instead, upon hybrid entities – complexes of meaningfully configured material objects and instruments operating in the world – science studies looks toward understanding the shifting material-semiotic entanglements exhibited by the phenomenal events studied by the sciences. Bachelard's "technophenomena" may, as we shall see, be thought of as material-semiotic entities.

31. Richard Rorty, *Contingency, Irony, and Solidarity* (Cambridge: Cambridge University Press, 1989).

32. Rorty would, and does, reject precisely such a view of science as providing descriptions or representations of a universalizable, objective natural world. (See the Introduction and Chapter 1 of his book.) On metaphor, science, and change, see James J. Bono, "Science, Discourse, and Literature: The Role/Rule of Metaphor in Science," in *Literature and Science: Theory and Practice*, ed. Stuart Peterfreund (Boston: Northeastern University Press, 1990), 59–89; and

also, Bono, "Locating Narratives"; Bono, "Why Metaphor?"; and Bono, "A Whiteheadian Future." For a more extended critical discussion of Rorty's views, see Nancy Fraser, "Solidarity or Singularity? Richard Rorty between Romanticism and Technocracy," Chapter 5 of her book, *Unruly Practices: Power, Discourse, and Gender in Contemporary Social Theory* (Minneapolis: University of Minnesota Press, 1989), 93–110.

33. While parallels are sometimes drawn between Bachelard's breaks and notions of ruptures or paradigm shifts in Kuhn and others, Bachelard's formulation of the phrase "epistemological break" is distinctive to him and carries a quite different force or meaning. See Gary Gutting, "Thomas Kuhn and French Philosophy of Science" in *Thomas Kuhn*, ed. Thomas Nickles (Cambridge: Cambridge University Press, 2003), 45–64, for a very useful discussion of the filiation and historical links between Bachelard and later thinkers. In my view, however, Gutting's attempt to elicit from Bachelard a view of scientific change compatible with, if not identical to, Kuhn goes much too far. By contrast, Hans-Jörg Rheinberger, "Gaston Bachelard: The Concept of 'Phenomenotechnique,'" Chapter 2 in his *An Epistemology of the Concrete: Twentieth-Century Histories of Life* (Durham: Duke University Press, 2010), 25–36, provides a more nuanced and accurate account of Bachelard's thought, one that I fully endorse.

34. Hans-Jörg Rheinberger, "Gaston Bachelard and the Notion of 'Phenomenotechnique,'" *Perspectives on Science* 13 (2005), 313–29, at 320. I am indebted to Rheinberger's article in this essay. See also his *On Historicizing Epistemology* (Stanford: Stanford University Press, 2010), 21–7.

35. Rheinberger, "The Concept of 'Phenomenotechnique,'" 32.

36. Gaston Bachelard, *The New Scientific Spirit* (Boston: Beacon Press, 1984), 12.

37. Bachelard, *The New Scientific Spirit*, 13. We can trace phenomenology as a term to Kant's eighteenth-century contemporaries; as a philosophical "school" or method it is generally associated with twentieth-century philosophers from Edmund Husserl to figures such as Martin Heidegger and Maurice Merleau-Ponty. While all attend, in some sense, to subjective experience and description of "phenomena" as central to the work of philosophy, the variety of concerns, problems, and approaches defy succinct characterization and will not be addressed here.

38. Rheinberger, "The Notion of 'Phenomenotechnique,'" 316.

39. Isabelle Stengers, "The Cosmopolitical Proposal," in *Making Things Public: Atmospheres of Democracy*, ed. Bruno Latour and Peter Weibel (Cambridge: MIT Press, 2005), 994–1003, 994.

40. See Isabelle Stengers, *Cosmopolitics I* (Minneapolis: University of Minnesota Press, 2010) and *Cosmopolitics II* (Minneapolis: University of Minnesota Press, 2011) for fuller articulation of the cosmopolitical. Note as well Stengers's important discussion of "political ecology" and its relation to scientific or technical practices in volume 1, 32–4.

41. Michel de Certeau, *The Practice of Everyday Life*, trans. Steven F. Rendall (Berkeley: University of California Press, 1984). For more extensive discussion of de Certeau, forgetting, and authority in connection with science studies, see

Bono, "Locating Narratives," 130–5, and Bono, "A Whiteheadian Future," 168–9.

42. Stengers, *Cosmopolitics I* and *II*.

43. Isabelle Stengers, *Thinking with Whitehead: A Free and Wild Creation of Concepts* (Cambridge: Harvard University Press, 2011), Chapter 16, 254–76. The philosophy of organism is the label Whitehead affixed to the cosmology elaborated in *Process and Reality*.

44. Whitehead, *Process and Reality*, 155.

45. See Alfred North Whitehead, *Adventures of Ideas* (New York: The Free Press, 1967).

46. See the articles contained in the *Isis* Focus section "History of Science and Literature and Science: Convergences and Divergences," ed. James J. Bono, *Isis* 101 (2010): 555–98, and, in addition to works cited earlier, Hannah Landecker, *Culturing Life: How Cells Became Technologies* (Cambridge: Harvard University Press, 2007).

9

ADAM FRANK

Reading Affect
Literature and Science after Klein and Tomkins

What can affect theory offer science studies?[1] This is at once a promising and a difficult question which asks us to think about where these two varied, vital, and notoriously multidisciplinary research domains meet, and how this meeting might be useful or fruitful. But posed this way, the question seems to grant priority to one over the other, as if that tobacco-chewing old-timer, *science studies*, wonders just what that sharply dressed new kid on the block, *affect theory*, can do. Of course, affect theory is no longer new, having emerged into the theoretical humanities twenty years ago by way of the promotion of the very different work of Gilles Deleuze and Silvan Tomkins, and having expanded to include a number of approaches to the study of affect and emotion.[2] Affect theory, in at least one of its guises and under a different name, has been around much longer than that, however, and has already played a significant role in the critical study of science and technology. The pages that follow explore an early encounter between these research domains in the work of Evelyn Fox Keller, whose field-changing contributions to feminist science studies began by making extensive use of that branch of psychoanalysis called object relations theory. Keller's work in the 1970s and '80s used psychoanalytic concepts to understand how "the cognitive claims of science are not themselves objective in origin but in fact grow out of an emotional substructure."[3] Before trying to answer this chapter's leading question, then, I will address the historical one: What has affect theory already offered science studies, feminist science studies in particular?

It is notable that Keller set these psychoanalytic commitments to one side in the 1990s. As she puts it in the introduction to *Secrets of Life, Secrets of Death* (1992), whose title essay is arguably her most profound interpretation of the emotional fantasies of modern science, "I have since [writing that essay] found it strategically impossible to proceed with psychodynamic explorations of scientific postures."[4] Keller moved away from psychoanalytic theory and an accompanying focus on gender, and toward a more thoroughgoing commitment to studying language and metaphor especially in the life sciences. At stake in this move, as Keller points out, was not the inadequacy of psychoanalysis but the changing orientation toward subjectivity itself in the humanities and social sciences of the time.

> For both good and bad reasons, most historians, philosophers, and sociologists of science have come to regard psychoanalysis, and even the very idea of the individual subject on which it depends, as something of an embarrassment. However... the "subject" on which at least traditional psychoanalysis depends is in no sense either independent of or an alternative to other forms of social structure (or "discourse"): Individual subjects are as much constituted by social structures as social structures are constituted by individual subjects, and the occlusion of one is as serious an error as the occlusion of the other, in science studies as elsewhere. Psychoanalysis, despite its problems and deficiencies, continues to provide some of our only tools for thinking about both individual and collective subjectivities (8–9).

By the early 1990s, psychoanalysis was (and had been for some time) losing its authoritative position across the disciplines in part because it was perceived to prioritize universalized subjects over contingent, historical structures. Its more thoughtful detractors suggested that psychoanalytic explanations, by moving too quickly between general human developmental trajectories and individual experiences, beliefs, and feelings, failed to capture cultural difference and historical change across and within groups or collectives. Nevertheless, Keller thought that an improved psychoanalysis should continue to play a significant role in any reciprocal account of the relations between subjects and collectives. At the same time she sought a way to bring nature back into science studies: "Where, and how, does the nonlinguistic realm we call *nature* enter into that process [the generation of knowledge]? How do 'nature' and 'culture' interact in the production of scientific knowledge?" (36).[5]

Just after Keller moved away from psychoanalysis (however begrudgingly) we see the emergence of affect theory with its keen interest precisely in the nonlinguistic aspects of aesthetic and epistemological experience, its attempt to conceptualize a role for biological and physiological knowledges in the humanities and social sciences, and its exploration of new tools for articulating connections and continuities between individual and collective experience. How might more recent affect theory help to develop the reciprocal explanatory accounts of scientific knowledge that Keller and other science studies practitioners seek? This chapter aims to answer this question by offering a reading of Keller's early work *A Feeling for the Organism* (1983) alongside several of her essays in *Reflections on Gender and Science* (1985). I make use of Silvan Tomkins's ideas as well as those of Melanie Klein and Wilfred Bion, Anglo-American writing that offers substantial, unorthodox revisions of Freud. Keller's own writings are endebted to a related but distinct branch of psychoanalytic theory, the work of D. W. Winnicott and other Independent Group object relations theorists, as well as to feminist uptakes of these thinkers. With the exception of the remarkable essay "From Secrets of Life to Secrets of Death" (to which I will return below), Keller's writing is more concerned with developmental schemas than it is with the epistemological questions that accompany an attention to Kleinian psychic dynamics. Affect theory, this chapter argues, can offer science studies a way to address the overlooked topic of subjectivity – to assess the roles of feeling, style, and motive in scientific thinking – as well as a way to take into account the performativity of our own interpretations. Perhaps a contemporary critical approach to Literature and Science can (re)introduce these ways of paying attention into science studies.

Subjectivity Out of Style

Keller's *A Feeling for the Organism: The Life and Work of Barbara McClintock*, first published in 1983, is many things: a biography of an important geneticist; a historical examination of changing career possibilities for women scientists in the twentieth-century United States; an intellectual overview of distinct, at times competing methodological and conceptual approaches to genetics; and a case study of consensus and dissent in science.[6] It is also, and for my purposes most importantly, a feminist analysis of the emotional dynamics at the root of scientific practice. Born in 1902, Barbara McClintock achieved remarkable success during the 1930s in the fields of cytology and genetics with her studies of the maize plant. A key figure in establishing "the chromosomal basis of genetics" (4), McClintock's importance was quickly recognized (she was elected to the National Academy of Sciences in 1944 and became president of the Genetics Society of America in 1945) but, as a woman scientist with limited career options, never secured a permanent university position. She accepted a full time research position at the Long Island Biological Laboratories at Cold Spring Harbor, a well-established if somewhat isolated research facility. Keller's book offers a rich, detailed account of McClintock's work, especially in the context of the emergence and success of molecular biology best represented by James Watson and Francis Crick's discovery of the role of DNA in the replication of genetic material in 1953. McClintock's work did not fit with the physics-inspired methods of molecular biology and its "central dogma,"

178

the unidirectional flow of information from DNA to RNA to protein. While she arrived at conclusions similar to the well-received work of Jacques Monod and François Jacob on the control mechanisms for protein production, her work contradicted the central dogma and was not understood. Only when the ideas she introduced concerning genetic transposition could be articulated in the language of molecular biology (in the mid-1970s) would McClintock's work be recognized and integrated into mainstream genetic research, leading to substantial acknowledgment (including a Nobel Prize in 1983).

Keller's book could be described as an investigation into distinct and competing paradigms in genetics, with the midcentury move toward molecular biology an example of the kind of paradigm shift that Thomas Kuhn made famous in *The Structure of Scientific Revolutions* (1962). In the book's preface, however, Keller distances her work from the Kuhnian focus on "the dynamics by which the [scientific] community forms and reforms itself" (xxi), focusing instead on an individual scientist in order to investigate "the nature of scientific knowledge and the tangled web of individual and group dynamics that define its growth" (xx). Here Keller evokes Charles Darwin's famous image of the tangled bank, an exemplary figure for the fundamental complexity and idiosyncrasy of relations between organism and environment. While McClintock's commitment to understanding the complexity of organisms in their contexts becomes an explicit theme in the book's final chapter, Keller's own commitment to these complex relations is everywhere expressed in the book's method and structure. Her ethnographic intellectual history (she interviewed McClintock and her family members, friends, and colleagues) weaves individual recollections together with larger histories of the institutions of scientific knowledge in a subtle and nuanced manner. What emerges is both McClintock's exemplarity as a superb scientist and, at the same time, her idiosyncrasy or status as a self-described "maverick."

Keller's focus on one woman's personal experience as indexing larger social and political structures is clearly informed by 1970s American feminism. At the same time, it is informed by the longer tradition of American Transcendentalism. Keller quotes Ralph Waldo Emerson's essay "Nature" in a discussion of McClintock's relationship with vision (118), and the portrait that emerges of this remarkably stubborn and independent-minded Yankee scientist reminded this reader of two other unusual women affiliated with that tradition and its aftermath, Emily Dickinson and Gertrude Stein. Keller's sensibility is broadly literary critical in that she explores (or reads) the work of an individual scientist (or author) to discover something about the workings of science more generally. Her important term is *style*: Keller examines McClintock's scientific style, her way of "synthesizing the uniquely twentieth-century focus on experiment with the naturalist's emphasis on observation ... What for others is interpretation, or speculation, for her is a matter of trained and direct perception" (xxi). This style of doing science is a consequence of an intimate relationship with the maize plant, a relationship that McClintock herself calls "a feeling for the organism." Keller's primary object of study, then, and the title of her book, is McClintock's scientific style and the nature of those emotional dynamics that, Keller suggests, should be exemplary of scientific practice: "like all good scientists, her understanding emerges from a thorough absorption in, even identification with, her material" (xxii).

The precise nature of McClintock's identification comes into focus in several key quotations. Consider first her orientation toward problem-solving with respect to "the whole picture": "What's compelling in these cases is that the problem is sharp and clear. The problem ... fits into the whole picture, and you begin to look at it as a whole ... So you get a feeling for the whole situation of which this is [only] a component part" (67). This orientation toward the whole organism and the functions of its various parts is accompanied by detailed micro-attention. McClintock responded to a colleague's wonder at her skilled use of the microscope this way: "Well, you know, when I look at a cell, I get down into that cell and look around" (69). As Keller puts it, this "dialectic between two opposing tendencies" (101) defines McClintock's style: "It was her conviction that the closer her focus, the greater her attention to individual detail ... the more she could learn about the general principles by which the maize plant as a whole was organized, the better her 'feeling for the organism'" (101). Keller recounts several stories of successful problem-solving, one of which involves the scientist's uncanny ability to assess structural alterations in a given plant's chromosomes by simply looking at the kernels of the plants themselves. McClintock accounts for this ability by comparing her mind to a computer: "'Without being able to know what it was I was integrating, I *understood* the phenotype.' What does understanding mean here? 'It means that I was using a computer that was working very rapidly and very perfectly'" (103). McClintock's mind works like a computational agent, processing and integrating vast amounts of data without conscious help; impressive qualitative results emerge from quantitative calculations that take place automatically (or unconsciously), a consequence of McClintock's proximity to and familiarity with her object of study. Thus the basis of McClintock's peculiar style is an identification that she permits to take place between two complex systems, her mind (qua computer) and the maize plant: "Her respect for the unfathomable workings of the mind was matched by her regard for the complex workings of the plant" (105).[7]

In the terms of affect theory, I would describe McClintock as entering a fully transferential relation with her object of study. Transference, in psychoanalysis, names "the terrain on which all the basic problems of a given analysis play themselves out: the establishment, modalities, interpretation and resolution of the transference are in fact what define the cure."[8] Classically, in Freud's work, the transference refers to the relationship between analyst and analysand in which the patient displaces childhood feelings of love and hate for a parent or caregiver onto the doctor. In Melanie Klein's understanding, these transferential relations draw on even earlier experiences of the infant with the mother, in particular with the breast that feeds and comforts (or fails to feed and comfort) the infant. These early experiences, Klein suggests, determine object relations that are comprised of projective and introjective identifications, psychic processes based on the infant's fundamental somatic experiences of taking something into the body and expelling something out of the body. For Klein, adult mental life is characterized by the continuous to-and-fro movements of projective and introjective identification, psychic movements of affect and feeling among and between selves and others that are based on early infantile experience. In his work during the 1960s and '70s, Wilfred Bion, one of Klein's most influential followers, used Klein's ideas to develop an innovative account of thinking based on the to-and-fro movements of identification that involves one set of ideas going to pieces before a new set of ideas can be synthesized or integrated around a "selected fact": "The selected fact is the name of an emotional experience, the emotional experience of a sense of discovery of coherence; its significance is therefore epistemological."[9]

McClintock's emphasis on integrating data unconsciously and the emotional aspects of problem-solving resonate with Bion's theory of the necessary roles that projective and introjective identification play in coming to knowledge, that is, the emotional aspects of thinking. Consider McClintock's response to a particularly recalcitrant problem. At first, "I wasn't seeing things, I wasn't integrating" (115), but after a short walk that permits her to experience some grief ("she 'let the tears roll a little'" [115]), she comes to think about the problem in a new way: "I must have done this very intense, subconscious thinking. And suddenly I knew everything was going to be just fine" (115). As Keller puts it, "She had brought about a change in herself that enabled her to see more clearly, 'reorienting' herself in such a way that she could immediately 'integrate' what she saw" (117). This reorientation leads to new perceptions when McClintock looks again at the chromosomes under the microscope:

> I found that the more I worked with them the bigger and bigger [they] got, and when I was really working with them I wasn't outside, I was down there. I was part of the system. I was right down there with them, and everything got big. I even was able to see the internal parts of the chromosomes – actually every-thing was there. It surprised me because I actually felt as if I were right down there and these were my friends (117).

Here is a childlike experience, the intense absorption that accompanies play and the to-and-fro of projective and introjective identification with a toy or miniature figure. Keller goes on: "She was talking about the deepest and most personal dimension of her experience as a scientist. A little later she spoke of the 'real affection' one gets for the pieces that 'go together': 'As you look at these things, they become part of you. And you forget yourself. The main thing about it is that you forget your-self'" (117).

Keller suggests that McClintock's scientific style is based on a set of emotional dispositions that she had developed as a child and that were reinforced by her experiences as a woman scientist: autonomy, self-determination, and the "capacity to be alone." This last phrase, the title of an early biographical chapter on McClinctock's family background, childhood, and adolescence, is also the title of an essay by D. W. Winnicott, one of the only citations to psychoanalytic writing in Keller's book.[10] Like Bion, Winnicott built on the work of Melanie Klein, especially her analysis of children using play technique and focus on early infantile relations with the mother. Unlike Bion, however, Winnicott rejected Klein's emphasis on the role of constitutional factors, especially aggression and the death instinct, in early development. Along with W. R. D. Fairbairn, Michael Balint, and John Bowlby, Winnicott belonged to the Independent Group, those analysts in the British Psychoanalytic Society who broke away from both the Kleinians and the Freudians.[11] Winnicott's ideas are in the background of Keller's depictions of McClintock's unusual self-sufficiency as a child, her tomboy identifications and, later, disinterest in conventional sexual trajectories, as well as her ability to become entirely absorbed in intellectual activity – even to the point where she forgets her own name. McClintock maintained a "childlike capacity for absorption throughout her adult life" (36), a capacity, Keller suggests, that served as "a wellspring of her creative imagination in science" (36).

An Improved Psychoanalysis

In *Reflections on Gender and Science*, published two years after the book on McClintock, Keller made explicit her psychoanalytic approach to the "emotional substructure" of science.[12] In several richly detailed and somewhat technical essays Keller brings together questions of objectivity in science with questions of objectification in psychic development, that is, the ways that infants and children come to perceive and acquire knowledge of objects in the world. I will briefly unfold the elements of Keller's use of this complex theory in a selective summary; my aim is to propose what I hope is a more helpful set of concepts for science studies that emerge from the work of Klein, Bion, and Tomkins. Keller's goal in these essays is twofold. Her first, diagnostic goal is to show how "the ideology of modern science ... carries within it its own form of projection: the projection of disinterest, of autonomy, of alienation" (70). In "Gender and Science," Keller uses classical Freudian theory to suggest that "our earliest experiences incline us to associate the affective and cognitive posture of objectification with the masculine, while all processes that involve a blurring of the boundary between subject and object tend to be associated with the feminine" (87). What follows from this, at least in classical Oedipal development, is a strict identification of the (boy) child with paternal authority to defend itself against being absorbed by the maternal environment, an absorption that is both desired and forbidden. But Keller turns away from Freud and toward Winnicott to show how the child's need to separate itself from its mother need not result in such a stark, gendered opposition. Winnicott's ideas about transitional objects and the potential space between infant and mother permit Keller to distinguish between an emotional maturity that can "allow for that vital element of ambiguity at the interface between subject and object" (84) and a more rigid or static psychic autonomy in which "objective reality is perceived and defined as radically divided from the subjective" (84).

Keller's second goal, then, which she pursues alongside her diagnostic one, is to develop alternatives to traditionally masculinist, alienated forms of scientific subjectivity and the forms of domination over nature that accompany these. In "Dynamic Autonomy: Objects as Subjects" and "Dynamic Objectivity: Love, Power, and Knowledge," Keller reconceptualizes autonomy and objectivity in a way that retains their value for science but tempers their emotional foundations. Again, Winnicott is important for this sketch of "a dynamic conception of autonomy [that] leaves unchallenged a 'potential space' between self and other ... [and] allows the temporary suspension of boundaries between 'me' and 'not-me' required for all empathic experience – experience that allows for the creative leap between knower and known"

(99). Keller turns to other analysts of the Independent Group (such as Fairbairn) as well as feminist writers who take up this analytic tradition (Nancy Chodorow, Carol Gilligan, Jessica Benjamin) to develop a revised account of autonomy that permits the more flexible identifications between subject and object that she sees McClintock engaging in. For Keller, dynamic objectivity names "a pursuit of knowledge that makes use of subjective experience . . . in the interests of a more effective objectivity" (117); similarly, dynamic autonomy acknowledges dependency relations with the maternal/natural environment even as it acknowledges the independence of this reality.

As important as Keller's use of these Independent Group theorists may be, I am not convinced by the particular account of development she gives, and I wonder especially at her choice to avoid the theory of Melanie Klein. Keller reproduces the struggle in classical Freudian theory to understand the emergence of the distinction between self and other and hence relationality as such. But for Kleinians, object relations exist from birth, as Robert Hinshelwood explains: "the ego exists at birth, has a boundary and identifies objects."[13] The infant may experience more integrated or more fragmented ego states, but these are infantile phantasies of integrity or fragmentation rather than any properties of the ego as described from a metapsychological perspective (that is, from the perspective of the analyst as theorist). As the infant matures, it develops through stages of increased stability or integration, established in often-difficult relation to the ego's self-splitting due to powerful destructive tendencies. Klein took up Freud's notion of the death instinct to explain and characterize these destructive tendencies, and proposed that at around the middle of the first year of life, the infant moves from one set of defenses against destructive impulses, what she called the paranoid-schizoid position (characterized by an intensive splitting of good objects from bad), toward another set of defenses associated with what she called the depressive position. In this position, "The good breast and the bad breast begin to be understood not as separate and incompatible experiences, but as different features of the mother as a more complex other, with a subjectivity of her own."[14]

Keller's criticism of object relations theory, that it fails "to perceive the mother as subject" (72), precisely overlooks the insight of the depressive position: Klein's idea that the infant begins to integrate what it had previously perceived as entirely good and entirely bad part-objects into a newly perceived, damaged or contaminated, but more realistic and separate whole object. Klein's account would have been helpful to Keller in that it avoids what she sees as a "fundamental flaw" of psychoanalysis, "the theory's preoccupation with autonomy as a developmental goal and its corresponding neglect of connectedness to others" (72). Indeed, the Kleinian focus on the idea of *position* rather than developmental *phase* or *stage* offers a route toward the dynamism Keller seeks in her descriptions of qualified forms of autonomy and objectivity. For Klein, psychic experience (of infant, child, and adult alike) is characterized by a fluctuating temporality: an individual may return again and again to dynamics characteristic of the paranoid-schizoid position (such as splitting), or to those associated with the depressive position (such as depressive anxiety and impulses to repair the object).[15] It is this fluctuating temporality that permits Bion to articulate his theory of thinking in terms of a movement back-and-forth between the relatively unintegrated psychic elements in the paranoid-schizoid position and the relatively more integrated elements in the depressive position around a "selected fact," and to consider thinking itself as suffused with motivation and emotional experience.

"My use of psychoanalytic theory," asserts Keller, "is premised on the belief that, even with its deficiencies, it has the potential for self-correction" (73). Keller treats psychoanalytic theory and practice as a helpful set of tools, "with the understanding that all its terms are subject to revision as we proceed" (73), revisions which themselves depend on new empirical and theoretical work by "the many other scholars thinking about the same issues" (73). My return to, as well as criticism of, Keller's use of object relations theory supports this attitude toward psychoanalysis. Specifically, I am suggesting that the Kleinian/Bionian branch of object relations theory, especially in its concerns with epistemology, has more to offer science studies than the Independent Group theorists. As I mentioned above, one main point of disagreement between these approaches is the value of Freud's idea of the death instinct. The Kleinians seem to be the only analysts to have accepted and elaborated this idea in their work. In my own critical and theoretical speculations I have proposed recasting at least some of the phenomena that Klein associated with the death instinct in Silvan Tomkins's terms of a variety of innate, negative affects that threaten any sense the infant (and sometimes the adult) may have of a more coherent and integrated self. According to Tomkins, whose theory of the affect system offers an alternative to Freud's drive theory, the negative affects may accompany experiences of extreme bodily destabilization: the rending cries of grief, the burning explosions of rage, the shrinking or vanishing compressions of terror, the transgression of the boundary between inside and outside the body in retching or disgust, all these wreak havoc with any more integrated body image or sense of self that the infant is in process of developing. Generally, I have found Tomkins's theorization of the affects compatible with and complementary to Kleinian/Bionian theory, especially insofar as both lines of thinking explore how affects motivate the constitution, maintenance, and dissociation of objects.[16]

Letting the Material Tell You Where to Go

Returning to Keller's book on McClintock with some of Tomkins's ideas in mind, consider the presence of the feeling of joy in the scientist's description of her work on transposition, work which took years to develop:

> It never occurred to me that there was going to be any stumbling block. Not that I had the answer, but [I had] the joy of going at it. When you have that joy, you do the right experiments. You let the material tell you where to go, and it tells you at every step what the next has to be because you're integrating with an overall new pattern in mind. You're not following an old one; you are convinced of a new one (125).

For Tomkins, positive affect plays a significant role in infant perception: he proposes that the affect of interest-excitement sustains infant attention and motivates "perceptual sampling," while enjoyment-joy lets the perception of an object remain in awareness longer, motivating a return to what is emerging, in perception, as a bounded object.[17] Joy, in this account, accompanies and indexes a recognition (of pattern, shape, volume, and so on) intimately tied to cognition and the act of composing new objects in perception. This recognition takes place in the midst of the infant's confusion and distractibility when faced with the enormous variety and complexity of environmental stimuli. Keller describes the tendency in McClintock's work for "complexity and confusion ... to grow rather than diminish. But there was always a direction in which she was headed" (126), a direction determined in part by her confidence and joy in "let[ting] the material tell you where to go" (125).

By contrast with the midcentury molecular biologists whose brash and irreverent confidence came from their powerfully simple models and their excitement at "turning biology into what they regarded as a bona fide science" (181), McClintock's remarkable confidence is based on her commitment to the fundamental complexity and strangeness of nature. "There's no such thing as a central dogma into which everything will fit," she insists. "It turns out that any mechanism you can think of, you will find – even if it's the most bizarre kind of thinking ... So if the material tells you, 'It may be this,' allow that. Don't turn it aside and call it an exception, an aberration, a contaminant" (179). For Keller, McClintock's embrace of the complexity of her object of study, her rejection of reductive, purifying models of explanation, and her naturalist methods of observation are all part of her scientific style. In the final chapter Keller describes this style in terms of "a special kind of sympathetic understanding" for which "the objects of her study have become subjects in their own right: they claim for her a kind of attention that most of us experience only in relation to other persons. 'Organism' is for her a code word ... the name of a living form, of object-as-subject" (200). Keller concludes her study with a call for a "deep reverence for nature, a capacity for union with that which is to be known" (201) as alternatives to science's traditional obsessions with domination, and considers McClintock's different images for control: Tibetan monks who have learned to regulate body temperature, hypnotic practices that experiment with control of autonomic bodily processes. These are versions of control that begin from subjective bodily experiences and, what accompanies this, an empathic identification between subject and object.

Currently several strands of science studies echo such an insistence on empathy, on holistic ways of knowing, and on cultivating a "love affair with the world" (205) (Keller cites the psychoanalyst Phyllis Greenacre here). While I find it impossible not to support such ideas in principle, I am skeptical about the performative value of such exhortations. At the same time, I am not convinced by any account of scientific knowledge that leaves out an understanding of those destructive impulses that, from a Kleinian perspective, play a crucial role in the urge to know or (what Klein called, after Freud) epistemophilia. Keller addresses precisely such questions of the role of destructive impulses in science in her essay "From Secrets of Life to Secrets of Death."[18] Here she describes a fundamental fantasy of modern science: to take over female procreative function, often through male anal power. Keller reads this fantasy by exploring the discourse of secrets (whether of life, death, or nature) across several images, stories, and cultural locations, including the Manhattan Project and the Watson-Crick discovery, as they express what she calls "womb envy," a concept that she interprets by turning to Klein's conceptualization of envy as the desire to spoil the good object precisely in its capacities to create and sustain life: "Whether supplanted by fantasies of anal production or by a light/life-generating activity of the mind, the real life-giving power of the woman – often indeed women themselves – is effectively absented ... [or] actively spoiled" (51). Sweeping, compelling, and incisive though Keller's account is, she nonetheless concludes the essay by questioning the value of its analysis: "Surely, the fantasies I describe can neither be seen as causal (in any primary sense) nor as inconsequential. Where then ... are we to place the role of such fantasies – fantasies that are in one sense private, but at the same time collectively enforced, even exploited, by collateral interests?" (55).

Recall, only after writing this essay did Keller move away from psychoanalytic discourse, as if her discovery of the central role for anality in the fantasies of science and technology proved too "embarrassing" to historians, philosophers, and sociologists of science.[19] Interestingly, in a curious analogy to McClintock, whose naturalist methods were displaced by the theoretical successes of molecular biology, Keller's own critical feminist blend of Marxism and psychoanalysis was displaced by a powerful sociological constructivism that obscured the role of subjectivity in any understanding of science. This obscuring of subjectivity in science studies continues today: some of the several recent turns to ontology across the theoretical humanities (especially those committed to "objects") are distinctly shy of, or embarrassed by, the possibility that affect and fantasy play important roles in creating or composing objects in, of, and for science. Indeed, it is surprising how little substantive, positive attention has been given in science studies to questions of subjectivity, by contrast with the considerable attention given either to questions of *the subject*, or to subjectivity as what must be controlled, managed, or bracketed in the development of varieties of *objectivity*.[20] Relatedly, it is not common to find science studies scholars discussing affect, aesthetics, or style as integral to practices and theories of knowledge-making in the sciences. Steven Shapin has made a similar point in the context of an argument for taking taste seriously as an object of study.[21] My own motivation in returning to Keller has been to reactivate a concern with subjectivity, to propose a helpful set of tools and terms to assist with this concern, and to remind science studies scholars of the necessary imbrication of epistemology with ontology in any critical approach to science.[22]

Finally, to answer the question that begins this chapter: Affect theory offers several things to science studies, and, in particular, a contemporary science studies that has not often made use of the enriched notions of subjectivity that have been available to scholars of literature and media. First, it foregrounds the basic (Marxist-materialist) premise that science is done by individuals as well as collectives, in historical and institutional circumstances over which they have limited control, and in which circumstances they nonetheless make consequential choices. These choices, which may or may not be experienced as choices, result in specific scientific styles; and these styles can be described and analyzed using the vocabulary of affect theory. Second, in addition to offering tools and techniques for describing scientific styles, affect theory can help us to investigate the role of negative and positive affects in the composition of objects of scientific knowledge, as well as the role of destructive and creative fantasies in motivating scientific knowledge. Third, affect theory emphasizes, not historical or developmental schemas but the variable temporalities and fluctuations of motivation, and the role these temporalities play in thinking and coming to knowledge. Finally, affect theory can and should accompany a critical attention to the performativity of analysis itself. Consider, in this context, the basic goal of interpretation in Kleinian therapy: to open up a space in which the most destructive impulses can be voiced and entertained so that the analysand can be free to engage in more varied creative and reparative activities. The main way of assessing whether an interpretation is correct is if it has beneficial effect for the analysand. To bring this fundamentally performative criterion into science studies would be to ask: When can the communication of an interpretation or analysis of science be beneficial, and when not? Not all interpretations need to be conveyed; sometimes, holding back interpretation may lead to its fuller development or to the discovery of circumstances that permit its communication to be more effective. Affect theory fosters ways of paying a refined and technical attention to the subjective and intersubjective aspects of knowledge-making in the sciences as well as in science studies.

NOTES

1. Thanks to Lisa Cartwright for asking me this question several years ago at the Science Studies Colloquium Series at the University of California, San Diego. This essay is a belated answer.
2. The emergence of affect theory in the humanities is often conveniently dated to the publication of two essays in 1995, Brian Massumi's "The Autonomy of Affect," *Cultural Critique* 31 (Autumn 1995), 83–109; and Eve Kosofsky Sedgwick and Adam Frank, "Shame in the Cybernetic Fold: Reading Silvan Tomkins," *Critical Inquiry* 21.2 (Winter 1995), 496–522. The large number of publications since, including *The Affect Theory Reader*, ed. Melissa Gregg and Gregory J. Seigworth (Durham: Duke University Press, 2010) and a handful of critiques of the affective turn, signals a consolidation of the field. At the same time, the lack of consensus concerning a theory of affect and the sheer variety of approaches undermine any sense of consolidation. My writing here focuses on the work of Silvan Tomkins, Melanie Klein, and Wilfred Bion. Other orientations toward affect theory would approach science studies differently.
3. Evelyn Fox Keller, *Reflections on Gender and Science* (New Haven: Yale University Press, 1985), 96.
4. Evelyn Fox Keller, *Secrets of Life, Secrets of Death: Essays on Language, Gender and Science* (New York: Routledge, 1992), 8.
5. In this she was not alone: Bruno Latour's concept of "circulating reference" (and his actor-network theory, more generally) and Andrew Pickering's notion of "the mangle" were both attempts to understand the complex reciprocal relations between and among what earlier sociologists of science tended to describe in terms of subjects and structures, not to mention nature(s). See Latour, "Circulating Reference: Sampling the Soil in the Amazon Forest," in *Pandora's Hope: Essays on the Reality of Science Studies* (Cambridge: Harvard University Press, 1999), 24–79, and Pickering, *The Mangle of Practice: Time, Agency, and Science* (Chicago: University of Chicago Press, 1995).
6. Evelyn Fox Keller, *A Feeling for the Organism: The Life and Work of Barbara McClintock* (New York: W. H. Freeman, 1983).

7. McClintock's mind-computer analogy, which took place in conversation with Keller in the 1970s, would have been unlikely in the 1930s when she was doing her earlier work on maize chromosomes. At that moment a "computer" most often meant a woman doing calculations by longhand. Thanks to Elizabeth Wilson for pointing out this anachronism to me.

8. Laplanche and Pontalis, *The Language of Psycho-Analysis*, trans. Donald Nicholson-Smith (New York: Norton, 1973), 455.

9. Wilfred Bion, *Learning from Experience* (London: Karnac Books, 1984), 73.

10. D.W. Winnicott, "The Capacity To Be Alone," *International Journal of Psychoanalysis* 39.5 (1958): 416–20. Winnicott is best known for his concept of the transitional object and the emergence of a holding environment between the "good-enough" mother and the infant that permits optimal development. See the essays collected in *Playing and Reality* (London: Tavistock, 1971).

11. This three-way split was a result of a series of debates that culminated in the Controversial Discussions of the early 1940s. See Pearl King and Rocardo Steiner, eds., *The Freud-Klein Controversies 1941–45* (London: Routledge, 1992). For a useful survey of the differences and relations between these and other branches of psychoanlaytic thought, see Stephen Mitchell and Margaret Black, *Freud and Beyond* (New York: Basic Books, 1995).

12. Evelyn Fox Keller, *Reflections on Gender and Science* (New Haven: Yale University Press, 1985), 96. See the introduction and three essays in "Part Two: The Inner World of Subjects and Objects."

13. Robert Hinshelwood, *A Dictionary of Kleinian Thought* (London: Free Association Books, 1991), 284. See the entries for "Ego" and "Self."

14. Mitchell and Black, *Freud and Beyond*, 94.

15. For an essay that argues for the relevance of these Kleinian positions for criticism, see Eve Kosofsky Sedgwick, "Paranoid Reading and Reparative Reading, or, You're so Paranoid, You Probably Think This Essay Is About You," in *Touching Feeling: Affect, Pedagogy, Performativity* (Durham: Duke University Press, 2003), 123–51.

16. For more on the compatibility between the work of Tomkins and Klein, as well as what I call "the compositional aspect of affect in perception," see the chapter on "Thinking Confusion" in my *Transferential Poetics, from Poe to Warhol* (New York: Fordham University Press, 2015).

17. On the roles of the positive affects in infant perception, see Silvan S. Tomkins, *Affect Imagery Consciousness, vol. 1, The Positive Affects* (Oxford: Springer, 1962), 347–9, 487–9.

18. In *Secrets of Life, Secrets of Death*. Also published in Mary Jacobus, Evelyn Fox Keller, and Sally Shuttleworth, eds., *Body/Politics: Women and the Discourses of Science* (New York: Routledge, 1990), 177–91.

19. Recall, too, that this is the same moment (circa 1990) as the emergence of queer theory, that form of interdisciplinary scholarship that, in its focus on sexuality and fantasy in developing anti-homophobic critical, philosophical, and pedagogical projects, similarly provoked embarrassment in the academy and beyond.

20. For examples of these approaches, see Ian Hacking, *Rewriting the Soul* (Princeton: Princeton University Press, 1995); and Lorraine Daston and Peter Galison, *Objectivity* (Cambridge: MIT Press, 2007).

21. Steven Shapin, "The Sciences of Subjectivity," in *Social Studies of Science* (2012) 42.2: 170–84.
22. To expand briefly on this last point: while remaining largely agnostic about the recent proliferation of ontological approaches, I am drawn to those that bear some genealogical relation to the traditions of US pragmatism (especially the work of William James) and the alternative forms of empiricism that accompany studies of affect and emotion in the nineteenth and twentieth centuries. My thinking along these lines has been informed by Steven Meyer's account of "poetic science" in *Irresistible Dictation: Gertrude Stein and the Correlations of Writing and Science* (Stanford: Stanford University Press, 2001).

PART IV

In Practice
Literary Studies and Science

10

WAI CHEE DIMOCK

The Global Turn
Thoreau and the Sixth Extinction

My essay is a meditation on Thoreau in the context of climate change and the loss of biodiversity, a global turn of events from which no one is exempt. In thinking about this as a development extending from the nineteenth century to our own time, I would like to begin at some distance from Thoreau, with a recent work by an ecomusicologist, Bernie Krause's *The Great Animal Orchestra* (2012).[1] Krause is something of a cult figure to music fans: the last guitarist recruited by the Weavers to replace Pete Seeger, he teamed up a bit later, with Paul Beaver, to form the legendary synthesizer team Beaver and Krause, providing electronic music for films such as *Rosemary's Baby* and *Apocalypse Now*. For the past forty years, though, his work has been primarily in bioacoustics, focusing especially on the sound ecology of endangered habitats. Wild Sanctuary, his natural soundscape collection, now has over 4,000 hours of recordings of over 15,000 species.[2]

Krause tells us that animals consistently outperform us when it comes to sound: they both hear and vocalize better than we do, and can also do more with sound than we can. One example he gives is the sound camouflage perfected by the spadefoot toad. This amphibian species, like many animals in the wild, does not vocalize separately, but does so as a group, "a synchronous chorus assuring a seamless protective acoustic texture" (178). Through this sound aggregation, they prevent predators such as foxes, coyotes, and owls from pouncing on one particular victim, since no single individual stands out.

Unfortunately, the complexity of this camouflage is such that any human interference, any artificially generated noise that falls outside the usual sound spectrum within this particular environment, is likely to disrupt it and undermine its working. Krause starts with this marvelous sound engineering, but by the time he is done it is no longer a happy story. When a military jet flew "low over the terrain nearly four miles west of the site," the sound camouflage was thrown off kilter. It took the toads between thirty to forty-five minutes to rebuild it. Krause reports, "My wife and I watched from our nearby campsite as a pair of coyotes and a great horned owl swept in to pick off a few toads during their attempts to reestablish vocal synchronicity" (180–1).

The death of a few spadefoot toads is probably no major disaster, but the larger narrative that comes out of *The Great Animal Orchestra* is disturbing in more ways than one, with an intimated ending that probably none of us would want to hear in full. Something much larger, more systemic, and more destructive than military jets is preying on these sound ecologies, upsetting their delicate balance, making them less and less able to function as they used to. Almost half of the habitats in which Krause made his recordings have now been seriously compromised or destroyed. His audio archives are all that is left of those once sound-rich environments.

Frogs Croaking

Bernie Krause is writing at a point in time when elegy is almost a default genre, one that speaks not only to our private and personal losses, but also to those losses that are sustained by the planet as a whole. While "elegy" is sometimes defined strictly, as a particular kind of lyric lamenting the death of a public personage or a loved one, historically it has been a broader genre, a meditation on nonsurvival, an *ubi sunt* tally of what was gone, common in Old English, and also in Norse, Homeric Greek, Hebrew, and Sanskrit.[3] At the same time, the genre has also been understood, from the very first, to have implications for those still on this earth, left to do the lamenting. "Elegies are for the living," Stuart Curran writes, "but how and why so can be a point of some dispute." And while the genre can be made to "cover any number of possible permutations," its principal charge is to speak for all humanity on the ground of our shared losses, to remind us that we are no longer defined by a "vital and buoyant present tense, but by what has been eroded from us and is left only in our memories, to taunt us with its inevitable absence."[4]

More recently, Timothy Morton has argued that elegy is a "quintessential mode of ecological writing," at work in prose no less than in poetry, to be found in the writings of Rachel Carson and the Dalai Lama no less than in Shelley and Keats. For elegy to address climate change, however, it must dwell in more than just one verb tense, looking both forward and backward, gesturing both to what could have been and to what might yet be. It must "mourn for something that has not completely passed, that perhaps has not even passed yet. It weeps for that which will have passed given a continuation of the current state of affairs."[5] *The Great Animal Orchestra* is elegiac in all these senses, its future perfect looming ahead, but not a foregone conclusion yet, and in part to be averted by retracing our steps, going back to a past that we are still not done with. Turning now from Krause to Thoreau is not only a journey back in time; it is also a "Janus-visaged" reckoning,[6] a surveying of the damage done, the better to take stock of where we are now. To devise a credible way to go forward, our increasingly fragile environment needs to be seen against one that was still relatively robust, beginning to suffer to some extent, but also holding the promise of different developmental pathways, different ways of coming to terms with systemic changes to the planet.

There is no better example of these cross-currents than the boisterous frog chorus in Chapter Four of *Walden*:

> In the mean while all the shore rang with the trump of bullfrogs, the sturdy spirits of ancient wine-bibbers and wassailers, still unrepentant, trying to sing a catch in their Stygian lake, – if the Walden nymphs will pardon the comparison, for though there are almost no weeds, there are frogs there, – who would fain keep up the hilarious rules of their old festive tables, though their voices have waxed hoarse and solemnly grave, mocking at mirth, and the wine has lost its flavor, and become only liquor to distend their paunches, and sweet intoxication never comes to drown the memory of the past, but mere saturation and waterloggedness and distention. The most aldermanic ... quaffs a deep draught of the once scorned water, and passes round the cup with the ejaculation *tr-r-r-oonk, tr-r-r-oonk, tr-r-r-oonk!* And straightway comes over the water from some distant cove the same password repeated.[7]

"Repeated": this is the keyword here, perhaps the single most important word in this nineteenth-century report on the natural environment. Nothing spectacular, just the sense that there will be more, that whatever is happening now will happen again, a dilation of time that makes the future an endless iteration of the present. All of this is suggested by the croaking of the bullfrog, so natural to that particular habitat and so eternal in its recurrence that it is unimaginable there would ever be a time when that sound would not be there. And because this is Concord, Massachusetts, there are none of the predators mentioned by Krause, no coyotes or big horned owls, and no military jets. The croaking of the frog, at least as Thoreau depicts it here, can luxuriate in the present precisely because the future is not yet a cause for concern.

Walden, it is often said, is a timeless text. It is true here in one sense, in that time seems to stand still for the bullfrog, an animal that has always been there and will always be there, free from the pressures of an end date. We know, of course, that *Walden* was written in the nineteenth century, but that chronological fact is not always the first thing that comes to mind for modern readers. This particular moment, though, with its sound-rich present taking for granted an unaltered future flowing from itself, does seem more "nineteenth-century" than some other moments. It is a luxury to be able to feel that way and will be increasingly hard to sustain in the centuries to come.

Among the casualties wrought by the escalating changes to the climate since the industrial revolution, a habitable and bountiful future must rank high. The now-familiar term "Anthropocene," coined in the 1980s by ecologist Eugene F. Stoermer and atmospheric chemist Paul Crutzen, names human behavior as the chief cause for the drastically altered conditions for life on the planet, so abrupt and unprecedented as to constitute a new geological epoch. A "sixth extinction" seems well underway, the elimination of a "significant proportion of the world's biota in a geologically insignificant amount of time."[8] Such massive die-offs had happened only five times in the 3.6-billion-year history of life on the planet. Each time, it took millions of years for life to recover, starting from scratch with single-celled organisms such as bacteria and protozoans.[9] The sixth extinction – if that is indeed what we are headed for – promises to be even more cataclysmic than the previous five. The work of just one species, it has already resulted in 140,000 species disappearing each year, and half the life-forms on Earth slated for extinction by 2100, according to E. O. Wilson, writing in 2002.[10] In the ten years that followed, Wilson's predictions have been more than borne out. Elizabeth Kolbert now reports that "it is estimated that one-third of all reef-building corals, a third of all fresh-water mollusks, a third of sharks and rays, a quarter of all mammals, a fifth of all reptiles, and a sixth of all birds are headed toward oblivion."[11]

Frogs turn out to have been the first to sound the alarm. Since the mid-1970s, herpetologists from all over the world have begun to hear, not the loud croaking of frogs, but an eerie silence, a deafening absence of sound. Researchers from North America, the United Kingdom, Australia, and New Zealand started comparing notes, puzzled by the fact that, in many of these cases, the disappearances were taking place apparently without encroaching human presence. There was no suburban development, or highways with life-threatening traffic. The frogs seem to be dying out on their own.

What makes these extinctions especially worrisome is that the frog is one of the oldest species on Earth. Its history is one hundred times longer than human history. This long duration suggests that the evolutionary history of amphibians is intertwined with the evolutionary history of the planet at every stage. Over their life cycles, they turn from tadpoles to frogs, moving from water to land, and changing from plant-eater to insect-eater, so they have something to tell us about almost every kind of habitat. And because their skins are permeable, they are the first to register any environmental degradation, and to do so across the widest range of variables. It is for this reason that they are the proverbial canary in the coal mine: their well-being is also a measure of the well-being of the planet.

On December 13, 1992, "The Silence of the Frogs" appeared on the cover of the *New York Times Magazine*, accompanied by a nine-page article by Emily Yoffe documenting the extinction or near-extinction of many amphibian species. Ten years later, an article appeared in *Proceedings of the National Academy of Sciences* with this title: "Are We in the Midst of the Sixth Mass Extinction? A View from the World of Amphibians."[12] The authors, David Wake and Vance T. Vandenburg, noted that, while mass extinctions are extremely rare, based on the collective observations of herpetologists around the world, they would have to conclude that this extreme scenario is indeed upon us. In 2009, PBS revisited the issue in a special program of *Nature* entitled "The Thin Green Line," showing that already one-third of all amphibian species have now vanished.[13]

In 2012, the *New York Times* reported that a killer had been identified: a fungus named chytrid, capable of infecting most of the world's approximately 6,000 amphibian species and wiping them out in a matter of weeks, resulting in "the worst infectious disease ever recorded among vertebrates in terms of the number of species impacted, and its propensity to drive them to extinction." Ironically, the principal carrier for this pathogen appears to be Thoreau's bullfrog, itself resistant to the fungus, and a popular food item around the world, fueling a global trade in amphibians. Human dietary habits, it seems, are responsible for the dissemination of this infectious agent, triggering mass extinctions as an unforeseen side effect.[14]

Disturbances in the Auditory Field

This is not a future Thoreau could have imagined. And yet, there is already something odd about his portrait of the frog, a noticeably archaic diction that suggests this species could be something of a relic – having a venerable past, but perhaps no longer securely inhabiting the present. The frogs are "wine-bibbers and wassailers," "quaff[ing] a deep draught" from the pond, accompanied by nymphs and the river Styx. These overdone classical allusions, rather than drawing us into the worlds of Homer and Ovid, keep us instead at arm's length, highlighting our own necessary modernity and necessary separation from the ancient world. It is in such moments, when time becomes segmented and disjointed, that the eternal present of *Walden* ceases to be eternal, and becomes more like a finite end game, points of no return, in which past and future are no longer one, in which the terminus is no longer a faithful replica of the starting point. It is worth noting in this context that, though still loudly croaking, the bullfrogs are in fact no longer what they used to be. Try as they might to "keep up the hilarious rules of their old festive tables," the wine has "lost its flavor," and their own voices have grown "hoarse and solemnly grave." Theirs is a narrative of progressive attrition, in which losses will occur as a matter of course, opening up gaps through which the growing distance between moderns and ancients would take on a significance also hitherto unimagined.

And, if this is true of Thoreau's relation to Homer and Ovid, it is even more true of his relation to the ancient authors of animal fables, a genre now almost exclusively associated with Aesop (620–560 BCE) but, for an avid reader like Thoreau, also trailing other, equally venerable traditions. These fables seemed to belong to the mythic past of humankind, passed down from times immemorial and flourishing in a variety of languages and cultures. As Laura Gibbs points out,

> The animal characters of Aesop's fables bear a sometimes uncanny resemblance to those in the ancient folktales of India collected both in the Hindu storybook called the *Panchatantra* (which later gave rise to the collection entitled *Kalila wa Dimnah*, a book which served as a source for many of the didactic animal stories in the Islamic mystical poet Rumi) and also in the tales of the Buddha's former births, called *jatakas*.[15]

Aesop's fables were first translated into English and published by William Caxton in 1484; the Sanskrit stories were translated into English in 1775, as *Fables of Pilpay*. In an undated entry in his commonplace book (what he kept before he started his journals), Thoreau pays tribute to both these Greek and Sanskrit antecedents, but then proceeded to tell an animal story of his own, pulling away from both:

> Yesterday I skated after a fox over the ice. Occasionally he sat on his haunches and barked at me like a young wolf ... All brutes seem to have a genius for mystery, an Oriental aptitude for symbols and the language of signs; and this is the origin of Pilpay and Aesop ... While I skated directly after him, he cantered at the top of his speed; but when I stood still, though his fear was not abated, some strange but inflexible law of his nature caused him to stop also, and sit again on his haunches. While I still stood motionless, he would go slowly a rod to one side, then sit and bark, then a rod to the other side, and sit and bark again, but did not retreat, as if spellbound.[16]

Pilpay and Aesop are mentioned by name, but there is in fact very little resemblance between Thoreau's encounter with the fox and their tried and tested, and easily recognizable forms of the fable. Pilpay's and Aesop's animals typically talk, and typically do so inside a frame story, coming with morals that are clearly stated. Thoreau's fox does not. Rather than fitting comfortably into a frame story, this animal is out there running wild in more senses than one, moving according to a logic of his own, not one that readily makes sense to humans. He is not the bearer of anything edifying, for he is himself a sealed book, an unyielding mystery. And yet the disturbance that he is producing in the auditory field is such that there does seem something that is crying out to be deciphered. Without language, but in some sense not dependent on it, this fox seems to gesture toward a signifying universe that proceeds by instincts and reflexes, a "language of signs" older than civilization and older than human language itself.

Sound is crucial. For even though the fox is not saying anything intelligible to humans, the auditory field here is in fact more volatile than it would have been had he been capable of speech. For Thoreau seems to go out of his way to create a sonic anomaly: this fox does not sound like a fox at all, his bark is like that of a young wolf. And he barks only when he is sitting on his haunches, while he is playing out an extended lockstep sequence with Thoreau himself. The man and the fox move strangely in tandem, two halves of the same ritual of speeding, stopping, and starting again, a dance of pursuit and flight, making humans and nonhumans part of the same rhythmic fabric.

And yet, this rhythmic fabric notwithstanding, the man and the fox are not in fact one; they are separated by the steadily maintained physical distance between them and by a gulf still more intractable. "The fox belongs to a different order of things from that which reigns in the village," Thoreau says, an order that is "in few senses contemporary with" socialized and domesticated humans.[17] All that Thoreau can say about a creature so alien is that his bark is more wolf-like than fox-like, a strange sonic misalignment that seems a metaphor for just how little the fox is attuned to us, thwarting the attempts by our ears to classify him, just as he runs counter to the rationality of human settlements in general.

In fact, though not itself hunted to extinction, the fox has less in common with humans than with the wolf, a creature systemically exterminated in New England. As Christopher Benfey points out, "Among the first laws instituted by the Puritan settlers of the Massachusetts Bay Colony in 1630 was a bounty on wolves, which Roger Williams, who fled the colony for its religious intolerance, referred to as 'a fierce, bloodsucking persecutor.'"[18] The gray wolf has been extinct in the state since about 1840, according to the Massachusetts Division of Fisheries and Wildlife.[19] Recalling that silenced species and reproducing a sound that is otherwise no longer heard, the fox points to an early loss of biodiversity in Massachusetts, one that speaks to the destructive work of humans.

This is not the only occasion where a lost world is hinted at through a mistaken sonic identity, a disorientation of the senses. Thoreau's celebrated encounter with the loon, in the "Brute Neighbors" chapter of *Walden*, features another instance. While Thoreau is single-mindedly pursuing this bird, his soundscape is once again strangely volatile, strangely misaligned, haunted by what ought not to have been there. First of all, there is a curious expansion of the sensorium, once again conjuring up a creature not otherwise to be found on Walden Pond:

> [The loon's] usual note was this demoniac laughter, yet somewhat like that of a water-fowl: but occasionally, when he had balked me most successfully and come up a long way off, he uttered a long-drawn unearthly howl, probably more like that of a wolf than any bird; as when a beast puts his muzzle to the ground and deliberately howls. . . . At length having come up fifty rods off, he uttered one of those prolonged howls, as if calling on the god of loons to aid him, and immediately there came a wind from the east and rippled the surface, and filled the whole air with misty rain, and I was impressed as if it were the prayer of the loon answered, and his god was angry with me; and so I left him disappearing far away on the tumultuous surface.[20]

The wolf can make an appearance here only because of an auditory conceit, a fancied likeness suggested by the ear. It might not have occurred to everyone, but Thoreau insists on it. And since this is the second time he is resorting to that conceit, it seems safe to surmise that, as with the earlier encounter with the fox, the point here seems to be to produce a disturbance, a break and a tear in the narrative fabric. The wolf-like sound, a "long-drawn-out unearthly howl," let out at just the moment when the loon has "balked [Thoreau] most successfully," could in fact be quite unnerving. Even though it is meant to be a note of triumph, an undertone of defiance, of unresolved hostility, and perhaps even of remembered pain seems to lurk just below the surface. It reminds us that the fate of the loon is not so different, after all, from the fate of the wolf, that peaceful coexistence with humans might be close to impossible for both of them.

Indeed, by the end of the nineteenth century, the loon would become locally extinct in eastern Massachusetts. Not till 1975 would a pair of loons be sighted again, nesting at Quabbin Reservoir. Today loons are listed on the Massachusetts Endangered Species Act as a Species of Special Concern.[21] Through a haunting of the ear, Thoreau seemed to have anticipated all of this. Hearing the wolf where he is not supposed to, he injects an edginess, an intimation of harm, into an otherwise idyllic setting.

In *Walden*, though, this intimation of harm is both deliberately staged and, just as deliberately, allowed to subside. In this world, still relatively benign, miraculous deliverances do occur, crises do get averted. And the intervening force is literally a *deus ex machina*, in the shape of the god of loons, signaling to Thoreau to leave the bird alone. The patently contrived nature of the denouement is perhaps the point: this is not meant to be entirely realistic or convincing. Any avoidance of harm that rests on this flimsy plot device is resting on a fiction that announces itself as such.

Here, then, is a story very different from those in Pilpay and Aesop. In those fables from antiquity, marked by relative harmony between humans and nonhumans, animals are there to teach us a lesson, and death is edifying, not traumatic. In a world where bad things happen only to those who are themselves at fault, harm is fully rationalized by the concept of "desert": it delivers a moral, and comes to an end when the consequences of a misdeed are embodied without fail by the culprit. If harm were to befall the loon, it is likely to take a very different form; and the precipitated response would also be savage and unappeasable, like the wolf-howl, with no edifying message to give it rational grounding, and nothing to hold it in check.

The Listening Cone

How to honor that kind of sound? Neither Pilpay nor Aesop is of much help here; the traditional animal fable cannot tell that kind of story. But Thoreau is not without alternatives, even among ancient texts. As Stanley Cavell points out, the genre closest to his temperament might turn out to be a genre regularly encountered in nineteenth-century New England, namely, the elegiac lamentations of the Old Testament prophets, especially Jeremiah and Ezekiel.[22] These are voices crying out in the wilderness – and doing so because their faculty of hearing is exceptional, because they have received in full what "the Lord said unto me." Hearing and lamenting are of supreme importance in the Old Testament, affirming the primacy of a sound-based environment and providing the language, the rhetorical structure, and above all the emotional fervor to mourn publicly devastations that are large scale, that defy our common-sense reckoning. Here is Jeremiah: "For the mountains will I take up a weeping and wailing, and for the habitations of the wilderness a lamentation, because they are burned up, so that none can pass through them; neither can men hear the voice of the cattle; both the fowl of the heavens and the beast are fled; they are gone."[23]

Thoreau speaks in these accents only very occasionally, and mostly outside the pages of *Walden*, as in this journal entry on March 23, 1856:

> Is it not a maimed and imperfect nature that I am conversant with? As if I were
> to study a tribe of Indians that had lost all its warriors ... I listen to a concert in

which so many parts are wanting . . . mutilated in many places . . . All the great trees and beasts, fishes and fowl are gone; the streams perchance are somewhat shrunk.[24]

The Jeremiah-like sound of this lamentation shows a Thoreau increasingly aware of the natural world as one "maimed" and "mutilated" by modernity: a modernity associated in *Walden* with the railroad, the "iron horse" with massive impact on the nineteenth-century landscape. Still, environmental degradation and species loss are not yet terms available to him.

Walden is in that sense an incomplete work, with future trajectories to be charted by others. Between 2003 and 2007 a team of scientists from Boston University and Harvard University decided to measure the biodiversity in Concord, Massachusetts, using Thoreau's plant database as a reference point. Their findings were reported in the *Proceedings of the National Academy of Sciences*. Of the species seen by Thoreau in the mid-nineteenth century, twenty-seven percent cannot be located, and an additional thirty-six percent persist in one or two populations where they are vulnerable to local extinction. Even more importantly, the scientists discover that the flowering time for many plant species have moved significantly earlier – by as much as six weeks – a change most likely triggered by global warming and strongly correlated with the extinction of some species. The article concludes: "climate change has affected and will likely continue to shape the phylogenetically biased pattern of species loss in Thoreau's woods."[25]

And just as there is a loss in plant species, the loss in the sound ecology is equally severe. It is this that prompts Maya Lin to build what she calls her "last memorial," a tribute to and repository of all the vanished sounds of the planet. Entitled "What Is Missing," and featuring, among other things, a huge "listening cone" filled with the sounds of loons and other birds from the Cornell Laboratory of Ornithology, this twenty-first-century elegy bears emphatic witness to what Thoreau has only intimated.[26]

NOTES

1. Bernie Krause, *The Great Animal Orchestra: Finding the Origins of Music in the World's Wild Places* (Boston: Little Brown, 2012). All page references to this work will be included in parentheses in the text.
2. See www.wildsanctuary.com/.
3. Anne L. Klinck, *The Old English Elegies: A Critical Edition and Genre Study* (Montreal: McGill-Queen's University Press, 1992), 124.
4. Stuart Curran, "Romantic Elegiac Hybridity," in *Oxford Handbook of the Elegy*, ed. Karen Weisman (Oxford: Oxford University Press, 2010), 239–50, at 238, 240.

5. Timothy Morton, "The Dark Ecology of Elegy," in *Oxford Handbook of the Elegy*, ed. Weisman, 251–71, at 251, 254.

6. Stuart Curran, *Poetic Form and British Romanticism* (Oxford: Oxford University Press, 1986), 28.

7. Henry D. Thoreau, *Walden*, ed. Lyndon Shanley (Princeton: Princeton University Press, 1971), 126.

8. Anthony Hallam and P. B. Wignall, *Mass Extinctions and Their Aftermaths* (Oxford: Oxford University Press, 1997), 1.

9. Richard Leakey and Roger Lewin, *The Sixth Extinction: Patterns of Life and the Future of Humankind* (New York: Anchor Books, 1996); Terry Glavin, *The Sixth Extinction: Journeys among the Lost and Left Behind* (New York: St. Martin's Press, 2007); Elizabeth Kolbert, "The Sixth Extinction? There Have Been Five Great Die-Offs in History. This Time, the Cataclysm Is Us," *New Yorker*, (May 25, 2009): www.newyorker.com/magazine/2009/05/25/the-sixth -extinction. See also Bill Marsh, "Are We in the Middle of a Sixth Mass Extinction?," *New York Times*, (June 6, 2012): www.nytimes.com/interactive /2012/06/01/opinion/sunday/are-we-in-the-midst-of-a-sixth-mass-extinction .html.

10. S. L. Pimm, G. J. Russell, J. L. Gittleman and T. M. Brooks, "The Future of Biodiversity," *Science* 269 (1995): 347–50. Edward O. Wilson, *The Future of Life* (New York: Knopf, 2002).

11. Elizabeth Kolbert, *The Sixth Extinction: An Unnatural History* (New York: Henry Holt, 2014), 17–18.

12. D. B. Wake and V. T. Vredenburg, "Colloquium Paper: Are We in the Midst of the Sixth Mass Extinction? A View from the World of Amphibians," *Proceedings of the National Academy of Sciences* 105 (2008): 11466–73. Available online at www.pnas.org/content/105/Supplement_1/11466.full.pdf.

13. PBS, "Frogs: A Thin Green Line," April 5, 2009: www.pbs.org/wnet/nature /episodes/frogs-the-thin-green-line/introduction/4763/.

14. John Upton, "Despite Deadly Fungus, Frog Imports Continue," *New York Times*, April 7, 2012: www.nytimes.com/2012/04/08/us/chytrid-fungus-in -frogs-threatens-amphibian-extinction.html. See also www.amphibianark.org /the-crisis/chytrid-fungus/.

15. Laura Gibbs, "Introduction," *Aesop's Fables: A New Translation by Laura Gibbs* (Oxford: Oxford University Press, 2002), ix–xxxi, at xix.

16. These commonplace book entries from 1837 to 1847 are in the first volume of the *Journals*. See Henry D. Thoreau, *Journal of Henry D. Thoreau*, vol. 1, ed. Bradford Torry and Francis H. Allen (Boston: Houghton Mifflin, 1949), 470.

17. Thoreau, *Journals*, 1: 470.

18. Christopher Benfey, "The Lost Wolves of New England," NYRDaily (blog), *New York Review of Books*, January 22, 2013: www.nybooks.com/daily /2013/jan/22/lost-wolves-new-england/.

19. "State Mammal List," Massachusetts Office of Energy and Environmental Affairs. www.mass.gov/eea/agencies/dfg/dfw/fish-wildlife-plants/state-mam mal-list.html.

20. Thoreau, *Walden*, 236.

21. "Loons, Lead Sinkers and Jigs," Massachusetts Office of Energy and Environmental Affairs: www.mass.gov/eea/agencies/dfg/dfw/hunting-fishing -wildlife-watching/fishing/loons-lead-sinkers-and-jigs.html.

22. Stanley Cavell, *The Senses of Walden: An Expanded Edition* (Chicago: University of Chicago Press, 1992), 19–20.

23. Jeremiah, 9:10.

24. Thoreau, *Journals*, 8: 221.

25. Charles G. Willis, Brad Ruhfel, Richard B. Primack, Abraham J. Miller-Rushing, and Charles C. Davis, "Phylogenetic Patterns of Species Loss in Thoreau's Woods Are Driven by Climate Change," *Proceedings of the National Academy of Sciences* 105:44 (November 4, 2008): 17029–33. Available online at www.pnas.org/content/105/44/17029.full.pdf.

26. Diane Toomey, "Maya Lin: A Memorial to a Vanishing Natural World," *Yale Environment 360*, June 25 2012: http://e360.yale.edu/feature/maya_lin_a_me morial_to_a_vanishing_natural_world/2545/. Also see www.whatismissing.net.

11

ALAN RICHARDSON

Literary Studies and Cognitive Science

Cognitive literary studies, a relatively new area at the interface of literary studies and the sciences of mind and brain, has yet to fully cohere as an interdisciplinary field. As a result, the still emerging field has proved difficult to define with any great precision. One working definition, though first proffered about a decade ago, can still be found relied upon in current introductions to the field.[1] It reads: "the work of literary critics and theorists vitally interested in cognitive science and neuroscience, and therefore with a good deal to say to one another, whatever their differences."[2] Unabashedly "soft," this definition not only affords a good deal of inclusiveness but also implies, correctly, that cognitive literary studies as yet lacks a unifying "theory" (or even preferred set of guiding theorists), constellating instead around a shared "stance."[3] In this way, it resembles the established field of feminist and gender studies, famously lacking a central body of theory and interrelated rather by a stance that might be summarized as, "gender differences matter, in understanding literary reading, writing, and the institution of literature itself." Similarly, one might say of cognitive literary studies, "the instantiation of minds in brains, bodies, and sociophysical environments matters, in understanding literary reading, writing, and literariness itself."

If one slightly alters the above working definition to read "the work of literary theorists and critics vitally interested in science," it might describe a central feature of another field: Literature and Science, the subject of this volume as a whole. The less surprising, then, that the two areas have found themselves in a relation of close proximity for some time. Initially, the relation proved a tense and rather unhappy one, as I can personally attest. As one working to establish cognitive literary studies as a distinct field in the late 1990s, along with several like-minded colleagues I attended at least one annual meeting of the Society for Literature and Science (as it was then called), in hopes of generating interest and perhaps a sense of common purpose. Our group panels and individual papers were received, however, with remarkable and quite unexpected hostility. Understandably enough, in retrospect: this was also the period of the "science wars," a set of overheated and widely reported debates that temporarily hardened positions and generated considerable defensiveness on both sides. As one well-meaning colleague explained to me at the SLS convention I attended in 1998, "our job isn't to learn from scientists; it's to show them where they're wrong."[4]

So much for anecdote. A number of criticisms that came up in the discussion periods of those early cognitive SLS sessions have since been advanced in print. Prominent among them: that cognitive literary studies illicitly buttresses its claims by cultivating an aura of "scientificity";[5] that "vital interest" in the sciences of mind and brain entails a commitment to empirical methodologies fundamentally at odds with the nature and history of literary interpretation;[6] that a cognitive approach cannot keep sight of literariness and "tends to dissolve the aesthetic into cognitive clarity";[7] that the relation between cognitive science and literary studies must inherently prove an "unequal" one with science in the dominant position and literary studies threatened by absorption or "consilience";[8] that the "universalist" assumptions of cognitive science, adopted by the cognitive literary critic, force the latter to abandon the discrimination of historical, cultural, gender, and ethnic differences that has done so much to transform literary studies since the 1980s.[9] More generally, for all its innovative and often unprecedented postulates and methods, the field of cognitive literary studies has been seen as "nostalgic" and "antitheoretical," especially in its allegedly pervasive opposition to poststructuralist, historicist, and contextualist paradigms.[10]

All of these charges have been persuasively answered – when they have not been anticipated – by cognitive critics. Essays and introductory chapters by Ellen Spolsky, Mary Crane, Patrick Colm Hogan, F. Elizabeth Hart, Alan Richardson, Lisa Zunshine, and Mark Bruhn especially come to mind.[11] However, versions of the same critiques continue to crop up, usually without reference to the critics just named, although their work would feature prominently in any account of mainstream cognitive approaches to literature. A second and equally vexing problem has been continued confusion between cognitive literary studies and another recently constituted field variously called evolutionary literary theory, biopoetics, and literary Darwinism, which in fact often *does* take an antitheoretical position, advocating instead consilience with evolutionary biology, the wholesale adoption of empirical method, and a decidedly junior status in relation to evolutionary psychology, heralded as a master discipline. Here, too, one after another cognitive literary critic has taken pains to distinguish these very different approaches and cognitive critics have been notable among those offering serious and sustained critiques of the work of literary Darwinists.[12] Yet this confusion persists as well: Michelle Ty, for example, writing on the "cognitive turn in literary studies," declares that cognitive literary studies routinely sets up "French theory" in particular, and poststructuralism in general, as its opposing approach, and a "straw man" at that.[13] This statement was published in 2010, eight years after Spolsky made the definitive argument for the complementarity of cognitive criticism and poststructuralism in her masterful essay, "Darwin and Derrida." Ignoring Spolsky, Ty points instead to statements by Joseph Carroll – whom she correctly identifies as a "literary Darwinist" but nevertheless groups with "cognitive" literary critics.

Having mentioned "mainstream" work in cognitive literary studies above, I should now indicate where that mainstream might be located. For, despite the admitted lack of a coherent program or agreed upon theoretical ground, cognitive literary studies does offer a series of paradigmatic examples. Rather than provide a survey of such work here, I would like instead to point to a representative twenty-first century study that exemplifies the dominant trend within cognitive literary and cultural studies, at least in the US, namely, Bruce McConachie's *Engaging Audiences: A Cognitive Approach to Spectating in the Theatre* (2008).[14]

To begin with, McConachie establishes a carefully calibrated relation to the scientific models and findings he selectively draws upon in establishing an original cognitive approach to theatrical texts and performances. Noting that, in the face of competing paradigms and models, no "Grand Theory" of mind and mental behaviors has yet to emerge from the mind and brain sciences, McConachie nevertheless finds some empirical findings robust enough to inspire a new account of theatrical spectatorship, without making any claim that his own method could be considered empirical rather than one of informed speculation (7). Moreover, he points out that at least some earlier accounts now seem scientifically implausible or "unreliable," including once authoritative semiotic or psychoanalytical approaches; many postulates, such as Lacan's "mirror phase," now look untenable in the light of several decades of experimental work in cognitive science (4, 81–2). We may not have anything like a full account of human cognition (contrary to the claims of literary Darwinists like Carroll), but we can at least "rule out impossibilities" (8).

McConachie also represents mainstream thinking among cognitive literary scholars in developing a view of cognition as both emotive and embodied. The conventional opposition of the terms *cognitive* and *emotive* has caused some confusion among those looking at cognitive literary studies from the outside, yet as McConachie notes, mind and brain researchers now generally "affirm that emotional drives undergird and sustain even the simplest of intellectual tasks"; the "old separations," going back at least to Plato, between reason and passion have been effectively breached (3). Similarly, another age-old – and related – dualism, the opposition between mind and body, has largely given way throughout cognitive science and neuroscience to various understandings of a fundamentally embodied mind, leading to the adoption of deliberately awkward hybrid terms like "mind/brain," intended to confront us with and challenge our own ingrained dualistic categories (4). Once this fundamental postulate has been accepted, it in turn leads to an acknowledgement of the mind/brain's implication in and shaping by the physical, social, and cultural environment in and through which it develops and which it must successfully negotiate in order to survive. We end up with an interactionist view of the human organism that empha- sizes the interplay of genetic inheritance and cultural situatedness, advancing a middle position between genetic determinism and "blank slate" style social constructionism, and recognizing certain "species-level commonalities" while putting forward cognitive flexibility as the single-most important aspect of the human genetic endowment (4, 17, 121–2).

These commitments lead McConachie in turn to an epistemological stance he terms, after George Lakoff and Mark Johnson, "embodied realism" (80). As Hart points out in her indispensable essay "The Epistemology of Cognitive Literary Studies," this position proves roughly compatible with such related formulations as the philosopher Hilary Putnam's "internal realism," and some version of it informs the work of a number of leading cognitive literary scholars. Hart usefully identifies a set of "minimal condi- tions" that accompany such "middle" positions between objective realism and blank-slate style relativism: "all of these critics operate from the position that there is such a thing as species-specific knowledge and that such knowl- edge must contribute substantially to our philosophical discussions about knowledge; yet they also recognize that all knowledge, including species- specific knowledge, is environmentally situated, context-dependent, and culturally indexed, i.e., subject to lesser or greater degrees of constructivity."[15] Within this broad area of consensus, however, one can in fact find a range of positions: mainstream cognitive critics occupy a middle- ground position in relation to the traditional (and by now sterile) realist/ relativist dichotomy, while the work of literary Darwinists like Carroll can be distinguished by hewing much more closely to the realist pole of the spectrum.[16]

Significantly for the purposes of this volume, Hart borrows her terminol- ogy here from a now classic essay in Literature and Science, "Constrained Constructivism," by N. Katherine Hayles, who in turn draws on the thinking of Donna Haraway, citing in particular her essay "Situated Knowledges."

Both theorists want to account for the "instrumental efficacy" of much scientific work without lapsing into a naïve scientific objectivism, a god's eye "view from nowhere" that discounts the embodiment and cultural situatedness of any human observer – or of any humanly designed and programmed instrument.[17] And, interestingly, both begin staking out the middle ground between relativism and "totalization" (Haraway 190) by talking about their dogs. Haraway, "walking with [her] dogs," begins thinking about what McConachie terms "species-level commonalities" (17), the differences in knowledge that follow from the differences between, say, "our bodies, endowed with primate colour and stereoscopic vision" and a dog's paucity of "retinal cells for colour vision" but "huge neural processing and sensory area for smells" (Haraway 190). Hayles writes more anecdotally about the repeated experience of scaring up rabbits with her dog Hunter, who "processes the world in a very different way" than Hayles herself (including a "limited color range" and a "vastly richer role" for scent), and yet manages to communicate with his human companion about a shared object of attention, however differently perceived and cognized. Different forms of embodiment – and the different sensory and neural organs that go with them – matter. Both theorists, then, begin from a postulate of "species-specific" knowledge, though only Hayles uses that term (29).

Limited to embodied, situated, species-specific knowledge, we must definitively abandon the old Platonic dream of objective knowledge; we are "always already within the theater of representations" (Hayles 28), forever trapped within Plato's cave. Yet, as Hayles argues, our constructions of the world remain constrained by the realities that we can never cognize directly but that indirectly make themselves felt. "By ruling out some possibilities – by negating articulations – constraints enable scientific inquiry to tell us something about reality and not only about ourselves" (32). This negative (as opposed to positivist) approach to epistemology enables us to build up a usable model of the world, constantly subject to revision to be sure, admittedly conditioned by our specific forms of embodiment and shaped by our sociocultural environment, yet ultimately "good enough": "enough consistencies obtain in the processing and in the flux to make recognition reliable and relatively stable" (32).

This dual commitment to embodiment and to sociocultural situatedness has crucial consequences for the relationship between cognitive literary studies and the various forms of poststructuralist criticism dominant in the academic study of literature at the time of its emergence. Although decisively departing from some postulates of "high" poststructuralist theory – such as the systemic arbitrariness of language and unqualified versions of social constructionism – cognitive literary studies (again, unlike most literary

Darwinism) does not reject the poststructuralist project altogether or claim that the study of literature needs to be reconceived from the ground up. As the work of Spolsky, Crane, Hart, Richardson, Hogan, Zunshine, Bruhn, and by now many others, including McConachie, makes clear, cognitive literary studies can take up and at times extend claims advanced by various forms of materialist, feminist, postcolonialist, and (new) historicist critique.

What some have called *cognitive historicism*, in fact, has proved one of the more vital areas within the new field and, because it overlaps significantly with work in Literature and Science, it deserves special attention here.[18] Cognitive historicism shares several basic assumptions with much new historicist criticism generally. Literary texts, for example, are not examined for the ways in which they might reflect the science of their time, but rather are seen as drawing on a common discursive lexicon, sharing in the work of developing and delineating innovative scientific conceptions, and at times even running ahead of science in this common work. Scientific texts, in turn, are examined not only for the ideas and methods they put forth but for their rhetorical aspects as well. Special attention gets paid to the ideological environment and implications of literary-scientific discourse and the ways that relevant scientific and literary developments may serve to further or, alternatively, contest the interests of dominant groups.

What features, then, make cognitive historicism *cognitive*? For one, recent developments in cognitive science and neuroscience can be recruited to serve as a lens through which to newly perceive the science of the past and to recapture some of the excitement and anxiety it provoked in its own time. So Crane, for example, helps her readers appreciate the pre-Cartesian, anti-dualistic tenor of some early modern theories of mind by means of comparison to roughly comparable developments in the "embodied" psychologies of the present.[19] "Roughly" needs to be stressed here: the analogies posed are always imperfect and the instructive differences between then and now garner particular attention. The point is not to naively project the present onto the past but to open up a new perspective on the past that is then developed with scholarly rigor. Such reopening can be especially effective when past accounts and representations of mind have been occluded or distorted by later historical developments. So, for example, critics like Richardson and Marcus Iseli have elicited a much larger range of Romantic-era scientific and literary versions of the unconscious mind than had critics self-limited to finding prefigurations of a Freudian unconscious, first by beginning from the comparatively broader and richer "cognitive unconscious" posited by contemporary neuroscience and cognitive science.[20] Vanessa Ryan makes a comparable case for the importance of "unconscious cerebration" in Victorian mind science and fiction alike in her book *Thinking without Thinking in the Victorian Novel*.[21]

The primary danger involved in cognitive historicist criticism, anachronism, can be (and usually is) avoided by means of the usual scholarly virtues: wide and deep reading in the relevant archives, noticing fine as well as broad distinctions, above all a willingness to find something exceeding or altogether different from whatever one had expected to find. Still, even work marked by careful scholarship can be accused of a "Whiggish" progressivism, prizing and therefore giving inordinate emphasis to those aspects of the past that most resonate with the present.[22] Perhaps the best response to this charge is to note how cognitive historicists have shown and inspired genuine and sustained interest in past scientific ideas and practices that would likely have remained undervalued otherwise. In addition, the best work in cognitive historicism can circle back to the present and show how twenty-first century scientific models can in fact be seen as limited or biased in comparison to some models excavated from the past. Bruhn, for example, brings models from cognitive linguistics to bear on theories and uses of metaphor in the Romantic era only to conclude that the Romantic materials suggest certain limitations of and possible future directions for cognitive linguistics.[23] Current scientific theories of dreaming have similarly been shown to be biased toward REM dreaming, at the expense of somnambulism and other "parasomnias," in comparison to the dream science of the eighteenth and early nineteenth centuries.[24]

A second feature of much cognitive historicism, and one that more radically differentiates it from other work in Literature and Science, begins from the assumption that the human brain, along with a range of basic cognitive functions, have not changed fundamentally since the beginnings of recorded culture. As McConachie writes of consciousness, for example, the "basic properties of consciousness evolved thousands of years ago and there is no reason to suspect that they have changed during recorded history," adding that biological evolution "rarely works that fast" (31). So something as basic as the limited amount of available attention ("about seven pieces" of information in a "single conscious gestalt"), found currently across cultures, can safely be projected into aesthetic practices and artifacts from the past (30). None of this implies, of course, that human experiences, representations, and technologies of attention have not changed significantly over historical time: Natalie Phillips's work on attention in the eighteenth century brilliantly shows otherwise.[25]

Incorporating such assumptions into cognitive literary study does not entail a flight from history but rather, as Mark Turner has argued, a "wider notion" of what counts as human history.[26] Supplementing the expected focus on culture and ideology found throughout literary studies since the 1980s, cognitive critics follow the mind and brain sciences in considering as well phylogenetic and ontogenetic history. Phylogenetic history, what some historians now term deep history, considers biological and cultural developments taking place over thousands or even "millions of years," while ontogenetic history considers the entire life course of the human individual, from developmental changes occurring in the womb through senescence and death. Again, rather than displacing what we ordinarily mean by cultural history, these additional perspectives serve to complicate and extend it: cognitive neuroscientists typically view cultural, phylogenetic, and ontogenetic history as "aspects of human history that do not operate independently."[27]

Crane's *Shakespeare's Brain*, still one of the most successful examples of a cognitive literary approach to the work of a past author, illustrates how all three forms of historical investigation can work together. Assuming that Shakespeare's brain shared basic patterns of functioning with brains as experimentally studied in the present, Crane can draw on work in cognitive linguistics and cognitive categorization theory, as well as work on language acquisition, to elicit previously unnoticed lexical patterns at work in a given Shakespeare play.[28] Yet, once she has identified a given set of "radial" lexical relationships, she analyzes these according to their significance in Shakespeare's time, paying attention to their historically changing definitions, their ideological significance, and special shadings of meaning related to the context of early modern theatrical production.

Importantly, however, Crane does not attribute conscious insight into the relevant brain processes she discusses to Shakespeare himself. Cognitive historicism makes little or no room for authorial intuition. Cognitive science and neuroscience, still more than did psychoanalysis, tend to emphasize how vast an extent of mental life remains closed to conscious introspection. It would make little sense, then, to claim special powers for past writers enabling them to somehow "anticipate" developments in mind and brain science lying hundreds of years in the future. At the same time, no one would accuse Shakespeare (or Jane Austen, or Henry James) of any deficiency in observing and analyzing human behavior and motivation. For cognitive historicism, however, even claiming acute powers of observation is rarely enough; where a rough correspondence occurs between a current scientific theory or finding and literary representations from a past era, scholarly investigation often reveals relevant (and previously unappreciated) formulations in the philosophical, medical, and/or psychological or proto-psychological discourses of that same era. Cognitive historicist scholarship can reveal how scientific hypotheses and experimental findings considered novel and unprecedented by scientists in the present – who have neither training nor motivation for studying the history of their fields – may in fact constitute new versions of ideas or observations from the past.

The dual interest in cultural diversity and species-level commonalities has led some cognitive literary critics to investigate certain human, cultural, or literary universals. *Universal* here does not imply a behavior found in every known culture, but rather a statistical universal: something occurring well beyond chance across geographically and genetically distinct cultures (that is, not reflecting a common historical origin or cross-cultural transmission).[29] Such universals need not be seen as hard-wired into the human brain and genome: they may instead reflect the capabilities and constraints that come with a shared basic body plan and neural architecture. For example, the constraints on conscious attention discussed above – up to seven items or "chunks" (like an area code) held in short-term memory at a time – may help account for a universal predilection for verse line lengths of no more than nine words, independently noted by several different cognitive critics.[30] Yet the *minimal* "universal" verse line length (about five words) cannot be accounted for in the same way, and might in fact inspire a new direction for cognitive psychological research into human attention.[31]

Hogan differentiates such statistical, empirically elicited universals from the *normative* universals that have sometimes accompanied chauvinistic claims to cultural centrality and superiority – Hogan in fact calls these "pseudouniversals."[32] Yet the experimental cognitive scientist's reliance on phrases like "normal human subjects" may seem to grate against poststructuralist appreciation for "heterogeneous multiplicities... incapable of being squashed into isomorphic slots," including the "multidimensional... topography of subjectivity" (Haraway 193). On one hand, common sense suggests that cognitive science needs some kind of shorthand for, say, not randomly including those blind from birth in studies of mental imagery, or expecting lefthanders to show the same kinds of brain hemisphere differences as righthanders. On the other, several decades of poststructuralist critique have taught us how readily the "normal" shades into the normative, suggesting that both a special wariness and a more careful vocabulary may be called for.

One should not underestimate the significance and the salutary influence, then, of recent work in cognitive literary studies associated with such terms as *neurodivergence, neurodiversity*, and *neurocosmopolitanism*. As developed by critics like Ralph Savarese and Nicola Shaughnessy, these terms represent an attempt to appreciate "cognitive difference" that refuses to pathologize, patronize, or exoticize such neurodivergent subjects as those with autistic spectrum condition (ASC).[33] Neurocosmopolitanism involves several strategies that could be more widely adopted by scholars of literature and cognition and, more broadly, of literature and science. One is to posit a spectrum or continuum model rather than a simple dichotomy between neurotypical and neurodivergent subjects, recognizing that individuals exhibit many different combinations of typical and divergent mental processing styles and capacities, and that a given neurotypical individual will experience starkly different cognitive modes over the life course, from preverbal infancy to the divergent cognitive styles associated with senescence.

A second strategy involves moving beyond a "deficit" model of neurodivergence. In her work with children exhibiting various forms of ASC, for example, Shaughnessy has found that a presumption of cognitive "difference" rather than disability has enabled the emergence and appreciation of unique abilities, including a high degree of artistic originality.[34] Savarese similarly cites the well-known success of Temple Grandin's "sensory-based problem solving" in pioneering new livestock technologies and quotes some dazzlingly original verses by the "autist" poet Tito Mukhopadhyay.[35] One might project a neurodivergent approach to creativity backward to Kay Jamison's study of bipolar illness and the "artistic temperament."[36] In the mode of cognitive historicism, one might also locate a neurocosmopolitanism *avant la lettre* in the Romantic appreciation for such cognitively different subjects as wild children, subjects deprived of language, and even those at the time termed "idiots," a tendency that found popular expression in works like William Wordsworth's "The Idiot Boy" and Mary Shelley's *Frankenstein*.[37]

Both Savarese and Shaughnessy engage in what the latter calls "practice-based research," not limiting their interest to texts and dramatic productions but working actively to elicit creative, and perhaps therapeutic, responses in subjects on the autistic spectrum (Savarese through poetry workshops, Shaughnessy through experimental, improvisational theater exercises).[38] Neither critic passively accepts the models and definitions proposed by scientific research on autism; both challenge and seek to revise the terms of autistic research through their own literary and practice-based investigations. Cognitive historicism, as noted above, also seeks to speak back to mind and brain research in the present, identifying limitations or biases in scientific research agendas through comparison with past models and formulations. At least since Spolsky's *Gaps in Nature* (1992), cognitive critics have been pointing out the kinds of simplification and distortion that frequently accompany the scientific practice of reducing or segmenting complex behaviors to narrow, neatly defined, and empirically testable bits.[39]

Whether mind and brain scientists are noticing such backtalk poses a different question, however, one that harks back to early criticism that cognitive literary studies, despite protestations to the contrary, takes a decidedly subordinate role in its partnership with cognitive science and neuroscience. One way to make sure that at least some cognitive scientists are paying attention, then, has been to collaborate with them. Cross-disciplinary collaboration is the norm in cognitive science and cognitive neuroscience, multidisciplinary fields that arose out of the recognition that progress in the mind and brain sciences had come to depend on multiple kinds of expertise. Although literary scholars have rarely been invited to join multidisciplinary research groups – even when such groups are studying traditionally literary topics like metaphor, narrative, or imagination – one can by now list a number of important exceptions. The study of "conceptual metaphor" and "conceptual integration" or "blending," for example, has been interdisciplinary from the start, the former developed through collaborations among Lakoff, Johnson, and Turner, bringing together disciplinary expertise in linguistics, philosophy, and literature, and the latter developed by Turner working together with the linguist Gilles Fauconnier.[40]

The psychological study of literary reading has also encouraged some notable collaborations across the traditional sciences/humanities divide. David Miall, a scholar of English literature, and Don Kuiken, a cognitive psychologist, both at the University of Alberta, have been publishing significant papers on a range of topics involved in literary reading since the early 1990s.[41] A second partnership, also at the University of Alberta, studies the comprehension of literary narratives, bringing together the critical perspectives of a cognitive psychologist, Peter Dixon, and a Romance languages scholar, Marisa Bortolussi.[42] Both collaborations have involved bringing empirical methods from cognitive psychology to bear on problems and issues arising from within literary studies; the research methodologies come largely from the psychology side, while the research agendas and specific hypotheses more often arise from literary theory and criticism. Each partnership has at times formed the nucleus of a larger interdisciplinary research group. Both realize the possibility of genuine two-way exchange among cognitive scientists and literary scholars; their work also underscores how, although cognitive literary studies need not adopt empirical methodologies, empirical approaches constitute one important aspect of the wider field.

Cognitive literary scholars have also, more recently, begun working with neuroscientific research groups on neuroimaging studies of the reading or spectating mind. Zunshine, for example, helped to design and implement a series of fMRI (functional magnetic resonance imaging) experiments testing her claim that adding levels of intentional "embedment" to fictional narratives slows down text processing (and may contribute to what we think of as literariness).[43] G. Gabrielle Starr, like Zunshine a professor of English originally trained as an eighteenth-century scholar, undertook postgraduate work in neuroscience in order to design and run (with two neuroscientist colleagues) fMRI studies of aesthetic reception; their work has been described both in Starr's important book on cognition and aesthetics (*Feeling Beauty*) and in peer-reviewed scientific journals.[44] Natalie Phillips, also an eighteenth-century specialist, has learned fMRI imaging techniques from neuroscientific colleagues and has undertaken her own series of fMRI experiments with subjects reading the fiction of Jane Austen under various task conditions.[45] The work of these scholar-researchers represents one important new direction for cognitive literary studies, one that not just softens but virtually erases the line between the study of literature and cognitive science. Yet informed speculation – drawing on traditional literary theory and criticism no less than cognitive science and neuroscience – continues to play a leading role in the work of each, not to mention in the emerging field as a whole. Even among those now trained to engage in laboratory studies, that is, cognitive literary studies has not become a predominately empirical endeavor.

Whatever the methodology, or array of methodologies, they employ, cognitive literary critics collectively subscribe to what their colleagues in psychology and linguistics term a "cognitive commitment."[46] Lakoff, writing as a linguist, defines this as a "commitment to make one's account of human language accord with what is generally known about the mind and brain from disciplines other than linguistics."[47] Notice, to begin with, that the cognitive commitment necessarily involves interdisciplinarity, extensive engagement with disciplines other than one's home discipline. Notice too that nothing in this formulation implies taking one or more of those other disciplines as a "master" – to seek "accord" does not mean to declare subservience – and that Lakoff assumes that linguistics will remain a distinct discipline and not become absorbed into other cognitive disciplines: "accord" does not entail "consilience." Yet for Lakoff the cognitive commitment involves more than a willingness to read relevant work in other disciplines: it "forces one," he stresses, to "be responsive to empirical results from cognitive and developmental psychology, cognitive anthropology, neurobiology, etc."[48] And, of course, for literary scholars making a cognitive commitment, this list would include cognitive linguistics and psycholinguistics as well.

In relation to literary studies, then, making a cognitive commitment does not mean giving up the autonomy of literature as a discipline; nor does it mean subordinating literary studies to the sciences of mind. And responsiveness to empirical results from other cognitive disciplines does not entail that all cognitive approaches to literature need to employ empirical methods. But if the cognitive commitment does not lead to exclusive adoption of scientific methods in literary studies, it does imply that cognitive literary scholars subscribe to a basic scientific world view, that is, some version of constrained constructivism, an epistemological stance now held in effect (if not in name) by most neuroscientists and cognitive scientists. Cognitive literary scholars similarly adopt what might be called a scientific attitude, including a willingness to abandon models, assumptions, and theories as soon as these can be shown to be empirically untenable. This includes, of course, models and assumptions adapted from other cognitive disciplines, no matter how well they seem to fit with literary studies or how invested one may have become in them.

Sharing an epistemological and theoretical stance with mind and brain scientists, cognitive critics stand apart from many of their colleagues in literature departments, any number of whom remain attached to "blank slate"-style social constructionism and continue to take their theoretical compass points from the work of early twentieth-century thinkers like Freud and Saussure. Partly for this reason, and partly due to the considerable difficulty of working across the humanities/sciences divide, cognitive literary studies remains a minority presence within the discipline as a whole, although its appeal seems to be growing among younger scholars in particular. Neither a science of literature nor a predominately empirical endeavor, it nevertheless seeks coherence with other cognitive disciplines and shows respect for (though by no means uncritical deference toward) empirical findings. Bringing cognitive science and literary studies into meaningful dialogue has by no means proved easy, yet a number of literary scholars, critics, and theorists have come to find it indispensable.

NOTES

1. See, for example, Lisa Zunshine, "Introduction," in *Introduction to Cognitive Cultural Studies*, ed. Zunshine (Baltimore: Johns Hopkins University Press, 2015), 1–33, at 1.
2. Alan Richardson, "Studies in Literature and Cognition: A Field Map," in *The Work of Fiction: Cognition, Culture, and Complexity*, ed. Richardson and Ellen Spolsky (Aldershot: Ashgate, 2004), 1–29, at 2.
3. Porter H. Abbot, "Cognitive Literary Studies: The 'Second Generation,'" *Poetics Today* 27.4 (Winter 2006): 711–22, at 713–14.
4. As the present volume attests this is certainly not a characteristic stance of Literature and Science today – nor, as the essays by Hayles and Haraway alluded to below indicate, was it uniformly adhered to at the time.
5. Hans Adler and Sabine Gross, "Adjusting the Frame: Comments on Cognitivism and Literature," *Poetics Today* 23.2 (2002): 195–220, at 209.

6. Tony Jackson, "Questioning Interdisciplinarity: Cognitive Science, Evolutionary Psychology, and Literary Criticism," *Poetics Today* 21.2 (2000): 319–47.
7. Adler and Gross, "Adjusting the Frame," 216.
8. Adler and Gross, "Adjusting the Frame," 212. Consilience, as developed by the sociobiologist E. O. Wilson in the book of that title, names an ambitious program to unify the social sciences and humanities with the physical sciences, the latter taking the leading role, and biology in particular serving as a master discipline in relation to the humanities. This program has been adopted by many within evolutionary literary studies, also known as literary Darwinism: see E. O. Wilson, *Consilience: The Unity of Knowledge* (New York: Knopf, 1998), and Joseph Carroll, "Wilson's Consilience and Literary Study," *Philosophy and Literature* 23.2 (1999): 393–413.
9. Adler and Gross, "Adjusting the Frame," 209.
10. Sabine Gross, "Cognitive Readings; or, The Disappearance of Literature in the Mind," *Poetics Today* 18.2 (1997): 271–97, at 279–80.
11. See especially Ellen Spolsky, "Darwin and Derrida: Cognitive Literary Theory as a Species of Post-Structuralism," *Poetics Today* 23.1 (2002): 43–62; Mary Thomas Crane, *Shakespeare's Brain: Reading with Cognitive Theory* (Princeton: Princeton University Press, 2001), 3–35; Patrick Colm Hogan, "Literary Universals," *Poetics Today* 18 (1997): 223–49; F. Elizabeth Hart, "The Epistemology of Cognitive Literary Studies," *Philosophy and Literature* 25.2 (2001): 314–34; Richardson, "Studies in Literature and Cognition"; Zunshine, "Introduction," 1–9; Mark Bruhn, "Introduction: Exchange Values: Poetics and Cognitive Science," *Poetics Today* 32.3 (2011): 403–60.
12. See, for example, Richardson, "Studies in Literature and Cognition," 12–14; Spolsky, "Frozen in Time?," *Poetics Today* 28.4 (2007): 807–16; and especially Jonathan Kramnick, "Against Literary Darwinism," *Critical Inquiry* 37 (2011): 315–47.
13. Michelle Ty, "On the Cognitive Turn in Literary Studies," *Qui Parle* 19.1 (2010): 205–19, at 214.
14. Bruce McConachie, *Engaging Audiences: A Cognitive Approach to Spectating in the Theatre* (New York: Palgrave MacMillan, 2008), hereafter cited in the text.
15. Hart, "Epistemology," 326.
16. Hart, "Epistemology," 328.
17. N. Katherine Hayles, "Constrained Constructivism: Locating Scientific Inquiry in the Theater of Representation," in *Realism and Representation: Essays on the Problem of Realism in Relation to Science, Literature, and Culture*, ed. George Levine (Madison: University of Wisconsin Press, 1993), 27–43, at 27; Donna Haraway, "Situated Knowledges: The Science Question in Feminism and the Privilege of Partial Perspective," in *Simians, Cyborgs, and Women: The Reinvention of Nature* (New York: Routledge, 1991), 183–201, at 195. Both essays hereafter cited in the text.
18. See Spolsky, "Cognitive Literary Historicism: A Response to Adler and Gross," *Poetics Today* 24.2 (2003): 161–83; Richardson, *The Neural Sublime: Cognitive Theories and Romantic Texts* (Baltimore: Johns Hopkins University Press, 2010), esp. 1–16; and Mark Bruhn and Donald R. Wehrs, *Cognition, Literature, and History* (New York: Routledge, 2014).

19. Crane, *Shakespeare's Brain*, esp. 116–155. Crane discusses her critical practice in "Cognitive Historicism: Intuition in Early Modern Thought," in *Introduction to Cognitive Cultural Studies*, ed. Zunshine, 15–33.

20. Richardson, *British Romanticism and the Science of the Mind* (Cambridge: Cambridge University Press, 2001), 39–65; Marcus Iseli, "Thomas De Quincey's *Subconscious*: Nineteenth-Century Intimations of the Cognitive Unconscious," *Romanticism* 20.3 (2014): 294–305.

21. Vanessa L. Ryan, *Thinking without Thinking in the Victorian Novel* (Baltimore: Johns Hopkins University Press, 2012).

22. George Rousseau, "Brainomania: Brain, Mind and Soul in the Long Eighteenth Century," *British Journal for Eighteenth-Century Studies* 30 (2007): 161–91, at 168.

23. Mark Bruhn, "Harmonious Madness: The Poetics of Analogy at the Limits of Blending Theory," *Poetics Today* 32.4 (2011): 619–62.

24. Richardson, "The Politics of Dreaming: From Diderot to Keats and Shelley," *Romantik* 1 (2012): 9–26.

25. Natalie Phillips, *Distraction: Problems of Attention in Eighteenth-Century Literature* (Baltimore: Johns Hopkins University Press, 2016).

26. Mark Turner, "The Cognitive Study of Art, Language, and Literature," *Poetics Today* 23.1 (2002): 9–20, at 18.

27. Turner, "Cognitive Study," 18.

28. Cognitive categorization theory draws on findings in cognitive psychology, cognitive anthropology, and neuroscience to describe the ways in which human subjects form perceptual, semantic, conceptual, social, and other kinds of categories. For a representative survey, see *Categorization in Cognitive Science*, ed. Henri Cohen and Claire Lefebvre (Amsterdam: Elsevier, 2005).

29. For an introduction to the study of cognitive universals, see Hogan, "Literary Universals."

30. Richardson, "Studies in Literature and Cognition," 11.

31. Hogan, "Literary Universals," 244.

32. Hogan, "Literary Universals," 225.

33. Ralph Savarese, "Neurocosmopolitan Melville," *Journal of Melville Studies* 15.2 (2013): 7–19, at 8.

34. Nicola Shaughnessay, "Imagining Otherwise: Autism, Neuoroaesthetics and Contemporary Performance," *Interdisciplinary Science Reviews* 38.4 (2013): 321–34, at 323, 331.

35. Savarese, "Neurocosmopolitan Melville," 29–30.

36. Kay Redfield Jamison, *Touched with Fire: Manic-Depressive Illness and the Artistic Temperament* (New York: Free Press, 1993).

37. Richardson, *British Romanticism*, 151–74.

38. Shaughnessay, "Imagining Otherwise," 323.

39. Spolsky, *Gaps in Nature: Literary Interpretation and the Modular Mind* (Albany: State University of New York Press, 1993), 209.

40. For an introductory overview, see Richardson, "Studies in Literature and Cognition," 4–7.

41. For a representative article, see David S. Miall and Don Kuiken. "The Form of Reading: Empirical Studies of Literariness," *Poetics* 25 (1998): 327–41.

42. For their most significant publication to date, see Marisa Bortolussi and Peter Dixon, *Psychonarratology: Foundations for the Empirical Study of Literary Response* (Cambridge: Cambridge University Press, 2003).

43. Zunshine, "Style Brings in Mental States," *Style* 45.2 (2011): 349–56.

44. G. Gabrielle Starr, *Feeling Beauty: The Sister Arts and the Neuroscience of Aesthetic Experience* (Cambridge: MIT Press, 2013); and Edward A. Vessell, G. Gabrielle Starr, and Nada Rubin, "The Brain on Art: Intense Aesthetic Experience Activates the Default Mode Network." *Frontiers in Human Neuroscience* 6.66 (2012): 1–17.

45. Phillips, "Literary Neuroscience and History of Mind: An Interdisciplinary fMRI Study of Attention and Jane Austen," in *Introduction to Cognitive Cultural Studies*, ed. Zunshine, 55–81.

46. Raymond W. Gibbs, Jr., *The Poetics of Mind: Figurative Thought, Language, and Understanding* (Cambridge: Cambridge University Press, 1994), 15–16; George Lakoff, "Cognitive Versus Generative Linguistics: How Commitments Influence Results," *Language & Communication* 11.1–2 (1991): 53–62.

47. Lakoff, "Cognitive Versus Generative Linguistics," 54.

48. Lakoff, "Cognitive Versus Generative Linguistics," 54.

12

TIM ARMSTRONG

Modernism, Technology, and the Life Sciences

"Oh, my God," he said, "we shall know each other now, shan't we? We shall know each other now."

D. H. Lawrence, "The Blind Man"

The "Life Sciences" are a loose disciplinary construction, only commonly used since the 1960s, that describes the various sciences applicable to living organisms and the systems that pertain to them: biology, genetics, medicine, environmental studies and other subfields. It is, nevertheless, a useful term to apply to the period of modernism, not least because *The Science of Life* (1929–30), the popular synthesis by H. G. Wells, Julian Huxley and G. P. Wells, is one point of origin for the term.[1] The period saw major developments and debates in many of the fields involved, as well as a growing understanding of the complexity of living systems. What Huxley in 1942 called the "modern synthesis" in evolutionary studies was one outcome of that understanding, but developments in ecology and biochemistry also contributed to knowledge of the internal and external systems governing human and animal life.[2]

Where biology stood out from the other sciences was in offering the promise of major intervention in human relations, making it a driving force in what we understand as modernity. In *Daedalus, or Science and the Future* (1923), the book which launched the Today & Tomorrow series and set the keynote of many futurological debates, J. B. S. Haldane wrote that "the biologist is the most romantic figure on earth at the present day" before imagining a future of abolished disease and medical enhancement.[3] Julian Huxley commented the same year that "the extension of control in biology will *inter alia* mean the alteration of the modes of man's experience itself."[4] When his brother Aldous Huxley discussed the impact of biological discovery in his BBC talk "Science and Civilization" almost a decade later, he focused on two areas that Haldane had singled out: eugenics and endocrinology, that is, the external management of populations by direct bodily control and by management of reproduction.[5] *Brave New World* (1932) is of course a response to those possibilities, yoking them to technologies of distraction and surveillance.

Huxley's relation to science was particularly intimate: he boarded at Haldane's house in Oxford. Much literary understanding of the life sciences, as in the case of physics and mathematics, was more patchy, intermittent and driven by local passions; manifesting itself into both treatments of science in literature and moments where science informs literary *techne*. Partially because of the rapidity of development, this was a field in which there were many popularizer sythesizers, working against the grain of the increasing specialism of scientific practice. There was also a tradition of experts – Haldane, Julian Huxley, Arthur Keith, Joseph Needham and many others – reflecting on the general implications of their specialisms, crossing what was only later seen as a barrier between "two cultures." Moreover the question of "life" itself – of the inheritance of vitalism, of the values of the body and its drives, its relation to human civilization – was central to many modernist discourses and their reform modes, often producing what could be called a "biological style," associated (in different ways) with D. H. Lawrence, William Carlos Williams, and Marianne Moore; with a number of young writers in Cambridge around 1930; and with other groupings that we would be less inclined to call "modernist."[6]

The Birth of Complexity

It could be argued that it was the new awareness of the complexity of life forms, both internally and in relation to their environment, that gradually edged out the last adherents of vitalism – the idea that life itself was separate from the rest of creation, expressed in a "soul" or other entity. As one summary put it in 1929, "In biology we do not analyse the complex into the simple, we are continually bringing to life greater complexity."[7] Georges Canguilhem calls this the "devitalizing" of life, linking it (in a slightly broader period) to "the intersection of a wide range of techniques: of micro-extraction and microddisection, or combinatorial algebra, or statistics, or electron microscopy, or enzyme chemistry."[8] A defensive campaign in support of vitalism would be waged – Eugenio Rignano would publish *Man Not a Machine* (1926) in the Today & Tomorrow series, espousing his version of Lamarckism – but as in many cases, the series itself provided a reply, Joseph Needham's *Man a Machine* (1927), and by the 1930s materialist explanations of the body were the norm.[9]

If the nineteenth-century conception of the animal or human body was largely mechanical and electrical, and tended to yoke it to disciplinary regimes such as Taylorism and various forms of biomechanics, the period

between the wars was marked by a stress on the role of biochemical trans-
mitters. The body had a "postal as well as a telegraphic system," sending
messages via the blood, as Sir Arthur Keith put it.[10] For Keith, this is an older
and more primitive system than the nerves. The hormones, as they were
christened by Ernest Starling of University College London in 1905, were
gradually isolated: thyroid hormone in 1915, insulin in 1921; oestrin, pro-
gesterone, androgens and testosterone by midcentury.[11] Otto Loewi's
experiments on the frog's heart in 1921 identified "Vagusstoff" (acetylcho-
line), establishing the existence of neurotransmitters, a chemical component
of nerve activity. The notion of "homeostasis," developed by Walter
B. Cannon to describe the neuro-endocrine system in 1926, was linked to
an emerging understanding of the body as a complex set of interrelated
nervous and chemical systems.[12] In embryology, a focus on the problems
of development and differentiation produced major research.
The development of tissue culture after Jacques Loeb's 1902 breakthrough
(by 1911 clotted plasma could be used as a medium for maintaining cell
growth indefinitely) was an added stimulus to biochemistry: life itself, it
seemed, could be treated in the laboratory.

Nowhere is complexity more apparent than in genetics. Darwin's
depiction of natural selection operating on random changes had produced a major challenge both to man's central place in the order of
things and ideas of a directional evolution. What Peter J. Bowler calls
the "Eclipse of Darwinism" had produced, by 1900, a number of competing neo-Lamarkian theories, many of them attempting to hold on to
a residue of purpose in evolution against the "new materialism."[13] With
the rediscovery and dissemination of Mendel's work in 1900 the direction
of genetics was set – T. H. Morgan's 1910–15 work on the *Drosophila*
gene rapidly produced a sense of the parameters of Mendelian inheritance, for example.

One implication of the new biology was a displacing of the human into
what might be called context. In "Philosophic Ants: A Biological Fantasy,"
a paper read to the Cambridge Heretics in 1922, Julian Huxley argued for
a "biological relativity" in which perception and being are related to environment; to think in these terms means to "quit our anthropocentricity."[14]
That "context" might be the human's own natural history; it is surely no
coincidence that arguably the most enthusiastic interwar popularizer of
Freud's ideas in the UK was Sir Arthur Tansley, the eminent ecologist.
In *The New Psychology and Its Relation to Life* (1920) he wrote,

> The human mind, then, is an organism, which like all organisms is continuously
> expressing the life that is in it by the discharge of energy. The form and

direction which the discharges take are determined absolutely by the structures of the organism – in the case of the mind by the complexes which are developed as the result of the interaction of the instincts with one another and with the whole mental environment.[15]

The "complexes" are themselves an internal version of biological complexity. In Tansley's own field, the influential concepts of "biological succession" and "climax community" espoused by the American ecologist Frederic Clements in the early 1900s – involving a form of ontogenetic thinking, a directionality directed at an ideal stable state – was gradually displaced by an ecology in which change is ever-present, and in which the pressures of modernity create a need to intervene in natural processes.[16]

What are the literary correlatives of "complexity" and the new biological thinking? The self "expressing the life that is in it by the discharge of energy" (as Tansley put it) is everywhere apparent in Lawrence, seen against the background of environments that nurture or hinder the self's exfoliation.[17] Lawrence's writings assert a fundamental biological reality that might be grasped, whether the life of a horse, or the influence of the sun on a naked body; or the chemistry of desire. Maurice, inserting Bertie's fingers into his empty eye-sockets in Lawrence's "The Blind Man," says, "Oh, my God ... we shall know each other now, shan't we? We shall know each other now."[18] Maurice's knowledge, in Lawrence's text, is not knowledge of Bertie's rationalizations and intellectual values, which Maurice rather despises; it is knowledge gained in the dark, among his animals, linked to touch, the blood and the genitals rather than to sight and science. For W. B. Yeats too "generation" is a "blind" force that must ultimately be accepted and affirmed:

> I am content to live it all again
> And yet again, if it be life to pitch
> Into the frog-spawn of a blind man's ditch,
> A blind man battering blind men.[19]

As Ronan McDonald argues, "A Dialogue of Self and Soul" is "enmeshed in biological struggle and the physical world," exemplifying a Darwinism at odds with Yeats's official opposition to the Darwinian and mechanistic worldview.[20] For Yeats, the "mere complexities" or "complexities of mire or blood" of "Byzantium" are, McDonald suggests, an index of the inescapably biological; the soul's desire for unity is pitted against complexity but can only be extracted from it via a posthumous untangling.[21] The essentially occult nature of Yeats's reaction to the science of his time – his replacement of its diverse forms of knowledge with the simplified structures of *A Vision* – testifies, among other things, to the difficulties of synthesis involved.

In such accounts the biological is not simply a category that includes the human; it in some senses obviates or undermines the values of consciousness and even language; true bodily knowledge becomes a plunge into the animal. In contrast, "complexity" for many writers may include an understanding of biology that locates it more firmly within the world of human knowledge, or at least an analysis of human existence that might inform literature. An example is Marianne Moore, who sustained an interest in natural history and evolution across her career, reading extremely widely from Humboldt and Darwin to Haldane and Robert Yerkes, attending lectures on the subject at the Brooklyn Institute and American Natural History Museum, and of course writing many poems on exotic and occasionally less exotic creatures. Moore's Darwinism informs her attitude to poetic evolution, including her sense of the exposure of her unauthorized first volume of poems, like Darwin's "naked pigeon," in the harsh environment of modernism; her own tendency to cut superfluous or non-functional, as she saw it, sections of her exfoliating poems, or perhaps simply to keep them evolving, for better or worse, like "Poetry" in its drift from thirty to three lines between 1919 and 1967.[22] And finally, there is her tendency to see the syllabic stanza-form as akin to a self-replicating genotype might be seen in terms of her concern with form as acted on by the "instinct" of the poet.[23]

Moore's letters provide examples of involved forms of biological thinking. A 1921 letter to Bryher moves from the feel of a snake's skin and muscles, "like the complicated orderly appearance of the ropes by which a ship's sails are tethered to the mast" to a comment on anachronism in literary form ("a great many trashy old time novels are being written today ... and the form annoys one along with the content"); followed by a comment on Dostoevsky's experimentation; and finally on to marriage ("in Turkey, monogomy is gaining as it is everywhere else").[24] What unites these observations is a mode of thought in which form and its mode of reproduction are considered across different fields. Consider the opening of "Virginia Britannia" (1935):

> Pale sand edges England's Old
> Dominion. The air is soft, warm, hot
> above the cedar-dotted emerald shore
> known to the red-bird, the red-coated musketeer,
> the trumpet-flower, the cavalier,
> the parson, and the wild parishioner. A deer-
> track in a church-floor
> brick, and a fine pavement tomb with engraved top, remain.[25]

Here there is a balance of environment (the New World) and inhabitants, with no real distinction between human, plant and animal; between nature and making. The poem describes a complex hybridization, a field through which the poet advances cautiously, as she watches a culture evolve.

The final word on writing as process akin to natural law can be provided by Lorine Niedecker's late-modernist poems of process and observation, and the formal adhesion to biology registered in her poem "Darwin." Its stanzas like Moore's are a template-shape thrusting forward with subtle variation, registering persons, creatures and their environments:

> the universe
> not built by brute force
> but designed by laws
> The details left
>
> to the working of chance
> "Let each man hope
> and believe
> what he can."[26]

In the universe of uncertainty depicted by Niedecker, the poem's gappy field is itself a form of environmental mapping; a place of dynamic interactions and a response to the human position between totality and local knowledge.

Biopolitics and World-Planning

If the embodied creative process of the individual was one focus for biological and environmental thinking, another was society more generally. J. B. S. Haldane wrote in 1927 that

> one gets the very strong impression that from the quantitative study of animal and plant associations some laws of a very unsuspected and fundamental character are emerging; laws of which much that we know of human history and economics only constitute special and rather complicated cases. When we see human history and sociology against a background of such simpler phenomena, it is hard to doubt that we shall understand ourselves and one another more clearly.[27]

Applying biological ideas to the "social organism" had been commonplace since Herbert Spencer, and despite early attacks on Spencer's metaphors from T. H. Huxley and cautions from leading scientists like H. S. Jennings about the incomplete state of knowledge, the study of animal behavior was readily applied to popular understandings of human societies between the wars, whether it was Pavlov's experiments with animal conditioning, the "totalitarian" hierarchy of primates at "Monkey Hill" in London Zoo, or the study of the behavior of ticks – all examples which suggested the potential malleability of human populations.[28] A number of writers, notably William Empson, were to follow Julian Huxley in exploring ant and termite societies as reflections of the human.[29]

The focus on biopolitics was related in turn to the fantasy of intervention. The Eugenics movement had, from its inception, proposed state intervention in human populations, and was supported by a range of writers on the left and right from George Bernard Shaw to W. B. Yeats.[30] Chemical enhancements of performance began with experiments on troops in World War I. Experiments in hormone therapy and gender reassignment date from the same period.

The greatest stimulus to such thinking was provided by H. G. Wells, who inspired many scientists to popularize their fields and speculate on human futures. In Chapter 9 of *An Experiment in Autobiography* (1934), "The Idea of a Planned World," he wrote of the chairs he would like to endow:

> From the biological point of view my Professors would be human ecologists; indeed Human Ecology would be a good alternative name for this new history as I conceive it . . . My new men and the students under them would be working out strands of biological, intellectual, economic consequences. Periods, nations and races they would consider only in so far as these provided them with material facts. They would be related to the older school of historians much as vegetable physiologists ecologists and morphologists are related to the old plant-flattening, specimen-hunting, stamen-counting botanists. The end of all intelligent analysis is to clear the way for synthesis. The clearer their new history became the nearer they would be to efficient world-planning. All this is very obvious to-day but it was by no means clear in 1900.

This is the Wells who berated Aldous Huxley for his parody of planning in *Brave New World*. In fact, Wells's ideas were in the mainstream in the 1930s, where the pressure of economic and political crisis pushed many toward notions of a rationally planned society: Julian Huxley became convinced of the need for an "organic" planned economy in the 1930s, and organizations as different as the American Technocracy movement and Mosley's British Union of Fascists proposed social, biological and economic "engineering."[31]

These ideas were not unopposed: eugenics in particular became less popular as the Nazi party applied it brutally in Germany. *Brave New World* is broad in its comedy, and it is, as David Bradshaw points out, ambivalent about the need for control of human societies – certainly Huxley was one of the many drawn to forms of technocracy and eugenics in the early 1930s, as civilization seemed to stutter, and the novel's world-controller is in the end a more self-conscious figure than the flawed rebels. But what seems to me most original in Huxley's satire is less the manipulation of test-tube babies than the stress on repressive desublimation: the control of the sexualized body via total expression of the body's needs; the attack on repression and any idealization of the sexual object, desire reduced to a comic and stereotyped pneumatics and an ant-like chemical feeding. Huxley's world is in fact one where the complexity of genetics and social action continues to throw up dissatisfaction; where control can only ever be a general scattering of biological energy.

Along with Wells, literary scientific writers who moved fluidly between real reputations in science, popular journalism and fiction include Edward Herron-Allen and Morley Roberts. The former (discussed briefly in the next section) was translator of Omar Khayyam, expert on the biological order of *foraminifera*, and (as Christopher Blayre) a writer of fantasy and science fiction. The latter was a man of letters as well as a writer of biological syntheses who forged close links with the anatomist Sir Arthur Keith. Keith in turn was part of a group of eminent scientists for whom the values attached to literature were important in sustaining a holistic view of biology and society, including E. Ray Lankester and Walter Langdon-Brown.[32] Langdon-Brown's specialism was endocrinology and the sympathetic nervous system. He was drawn to it, Christopher Lawrence argues, because of a holism which enabled parallels between society and the body as integrated and balanced (or, in contrast, subject to pathological imbalances): "Brown used the endocrine system to bring together mind and body, individual and society, man and animal, and past and present and to integrate all these into a single biological domain."[33] Thus he could write on the "biology of social life," and explore, in his essays, a range of topics linking medicine and culture.[34]

Morley Roberts is a particularly interesting case, not least because he received a warmer welcome from scientists seeking synthesis than he did from literary culture. Julian Huxley for example cites Roberts approvingly in *Essays of a Biologist* (1923), as an author who attempts to link sociology and biology, and in 1934 five scientists wrote to the *Times* pointing out the importance of his *Malignancy and Evolution* to the study of cancer.[35] Roberts shared a version of qualified Lamarckism with Rignano and other theorists of "emergent evolution."[36] In the 1930s he developed a "Political Ecology" expressed in such texts as *Bio-politics: An Essay in the Physiology, Pathology and Politics of the Social and Somatic Organism* (1938) and *The Behavior of Nations: An Essay on the Conduct of National Organisms in the Nutritional Field* (1941). In his texts, societies are dynamic organisms comprised of competing specialized parts and nations similarly struggle for resources in an anarchic world.[37]

In Roberts's case, we are at some distance from the fantasies of planned intervention promoted by Wells: the situation is one of perpetual struggle. The novelistic equivalence of this worldview is provided by an author like Theodore Dreiser, who was strongly influenced by Jacques Loeb's mechanistic worldview. Dreiser declared in a 1936 interview that he was interested in "speculative biology."[38] His characters struggle blindly in the present, uninterested in the past, and are driven by passions they barely comprehend. This is from *The Stoic* (1947), the last volume of his Cowperwood trilogy. The aging financier and his lover Berenice are visiting Canterbury, where she becomes engrossed in the tombs in the cathedral:

> Cowperwood, who saw things in the large, could scarcely endure this minutae. He was but little interested in the affairs of bygone men and women, being so intensely engaged with the living present. And after a time he slipped outside, preferring the wide sweep of gardens, with their flower-lined walks and views of the cathedral. Its arches and towers and stained-glass windows, this whole carefully executed shrine, still held glamor, but all because of the hands and brains, aspirations and dreams of selfish and self-preserving creatures like himself ... Was any man noble? Had there ever been such a thing as an indubitably noble soul? He was scarcely prepared to believe it. Men killed to live – all of them – and wallowed in lust in order to reproduce themselves. In fact, wars, vanities, pretenses, cruelties, greeds, lusts, murder, spelled their true history, with only the weak running to a mythical saviour or god for aid.[39]

The lack of interest in the past; the struggle in a new environment – Cowperwood has moved to London to invest in the underground system – are the keynotes.

But one should also note that one result of evolutionary thinking, and of the kind of futurology promoted by the Today & Tomorrow series edited by C. K. Ogden, was an expansion of *uncertainty*. Evolution was, Darwin implied, a catalogue of destruction; even humankind would pass away. Before that happened, radical changes might occur; biology might wander down unanticipated pathways; human populations and environment might shift radically. That too was canvased by science fiction: Well's own pessimistic projections of degeneration in *The Time Machine* haunt his desire for planning. Katharine Burdekin's *Proud Man* (1934), to take another example, describes a time-traveler (the "person") from a future society in which there is no gender and people are self-fertilizing mind-readers; the same writer's *The End of this Day's Business* – published many years after it was written –

describes an inverted future society ruled by woman in a kind of benign fascism, in which men are regarded as the hapless weaker sex. Closer to the period's present, the Harlem Renaissance author George S. Schuyler's *Black No More: Being an Account of the Strange and Wonderful Workings of Science in the Land of the Free, AD 1933–1940* (1931) describes an African American scientist who invents a process for turning black people white, with hilarious consequences, not least an inability to identify "race" biologically or culturally. Inherited certainties of gender and race were unfixed, and world-planning in that context seeks to stabilize that which is dangerously contingent.

Engineering Bodies: Bottled Babies and Pickled Glands

Despite the uncertainties described above, a purposive Lamarckism often persisted in the analysis of technology as it applied to the body. In such texts as J. D. Bernal's *The World, the Flesh and the Devil* (1929), the body is refigured in terms of its technological extensions. Responding to this in his critique of scientific and technological modernity in *The Art of Being Ruled* (1926), Wyndham Lewis attacked what he called "biologic transformation" – the idea of the extension of human capacities which he saw in the Futurists and in Haldane's *Daedalus* – as unhelpful in human terms, pointing out (after Locke) that hearing a thousand times more acutely would only mean we existed in a roar of distraction.[40] The question of to what extent the human might be reconfigured by medical technologies remained open.

Hormones, as we have already noted, were central to notions of social-biological engineering, suggesting a direct access to human emotions at a primitive level. Charles Duff's play *Mind Products Limited: A Melodrama of the Future* (1932) satirizes the notion of social control primed by endocrines; as does *Brave New World* the same year. Experimentation with the individual application of hormone therapy was common: the Steinach Operation undertaken by Freud and Yeats in the interests of rejuvenation is perhaps the best-known example. Novels of the 1920s like Gertrude Atherton's *Black Oxen* (1923) show a lively interest in rejuvenation technologies, but by the end of the decade glandular extracts were as likely to be depicted as quackery. Angus McLaren lists a succession of novels that deal with rejuvenation techniques, increasingly the vehicle for satire: C. P. Snow's *New Lives for Old* (1933), M. E. Mitchell's *Yet in My Flesh* (1933), John Gloag's *Winter's Youth* (1934), and Huxley (again) in *After Many a Summer* (1939).[41] In the latter, deferred aging is investigated by the scientist Dr. Obispo. When he tracks down the pioneering Earl of

Gonister, who has treated himself with raw carp intestines, he finds a 200-year-old ape hidden in caverns beneath his ancestral home: the end result predicted by the theory of neotony, in which evolutionary progress is achieved by the deferring of adult characteristics (so the human is a "foetal ape" that normally dies before maturity).[42]

Imaginations of experiments with gender are a particularly fertile area, though they take predictably gendered lines. As McLaren points out, the role of female hormones was a particularly important area in the 1920s.[43] Christopher Blayre's *The Cheetah-Girl* appeared only in a privately printed edition of twenty-five in 1923, understandably given its sex with a thirteen-year-old, lesbianism, as well as the interspecies procreation hinted at in the title. Referencing E. Ray Lankester's classic experiments on parthenogenesis in sea urchins, it explores the idea that "the action of the spermatozoon is primarily mechanicity, it merely perforates and excites the ovum and 'sets it going,' so to speak, and may therefore be replaced by artificial and mechanical means."[44] If this is the case, "why should there be any limits to the possibility of miscegenation?" (249). Thus the cheetah-human cross: "[t]he serum of the one accommodated the corpuscles of the other without any trace of haemolysis" (284). The result is a being at once sexy and shocking, the wife (and experimental animal) whom at novel's end the narrator promises to kill.

If the feminine is the field of experiment, masculine accounts – as in Yeats's Steinach Operation – tend to focus on the extension of personal power. Masculine glands are explored by the Harlem Renaissance writer, Rudolph Fisher in his detective novel *The Conjure-Man Dies* (1932). Fisher, who gained an MA in biology at Brown and graduated from Harvard Medical School, describes the African prince and scientist Frimbo, who can seemingly read the future and declares that "Psychology is really a branch of biology."[45] He and the African American doctor Archer, who declares himself insufficiently up on endocrines, discuss "the hopelessness of applying physio-chemical methods to psychological problems" (127). Nevertheless Frimbo keeps "male glands" in jars, and what enables him to lift himself out of "the common order of things" and transcend causality is the secret "rite of the gonad." As he explains,

> The germplasm, of which the gonad is the only existing sample, is the unbroken heritage of the past. It is protoplasm which has been continuously maintained throughout thousands of generations ... It is therefore the only matter which brings into the present every influence which the past has imprinted upon life. He who can learn its use can be master of his past. And he who can master his past, that man is free. (159)

Here he sounds something like Propter, Huxley's version of the science writer and philosopher Gerald Heard in *After Many a Summer*, setting the determined past against an eternity of possibility. Freedom, in the novel, includes the freedom to walk toward a death produced by Frimbo's own (adulterous) bodily urges.

Equally fascinating was the idea that the production of humans could be directly engineered, as they are in Huxley's novel; that reproduction could become production. John Hargrave's *The Imitation Man* (1931) is one of a range of novels on test-tube babies published in the interwar period, initiated perhaps by the "rows upon rows of gravid bottles" in "vast state incubators" predicted in Aldous Huxley's *Crome Yellow* (1921).[46] Hargrave, as leader of the eccentric group known as the Kindred of the Kibbo Kift, may be the original of Webley in Huxley's *Point Counter Point* – in which case it is interesting to speculate whether Huxley was aware of *The Imitation Man* as he wrote *Brave New World*.[47] The imitation man is Charles Chapman, a homunculus created in a bottle buried in a pile of horse dung by the chemist Harold Chater. He feeds off pure energy ("actinic rays") and quickly grows into splendid manhood, then is exploited by the biologist Mostyn, who combines with the financier Sir Betram Emmet and uses Chapman's extreme empathetic power – effectively mind-reading – to take over much of the world's business. But Chapman eventually outgrows his sponsors and becomes a virtual dictator. Finally, when he marries his first love, Chater's sister Ella, he is burned up in the "act of love," returning to "elemental salts."

The most marked feature of Chapman is mimesis: he imitates others, enacting their desires – blurting out Chater's obsession with a shop-girl and wooing her; ordering luxuries dreamed of by the housekeeper. He learns language in a manner akin to that later described in B. F. Skinner's *Verbal Behavior* (1957), absorbing cues. This can produce wildly inappropriate responses – initially random; later poorly judged, as when he uses the brutal language of a working class couple with Ella: "I knew what *yew* was after all along."[48] But eventually he has assimilated so many people that he comes to approach the status of everyman; his discourse ceases to be random and is smoothed like a pebble. This produces a simulacrum of free will:

> At first he had no mind of his own, and so unknowingly took on the mental mechanics of others. He had no feelings of his own, but received the sensations of others. He had no will of his own, but by degrees the wills of others engraved within him an average will. The will of one person would counterbalance or

cancel out the will of someone else ... But all the time one general quality was being stamped into Mr. Chapman. He began, at last, to feel that he was "himself." He was nothing of the sort, of course. He was everybody else, but never himself.

(206–7)

This is akin to the self elicited by compulsory intersubjectivity in *Brave New World*. Chapman is at the same time a perfect emblem of democracy and a parody of that democracy; a leader who can absorb the will of the crowd but who has nothing to add to its views; whose self-assertion is without content. He merely *is* the situation rather than intervening in it. It is significant that his demise is linked to sexual passion – he cannot incorporate "nature's increase," as Ezra Pound would have put it; nothing grows from him.[49] The constructed human is merely a statistical person rather than an extension of the human.

The Uses of Pathology

Oscar Wilde, while still at Oxford in the late 1870s, noted that the "science of society ... rests on the science of life: sociology on Biology," before moving on to note "the increased differentiation of function and structure" in evolution.[50] *The Picture of Dorian Gray* can be read as an illustration of August Weismann's distinction between unchanging germ-cell and time-bound soma.[51] But it also is an illustration of a pathology: in producing himself as artwork, Dorian has interrupted the dynamic process of evolution. Indeed, Wilde's work and its reception reflects the shift in conceptions of "genius" that took place in the work of Nietzsche, Max Nordau and others, in which rather than representing the "central" human, the genius is "sick," living close to madness and exclusion.

Contemporary popular biology reinforced this view that the pathological may be productive. Morley Roberts emphasized accident, mistake, and stress in evolution, with many evolutionary developments being triggered, in his view, by a response to a pathological development: the nervous system, for example, was produced by a cellular invasion from outside the body.[52] His work finds an echo in C. P. Donnison's *Civilization and Disease* (1937), with an introduction by Langdon-Brown, which depicts civilization as a permanent state of excess in "the kinetic system, in which the brain, thyroid gland, adrenal glands and the sympathetic nervous system have become hyper-active."[53] Roberts concurred, seeing the body in terms of perpetual internal glandular warfare rather than a well-integrated homeostasis.

Haldane was also willing to understand the evolution of literature as paralleling that of biology in its move toward complexity and over-elaboration:

> To my mind the closest analogy to the evolution of a given group is the history of art and literature of a civilization. The clumsy primitive forms are replaced by a great variety of types. Different schools arise and decline more or less rapidly. Finally, a period of decline sets in, characterized by archaism like that of the last ammonites. And it is difficult not to compare some of the fantastic animals of the declining periods of a race with the work of Miss Sitwell, or the clumsy but impressive with that of Epstein.[54]

For Walter Langdon-Brown, the childishness of modern writing is evidence of neotony, or an extended childhood.[55] As he noted in a 1931 in a study of anorexia, referencing Keith, "the tendency to carry youthful characters into adult life has played a large part in the evolution of human races." While this is seen as detrimental in the anorexic's refusal of adulthood, the payoff is "a plasticity out of which higher characteristics can be moulded."[56] Biological openness finds its correlative in literary experiment.

A final example of productive pathology can be provided. William Carlos Williams in *A Novelette* (1932), writes the flu epidemic of 1929 into his prose, weaving sickness as inspiration and botany into a poetics of plant life in which, say, the great mullein is an emblem of noble ruin. Williams describes the epidemic itself as both a distraction and the reassignment and refocusing of attention. He even finds a physiological basis for the equation of epidemic and the release of static constellations of knowledge, noting that the strong toxins of flu create a state of useful fatigue:

> After the flu a weakness persists that is out of all proportion to the coincident anatomical changes, proving the effects of an evanescent poison of great intensity. Also proving that all the information that is static in the liberal arts and sciences can, by intelligent understanding, be made active – loosed from a cupboard of dullness – Thus fatigue, so called, dulls the perception. It is hard to keep on a basis of actuality.
>
> Sycamore trees shed their bark differently from most others, by patches, leaving a green of yellow freshness for the beginning year. Nijinski's tights.[57]

In this text Surrealism is an "epidemic" that will infect America, renewing the word; it is a rebirth and a collision with the modern world (literally, in the text, a car crash). Williams' style, with its disconnected observations, figured as a response to (and indeed an anticipation of) that epidemic.

This chapter has necessarily ranged over a number of loosely connected examples, seeking points of entry into a confluence of science and literature that has barely been defined, and in which more work is needed. What unites the examples, it seems to me, is a sense of the contingency and malleability of the human; both an uncertainty about the complex possibilities raised by science and a desire to grasp those possibilities. The life sciences were building, in the period, a dominant role in the understanding of human beings, but the syntheses on offer were less certain. Literature's relation to these debates ranges from the productivity of styles interpenetrated by medical or evolutionary ideas (Moore, Williams, and others) to the speculative, and often pessimistic, description of possible worlds transformed by science (Huxley, Burdekin and others). This in turn reflects a fundamental uncertainty in the face of scientific hegemony, which both threatened a cultural dominance and offered exciting possibilities of cultural change, as well as new forms of knowledge and *praxis*.

In this sense, the period of what we call modernism (albeit a disparate and conflicted body or writing) is one of openness to possible futures, as signaled by the rise of science fiction in the period from 1926. In the postwar world, biology and genetic research become more specialized and distant from literary culture, and the study of the human more influenced by cybernetics and systems theory of the kind developed at MIT by the mathematician Norbert Wiener – himself a Harvard acquaintance of T. S. Eliot who worked briefly in Cambridge in the mid-1920s. The world that the life sciences posited became more distinct and defined by disciplinary needs, and speculation rarer. Science continues to give rise to utopian forms of thinking – on forms of chemical enhancement, genetic manipulation and body-extension; on technology and the posthuman; on networked groupings – but it is a notable fact of recent more dystopian texts, by William Gibson, David Mitchell, or Gary Shteyngart, say, that they deal with near futures which are closely and consciously modeled on our own time and preoccupied with state and corporate control. That bespeaks, perhaps, a relative pessimism about the potential of technology and biology, which reflects a more closed cultural field.

NOTES

1. See H. G. Wells, Julian Huxley, and G. P. Wells, *The Science of Life: A Summary of Contemporary Knowledge about Life and Its Possibilities*, 3 vols. (London: Amalgamated Press, 1929–30).
2. See Julian Huxley, *Evolution: The Modern Synthesis* (London: George Allen and Unwin, 1942). The "Modern Synthesis" involved the integration of Darwinian and Mendelian thought within a scientific paradigm involving genetics, statistics, the study of populations, ecology and paleontology.

3. J. B. S. Haldane, *Daedalus, or Science and the Future* (London: Kegan Paul, Trench & Trubner, 1923), 77. The Today & Tomorrow series – a combination of futurology and provocative essay – was published by Kegan Paul (and E. P. Dutton in the US) between 1923 and 1931, and developed by the linguist and philosopher C. K. Ogden, who was central to the Cambridge dialogue between the arts and science and later responsible for the development of Basic English.

4. Julian Huxley, *Essays of a Biologist* (London: Chatto & Windus, 1923), viii.

5. Aldous Huxley, "Science and Civilization," in *The Hidden Huxley*, ed. David Bradshaw (London: Faber & Faber, 1994), 105–14.

6. On Cambridge, see kitt price [Katy Price], "Finite but Unbounded: Experiment Magazine, Cambridge, England, 1928–31," *Jacket* 20 (2002), http://jacketmagazine.com/20/orice-expe.html.

7. Herbert Wildon Carr, "Life and Matter," *The Realist* 2:2 (1929): 196.

8. Georges Canguilhem, "On the History of the Life Sciences since Darwin," in *Ideology and Rationality in the History of the Life Sciences*, trans. Arthur Goldhammer (Cambridge, MA: MIT Press, 1988), 117.

9. Lamarckism, the belief derived from the French biologist Jean-Baptiste Lamarck that acquired characteristics may be transmitted to offspring, enjoyed a resurgence in the early twentieth century: see Peter J. Bowler, *The Eclipse of Darwinism: Anti-Darwinian Evolution Theories in the Decades Around 1900* (Baltimore: Johns Hopkins University Press, 1992). The idea that evolution may be purposive or teleological similarly appealed to many writers, often linked to versions of orthogenesis: the idea that evolution represents a linear in-folding according to some inner force or principal of design.

10. Arthur Keith, *Engines of the Human Body*, 2nd ed. (London: Williams & Norgate, 1925), 222.

11. A. F. Hughes, "A History of Endocrinology," *Journal of the History of Medicine and Allied Sciences*, 32 (1977): 292–313.

12. V. C. Medvei, *The History of Clinical Endocrinology: A Comprehensive Account of Endocrinology from Earliest Times to the Present Day*, rev. ed. (Carnforth: Parthenon Press, 1993), 415.

13. Peter J. Bowler, *Science for All: The Popularisation of Science in Early Twentieth-Century Britain* (Chicago: University of Chicago Press, 2009), 50.

14. Huxley, *Essays of a Biologist*, 200–1.

15. Arthur G. Tansley, *The New Psychology and Its Relation to Life* (London: Allen & Unwin, 1920), 71.

16. See Peder Anker, *Imperial Ecology: Environmental Order in the British Empire, 1895–1945* (Cambridge: Harvard University Press, 2001).

17. On Lawrence's "bio-centrism," see Margot Norris, *Beasts of the Modern Imagination: Darwin, Nietzsche, Kafka, Ernst, & Lawrence* (Baltimore: Johns Hopkins University Press, 1985).

18. D. H. Lawrence, "The Blind Man," in *England, My England and Other Stories*, ed. Bruce Steele (Cambridge: Cambridge University Press, 1990), 46–63, at 62.

19. W. B. Yeats, "A Dialogue of Self and Soul," in *The Collected Works of W. B. Yeats, Vol. 1: The Poems*, 2nd edn, ed. Richard J. Finneran (New York: Scribner, 1997), 236.

20. Ronan McDonald, "Darwinian Traces in Yeats's Poetry," in *Science in Modern Poetry: New Directions*, ed. John Holmes (Liverpool: Liverpool University Press, 2012), 160.

21. Yeats, *Poems*, 252.

22. See, for example, Susan McCabe, "Survival of the Queerly Fit: Darwin, Marianne Moore, and Elizabeth Bishop," *Twentieth-Century Literature* 55.4 (2009): 547–71; Robin G. Schulze, "Textual Darwinism: Marianne Moore, the Text of Evolution, and the Evolving Text," *Text* 11 (1998): 270–305.

23. See Robin G. Schulze, *The Degenerate Muse: American Nature, Modernist Poetry, and the Problem of National Hygiene* (New York: Oxford University Press, 2013), 171–8. Moore's stanza patterns often involve a syllabic grid that is replicated – an almost mathematical pattern that is independent of the traditional arrangements of stress or rhyme.

24. Moore to Bryher, August 31, 1921, in *The Selected Letters of Marianne Moore*, ed. Bonnie Costello, Celeste Goodridge and Cristanne Miller (New York: Alfred A. Knopf, 1997), 176–7.

25. *The Poems of Marianne Moore*, ed. Grace Schulman (New York: Viking, 2003), 212.

26. Lorine Niedecker, "Darwin," in *Collected Works*, ed. Jenny Penberthy (Berkeley: University of California Press, 2002), 299. The lines cited by Niedecker are from a letter that Charles Darwin wrote to the American botanist, Asa Gray, dated May 22, 1860. See www.darwinproject.ac.uk/letter/DCP-LETT-2814.xml.

27. J. B. S. Haldane, "The Future of Biology," in *Possible Worlds* (London: Evergreen, 1940), 134–48, at 137.

28. See Jonathan Burt, "Violent Health and the Moving Image: London Zoo and Monkey Hill," in *Animals in Human Histories: The Mirror of Nature and Culture*, ed. Mary J. Henninger-Voss (Rochester: University of Rochester Press, 2002), 258–94; Charlotte Sleigh, *Six Legs Better: A Cultural History of Myrmecology* (Baltimore: Johns Hopkins University Press, 2007).

29. See kitt price [Katy Price], "William Empson, Ants and Aliens," in *Science in Modern Poetry*, 116–29, as well as price's essay in the present volume; and Tim Armstrong, "The Human Animal: Biological Tropes in Interwar Poetry," in *Science in Modern Poetry*, 101–15.

30. See Donald J. Childs, *Modernism and Eugenics: Woolf, Eliot, Yeats and the Culture of Degeneration* (Cambridge: Cambridge University Press, 2001).

31. On Huxley, see Peder Anker, *Imperial Ecology*, 204–8; on the United States, Edwin T. Layton, *The Revolt of the Engineers*, 2nd ed. (Baltimore: Johns Hopkins University Press, 1986).

32. See Joseph Lester, *E. Ray Lankester and the Making of Modern British Biology* (Oxford: British Society for the History of Science, 1995).

33. Christopher Lawrence, "A Tale of Two Sciences: Bedside and Bench in Twentieth-century Britain," *Medical History*, 43 (1999): 421–49, at 443.

34. See, for example, Sir Walter Langdon-Brown, "The Biology of Social life," in *Thus We Are Men* (London: Kegan Paul, Trench, Trubner, 1938), 11–31.

35. Storm Jameson, *Morley Roberts: The Last Eminent Victorian* (London: Unicorn Press, 1961), 36; Christopher Lawrence, "Still Incommunicable: Clinical Holists

and Medical Knowledge in Interwar Britain," in *Greater than the Parts: Holism in Biomedicine 1920–1950*, ed. Christopher Lawrence and George Weisz (New York: Oxford University Press, 1998), 94–111; Julian Huxley, *Essays of a Biologist*, 75.

36. See C. Lloyd Morgan, *Emergent Evolution* (London: Williams and Norgate, 1923).

37. See Rhodri Hayward, "The Biopolitics of Arthur Keith and Morley Roberts," in *Regenerating England: Science, Medicine and Culture in Inter-war Britain*, ed. Christopher Lawrence and Anna-K. Mayer (Amsterdam: Rodophi, 2000), 251–74.

38. *Theodore Dreiser Interviews*, ed. Frederic E. Rusch and Donald Pizer (Urbana: University of Illinois Press, 2004), 293.

39. Theodore Dreiser, *The Stoic* (London: Doubleday, 1947), 137.

40. Wyndham Lewis, *The Art of Being Ruled*, ed. Reed Way Dasenbrock (Santa Rosa: Black Sparrow Press, 1989), 191.

41. Angus McLaren, *Reproduction by Design: Sex, Robots, Trees, and Test-tube Babies in Interwar Britain* (Chicago: University of Chicago Press, 2012), 94–9; Susan Merrill Squier, *Babies in Bottles: Twentieth-Century Visions of Reproductive Technology* (New Brunswick: Rutgers University Press, 1994).

42. On literary responses to neoteny, see Tim Armstrong, "The Human Animal," 112–15.

43. Angus McLaren, *Reproduction by Design*, 100.

44. Christopher Blayre [Edward Herron-Allen], *The Cheetah-Girl* (London: privately printed, 1923), 249.

45. Rudolph Fisher, *The Conjure-Man Dies: A Mystery Tale of Dark Harlem* (New York: Covici-Friede, 1932), 106.

46. Aldous Huxley, *Crome Yellow* (1921: London: Chatto & Windus, 1949), 47.

47. David Bradshaw, "Huxley's 'Tinpot Mussolini' and the KKK's 'White Fox': A New Source for Everard Webley and the Brotherhood of British Freemen in 'Point Counter Point,'" *Aldous Huxley Annual* 2 (2002): 146–59.

48. John Hargrave, *The Imitation Man* (London: Gollancz, 1931), 129.

49. "Usury kills the child in the womb / And breaks short the young man's courting / Usury brings age into youth; it lies between the bride / and the bridegroom / Usury is against Nature's increase." *The Cantos of Ezra Pound* (New York: New Directions, 1996), 250.

50. *Oscar Wilde's Oxford Notebooks: A Portrait of Mind in the Making*, ed. Philip E. Smith and Michael S. Helfand (Oxford: Oxford University Press, 1989), 109.

51. See Michael Wainwright, *Toward a Sociobiological Hermeneutic* (New York: Palgrave Macmillan, 2012), 25–48.

52. Morley Roberts, *Malignancy and Evolution: A Biological Inquiry into the Nature and Causes of Cancer* (London: Eveleigh, Nash & Grayson, 1926) and *The Serpent's Fang: Essays in Biological Criticism* (London: Eveleigh, Nash & Grayson, 1930).

53. C. P. Donnison, *Civilization and Disease* (London: Ballière, Tindall and Cox, 1937), 77–8.

54. J. B. S. Haldane, "Darwinism Today," in *Possible Worlds*, 33–50, at 49.
55. Walter Langdon-Brown, "Myth, Phantasy and Mary Rose," in *Thus We Are Men*, 123–51.
56. *Anorexia Nervosa: A Discussion* (London: W. Daniel, 1931), 17.
57. William Carlos Williams, *Imaginations*, ed. Webster Schott (London: MacGibbon & Kee, 1970), 296.

13

REVIEL NETZ

The Long History of Cognitive Practices
Literacy, Numeracy, Aesthetics

This is the penultimate chapter of the present collection: it is there to provide a starting point – in the first instance, for the final chapter. To have Literature and Science, one needs to have literature and to have science. Both, in a sense, were Greek inventions. In this chapter I survey some of the issues concerning literature and science in Greek antiquity and their legacy. The title refers to literacy, numeracy and aesthetics, and one needs to bring to bear all three vectors. At heart is a question of media: at a given historical moment, how does one produce literature and how does the literary medium interface with that of science? How is all of that perceived by a mind that forms an aesthetic judgment?

Greek Science and Literature: A Miniature Map of Genre

The antiquated heresy above – literature and science, Greek inventions – is a valid, albeit contingent fact about the West. Literature, as well as science, could have been otherwise, and were indeed different in other civilizations. And yet, the system of genres we still refer to most naturally goes back to a series of choices made in classical Greece.

Such were the Greek genres. Poetry was of central value, epos being the most canonical, lyric presenting a more personal and precarious voice just beneath it. The main form of cultural expression otherwise was drama (or, in prose, speech). Such genres obtained their cultural currency from their association with the public performances of the Greek city-state. Here is a first observation: for the premodern West – for the heirs to the Greeks – the field of the literary meant, essentially, written works whose format or values somehow reflected acts of performance.

Alongside performances, the Greek city-states gave rise to forms of writing that were more purely written, and for which performance was less essential. Some early works were liminal in this regard: Herodotus could have recited his history, Plato certainly echoed the lived experience of Socratic performance, and many Hippocratic treatises of medicine are, effectively, speeches. But very early on, philosophy as well as medicine became primarily written forms (history, however, would always maintain its liminal position and its tight relation to the representation of political speech).

The exact sciences, in particular, would rely essentially on the written tool of the diagram and would thus be a writing-based genre *par excellence*: they are thus the most purely scientific of the scientific genres and will form the main theme of this chapter.

In sum, a bifurcation: some genres, effective through their evocation of performance and so, perhaps, more a matter of emotional affect; others, effective through their transmission of written content and so, perhaps, more a matter of cognitive computation. Western literary culture is shot through with a binary dialectic, performance against writing manifesting itself, in the largest scale, in the opposition between literature against science; within literature itself, the same opposition is reflected as the division of poetry against prose.

Here, then, is the Western (Greek) model of literary culture:

Performance:Writing::Literature:Science::Poetry:Prose

Performance is to writing as literature is to science and poetry is to prose.

We have thus located literature and science in terms of media – in other words, at the interface of literary and scientific media. A few further comments are required.

Greek civilization – emerging as it did from the small city-state, sometimes democratic and mostly sunny – was organized around public, open-air events. At the same time, this was also, in relative terms, a highly literate society. The Greeks imported an easy-to-learn alphabet from the Phoenicians, and a plentiful writing surface (papyrus) from the Egyptians. Starting at the classical era, this was a civilization awash with writing, accessible to a significant fraction of male city-dwellers. That the Greeks were less literate than their modern counterparts is beside the point. It is essential to note the vast difference between the civilization of the ancient near east (where writing was a scribal prerogative) and that of the Greek city-state, where writing and education were, literally, synonymous. It should be emphasized that while medieval parchment was rare and expensive, the ancient papyrus was, once again relatively speaking, neither. The thousands of scraps of literary papyri dug out of a small corner of the Mediterranean world (Upper Egypt), stand for millions upon millions of ancient rolls. These rolls were distributed in many private libraries, book collecting being a practice almost as common as reading itself. Alexandria did possess a royal library, but even in that city, most books would have been distributed in many private hands. In some ways, the scale of ancient civilization was surprisingly modern.

Thus, a civilization highly performative *and* highly written is also highly literary *and* highly scientific.

The seminal contributions of Greek civilization do not need to be rehearsed here. To praise Greek literature is to reaffirm a cultural choice to valorize a particular canon. This choice began with the Greeks themselves (who codified early on a clear set of canonical authors: Homer, the three tragedians, Pindar and other lyric poets, Demosthenes and the other orators ...). The following fact – contingent, socially constructed, nevertheless a fact – should be remembered: this choice was indeed reaffirmed in many different ways across many layers of European civilization, well into the twentieth century.

The same is no less true for science though, in that case, it would be even more fraught with danger to suggest that the choice to valorize a particular canon was in some sense contingent. Could we have had a different science? Is science, then, no less contingent than literature? Certainly so, in terms of its cultural expression. The Greeks came up with certain idiosyncratic approaches to science. Proof was valued above usefulness, hence a unique approach to the mathematical sciences. For most other early cultures, mathematics was a matter of practices of calculation. For the Greeks, mathematics was a matter of demonstrations about figures. Argument and demonstration are known in other civilizations but it was left to the Greeks to devise a specialized written form where one goes through a text, being compelled to affirm its validity throughout, overpowered by the sheer power of deductive logic.[1] This new type of genre – Greek mathematics – would exercise a profound influence on many later forms of writing.

In most civilizations, arguably also among the Greeks, the most important form of science is that of medicine. Even there, for the Greeks, argument and persuasion were valued no less than the practices of healing itself. In all of this we probably see traces of the practices of public performance – that is, public persuasion – of the Greek city-state. At any rate, a demonstrative, argumentative science would prove irresistible: having been exposed to persuasion, how could you now produce science that would *not* aim to persuade? Later scientific practices in the West are all heirs to Euclid and to Hippocrates.

I have noted the relatively marginal role of calculation, relative to proof, in Greek mathematics. It should be emphasized that calculation was marginal to Greek mathematical writing as a matter of media. Mathematics was written, organized around diagrams depicting geometrical figures. But calculation was not written, but rather manipulative. The basic form of calculation was based on the Mediterranean abacus, a system where small tokens, transposed and substituted with each other, stand for arithmetical calculation. A system of such tokens was noticeable everywhere where the Greeks handled numeracy – in their politics (voting was done with specialized kinds of tokens) and the economy (there, another Greek invention was that of the coin – a token of counting used for the calculation of economic transactions). The Greeks could of course write down the results of calculation but the act of calculation was just that – an act. For us, numbers are written traces and so semiotically they are at the same level as writing itself. For the Greeks, numbers were concrete manipulated entities, of a different semiotic order from the written trace. Calculation, one can almost say, belonged to the world of public performance. However, we learn something important by noting that even though performative, calculation, for the Greeks, was not valorized. What the Greeks valued was *performed speech*. Purely embodied, artifactual acts of performance were valued less than writing.

In the brief statement above we have noted the historical significance of the Greek arrangement of genres, as well its semiotic setting, always against the dialectic of writing and performance. Before concluding this miniature map a word should be said about our evidence. Greek writing was plentiful. As a consequence, much remains, and much more is lost. About 270 authors survive from Greek antiquity, of which no more than several dozen are clearly the authors of pure "literature." While the West always valued the canonical authors of Greek epic, drama and speech, it did not preserve more than a few canonical authors of those genres. Otherwise, practically everything else extant from the Greek belongs to the various technical genres: so, for instance, many works are extant by ancient grammarians (indeed, even the canonical works survived in Byzantium largely because they were entrenched as part of the educational process of Greek letters, hence almost works of "grammar": during part of its transmission, Greek literature became *all* technical). This is but a fraction of the work of thousands of ancient authors, and many more ancient works, now lost. However, our evidence is fairly representative of ancient tastes (as we can judge from the evidence of the papyri) and spread across many genres. We can learn about the Greeks and let us now proceed to look in more detail at two key examples of ancient scientific writing – of Greek science-as-literature.

A Sample of Two

Archimedes and the Exact Sciences. About thirty ancient Greek authors in the exact sciences are extant (over ten percent of the total authors extant!).

From several of these we even have substantial corpora that allow us to reconstruct a literary persona. In only one case – that of Archimedes – we can also see the ancient construct of the biographical author (note that, in this case, skepticism concerning the "biographical author" is a matter of fact, not theory[2]: the biographical evidence for Archimedes is mostly apocryphal). The biography presents an enigmatic person, isolating himself with his diagrams, that are not to be disturbed, asserting his science in gnomic, hyperbolic terms ("Give me a place to stand, and I shall move the earth" or just, simply, "Eureka!"). All of this, it turns out, is consonant with the extant body of work. In the extant treatises – ten, even without counting fragmentary works and those known only via translation – we see a science that strikes out in surprising ways, marked with literary qualities. Indeed, the literary character of Archimedes's science may well be related to the poetics of the literature of his time.

Archimedes was active in the third century BCE, the century following the consolidation of the Greek canon. It was a time when Greek culture expanded from the core areas of the Greek city-states, to the new Hellenistic kingdoms of Alexander's heirs: postcanonical, postdemocratic, postperformative. It was an era where literature itself became more written, and also more scientific. The great flowering of Greek science took place then, and indeed, from the third century BCE, the bulk of our extant literature is mathematical: the original poetry of this era always stood in the shadow of the preceding canon. Still, authors such as Callimachus, Aratus, Theocritus and Apollonius of Rhodes created their new version of Greek poetry, which did survive (if in a somewhat qualified sense) as an appendix, as it were, to the Greek canon (indeed, this Hellenistic poetry was especially important, as a model, for Latin authors and through this route gained an important influence on European literatures). This poetry is marked above all by the hybridization of genre, a phenomenon marked for its questioning of performance. For if genre is no longer respected, this must mean that we no longer compartmentalize literary works according to their distinct contexts of performance. Apollonius's *Argonautica* evokes both epos and drama; Theocritus brings epos down to the level of mime; in both Aratus and Callimachus, epic traditions are combined with prose, scientific practices. Since the poetics emphasize such breaking of genres, it becomes natural to mark, not mask, the heterogeneity of one's text. Solecism is celebrated, surprise becomes a key poetic technique.

As noted, many poets of the time bring together, precisely, the literary and the scientific. It is thus perhaps not shocking that the sciences, themselves, should be marked by contemporary literary tendencies. In Archimedes we see a mathematical science marked by the breaking of generic boundaries, always intent on surprise.

Archimedes's *On the Sphere and the Cylinder*, Book I, begins with an announcement of a remarkable result: the surface of a sphere is equal to four times the circle at its equator; its volume is two-thirds the cylinder circumscribing it. This is as close to the squaring of the circle as one can get (it is, as it were, nearly a cubing of the sphere), in and of itself a surprising result. Having announced the result, Archimedes proceeds to prove it. However, he says nothing on spheres. Instead, he derives various abstract results in proportion, then in the geometry of polygons, then in the measurement of cones, then in the proportions of lines insides polygons inside a circle; each of these argumentative segments is pursued independently, without any motivation, and in sharp departure from the preceding segments. Nothing seems to contribute to the main theme. Heterogeneity is maximized. Then, a thought experiment: take a circle and a polygon and rotate them in space and the result is a system composed of cones inside a sphere. It becomes obvious that all the preceding results were mere preparation and that all combine together for the measurement of the sphere in terms of cones, proportions, and polygons within circles.

This is masterly authorial control over narrative, achieving maximum elegance and surprise. "Authorial," for this was Archimedes's *choice*. He could have presented the thought experiment right at the beginning, making the development more transparent (perhaps, more pedagogically useful) and yet less effective as surprise. We find what his choices were – we notice the role of choice even in mathematics, the realm of necessity – and we recognize why it should have a poetics: because its authors exercise control over its manner of writing.

Heterogeneity is a widespread theme in Archimedes. His surprising combinations often involve the straight and the curved (so, many variations on squaring the circle: for instance, measuring areas contained under a parabolic segment). Most remarkable is his tendency to bring together the concrete and the abstract, the physical and the mathematical. In *Planes in Equilibrium*, Archimedes considers plane areas as if they were physical objects laid on the balance; in *Floating Bodies*, he consider certain solids for their behavior (understood in purely mathematical terms) as if immersed in a body of liquid. The consequences of such thought experiments for the history of modern science would be enormous, but we note the aesthetic effect of the combination of apparently distinct categories, which in this case cross almost a metaphysical boundary. Archimedes experimented not merely with genres, but with entire ontologies.

All of this – in Archimedes as in Greek mathematics as a whole – is laid out in a heavily formulaic genre, seemingly denuded of literary embellishment. There is no metaphor as such (although there is some effective play with neologism), word choice is extremely constrained so that there is no prosody or alliteration. The emphasis on the written form, mentioned above, gives rise to a nearly coded language: one keeps referring to terms within a diagram, through letter labels attached to them, so that the language is already reminiscent of our own, symbolic language of science: triangle ABC, square ABCD ... Yet, it should be emphasized, the Greeks never use the modern symbolic expressions of modern algebra. Instead, their formulaic language is based on verbal patterns, the repeated utterance of fixed phrases: "let a line AB be drawn through A, parallel to CD ... " While it might be wrong to read any "orality" into this formulaic language (those are not the formulae of the Homeric bard), their repeated use has cognitive and semiotic parallels to the use of formulaic language elsewhere in literature. By writing with formulaic expressions, the author and the reader can easily parse the text (just as oral poets use their own formulae so to construct their text with greater ease). This supports the cognitive effect of rapid, synoptic perception of the train of thought, crucial for the cognitive effect of deductive persuasion.

In general, in the remarks above concerning Archimedes's style, the emphasis was on the aesthetics of a particular variety of Greek mathematics. One can address the aesthetics of mathematical texts in broader terms, considering, for instance, the sense of closure obtained by proof as such. In the most general terms, mathematical proof operates by finding equivalences: two triangles are similar; which means that four lines are in proportion. The gap between seemingly distant expressions (similarity of triangles, proportion of line segments) and their resulting equivalent logical content – ultimately, a gap of signifier and signified – endows mathematical texts with a rich semiotic and poetic structure. The typical form this duality takes in Greek mathematics is the duality of abstract proportions and concrete geometrical figures – and it is starting from this duality that Archimedes builds his many double structures.

So much for mathematics, and for Archimedes.

Galen and Medicine. Only about ten authors are extant from Greek medicine, even though in all likelihood there were significantly more medical authors in antiquity than there were mathematical ones. The reasons for this discrepancy are complex, but the main observation must be that there was less room to copy Greek medicine in the Middle Ages, as so much of it was occupied by Galen. This Roman-era author (second century CE) came to occupy a position in Western medicine comparable only to that of Aristotle in philosophy. His roughly two million extant words form the greatest corpus surviving from pagan antiquity, and even these are not his complete works. We witness, then, a physician who spent his life *writing*. This does not mean he did nothing else. While many of his extant works have a very written, encyclopedic character (so, especially, his collections of pharmacological information), in many of them we see Galen as a very active performer, addressing his patients, discursing in public, above all engaged in an anatomical theater whose drama is clearly present to the reader's mind. Indeed, in some of these works we see the traces of the circus – Galen, studying the heart of the elephant!

Galen provides a sense of his embodied performances – by insisting on his own embodied presence. Not only the most prolific, this may well be the most subjective author from antiquity, and these two may be connected: in this case, writing and life converge. Galen is famous for his unique autobibiliographic writings. In not one but two occasions ("My Own Books," "The Order of My Own Books"), Galen set out to present his entire written corpus in rational order, providing along the way an account of how the works came to be written. This, indeed, is one of the earliest examples we have of the writing of autobiography. The explanations for this original practice are many and of course one of them must be an enormous ego (whose palpable presence makes Galen an amusing author to read, if sometimes inadvertently). The serious purpose was to prevent the circulation of spurious works – and to make sure that the works that are read, are used in the correct educational order. Those texts were in part works of instruction, whose main purpose, however, once again, was to become like Galen – to learn how to accumulate the embodied experience that makes it possible to be a doctor as good as Galen. For medicine, for Galen, was enacted through the doctor's body: touching many bodies so as to confirm their precise heat, thus making the physician's hand into a kind of a scientific instrument, a thermometer; experiencing time and again as many as possible varieties of pulse, so as to make the same hand also into a sphingometer. Above all, to cut and discern body after body, so as to make one's mind into an anatomical atlas. Only once you've become a walking, embodied science of medicine – a body of writing – do you become a full Galenic doctor. We see then why Galen's writings have to be so prolific: he aims to reconstruct his entire subjectivity as a written form, laying out a lifetime of observation, all of it in vivid descriptive detail.

Indeed, Galen's science was practiced on the bodies of animals, dissected and vivisected, all of it described in gory detail and often performed in public in its full gory mess. The sense of performance is in part due to the culture of the circus; more seriously, we see Galen, once again, as heir to the culture of

Greek demonstration: Galen's medical performance gives rise to the idea of the experiment, and by cutting a nerve one cuts down an opponent's theory, the surgeon's knife always there as a tool of physical and discursive violence.

Neutral discursive prose is found in the more descriptive passages but typically we see Galen engaged in polemic. One of his key techniques is a double apostrophe, inviting an imaginary audience to judge between him and an imagined opponent. Of course, Galen's era – that of the high empire – is also the high point of ancient rhetoric (the Second Sophistic). Galen learned his rhetoric. In context, the use of apostrophe reads as more than a rhetorical device. Put together with the emphasis on reconstructing Galen's subjective experience, and with the many descriptions, apostrophe enhances the sense of a vivid personal encounter, not only with Galen but with an entire array of Greek doctors and philosophers in debate. To the extent that Galen's work – and, by extension, that of Greek medicine as a whole – participates in an aesthetic literary endeavor, this is through the practice of rhetoric, and one of the lasting achievements of Greek medicine (alongside Greek philosophy) was to make the bite of critical debate participate in the pursuit not only of persuasion, but also of truth. In his own mind, Galen excelled in that pursuit, won all debates. This was never the sense of his contemporaries and in fact Galen had few followers. His written works did survive and later doctors – Oribasius, in the fourth century CE – chose Galen as the foundation of his medical encyclopedia. Hailing from a culture of debate, Galen's works would thrive in a different literary culture, that of the scientific canon, on which more shortly.

As with mathematics, the literary aspects of Greek medicine are not restricted to one author or one era. Indeed, Greek medicine produced an early canonical set of works, those ascribed to Hippocrates. Remarkable in their authorial status (already the ancients recognized that the attributions were at least in part spurious), these works span a range of genres such as medical speeches, medical aphorisms (perhaps the most influential of all ancient medical works), and medical case histories. This last genre is indeed among the important literary legacies of ancient medical writing: spare and precise in its original Hippocratic form, it will give rise to a genre still elaborated today. Freud's *Dora* has, among its many fathers, Hippocrates himself.[3] Indeed, several of the case histories in the Hippocratic corpus are of female patients but, more important, a discussion of gender and sexuality is an absolute obsession for ancient medical and biological writings (for this tradition, philosophical sources are no less important). The ancients developed an ontology of the body based on vessels and liquids, on the basis of which is built a complex economy of gender. The wet female will have an important role to play through the later history of Western culture.

Transformations

As noted above, Galen emerges from a world of polemic: he envisages himself surrounded, in the Rome in which he practiced through much of his career, by opponent philosophers and medical authorities, few following him though all, at least in Galen's fantasy, defeated in debate. And as also noted, this fits the thriving rhetorical scene of the second century CE. In the fourth century CE and later, Galen's works became canonized and taken to be the culmination of a largely undoubted medical truth. This transition was pervasive in ancient culture as a whole. Later readers, from the Middle Ages to our own age, take Aristotle to be a canonical author. In fact he was somewhat neglected in the Hellenistic era, revived in the Roman imperial era and made a canonical author only in late antiquity. Astronomy for later readers was "Ptolemaic," and Kuhn, famously, built a structure of a "Scientific Revolution" out of the opposition between an ancient Ptolemaic paradigm and a modern, Copernican one.[4] In fact, there was no canonical astronomy in antiquity itself, different models of the heavens circulating in competition well into Ptolemy's own time (indeed, Ptolemy's model itself underwent changes during his career). Ptolemy's canonicity, once again, appears to have been primarily a late ancient practice. Now, this should be distinguished carefully from the case of the literary, performative genres, which indeed underwent their canonization already in the classical era itself. For about seven centuries – from the time of Aristotle (who already assumes the dramatic canon) to that of Oribasius (who created Galen's canon) – there was a performative, literary canon but no purely literate, scientific canon. (Thus, the nonperformative and purely literate ancient novel did not seem to go through a canonization in antiquity itself, and since late antiquity did not chose a canonical corpus of ancient novels, the genre largely disappeared: this is a major contrast between the ancient and the modern novel, underscoring the position of the novel, in antiquity itself, as somewhat affine to that of technical and nonliterary genres.) This is the context for the many ancient scientific debates: science is where one could aim to dominate one's rivals.

With late antiquity, that changed and the structure of literature, as such, became predicated on the notion of the canon. Homer, in epos; and so Galen, in medicine.

The causes for this transformation are diverse. It seems to go hand-in-hand with a major media transformation, from roll to codex and from papyrus to parchment. This in turn goes hand-in-hand with the rise of scriptural religion. From a culture where the main ideal is that of performance, the Mediterranean became a culture fixated upon the pages of a venerated book. Little wonder, perhaps, that books became embellished, fetishized, canonized. With the invention of the codex, the history of literature becomes, literally, the history of the book.

The arrival of the book brought science and literature closer together: in the Middle Ages, both were, basically, canons, to be learned and venerated. The marginalia on the Venetus Homer codex, with their accumulation of scholia, are not all that different from the extra diagrams accumulating on the margins of Euclid's manuscripts. An important difference is in terms of cultural range: while science and philosophy were massively translated from Greek to Arabic, often via Syriac, literature was not (Borges's Averroës, in his Cordoba, ponders the meaning of Aristotle's *Poetics*, suffering from the lack of any access to the ancient dramatic poets).[5] This is exactly complementary to another major project of cultural transmission – the Latin appropriation, within antiquity itself, of Greek literary models. Vergil imitated Homer (via Apollonius of Rhodes), Ovid imitated Callimachus. Such imitations endured and created a Latin mirror-canon of the literary genres. Latin imitations of Greek science were rare and endured to the extent that they broke, in fact, new literary ground (as with Lucretius's *De Rerum Natura*, a wildly original exercise, turning Epicurus's straightforward prose into poetry). It was only late in the Middle Ages, and mostly via Arabic sources, that the Latin West slowly acquired its scientific canon.

The parchment codex transformed the media of literate culture, creating the civilization of the Middle Ages. The Middle Ages, in turn, will give rise to a new culture of paper. Invented in China, paper was introduced early to the Muslim world and eventually, in the High Middle Ages, reached Europe. Papyrus was plentiful, parchment scarce; paper, made ultimately from plant fibers (always at an advantage compared to animal products, such as parchment) made writing plenty, again. There is much more writing now extant from the medieval Muslim world than from the European Latin one, primarily an opposition between paper and parchment. In the medieval Muslim world we also witness the appropriation of another Eastern technique (this time, a South Asian invention), that of the decimal position writing of numbers. This is closely tied to paper culture, as the key significance of decimal position writing is that it makes it possible to manipulate numbers not only via concrete counters, but also via written traces. The algorism is a technique of transposing the concrete abacus into the space of the page: making the page, in fact, manipulative.

Just as parchment and scriptural religion brought literature and science together, so paper and the algorism set them asunder. The practice of the algorism – writing numerals so as then to move them around and cross them out, cutting and copying results along the space of the page – implies a new attitude to the written medium, distinct from the passive veneration of the scriptural word. The scientific notebook emerges naturally out of the new practices of calculation and in early modern Europe it is already widespread (alongside other new practices of paper-based, manipulative literacy, such as the card game and the promissory note). The book as cultural artifact – as against the notebook as a tool of trade. Leonardo would produce only note-books, never a finished scientific book; authors such as Kepler and Galileo would become published authors (with remarkable literary finish, echoing and reviving the Archimedean traditions), but their published – and now, printed, books – would carry the mark of a scientific practice immersed in the notebook, with results tried out and experiments accumulated. The notebook carries the germs of the laboratory and with it, a new depar-ture, where science diverges from literature. Scientific practice is now per-formed, whereas the reading of literature has moved, in the modern era, decidedly into the private realm of bourgeois consumption. The media sys-tem of science and literature in modern Europe now neatly reversed.

Conclusion

Taking several broad strokes, this chapter postulated various configurations and transformations of literature and science in the West, from Greek anti-quity to early modern Europe. None of these was argued for in any detail, and none should be considered as more than tentative. Let me sum up some key thoughts. To begin with, literature and science take place in the mind; they are mental, cognitive phenomena. This does not have the consequence of making them a-historical but, precisely to the contrary, this makes them share in a related historical trajectory. Cognition must take place in the material world and so has to be mediated by material, cognitive tools – media and genres – that are historically formed. Hence the historicity of literature and science as well as their relatedness. Second, since science is a cognitive, mental phenomenon, taking place within media and genres, it is natural that it can be analyzed, among other things, on aesthetic grounds: the surprise of an Archimedean proof, the bite of a Galenic piece of rhetoric. Third, and reinforcing the overall relatedness of literature and science, cultural practices at any given place and time form a system: if certain practices are common in one part of the system, but not in another, this tends to mark the parts of the system as such and to endow the practices with meaning. Thus we noted the binary structure of the performed and the written, in classical Greek antiquity, informing the very formation of a binary opposition that will eventually give rise to "literature" and "science"; and the transformation of such oppositions through the changing configurations of the genres, as new media and cognitive tools become available, as literacy and numeracy expand and transform, and as a new literary form gradually comes into being, approaching our modern "science."

NOTES

1. I have discussed this cognitive effect of Greek mathematical writing in Reviel Netz, *The Shaping of Deduction in Greek Mathematics* (Cambridge: Cambridge University Press, 1999).

2. I have in mind of course Roland Barthes's 1967 "Death of the Author" and Michel Foucault's 1969 "What Is an Author?" See Roland Barthes, *Image Music Text* (London: Fontana Press, 1977), 142–8, and Michel Foucault, *Language, Counter-Memory, Practice: Selected Essays and Interviews*, ed. Donald Bouchard (Ithaca: Cornell University, 1977), 113–38. Those seminal articles extend the more basic claim of the New Criticism (that the intentions of the biographical author are irrelevant for the understanding of the text) to emphasize the inherently arbitrary nature of the cultural choice to make the category of the author into the primary unit according to which works are classified (the main identity of *Anna Karenina* being "by Leo Tolstoy," with this classification supposedly providing us with insight into the work's making). Bizarrely, both Barthes and Foucault seem to have considered this centrality of the author as a fundamentally modern, perhaps capitalist phenomenon; it is in fact, specifically, a Greek invention.

3. Sigmund Freud, *Dora: An Analysis of a Case of Hysteria* (New York: Simon and Schuster, 1997).

4. I am referring – wait for it – to Thomas Kuhn's 1962 *Structure of Scientific Revolutions*, the foundational text of the discipline of the History and Philosophy of Science; see *The Structure of Scientific Revolutions* (Chicago: University of Chicago, 1962). Kuhn considered it essential to a "Science" that it was in possession of a paradigm, while famously employing a polysemic concept of "paradigm." Two central meanings were those of a shared metaphysical commitment, and a shared set of practices. It should be emphasized that Greek scientists, generally speaking, did develop a shared set of practices but, prior to late antiquity, it would be a stretch to describe them as possessing a shared metaphysical system. The ancients themselves were *not*, as a group, Aristotelian-Ptolemaic-Galenic!

5. See Jorge Luis Borges, "Averroës's Search," in *Labyrinths: Selected Stories and Other Writings*, ed. Donald A. Yates and James E. Irby (New York: New Directions, 2007), 148–55.

STEVEN MEYER

Futures Past and Present
Literature and Science in an Age of Whitehead

The cognitive practices addressed by Reviel Netz in the previous chapter emerged within very specific locales of the ancient world. How can such emergence possibly be tracked, it might be objected, in light of all that has transpired in the interim and the obscurity of the fragmentary traces that have survived? Yet Netz demonstrates that careful attention to practice, so central to second-wave Literature and Science, does in fact possess the capacity to produce more exact characterizations of what is now ancient history. And not as it may currently appear from the vantage of the early twenty-first century, filtered through millennia alternating neglect and recovery, but as the cognitive practices in question would have been experienced in the course of their emergence, even – here science fiction may serve as a guide – when they largely remained something still to come. For it is only with some such sense of the distinctive ways presentness and futurity are experienced at any particular time that it becomes possible to investigate the emergence of cognitive skills in relation to contexts in which they still seemed genuinely new.[1] How did members of specific communities come to do certain things? What techniques or strategies did they utilize? How did cognitive modes of abstraction, generalization, and demonstration, for instance – characteristic no less of literature than of science – actually emerge within concrete practices? Ultimately such skills take specialized literary, scientific, and artistic forms, yet so long as they remain *in the making* (and one aspires to investigate them in the process of being made, in laboratory or studio, in the field, on the page), they fall directly within the purview of second-wave Literature and Science and the range of approaches described, and exemplified, in this *Companion*.

Turning to Alfred North Whitehead – mathematician, physicist, philosopher of science, speculative philosopher in the half century between 1888 and 1941, hence just *prior* to the advent of first-wave Literature and Science – for an account of the evolution of modern science consistent with developments in the humanities and in Literature and Science in recent years may seem counterintuitive, to say the least.[2] Yet features of second-wave Literature and Science emphasized throughout the accounts in the present volume were typically already stressed by Whitehead nearly a century ago. Such features include: an emphasis on triangulation and robustness; criticism of the fact/value dichotomy and the concomitant bifurcation of nature; commitment to ontological pluralism; suspicion of the toxic mixture of professionalization and specialization and the ensuing two-cultures paradigm (without denying frequent mutual isolation due to specialization and the resulting appearance of sharp divides among the sciences and humanities); an expanded and expansive empiricism; a distrust of the tendency of critique (critical theory) to presume to do without speculation (speculative philosophy); criticism of excessive infatuation with epistemology (which is not the same as wholesale dismissal of epistemological concerns); focus on the affective, cognitive, and technological aspects of practice; a turn from the physical to the life sciences as a model science (including the more life-science-like aspects of the physical sciences). To be sure, we are dealing here with a general tendency in second-wave Literature and Science, rather than a uniform set of features, and contestations among practitioners form an essential part of the story.

The following pages spell out an argument first formulated by Whitehead in his 1925 Lowell Lectures, *Science and the Modern World*, and which he quietly assumed thereafter in his philosophical investigations.[3] It involves a *further* transformation beyond the newly modernized science with which Netz concludes Chapter 13 and which the opening chapters of this volume also variously contextualize: a transition from the mode of inquiry that, with the emergence of modern science in the seventeenth century, came to dominate secular accounts of the natural world in the West to an alternate mode of scientific inquiry that by the early twentieth century was inextricably woven into the practices of multiple sciences. Certainly it is possible to trace these changes separately within different sciences, yet in *Science and the Modern World* Whitehead provided a richer, increasingly interinanimated group portrait, where the transformation occurs in the interstices among the sciences and between scientific practices and literary practices. For this philosopher-scientist at least, what was happening was unavoidably, ineluctably, a tale of literature and science.

An Age of Science?

In line with cognitive history of the sort exemplified in the previous chapter, these closing remarks posit an Age of Whitehead not in order to imagine what it *could have been like* but as a speculative tool for inquiry into current circumstances –in particular regarding the extent that such an age is still in the process of being realized. How accurate, one may begin by asking, is it to characterize our age as an Age of Science, as is so frequently done – for instance, by Hilary Putnam in the recent collection, *Philosophy in an Age of Science*?[4] Suppose we were instead to characterize it as a time in which an understanding of science – and of Literature and Science – pretty much in line with that proposed by Whitehead permits a richer grasp of what is actually happening around us than other accounts make available. Hence an Age of Whitehead. The existence of such an age would likely have surprised Putnam, who expressed little interest in his Harvard predecessor despite Whitehead's having argued in similar terms to those Putnam used three-quarters of a century later in a celebrated set of lectures on "the collapse of the fact/value dichotomy."[5] Obviously, in order to claim, as Whitehead did, that what he called "lures for feeling" operate at the deepest strata of the universe, the positivist credo divorcing fact from value has to go.[6]

Putnam's lack of interest in Whitehead is hardly surprising; what is so is the abiding interest in Whitehead that runs through science studies. Donna Haraway was not kidding when two decades ago she speculated that "this philosopher-mathematician lurks in the tissues of many a resister to gene fetishism in feminist science studies and elsewhere."[7] With his concept of the lure for feeling Whitehead was addressing the mechanisms – "organic mechanisms" he called them – whereby emergence doesn't just become possible but actually occurs. Many important twentieth-century developments in the life sciences, for instance, such as the concept of autopoiesis proposed by Humberto Maturana and Francisco Varela or C. H. Waddington's epigenetic landscape, may readily be viewed as applications of Whitehead's more general scheme – or alternately as extensions of his own investigation of emergent processes in terms of what he called his "cell theory of actuality."[8] Where the father of evolutionary developmental biology ("Evo-Devo") is concerned, this is only to be expected as Waddington deliberately applied Whiteheadian conceptualization to his biological investigations across his entire career.[9] Yet Waddington is certainly the exception in this regard; and positing an Age of Whitehead would seem to require that investigators like him somehow prove *exemplary*.

One obvious problem with regarding ours as an Age of Science is that its age is beginning to show: it has been around for an awfully long time, at least since Newton if not Galileo. To be sure, as Bruno Latour argues in *An Inquiry into Modes of Existence*, the Moderns – as he calls Europeans living, thinking, imagining under the sign of modern science, and more generally Westernized inhabitants of planet Earth – have not proved especially trustworthy regarding how they have spoken *about* themselves.[10]

In his account Latour lines up nicely (as he is entirely aware) with the attempt Whitehead was already making in the US in the mid-1920s to correct certain features of the self-description and self-understanding of modern science – with the objective, as Whitehead put it, of "widening the scientific scheme in a way that is useful for science itself."[11]

Here are several pertinent quotes from *Science and the Modern World*:

> [T]he scheme of scientific ideas which has dominated thought [since the seventeenth century] involves a fundamental duality, with *material* on the one hand, and on the other hand *mind*. In between there lie the concepts of life, organism, function, instantaneous reality, interaction, order of nature, which collectively form the Achilles heel of the whole system. (57)

(This duality of material and mind supports what Whitehead elsewhere referred to as the "bifurcation of nature" into a "causal nature" and an "apparent nature" – "the conjecture and ... the dream," respectively.)[12] To continue:

> The progress of science has now reached a turning point. The stable foundations of physics have broken up: also for the first time physiology is asserting itself as an effective body of knowledge, as distinct from a scrap-heap. The old foundations of scientific thought are becoming unintelligible. Time, space, matter, material, ether, electricity, mechanism, organism, configuration, structure, pattern, function, all require reinterpretation. What is the sense of talking about a mechanical explanation when you do not know what you mean by mechanics? (16)

Finally, in response to lines of Wordsworth that exemplify, in Whitehead's careful, technical phrasing, "a feeling for nature, as exhibiting entwined prehensive unities, each suffused with modal presences of others" (phrasing that incorporates important elements of the alternative explanatory scheme he was then in the process of developing):

> In thus citing Wordsworth, the point which I wish to make is that we forget how strained and paradoxical is the view of nature which modern science imposes on our thoughts. Wordsworth, to the height of genius, expresses the concrete facts of our apprehension, facts which are distorted in the scientific analysis. Is it not possible that the standardised concepts of science are only valid within narrow limitations, perhaps too narrow for science itself? (84)

There is much to consider here; and Whitehead went on to think a great deal about how one might answer such questions. In these closing remarks we will be concerned less with the specifics of his answers than with the challenge he poses (to himself in the first instance) regarding possible limits that inhere in the undeniably constructive constraints of modern scientific self-conception.[13] Pointing out the narrowness in question and arguing for more expansive limitations (by no means the same as proposing to do away with limits or constraints of any sort), that's the objective.

A Generalized Science of Organisms

Often it proves unhelpful to quarantine certain – poetic – practices from other – scientific – ones, because doing so makes it all the more difficult to register their precise nature and we comes away with idealized versions of them.[14] Whitehead helps us understand what is involved in such circumstances in his juxtaposition, on the one hand, of what he takes to be the quite reasonable criticism of Wordsworth and Shelley directed at rigid Enlightenment portrayals of scientific practices and, on the other hand, of the largely unanticipated transformations in late nineteenth- and early twentieth-century science which he carefully characterized in *Science and the Modern World* in terms consistent with those employed in the Romantics' poetry, whose lead he follows here. That these transformations, in physiology and physics alike, can *best* be so understood does not of course mean that they *were* so understood. Whether this happened in individual cases depended on the extent that one had successfully rid oneself of assumptions concerning the so-called bifurcation of nature. The chief issue at hand turned out to be that it really was not very difficult to explain non-bifurcative practices in bifurcative terms. And one consequence has been that, at least from a Whiteheadian perspective, it has been all too easy for modern science – that is to say, the full pluralistic spectrum of twentieth- and twenty-first-century sciences – to continue in its transformational ways even as scientists and students of science continued to frame their conclusions in the outmoded terms, too rigid for the phenomena at hand, of One Science or *the* one science.

Although the Unity of Science movement that emerged from logical positivism in the 1930s and 1940s has gone the way of logical positivism, traces of the approach still remain in works like E. O. Wilson's *Consilience: The Unity of Knowledge* (1998).[15] In an essay on "The Disunities of the Sciences," Ian Hacking has proposed a pluralistic alternative to the Unity of Science that while it does not require science to be One Thing does insist on "the *unifiability* of the sciences": "we are completely surrounded by unifications of science incarnate, material testimony to the metaphysical thesis that all phenomena should be interconnected. Entrepreneurial inventors, not only the legendary Edison or Gates, but also myriad more humble people in machine shops or biotech labs, put together bits of purified phenomena to produce new pieces of reliable technology."[16] Hacking cites testimony to this end from "our greatest unifier," James Clerk Maxwell, although the evidence in question does not concern electromagnetism, as one might have expected, but the telephone as "an instance of the benefit to be derived from the cross-fertilization of the sciences" (70). What Hacking and Maxwell are promoting is of course not a situation where "all phenomena [are monistically] interconnected," each with each and all with all, as William James might say, but rather a pluralism where every phenomenon is only connected with *some* others – all are connected, yet none are connected with all. The result is a great deal of often unexpected overlap without it all adding up to a single monist universe or single unifying approach: no One Thing, neither universe nor science.

Several unhappy consequences follow from this disjunction between the actually pluralistic nature of so much transformational science of the past century and a half and the still dominant conception of science as "unified." For instance, while on Whitehead's account (an account shared by Latour, Stengers, and Haraway, among others) science has developed in a fairly steady, non-paradigm-shifting sort of way,[17] so long as we retain a bifurcative framework, the history we tell of modern science, and of the Moderns, can only be revolutionary in structure. By positing occasional revolutionary change we are thereby able to catch up with the more gradual change that has actually been proceeding – as James Bono argues in Chapter 8 – much less disconnectedly. In other words, a Whiteheadian explanatory scheme does not conform to what remains the favored understanding and self-understanding of modern science, that it is at once revolutionary (perhaps increasingly so) and remains the same thing it has been since the seventeenth century – namely, "modern" science. This dynamic of ever-advancing modernization would seem to distinguish science from other cognitive practices, such as those exhibited in poetry, for instance – yet poetry too has been subject to its own science-inflected rhetoric of modernization ("make it new!").[18]

In science studies as well (and related disciplines including Literature and Science) we seem to undergo revolutions in quick succession, "turn" after "turn" after "turn": semiotic, ontological, nonhuman, and the like. Although the rhetoric is unambiguous, the term "revolution" itself possesses a pair of senses that pertain respectively to either side of the contrast at issue: a sharp break or revolt and a rotation or (re)turn. In actual practice of course the two senses are often joined, as in the possibly revolutionary tinge that may adhere to assertions of a novel "turn." Consider, for example, the proposals in Chapters 6 and 7 regarding the posthuman turn. In the first place, these are by no means held to be true even by all the contributors to the present volume. As such, they contribute to a lively argument, of the sort that any collection of essays claiming to be pluralistic in format had better offer. In the case of the posthuman – and of the terminology of the Anthropocene that often accompanies it – two fine places to begin are Donna Haraway's latest treatise, *Staying with the Trouble: Making Kin in the Chthulucene* (2016), and a 2013 interview with Isabelle Stengers, "Matters of Cosmopolitics: On the Provocations of Gaia."[19] Although Bruno Latour also rejects the assertion of an "'anthropic origin' of global warming" implicit in the term Anthropocene – "who can claim to speak for the human in general?" – in his recent Gifford Lectures he proposes that "to stay with the trouble it's better to stay with the word."[20] Arguments for the posthuman, like arguments for the *post*-anything may rely too much on the logic of bifurcation that the phrasing itself renders well-nigh unavoidable. By contrast, investigations like Latour's regarding the *inseparability* of human and nonhuman actors presume a very different logic – one that is more expansive in nature, on the robust or speculative empiricist model, for instance, of Whitehead's extension to nonhumans of the value we readily, if too often not readily enough, attribute to humans (while neither anthropomorphizing the nonhumans nor de-anthropomorphizing the humans).[21] By the same token, Stengers and Latour are not at all interested in dismissing subjectivity or objectivity (as some might imagine) but rather in better understanding how these are achieved, that is, the basis of their success as achievements – according to a constructivist logic that the better *understanding* and the successful *achievement* each exhibit.[22] Adam Frank's analysis of subjectivity in Chapter 9 operates along similar lines.

Here one might hazard a related conjecture. If the language of revolution shared by many scholars of Literature and Science with scientists blessedly ignorant of the scholars' endeavors largely serves rhetorical purposes (in the least attractive sense of "rhetoric," namely, *papering over confusions*), might it not in so doing also facilitate the decidedly non-revolutionary consolidation of scientific research within the vast social organization of Big Science?[23] And thereby, if Stengers is correct, massively limiting the potential – the range of possibilities – of scientific practices, replacing these with other sorts of social practice more germane to what Latour in *An Inquiry into Modes of Existence* calls the Modernizing Front than to the pursuit of objective knowledge, which for both Latour and Stengers marks successful scientific practice. This, one may surmise, is why Stengers speaks of modern science as dying, as something that can die, instead of turning into something else – living on in a new form.[24]

Among the many transformations in modern science that Whitehead himself experienced were those in physics from Maxwell to Einstein and Bohr; others that thoroughly redefined mathematics in the second half of the nineteenth century; and physiology's metamorphosis between Claude Bernard at midcentury and William James a quarter century later in at least four respects: (1) as an experimental science; (2) with regard to what Joan Richardson in Chapter 4 calls "the Darwinian information"; (3) in relation to developments in the new scientific psychology, by no means exclusively positivistic; and (4) in the context, as Edward Reed charmingly put it, of new strains of philosophy (phenomenological, analytic, and Jamesian) themselves emerging in response to the new psychology – rather than the reverse.[25] The great challenge, then, that Whitehead presented in his philosophical writings – the "lure for feeling" he passed on to his readers, thereby "infecting" us – lies in this juxtaposition of what he termed "the romantic reaction" to Enlightenment science and the massive changes in Victorian and post-Victorian science that occurred in his lifetime.[26] ("Infect" is one of Whitehead's preferred terms in *Science and the Modern World*, where it is typically used in a wholly positive sense. The related conception of a "lure for feeling" is inseparable from Whitehead's understanding of propositions, which he generalized from their usual logical context to phenomena with a distinct "role ... in the actual world." As he observed in *Process and Reality*, a proposition "is a datum for feeling, awaiting a subject feeling it" and as such a lure for feeling, understood pluralistically: "many subjects may feel it with diverse feelings, and with diverse sorts of feelings." By contrast with how a proposition is judged in the world of logicians, "[i]n the real world," he famously noted, "it is more important that a proposition be interesting than that it be true."[27] However, as he later added, one of the most interesting things about a proposition is that it may be true.)

The old foundations of scientific thought, Whitehead thus announced, *are becoming unintelligible. Time, space, matter, material, ether, electricity, mechanism, organism, configuration, structure, pattern, function, all require reinterpretation. What is the sense of talking about a mechanical explanation when you do not know what you mean by mechanics?* In Chapter 4 of *Science and the Modern World* ("The Eighteenth Century"), as the reader will recall, this is further elaborated:

> In my previous lecture I traced the evolution, during the seventeenth century, of the scheme of scientific ideas which has dominated thought ever since. It involved a fundamental duality, with *material* on the one hand, and on the other hand *mind*. In between there lie the concepts of life, organism, function, instantaneous reality, interaction, order of nature, which collectively form the Achilles heel of the whole system. (57)

Later, in speaking of the eighteenth-century empirical idealist, Bishop Berkeley, and his "fail[ure] to affect the main stream of scientific thought,"

Whitehead noted that "[i]t flowed on as if he had never written. Its general success made it impervious to criticism, then and since. The world of science has always remained perfectly satisfied with its peculiar abstractions. They work, and that is sufficient for it." "The point before us," he continued, "is that this scientific field of thought is now, in the twentieth century, too narrow for the concrete facts which are before it for analysis. This is true even in physics, and is more especially urgent in the biological sciences" (66). What was called for, then, was a *"widen[ing of] the scientific scheme in a way that is useful for science itself"* (68, emphasis added).

It is with this thread behind (and before) us, as we make our way through Whitehead's Lowell Lectures – delivered in Boston to the general public a half year after his arrival at Harvard – that we reach the set of observations which conjoin the critique of Enlightenment science by Wordsworth and Shelley and the subsequent scientific transformations that Whitehead believed were best understood by attending to the poets' more positive speculations alongside their poetic practices. A few more quotations are in order. First, from Chapter 5, "The Romantic Reaction": Wordsworth's "constant theme," we read, "is that the important facts of nature elude the scientific method. It is important therefore to ask, what Wordsworth found in nature that failed to receive expression in science," at least in the dominant understanding of modern science since the seventeenth century. "I ask this question," Whitehead remarked, "in the interest of science itself; for one main position in these lectures is a protest against the idea that the abstractions of science are irreformable and unalterable" (83). The next page he added, in a sentence already quoted: "In thus citing Wordsworth, the point which I wish to make is that we forget how strained and paradoxical is the view of nature which modern science imposes on our thoughts." Indeed, Whitehead found aspects of Einstein's description of the general theory of relativity circa 1920 paradoxical in precisely this objectionable sense – although the basis for his concern has rarely been appreciated.[28]

On one hand, we overlook the "strained and paradoxical" aspects of "the view of nature which modern science imposes on our thoughts"; on the other, Whitehead wondered, "Is it not possible that the standardised concepts of science are only valid within narrow limitations, perhaps too narrow for science itself?" (84). Still in Chapter 5: "we gain from the poets the doctrine" – here alluding to both Wordsworth and Shelley – "that a philosophy of nature must concern itself at least with these six notions: change, value, eternal objects, endurance, organism, interfusion" (88). Whitehead is calling for nothing short of a science consistent with poetic values. By the same token, he made use of the resources of poetic description to convey a world composed of what he termed "organic mechanisms," and "actual occasions" (or "entities"): a world in which the bifurcation of nature no longer held, in which fact and value were not treated as dichotomous, and on the basis of which transformations in and of the domain of science that by 1925 had become unmistakable could be appreciated without relying on paradoxical formulations. It should be noted that this is by no means to identify Wordsworth's poetry as in any strict sense a mode of scientific inquiry, nor is it to claim that in his poetry Wordsworth anticipated any particular scientific transformations.

Nor does a statement like the following, from the next chapter ("The Nineteenth Century"), entail the replacement of science by poetry. There Whitehead was speaking critically of vitalism, which he understood, first, as "accept[ing] the fact of mechanism," that is to say, the traditional understanding of "mechanism [as] based upon materialism" – as Whitehead did not – and, second, as introducing "an additional vital control ... to explain the actions of living bodies." This "appeal to mechanism on behalf of biology," he explained, "was in its origin an appeal to the well-attested self-consistent physical concepts as expressing the basis of all natural phenomena." By 1925 things were different: for "at present there is no such system of concepts" in physics. Instead – and this is where Whitehead introduced what one might term *a generalized science of organisms* – "[s]cience is taking on a new aspect which is neither purely physical, nor purely biological. It is becoming the study of organisms. Biology is the study of the larger organisms: whereas physics is the study of the smaller organisms" (102–3).

In the early 1940s the great biochemist (and sinologist) Joseph Needham observed of Whitehead's statement that it remained "one of his most famous and influential passages."[29] Needham was still dwelling on the implications of this generalized science a dozen pages later when he proposed: "The epigram of old John Scott Haldane, neo-vitalist though he was, is coming true: 'If physics and biology one day meet, and one of the two is swallowed up, that one will not be biology'" (268). Needham continued: "In justice we should add that though it might perhaps be classical physics, it will not be physics itself, either; the two disciplines constituting indeed a Hegelian-Marxist contradiction, of which the philosophy of organism is the synthesis." (He then proceeded to offer several examples, "from [his] own field, of the way in which the newer attitude is changing previous conceptions.") Arguably, after seventy-five years of additional transformative developments in modern science – confirming Whitehead's sense of the sea change he had witnessed, reaffirmed by Needham – it remains true that not only was the new physics irreducible conceptually to the old physics but the new biology was irreducible to the new physics. No single science possessed the conceptual key capable of unlocking all the others!

Why *arguably*? In brief, because the establishment, for instance, of molecular biology in the 1930s and 1940s, combining aspects of formerly biological and physical sciences, and in the same decades of the no less significant modern synthesis in evolutionary biology – discussed in Chapter 12 by Tim Armstrong – might well give the impression of everything ultimately coalescing into a single master science. A similar imperative may seem to operate in fundamental physics with attempts to align gravitational, electromagnetic, strong nuclear and weak nuclear interactions. Whitehead's point was that what was actually emerging was a whole slew of complementary and in many cases overlapping sciences, sharing certain features, yet not conceptually requiring a bifurcated nature. Even so, it was always possible to paper over the changes so long as one was able to tolerate the "strains and paradoxes" that followed.

Whitehead had much more to say about the nature of this heterogeneous generalized science combining physics and biology (and, presumably, additional sciences ranging from chemistry to ecology) – in fact, he was really only beginning to develop his theme. In subsequent chapters in *Science and the Modern World* he would fill out how the concept of organism could be applied to relativity and quantum theory, and four years later, in *Process and Reality*, would further develop a "philosophy of organism," as he called it, designed to establish generic concepts appropriate to the full spread of practices and technologies of the specific forms of scientific investigation (and not just of scientific investigation). At the same time he replaced the concept of organism with the twofold conceptualization of an "actual occasion" and of "societies" made up of such occasions. Whereas in *Science and the Modern World* Whitehead had posited organisms as being "incapable of further analysis," now, in *Process and Reality*, he found himself obliged to go deeper –interpreting any organism, in the most general sense, as isomorphic with this generalized sense of society.[30] As Isabelle Stengers has suggested, the general science of organisms thereby becomes a generalized sociology.

The decision to retain the term "organism" in the subsequent "philosophy of organism" even after he had largely ceased to use it in his own analytic practice – except when speaking of the organism-environment dyad[31] – makes it impossible to conceive of Whitehead's metaphysics as designed to apply fundamentally to physics and not, at an equally fundamental level, to the life sciences. Alternative phrasings such as "the philosophy of occasion" or "philosophy of the event" would have suggested something very different – and on Whitehead's reading of scientific developments in his lifetime, something very mistaken. The term's biological underpinnings are clear from

Science and the Modern World, where, so far as relations between organisms and environment are concerned, it is used in an explicit if nontraditional Darwinian sense, in addition to its being directly associated with "[t]he cell theory and Pasteur's work" (100). (The latter, we are informed, "introduced the notion of *organism* into the world of minute beings.") As already mentioned, Whitehead also characterized the generalized account in *Process and Reality* as a "cell theory."

A third contributing factor to Whitehead's distinctive understanding of organism derives from post-Bernard experimental physiology. Traces enter directly into the extended account in *Process and Reality* of the internal functioning of individual actual occasions, as well as of societies composed of multiple actual occasions, and of societies of societies. Already in Chapter 9 of *Science and the Modern World* – it is titled "Science and Philosophy" – Whitehead proposed that "[a]s long as men thought in terms of physical notions for the objective world and of mentality for the subjective world, the setting of the problem, as achieved by Descartes, sufficed as a starting point. But the balance has been upset by the rise of physiology" (147). "The career of William James," Whitehead observed, "is an example of this change in standpoint." As was his own career, despite the fact that as a scientist he operated chiefly with physical and mathematical concepts. That Whitehead and James could arrive at so similar a place despite such diverse starting points itself testifies to the viability of a generalized science of organisms. Indeed, it is the simultaneous viability and unlikelihood (at least in the traditionally bifurcative terms of modern science) that Whitehead set out to explain in the often startling twists and turns that the philosophy of organism required of him.

It Must Apply to Our Aesthetic Experiences

The tension Whitehead observed between traditional modes of taxonomizing modern science (and varieties of knowledge more broadly) and an emerging nontraditional generalized science has if anything increased since, and his analysis of the tension, together with his proposed redescription of scientific practices in terms of the generalized science of organisms, has become if anything more pertinent. The line of argument followed in these concluding pages suggests, however, that it is not enough to stick to a generalized *science* of the sort Whitehead envisaged. "I am trying to evolve one way of speaking," he wrote in 1928 to his son about the Gifford Lectures he was then in the process of preparing – these became *Process and Reality* – "which applies equally to physics, physiology, psychology, and to our aesthetic experiences."[32] Three sciences lined up with something framed within a clearly very different category: *our aesthetic experiences*. A single manner of speaking, in other words, applied to an irreducibly pluralistic variety of forms of knowledge and components of experience.

When, in *Science and the Modern World*, Whitehead spoke of the need to *widen the scientific scheme in a way that is useful for science itself*, he was expanding on a passage a couple of pages earlier, concerning "the main stream of scientific thought," of which only part has already been cited:

> The point before us is that this scientific field of thought is now, in the twentieth century, too narrow for the concrete facts which are before it for analysis. This is true even in physics, and is more especially urgent in the biological sciences. Thus, in order to understand the difficulties of modern scientific thought and also its reactions on the modern world, we should have in our minds some conception of a wider field of abstraction, a more concrete analysis, which shall stand nearer to the complete concreteness of our intuitive experience.

"Such an analysis," he added, "should find itself a niche for the concepts of matter and spirit, as abstractions in terms of which much of our physical experience can be interpreted" (66–7). In this way the "peculiar abstractions" which had hitherto dominated the discourse of modern science (*matter* and *spirit*, but also, as Latour and Stengers have demonstrated, *objectivity* and *subjectivity*) may be altered or reinterpreted without thereby being dismissed out of hand.

Instead of being taken, or mistaken, for concrete phenomena, abstractions like these will find places in "a wider field of abstraction" of the sort entertained in a generalized science of organisms – a strictly scientific scheme permitting "a more concrete analysis" than that premised on the traditional conception of physics as a discrete science (including presumably any conception of biology as ultimately reducible to physics). As such, it would "stand nearer to the complete concreteness" captured, for Whitehead, in Wordsworth's poetry – and for other students of science in the compositions of writers like Henry James or Wallace Stevens or Gertrude Stein.

What, then, of Whitehead's characterization of his philosophical endeavor as an attempt to *evolve* a generalized account (the philosophy of organism) capable of being "applie[d] equally" to a range of sciences that fall under the rubric, it seems fair to say, of a generalized science of organisms as well as to "our aesthetic experiences" – falling outside the scientific rubric although by no means divorced from it? In choosing the verb "evolve" ("I am trying to evolve one way of speaking"), Whitehead signals his rejection of the view of philosophy as being "the forerunner of science," as Stengers has put it.[33] "[S]uch a distribution of roles" – as when, for instance, Whitehead's own "speculative philosophy" is conceived "as a forerunner of a new, 'enlightened,' scientifically grounded conception of the world" – "insults both science and philosophy," Stengers observes (44). It "entails that sciences forget the [specific] constraints that mobilize them, and that philosophy forgets the difference between philosophical concepts [each composed, like any form of 'knowledge-production,' directly in response to 'the question that it tries to answer'] and ... the kind of neutral statement that comes from nowhere and that could be called a 'conception of the world.'" Therefore when Whitehead characterized himself as actively engaged in "*evolv*[*ing*] one way of speaking," he was acknowledging the provisional nature of even so intricately argued a work as *Process and Reality*, ever subject to revision as was Darwin's own magnificent account of evolution – on the basis of ever more expansive empiricist inquiry.[34]

Besides setting himself against all accounts that stressed the ultimate nature of "materialistic mechanism," Whitehead also resisted any sharp division of life from nonlife.[35] To this end he developed the expressly nonvitalist concept of "organic mechanism" – what Donna Haraway in her first book, on 1930s developmental biologists including Joseph Needham, termed *a nonvitalist organicism*.[36] It is precisely in this regard, as well as to the extent that he was able to avoid surreptitiously reinstating the bifurcation of nature in the interstices of his scheme, that Whitehead offers such a compelling model of the many overlapping features of contemporary scientific practices – pluralistic science in an Age of Whitehead – which we may otherwise too hastily identify or bifurcate. Rather than insisting on radical breaks – between the human and posthuman or between the new physics of the twentieth and twenty-first centuries and the new physics of the seventeenth – he provided a richly evolutionary model, one that emphasized rhythmic continuity in discontinuity, from occasion to occasion, within cycles of cycles of cycles.

An Age of Whitehead, then. Not something to be prophesied in the manner, for instance, of the population geneticist J. B. S. Haldane – son of John Scott Haldane, referenced some pages back by Joseph Needham, and discussed by Tim Armstrong in Chapter 12 – in *Daedalus, or Science and the Future* (1924) and *Possible Worlds* (1927).[37] In *Explaining the Universe* (2002), John Charap may cite Haldane with approval: "As J. B. S. Haldane wrote in *Possible Worlds and Other Papers*, 'I have no doubt that in reality the future will be vastly more surprising than anything I can imagine. Now my own suspicion is that the universe is not only queerer than we suppose, but queerer than we can suppose.'"[38] For Whitehead, however, Haldane's final clause indicates a willful abdication of rational thought through the embrace of a *strained and paradoxical* bifurcated nature, as he himself refused to do. Instead, the speculative proposition of "an Age of

Whitehead" provides the occasion for construction envisaged, as Stengers does in Chapter 1, as an art of consequences.

The present – concluding – chapter has focused on several parameters of the challenge Whitehead posed, and found already posed in developments in literature and science, to traditional accounts of modern science. The contributors to the *Companion* have each taken up the same challenge, which – to vary an earlier formulation – concerns limits that inhere in the constructive constraints of the modern sciences as well as more expansive limitations located in practices alternately scientific, literary, and literary critical (together with those that characterize the richly sociological interdiscipline of science studies). What Literature and Science specifically adds to these practices, as the chapters demonstrate in such diverse ways, is a further set of possibilities that emerges when specific domains within each of the four quadrants (literature, science, science studies, and literary studies) are found – or is it made? – to overlap, often in conjunction with disciplinary pursuits unnamed though not unfelt.

Before closing, a few words about the volume's epigraph. It is not just a quotation but the quotation of a quotation: of the bioaesthetician Susanne Langer (Whitehead's student and author of the all-time best-selling US work of academic philosophy – more than half a million copies sold – from which the sentence is taken) as cited by the Bollingen Prize-winning poet, and MacArthur Fellow, Jay Wright. In the citation Wright has made two changes. One appears fairly meaningless (although before we dismiss the gesture, we should recall the observation in Chapter 7 of the present volume concerning contemporary posthermeneutic ambitions): Langer's "sense-data" has become Wright's "sense data." The significance of the other is easier to make out. "And the triumph of empiricism in science," Langer wrote, "is jeopardized by the surprising truth that *our sense-data are primarily symbols*"; "And the triumph of empiricism," Wright proposes instead, "is jeopardized by the surprising truth that *our sense data are primarily symbols*."[39] By removing the limitation to science Wright has broadened the range of empiricism considerably, as the contributors to this volume also seek to do, if not all to the same degree and in the same regard. With the change Wright responds to a shadow that crossed Langer's account at just this point. "*And*," the sentence had begun, pointing back to the directly preceding statement: "The problem of observation" – the problem traditionally associated with empiricism – "is all but eclipsed by the problem of meaning." Indeed, Langer's paragraph that included the sentence revised by Wright had itself begun: "This is bad, of course, for a thoroughgoing empiricism" (20). Yet is it really so bad? Is it not possible that rather than a dire threat being posed to empiricism, what is called for instead is an empiricism that is itself *more truly thoroughgoing*?

Like so many of the contributors to the present volume (and the subjects of their contributions) Wright practices an expansive empiricism. Consequently the situation may not be quite so bad, inasmuch as "the surprising truth" described by Langer can also be viewed as calling forth a constructive art of consequences, and Wright is prepared in his poetry to respond in kind. In other words, Wright possesses speculative tools and practices that enable him to introduce an expanded empiricist spin or twist into the equation. For the more traditional, more rigid, empiricist, by contrast, Langer's surprising truth is definitely bad news, and likely to lead to one or another Humean or Kantian solution that continues to assume the bifurcation of nature – whether rendered in the skeptical terms native to traditional empiricism (for instance, of apparent causation reduced to mere correlation) or in idealist terms like those marshaled by Kant in response to Hume (as some manner of projection from the mind outward).

Consider, then, half a dozen examples of the sort of phenomenon Langer was alluding to in her expression of concern, drawn from a like number of chapters in the *Companion*. Are the contributors responding as if they suddenly find themselves in jeopardy, or do they treat the circumstances as providing new opportunities for synthesis and analysis? Do they interpret the situation along more rigidly empiricist or more expansively empiricist lines? Thus:

> The particulars of *Hamlet* are the kind that tempted thinkers raised on Aristotle, and all that that name meant for the scholars of the time, to veer into occult territory: ghosts were among the limit cases – with comets, magnetism, phosphorescence and the metamorphosis of caterpillars into butterflies – of an empirical science based on faith in the legibility of the sensible world. For instance, Bacon's Idols of the Tribe: for "humane sense is fa[l]sely affirm'd to be the measure of things. On the Contrary, all the conceptions both of sense and reason are taken from the Analogy of man, not the analogy of the Universe." The ghost looks like my father because all I can see is human things (Chapter 2);
>
> In short, race, sexuality, and the social body are intimately interwoven in Darwin's eyes, constantly in flux and dependent upon the relative perspective of the observer – including the naturalist (Chapter 3);
>
> one phrase taken very much to heart was the simple mistranslated comment, "there is nothing outside of the text." In *Of Grammatology* (1967), Derrida wrote "*il n'y pas de hors-texte*," which would more felicitously be translated "there is no outside-text," itself a startling and profound claim, but one without the broader ontological implications of the more trendy version. (If there is

nothing outside the text, then being is only accessible through language.) (Chapter 6);

Thomas Kuhn's *Structure of Scientific Revolutions* is famous for its downgrading of a cumulative understanding of discovery. Although "normal science ... is a highly cumulative enterprise," "the view of science-as-cumulation is entangled with a dominant epistemology that takes knowledge to be a construction placed directly upon raw sense data by the mind" (Chapter 7);

Kuhn nonetheless accepts the premise that "interpretation" is a process that occurs *after* observation/seeing. By accepting this premise, he has no alternative but to root change in science in sudden perceptual shifts in seeing. Yet, it can be argued that how we see depends upon how we orient ourselves to the world of fluxes and flows – the phenomenal flow of experience – through what Whitehead would call "lures for feelings" (Chapter 8);

what I call "the compositional aspect of affect in perception" (Chapter 9).

To conclude: Just as Whitehead thought with Wordsworth, and Stengers (like Haraway) thinks with works of SF, and Latour thinks with the novelist Richard Powers – and Wordsworth, writers of SF, and Powers all themselves think and thought with the sciences of their days, real and imagined, present and future, achieved and possibly still to be achieved – so does the interfield of Literature and Science model what, following William James, may be termed a pluralistic universe.[40] Or, if one prefers, Stengers's "messy universe," Devin Griffiths's "Darwinian world," kitt price's "poetic adventures in Einstein's universe." As Joan Richardson proposes, it was hardly due to chance that Henry James so readily embraced the rich pragmatist framework spelled out by his scarcely older brother on the basis of a life saturated with the science and philosophy (sciences and philosophies) of *their* day. And if William, by contrast, was unenthusiastic about Henry's late novels, despite their being so close in spirit to his expanded empiricism, that just goes to show the thoroughly pluralistic nature of their world and ours – overlap everywhere, unities only partial, local, various, ever an achievement, assuredly not established once and for all. (Such that even this proposition can hardly be established impartially!)

NOTES

1. See Reviel Netz, *The Shaping of Deduction in Greek Mathematics: A Study in Cognitive History* (Cambridge: Cambridge University Press, 1999), and Isabelle Stengers, *Cosmopolitics I and II* (Minneapolis: University of Minnesota Press, 2010–11).

2. Alfred North Whitehead, "On the Motion of Viscous Incompressible Fluids: A Method of Approximation," *Quarterly Journal of Pure and Applied Mathematics* 23 (1888): 78–93; "Mathematics and the Good" and "Immortality," in *The Philosophy of Alfred North Whitehead*, ed. Paul Arthur Schilpp (Evanston: Northwestern University Press, 1941), 666–700.

3. Alfred North Whitehead, *Science and the Modern World* (New York: Free Press, 1967).

4. Hilary Putnam, *Philosophy in an Age of Science: Physics, Mathematics, Skepticism*, ed. Mario De Caro and David Macarthur (Cambridge: Harvard University Press, 2012).

5. Hilary Putnam, *The Collapse of the Fact/Value Dichotomy and Other Essays* (Cambridge: Harvard University Press, 2002).

6. Alfred North Whitehead, *Process and Reality*, corrected ed., ed. David Ray Griffin and Donald W. Sherburne (New York: Free Press, 1978), 85–8.

7. Donna J. Haraway, *Modest_Witness@Second_Millennium.FemaleMan©_Meets_ OncoMouse™: Feminism and Technoscience* (New York: Routledge, 1997), 297.

8. Whitehead, *Process and Reality*, 256; Humberto R. Maturana and Francisco J. Varela, *Autopoiesis and Cognition: The Realization of the Living* (Dordrecht: Reidel, 1980); Conrad H. Waddington, *The Strategy of the Genes: A Discussion of Some Aspects of Theoretical Biology* (London: Allen & Unwin, 1957). Also see James J. Bono, "Perception, Living Matter, Cognitive Systems, Immune Networks: A Whiteheadian Future for Science Studies," *Configurations* 13 (2005): 135–81.

9. Conrad H. Waddington, "Fifty Years On," *Nature* 258.6 (November 6, 1975): 20–1.

10. Bruno Latour, *An Inquiry into Modes of Existence: An Anthropology of the Moderns* (Cambridge: Harvard University Press, 2013); also see modesofexis tence.org.

11. Whitehead, *Science and the Modern World*, 68.

12. Alfred North Whitehead, *The Concept of Nature* (Cambridge: Cambridge University Press, 1993), 30–1. Also see Whitehead, *Process and Reality*, 289–90.

13. The reader curious for more technical detail regarding Whitehead's argument may begin with James Bono's discussion in Chapter 8 of several observations by Isabelle Stengers and then proceed directly to Stengers's masterful *Thinking with Whitehead: A Free and Wild Creation of Concepts* (Cambridge: Harvard University Press, 2011). A great deal of recent work on Whitehead bears on the concerns of Literature and Science. This would include Keith Robinson, ed., *Deleuze, Whitehead, Bergson: Rhizomatic Connections* (Basingstoke: Palgrave MacMillan, 2009); Steven Shaviro, *Without Criteria: Kant, Whitehead, Deleuze, and Aesthetics* (Cambridge: MIT Press, 2009); Michael Halewood, *A. N. Whitehead and Social Theory: Tracing a Culture of Thought* (London: Anthem Press, 2011); Brian Massumi, *Semblance and Event: Activist Philosophy and the Occurrent Arts* (Cambridge: MIT Press, 2011); Roland Faber and Andrew Goffey, eds., *The Allure of Things: Process and Object in Contemporary Philosophy* (London: Bloomsbury, 2014); Nicholas Gaskill and A. J. Nocek, eds., *The Lure of Whitehead* (Minneapolis: University of Minnesota Press, 2014); Mark B. N. Hansen, *Feed-Forward: On the Future of Twenty-First-Century Media* (Chicago: University of Chicago Press, 2015); and Brian G. Henning, William T. Myers, and Joseph D. John, eds., *Thinking with Whitehead and the American Pragmatists: Experience and Reality* (Lanham, MD: Lexington Books, 2015). Much relevant material is available online at the Whitehead Research Project; see https://whiteheadresearch.org/.

14. With regard to the transgeneric writing of Gertrude Stein, for example, see Steven Meyer, *Irresistible Dictation: Gertrude Stein and the Correlations of*

Writing and Science (Stanford: Stanford University Press, 2001); and, more recently, "The Scientific Imagination of U.S. Modernist Fiction," in *The Cambridge Companion to the American Modernist Novel*, ed. Joshua L. Miller (Cambridge: Cambridge University Press, 2015), 137–56.

15. E. O. Wilson, *Consilience: The Unity of Knowledge* (New York: Knopf, 1998).

16. Ian Hacking, "The Disunities of the Sciences" in *The Disunity of Science: Boundaries, Contexts, and Power*, ed. Peter Galison and David J. Stump (Stanford: Stanford University Press, 1996), 37–74, at 70, emphasis added.

17. See Chapters 7, 8, and 13 for criticisms of the Kuhnian account of paradigm change.

18. See Michael North, *Novelty: A History of the New* (Chicago: University of Chicago Press, 2013), 162–71, for the quite surprising history of this phrase – including the "spurious" exclamation mark.

19. Donna Haraway, *Staying with the Trouble: Making Kin in the Chthulucene* (Durham: Duke University Press, 2016), and "Matters of Cosmopolitics: On the Provocations of Gaia," Isabelle Stengers in conversation with Heather Davis and Etienne Turpin, in *Architecture in the Anthropocene: Encounters among Design, Deep Time, Science and Philosophy*, ed. Etienne Turpin (Ann Arbor, MI: Open Humanities Press, 2013), 171–82: http://quod.lib.umich.edu/o/ohp/12527215.0001.001/1:19/–architecture-in -the-anthropocene-encounters-among-design?rgn=div1;view=fulltext.

20. Bruno Latour, *Facing Gaia: Eight Lectures on the New Climatic Regime* (Cambridge: Polity Press, 2017).

21. Whitehead, *Science and the Modern World*, 93–4; Bruno Latour, *Politics of Nature: How to Bring the Sciences into Democracy* (Cambridge: Harvard University Press, 2004), 70–82. Also see Bruno Latour, *Reassembling the Social: An Introduction to Actor-Network-Theory* (Oxford: Oxford University Press, 2005), 72.

22. Isabelle Stengers, "Experimenting with Refrains: Subjectivity and the Challenge of Escaping Modern Dualism," *Subjectivity* 22 (2008): 38–59; Bruno Latour, "Circulating Reference: Sampling the Soil in the Amazon Forest," in *Pandora's Hope: Essays on the Reality of Science Studies* (Cambridge: Harvard University Press, 1999), 24–79.

23. Peter Galison and Bruce Hevly, eds., *Big Science: The Growth of Large-Scale Research* (Stanford: Stanford University Press, 1992).

24. Isabelle Stengers, *Another Science is Possible: A Manifesto for Slow Science* (Cambridge UK: Polity Press, 2018).

25. Edward S. Reed, "The Generation of 1879, or How Philosophy Emerged from Psychology," in *From Soul to Mind: The Emergence of Psychology, from Erasmus Darwin to William James* (New Haven: Yale University Press, 1997), 184–200.

26. Whitehead, *Science and the Modern World*, 75.

27. Whitehead, *Process and Reality*, 259.

28. Alfred North Whitehead, *Principle of Relativity* (New York: Barnes & Noble Books, 2005); also see Steven Meyer, "Principles of Relativity: Whitehead v. Russell," in *1922: Literature, Culture, Politics*, ed. Jean-Michel Rabaté (Cambridge University Press, 2015), 235–47. Among the many important essays by Ronny Desmet on Whitehead's alternate interpretation of general relativity,

probably the best place to start is "Whitehead and the British Reception of Einstein's Relativity: An Addendum to Victor Lowe's Whitehead Biography," *Process Studies Supplements* Issue 11: www.ctr4process.org/publications/process-studies-supplements.

29. Joseph Needham, "A Biologist's View of Whitehead's Philosophy," in *The Philosophy of Alfred North Whitehead*, 2nd ed., ed. Paul Arthur Schilpp (La Salle, IL: Open Court, 1951), 241–71, at 255–6.

30. Whitehead, *Science and the Modern World*, 103.

31. As, for example, in Chapter IV of the second part of *Process and Reality*, titled "Organisms and Environment."

32. Cited in Victor Lowe, *Alfred North Whitehead: The Man and His Work, Vol. II: 1910–1947*, ed. J. B. Schneewind (Baltimore: Johns Hopkins Press, 1990), 333.

33. Isabelle Stengers, "A Constructivist Reading of Process and Reality," in Gaskill and Nocek, eds., *The Lure of Whitehead*, 43–64, at 43.

34. In a superb feat of critical and speculative reconstruction, Lewis S. Ford has documented the extent of the revisionary processes that coursed through the compositions leading up to *Process and Reality*; see Ford, *The Emergence of Whitehead's Metaphysics, 1925–1929* (Albany: State University of New York Press, 1984).

35. Whitehead's criticisms of "the theory of materialistic mechanism" (73) may be found clustered throughout Chapters 3–5 of *Science and the Modern World*.

36. Donna J. Haraway, *Crystals, Fabrics, and Fields: Metaphors of Organicism in Twentieth-Century Developmental Biology* (New Haven: Yale University, 1976), 4. "I would term the doctrine of these lectures the theory of *organic mechanism*," Whitehead proposed; see Whitehead, *Science and the Modern World*, 80.

37. J. B. S. Haldane, *Daedalus, or Science and the Future* (London: Kegan Paul, Trench, Trubner, 1924) and *Possible Worlds* (New Brunswick: Transaction Publishers, 2009).

38. John M. Charap, *Explaining the Universe: The New Age of Physics* (Princeton: Princeton University Press, 2002), viii.

39. Susanne K. Langer, *Philosophy in a New Key: A Study in the Symbolism of Reason, Rite, and Art* (Cambridge: Harvard University Press, 1979), 21; and Jay Wright, *Transfigurations: Collected Poems* (Baton Rouge: Louisiana State University Press, 2000), 475. Langer's volume is dedicated to Whitehead – "my great Teacher and Friend."

40. William James, *A Pluralistic Universe: Hibbert Lectures at Manchester College on the Present Situation in Philosophy* (Lincoln: University of Nebraska Press, 1996).

Science Fiction to Science Studies

Abram, David. *The Spell of the Sensuous: Perception and Language in a More-Than-Human World.* New York: Vintage Books, 1997.

Debaise, Didier. *Un empirisme spéculatif. Lecture de Procès et realité de Whitehead.* Paris: Vrin, 2006.

Despret, Vinciane. *What Would Animals Say If We Asked the Right Questions?* Minneapolis: University of Minnesota Press, 2016.

Goody, Jack. *Renaissances: The One or the Many?* Cambridge: Cambridge University Press, 2010.

Haraway, Donna J. *When Species Meet.* Minneapolis: University of Minnesota Press, 2008.

——— "SF: Science Fiction, Speculative Fabulation, String Figures, So Far." *Ada: A Journal of Gender, New Media, and Technology* 3 (2013). http://adanewmedia.org/2013 /11/issue3-haraway/2.

Lapoujade, David. *William James: Empiricism and Pragmatism,* translated by Thomas Lamarre. Durham: Duke University Press, forthcoming.

Prigogine, Ilya, and Isabelle Stengers, *Order Out of Chaos: Man's New Dialogue with Nature.* Toronto: Bantam Books, 1984.

Russ, Joanna. *To Write Like a Woman: Essays in Feminism and Science Fiction.* Bloomington: Indiana University Press, 1995.

Shaviro, Steven. *Discognition.* London: Repeater Books, 2015.

Starhawk. *Dreaming the Dark: Magic, Sex, and Politics.* Boston: Beacon Press, 1982.

——— *Truth or Dare: Encounters with Power, Authority, and Mystery.* San Francisco: HarperCollins, 1987.

Stengers, Isabelle. "Experimenting with Refrains: Subjectivity and the Challenge of Escaping Modern Dualism." *Subjectivity* 22 (2008): 38–59.

Stengers, Isabelle. "Matters of Cosmopolitics: On the Provocations of Gaia" [Isabelle Stengers in Conversation with Heather Davis and Etienne Turpin]. *Architecture in the Anthropocene: Encounters among Design, Deep Time, Science and Philosophy,* edited by Etienne Turpin, 171–82. Ann Arbor, MI: Open Humanities Press, 2013. http://quod.lib.umich.edu/o/ohp/12527215.0001.001 /1:19/–architecture-in-the-anthropocene-encounters-among-design?rgn=div1 ;view=fulltext.

Stengers, Isabelle. "Speculative Philosophy and the Art of Dramatization." In *The Allure of Things: Process and Object in Contemporary Philosophy*, edited by Roland Faber and Andrew Goffey, 188–217. London: Bloomsbury, 2014.

Stengers, Isabelle, and Bruno Latour. "The Sphinx of the Work." In *The Different Modes of Existence*, edited by Etienne Souriau, 11–90. Minneapolis: Univocal Publishing, 2015.

Shakespeare and Modern Science

Albanese, Denise. *New Science, New World*. Durham: Duke University Press, 1996.

Campbell, Mary Baine. *Wonder and Science: Imagining Worlds in Early Modern Europe*. Ithaca: Cornell University Press, 1999.

Crane, Mary Thomas. *Losing Touch with Nature: Literature and the New Science in the Sixteenth Century*. Baltimore: Johns Hopkins University Press, 2014.

Daston, Lorraine, and Katharine Park. *Wonders and the Order of Nature, 1150–1700*. New York: Zone, 1997.

eds. *The Cambridge History of Science. Vol. 3: Early Modern Science*. Cambridge: Cambridge University Press, 2006.

Floyd-Wilson, Mary. *Occult Knowledge, Science, and Gender on the Shakespearian Stage*. Cambridge: Cambridge University Press, 2013.

Gatti, Hilary. *The Renaissance Drama of Knowledge: Giordano Bruno in England*. London and New York: Routledge, 1989.

Goldberg, Jonathan. *The Seeds of Things: Theorizing Sexuality and Materiality in Renaissance Representations*. New York: Fordham University Press, 2009.

Hallock, Thomas, Ivo Kamps, and Karen L. Raber, ed. *Early Modern Ecostudies: From the Florentine Codex to Shakespeare*. New York: Palgrave Macmillan, 2008.

Hallyn, Fernand. *La structure poetique du monde: Copernic, Kepler*. Paris: Seuil, 1987.

Lipking, Lawrence. *What Galileo Saw: Imagining the Scientific Revolution*. Ithaca: Cornell University Press, 2014.

Marchitello, Howard. *The Machine in the Text: Science and Literature in the Age of Shakespeare*. Oxford: Oxford University Press, 2011.

Mazzio, Carla, ed. Shakespeare and Science. Special issue of *South Central Review* 26:1–2 (Spring/Summer, 2009).

Paster, Gail Kern. *Humoring the Body: Emotions and the Shakespearian Stage*. Chicago: University of Chicago Press, 2004.

Serres, Michel. *Les cinq sens*. Paris: Grasset, 1985. Translated by Margaret Sankey and Peter Cowley. *The Five Senses: A Philosophy of Mingled Bodies*. New York: Continuum, 2008.

West, William N. *Theatres and Encyclopedias in Early Modern Europe*. Cambridge: Cambridge University Press, 2002.

Darwin and Literature

Amigoni, David. *Cults, Colonies, and Evolution: Literature, Science and Culture in Nineteenth-Century Writing*. New York: Cambridge University Press, 2007.

Beer, Gillian. *Darwin's Plots: Evolutionary Narrative in Darwin, George Eliot, and Nineteenth-Century Fiction*. Cambridge: Cambridge University Press, 2000.

Browne, Janet. *Voyaging*. Princeton: Princeton University Press, 1996.

The Power of Place. New York: Knopf, 2002.

Darwin, Charles. *The Autobiography of Charles Darwin, 1809–1882. With Original Omissions Restored*, edited by Nora Barlow. New York: Harcourt, Brace, 1959.

Dawson, Gowan. *Darwin, Literature and Victorian Respectability*. Cambridge: Cambridge University Press, 2007.

Desmond, Adrian, and James Moore. *Darwin: The Life of a Tormented Evolutionist*. New York: W. W. Norton, 1994.

Griffiths, Devin. *The Age of Analogy: Science and Literature between the Darwins*. Baltimore: Johns Hopkins University Press, 2016.

Grosz, Elizabeth A. *The Nick of Time: Politics, Evolution, and the Untimely*. Durham: Duke University Press, 2004.

Harley, Alexis. *Autobiologies: Charles Darwin and the Natural History of the Self*. Lewisburg, PA: Bucknell University Press, 2015.

Levine, George Lewis. *Darwin the Writer*. Oxford: Oxford University Press, 2011.

Rauch, Alan. *Useful Knowledge: The Victorians, Morality, and the March of Intellect*. Durham: Duke University Press, 2001.

Ruse, Michael, ed. *The Cambridge Encyclopedia of Darwin and Evolutionary Thought*. Cambridge: Cambridge University Press, 2013.

Ruse, Michael. *Darwinism and Its Discontents*. Cambridge: Cambridge University Press, 2006.

William James, Henry James, and the Impact of Science

Cavell, Stanley. *This New Yet Unapproachable America: Lectures after Emerson after Wittgenstein*. Chicago: University of Chicago Press, 2013.

Clark, Andy. "Magic Words: How Language Augments Human Computation." In *Language and Thought: Interdisciplinary Themes*, edited by Peter Carruthers and Jill Boucher, 162–83. Cambridge: Cambridge University Press, 2003.

Croce, Paul Jerome. *Science and Religion in the Age of William James. Vol. 1: Eclipse of Certainty, 1820–1880*. Chapel Hill: University of North Carolina Press, 1995.

Dickstein, Morris, ed. *The Revival of Pragmatism: New Essays on Social Thought, Law, and Culture*. Durham: Duke University Press, 1998.

Gavin, William Joseph. *William James and the Reinstatement of the Vague*. Philadelphia: Temple University Press, 1992.

Hocks, Richard A. *Henry James and Pragmatistic Thought: A Study in the Relationship between the Philosophy of William James and the Literary Art of Henry James*. Chapel Hill: University of North Carolina Press, 1974.

Lewis, R. W.B. *The Jameses: A Family Narrative*. New York: Farrar Straus and Giroux, 1991.

McDermott, John. J., ed. *The Writings of William James: A Comprehensive Edition*. Chicago: University of Chicago Press, 1977.

The Drama of Possibility: Experience as Philosophy of Culture. New York: Fordham University Press, 2007.

Menand, Louis. *The Metaphysical Club: A Story of Ideas in America*. New York: Farrar Straus and Giroux, 2001.

Poirier, Richard. *Poetry and Pragmatism*. Cambridge: Harvard University Press, 1992.

Posnock, Ross. *The Trial of Curiosity: Henry James, William James, and the Challenge of Modernity*. Oxford: Oxford University Press, 1991.

Richardson, Joan. *A Natural History of Pragmatism: The Fact of Feeling from Jonathan Edwards to Gertrude Stein*. Cambridge: Cambridge University Press, 2007.

Richardson, Robert D. *William James: In the Maelstrom of American Modernism*. Boston: Houghton Mifflin Harcourt, 2006.

Whitehead, Alfred North. *Science and the Modern World*. New York: Free Press, 1967.

Empson's Einstein: Science and Modern Reading

Beer, Gillian. "Eddington and the Idiom of Modernism." In *Science, Reason, and Rhetoric*, edited by Henry Krips, J. E. McGuire and Trevor Melia, 295–315. Pittsburgh: University of Pittsburgh Press, 1995.

 Open Fields: Science in Cultural Encounter. Oxford: Oxford University Press, 1996.

Bradshaw, David. "The Best of Companions: J.W.N. Sullivan, Aldous Huxley, and the New Physics. [Part One]." *Review of English Studies* NS 47.186 (1996): 188–206.

Cain, Sarah. "The Metaphorical Field: Post-Newtonian Physics and Modernist Literature." *Cambridge Quarterly* 28 (1999): 46–64.

Ebury, Katherine. *Modernism and Cosmology: Absurd Lights*. Basingstoke: Palgrave, 2014.

Eddington, Arthur. *The Nature of the Physical World*. Cambridge: Cambridge University Press, 1928.

Empson, William. *Complete Poems*, edited by John Haffenden. London: Allen Lane, 2000.

Galison, Peter. *Einstein's Clocks and Poincaré's Maps: Empires of Time*. New York: Norton, 2003.

Henderson, Linda Dalrymple. *The Fourth Dimension and Non-Euclidean Geometry in Modern Art* (Cambridge: MIT Press, 2013, rev. ed.).

Leane, Elizabeth. *Reading Popular Physics: Disciplinary Skirmishes and Textual Strategies*. Aldershot: Ashgate, 2007.

McCormmach, Russell. *Night Thoughts of a Classical Physicist*. Cambridge: Harvard University Press, 1982.

Parkinson, Gavin. *Surrealism, Art, and Modern Science: Relativity, Quantum Mechanics, Epistemology*. New Haven: Yale University Press, 2008.

Price, Katy. "Finite But Unbounded: Experiment magazine, Cambridge, England, 1928–31." *Jacket* 20 (2002): http://jacketmagazine.com/20/price-expe.html.

Richards, I. A. *Science and Poetry*. London: Kegan Paul, 1926.

Russell, Bertrand. *ABC of Relativity*. London: Kegan Paul, 1925.

Stanley, Matthew. *Practical Mystic: Religion, Science and A.S. Eddington.* Chicago: University of Chicago Press, 2007.

Steinman, Lisa. *Made in America: Science, Technology and American Modernist Poets.* New Haven: Yale University Press, 1987.

Thorne, K. S. *Black Holes and Time Warps: Einstein's Outrageous Legacy.* New York: Norton, 1994.

Whitworth, Michael. *Einstein's Wake: Relativity, Metaphor, and Modernist Literature.* Oxford: Oxford University Press, 2001.

Science Studies and Literary Theory

Alaimo, Stacy and Susan Hekman, eds. *Material Feminisms.* Bloomington: Indiana University Press, 2008.

Clarke, Bruce and Mark B. N. Hansen, eds. *Emergence and Embodiment: New Essays on Second-Order Systems Theory.* Durham: Duke University Press, 2009.

Haraway, Donna. *The Haraway Reader.* New York: Routledge, 2004.

Manifestly Haraway. Minneapolis: University of Minnesota Press, 2016.

Harding, Sandra G. *The Science Question in Feminism.* Ithaca: Cornell University Press, 1986.

Hayles, N. Katherine. *My Mother Was a Computer: Digital Subjects and Literary Texts.* Chicago: University of Chicago Press, 2010.

How We Think: Digital Media and Contemporary Technogenesis. Chicago: University of Chicago Press, 2012.

Keller, Evelyn Fox. *Making Sense of Life: Explaining Biological Development with Models, Metaphors, and Machines.* Cambridge: Harvard University Press, 2002.

Latour, Bruno. *Science in Action.* Cambridge: Harvard University Press, 1987.

Otis, Laura. *Membranes: Metaphors of Invasion in Nineteenth-Century Literature, Science, and Politics.* Baltimore: Johns Hopkins University Press, 2000.

Plotnitsky, Arkady. *Complementarity: Anti-Epistemology after Bohr and Derrida.* Durham: Duke University Press, 1994.

Rasch, William and Cary Wolfe, eds. *Observing Complexity: Systems Theory and Postmodernity.* Minneapolis: University of Minnesota Press, 2000.

Schleifer, Ronald. *Intangible Materialism: The Body, Scientific Knowledge, and the Power of Language.* Minneapolis: University of Minnesota Press, 2009.

Smith, Barbara Herrnstein. *Scandalous Knowledge: Science, Truth and the Human.* Durham: Duke University Press, 2006.

Squier, Susan Merrill. *Poultry Science, Chicken Culture: A Partial Alphabet.* New Brunswick: Rutgers University Press, 2011.

From Writing Science to Digital Humanities

Bloor, David. *Knowledge and Social Imagery.* 2nd ed. Chicago: University of Chicago Press, 1991.

DeLanda, Manuel. *Intensive Science and Virtual Philosophy.* New York: Continuum, 2003.

Philosophy and Simulation: The Emergence of Synthetic Reason. New York: Bloomsbury, 2015.

Doyle, Richard. *Wetwares: Experiments in Postvital Living*. Minneapolis: Minnesota University Press, 2003.

Elman, Benjamin A. *On Their Own Terms: Science in China, 1550–1900*. Cambridge: Harvard University Press, 2005.

Foucault, Michel. *Security, Territory, Population: Lectures at the Collège de France, 1977–1978*. New York: Picador/Palgrave, 2007.

Gitelman, Lisa, ed. *Raw Data Is an Oxymoron*. Cambridge: MIT Press, 2013.

Guattari, Félix. *The Machinic Unconscious*. Los Angeles: Semiotext(e), 2007.

Hacking, Ian. *The Social Construction of What?* Cambridge: Harvard University Press, 1999.

Johnson, John. "Machinic Vision." *Critical Inquiry* 26 (Autumn 1999): 27–48.

The Allure of Machinic Life: Cybernetics, Artificial Life and the New AI. Cambridge: MIT Press, 2008.

Kittler, Friedrich. "Theoretical Presuppositions." In *Optical Media*, 29–46. Cambridge: Polity Press, 2010.

Kuhn, Thomas S. *The Road Since Structure: Philosophical Essays, 1970–1993, with an Autobiographical Overview*. Chicago: University of Chicago Press, 2000.

Latour, Bruno. *An Inquiry into Modes of Existence: An Anthropology of the Moderns*. Cambridge: Harvard University Press, 2013.

Mindell, David A. *Between Human and Machine: Feedback, Control, and Computing before Cybernetics*. Baltimore: Johns Hopkins University Press, 2002.

Rheinberger, Hans-Jörg. "Experimental Systems, Graphematic Spaces." In *Inscribing Science: Scientific Texts and the Materiality of Communication*, edited by Timothy Lenoir, 285–303. Stanford: Stanford University Press, 1998.

An Epistemology of the Concrete: Twentieth-Century Histories of Life. Durham: Duke University Press, 2010.

Sha Xin Wei. *Poiesis and Enchantment in Topological Matter*. Cambridge: MIT Press, 2013.

Tartar, Helen and Andrew Wachtel, eds. *Writing/Écriture/Schrift*. Special issue of *Stanford Literary Review* 9 (1992).

Science Studies as Cultural Studies

Barad, Karen. *Meeting the Universe Halfway: Quantum Physics and the Entanglement of Matter and Meaning*. Durham: Duke University Press, 2007.

Biagioli, Mario, ed. *The Science Studies Reader*. New York: Routledge, 1999.

Bowker, Geoffrey C. and Susan Leigh Star. *Sorting Things Out: Classification and Its Consequences*. Cambridge: MIT Press, 1999.

Daston, Lorraine and Peter Galison. *Objectivity*. New York: Zone Books, 2007.

Galison, Peter. *Image and Logic: The Material Culture of Twentieth-Century Physics*. Chicago: University of Chicago Press, 1997.

Golinski, Jan. *Making Natural Knowledge: Constructivism and the History of Science*. Cambridge: Cambridge University Press, 1998.

Haraway, Donna J. *Simians, Cyborgs, and Women: The Reinvention of Nature.* New York: Routledge, 1991.

Hess, David J. *Science Studies: An Advanced Introduction.* New York: New York University Press, 1997.

Kuriyama, Shigehisa. *The Expressiveness of the Body and the Divergence of Greek and Chinese Medicine.* New York: Zone Books, 1999.

Landecker, Hannah. *Culturing Life: How Cells Became Technologies.* Cambridge, MA: Harvard University Press, 2007.

Latour, Bruno. *We Have Never Been Modern.* Cambridge: Harvard University Press, 1993.

Lederman, Muriel and Ingrid Bartsch, eds. *The Gender and Science Reader.* New York: Routledge, 2001.

Lenoir, Timothy. *Instituting Science: The Cultural Production of Scientific Disciplines.* Stanford: Stanford University Press, 1997.

Müller-Wille, Staffan and Hans-Jörg Rheinberger. *A Cultural History of Heredity.* Chicago: University of Chicago Press, 2012.

Pickering, Andrew. *The Mangle of Practice: Time, Agency, and Science.* Chicago: University of Chicago Press, 1995.

Rheinberger, Hans-Jörg. *Toward a History of Epistemic Things: Synthesizing Proteins in the Test Tube.* Stanford: Stanford University Press, 1997.

Stengers, Isabelle. *Cosmopolitics I* and *Cosmopolitics II.* Minneapolis: University of Minnesota Press, 2010; 2011.

Reading Affect: Literature and Science after Klein and Tomkins

Bion, Wilfred. *Attention and Interpretation.* New York: Basic Books, 1970.

Second Thoughts: Selected Papers on Psychoanalysis. London: William Heinemann, 1967.

Demos, Virgina. *Exploring Affect: The Selected Writings of Silvan Tomkins.* Cambridge: Cambridge University Press, 1995.

Fausto-Sterling, Anne. *Sex/Gender: Biology in a Social World.* New York: Routledge, 2012.

James, William. "What Is an Emotion?" *Mind,* 9 (1884): 188–205.

"The Place of Affectional Facts in a World of Pure Experience." In *Essays in Radical Empiricism,* 137–54. Lincoln: University of Nebraska Press, 1996.

Keller, Evelyn Fox. *The Mirage of a Space between Nature and Nurture.* Durham: Duke University Press, 2010.

Refiguring Life: Metaphors of Twentieth-Century Biology. New York: Columbia University Press, 1995.

Klein, Melanie. *Envy and Gratitude and Other Works, 1946–1963.* New York: Free Press, 2002.

Sedgwick, Eve Kosofsky. *Touching Feeling: Affect, Pedagogy, Performativity.* Duke University Press, 2003.

Epistemology of the Closet. Berkeley: University of California Press, 1990.

Sedgwick, Eve Kosofsky and Adam Frank, ed. *Shame and Its Sisters: A Silvan Tomkins Reader.* Duke University Press, 1995.

Spillius, Elizabeth Bott, Jane Milton, Penelope Garvey, Cyril Couve and Deborah Steiner. *The New Dictionary of Kleinian Thought*. New York: Routledge, 2011.

Tomkins, Silvan S. *Affect Imagery Consciousness*. Vols. 1–4. New York: Springer, 1962–3, 1991–2.

Wilson, Elizabeth A. *Gut Feminism*. Durham: Duke University Press, 2015.

Psychosomatic: Feminism and the Neurological Body. Duke University Press, 2004.

Winnicott, D. W. *Playing and Reality*. New York: Routledge, 2005.

The Global Turn: Thoreau and the Sixth Extinction

Adelson, Glenn, James Engell, Brent Ranalli, and K. P. Van Anglen, ed. *Environment: An Interdisciplinary Anthology*. New Haven: Yale University Press, 2008. Companion website: www.environmentanthology.org/.

Goodbody, Alex and Kate Rigby, ed. *Ecocritical Theory: New European Approaches*. Charlottesville: University of Virginia Press, 2011.

Heise, Ursula, Jon Christensen and Michelle Niemann, ed. *The Routledge Companion to the Environmental Humanities*. New York: Routledge, 2017.

Klein, Naomi. *This Changes Everything: Capitalism vs. the Climate*. New York: Simon & Schuster, 2015.

Latour, Bruno. *Facing Gaia: Eight Lectures on the New Climatic Regime*. Cambridge: Polity Press, 2017.

McNeill, J. R. *The Human Web: A Bird's Eye view of Human History*. New York: Norton, 2003.

Nixon, Rob. *Slow Violence and the Environmentalism of the Poor*. Cambridge: Harvard University Press, 2013.

Scranton, Roy. *Learning to Die in the Anthropocene: Reflections on the End of a Civilization*. San Francisco: City Lights, 2015.

Tsing, Anna Lowenhaupt. *The Mushroom at the End of the World*. Princeton: Princeton University Press, 2015.

Weisman, Alan. *The World without Us*. New York: St. Martin's Press, 2007.

Westling, Louise, ed. *The Cambridge Companion to Literature and the Environment*. Cambridge: Cambridge University Press, 2014.

Wilson, Edward O. *Half-Earth: Our Planet's Fight for Life*. New York: Liveright, 2016.

Literary Studies and Cognitive Science

Crane, Mary Thomas. *Shakespeare's Brain: Reading with Cognitive Theory*. Princeton: Princeton University Press, 2001.

Dissanayake, Ellen. *Art and Intimacy: How the Arts Began*. Seattle: University of Washington Press, 2000.

Herman, David. *Storytelling and the Sciences of Mind*. Cambridge: MIT Press, 2013.

Hogan, Patrick Colm. *The Mind and Its Stories: Narrative Universals and Human Emotion*. Cambridge: Cambridge University Press, 2003.

Lakoff, George and Mark Johnson. *Philosophy in the Flesh: The Embodied Mind and Its Challenge to Western Thought*. New York: Basic Books, 1999.

Miall, David S. *Literary Reading: Empirical and Theoretical Studies*. New York: Peter Lang, 2006.

Phillips, Natalie M. *Distraction: Problems of Attention in Eighteenth-Century Literature*. Baltimore: Johns Hopkins University Press, 2016.

Richardson, Alan. *The Neural Sublime: Cognitive Theories and Romantic Texts*. Baltimore: Johns Hopkins University Press, 2010.

Richardson, Alan and Ellen Spolsky, eds. *The Work of Fiction: Cognition, Culture, and Complexity*. Aldershot: Ashgate, 2004.

Scarry, Elaine. *Dreaming by the Book*. New York: Farrar, Strauss, and Giroux, 1999.

Spolsky, Ellen. *Gaps in Nature: Literary Interpretation and the Modular Mind*. Albany: State University of New York Press, 1993.

Starr, G. Gabrielle, *Feeling Beauty: The Sister Arts and the Neuroscience of Aesthetic Experience*. Cambridge: MIT Press, 2013.

Turner, Mark. *The Literary Mind*. New York: Oxford University Press, 1996.

Zunshine, Lisa. *Why We Read Fiction: Theory of Mind and the Novel*. Columbus: Ohio State University Press, 2006.

　ed. *Introduction to Cognitive Cultural Studies*. Baltimore: Johns Hopkins University Press, 2010.

　ed. *The Oxford Handbook of Cognitive Literary Studies*. Oxford: Oxford University Press, 2015.

Modernism, Technology, and the Life Sciences

Armstrong, Tim. *Modernism, Technology and the Body*. Cambridge: Cambridge University Press, 1998.

Bowler, Peter J. *Science for All: The Popularisation of Science in Early Twentieth-Century Britain*. Chicago: University of Chicago Press, 2009.

Clarke, Bruce. *Dora Marsden and Early Modernism: Gender, Individualism, Science*. Ann Arbor: University of Michigan Press, 1996.

Gordon, Craig A. *Literary Modernism, Bioscience, and Community in Early 20th Century Britain*. Houndmills: Palgrave Macmillan, 2007.

Holmes, John, ed. *Science in Modern Poetry: New Directions*. Liverpool: Liverpool University Press, 2012.

Martin, Kirsty. *Modernism and the Rhythms of Sympathy: Vernon Lee, Virginia Woolf, D.H. Lawrence*. Oxford: Oxford University Press, 2013.

McLaren, Angus. *Reproduction by Design: Sex, Robots, Trees, and Test-Tube Babies in Interwar Britain*. Chicago: University of Chicago Press, 2012.

Norris, Margot. *Beasts of the Modern Imagination: Darwin, Nietzsche, Kafka, Ernst, and Lawrence*. Baltimore: Johns Hopkins University Press, 1985.

Parrinder, Patrick. *Utopian Literature and Science: From the Scientific Revolution to Brave New World and Beyond*. Houndmills: Palgrave Macmillan, 2015.

Randall, Bryony. *Modernism, Daily Time and Everyday Life*. Cambridge: Cambridge University Press, 2007.

Wainwright, Michael. *Toward a Sociobiological Hermeneutic*. New York: Palgrave Macmillan, 2012.

The Long History of Cognitive Practices: Literacy, Numeracy, Aesthetics

There is no up-to-date historical introduction to ancient science. However, there is an excellent, brief introduction to the question of the historical and cognitive context for the specific contribution made to science by the Greeks:

Lloyd, Geoffrey E. R. *Demystifying Mentalities*. Cambridge: Cambridge University Press, 1990.

In general, the best resource now for the study of ancient science is

Keyser, Paul T. and Georgia L. Irby-Massie, ed. *Encyclopedia of Ancient Natural Scientists: The Greek Tradition and Its Many Heirs*. London: Routledge, 2009.

And there is also a masterful study of genre in ancient science:

Asper, Markus. 2007. *Griechische Wissenschaftstexte: Formen, Funktionen, Differenzierungsgeschichten*. Stuttgart: Franz Steiner, 2007.

The cognitive study of Greek mathematics was pioneered by

Netz, Reviel. *The Shaping of Deduction in Greek Mathematics: A Study in Cognitive History*. Cambridge: Cambridge University Press, 1999.

And a useful variation on the same approach can be found in

Acerbi, Fabio. *Il silenzio delle sirene: La matematica greca antica*. Rome: Carocci, 2010.

A study in the aesthetic character of Greek mathematics is

Netz, Reviel. *Ludic Proof: Greek Mathematics and the Alexandrian Aesthetic*. Cambridge: Cambridge University Press, 2009.

The interface between literature and medicine has been explored most effectively by

Holmes, Brooke. 2010. *The Symptom and the Subject: The Emergence of the Physical Body in Ancient Greece*. Princeton: Princeton University Press, 2010.

We now have an entire array of scholarship on Galen, for which a very accessible introduction may be found in

Mattern, Susan P. *The Prince of Medicine: Galen in the Roman Empire*. Oxford: Oxford University Press, 2013.

Going beyond Galen, we are fortunate in that one of the major lost Greek medical authors – Herophilus – has been studied so magisterially by von Staden, that this study can be taken, effectively, as the best introduction available to the study of ancient medicine:

von Staden, Heinrich. *Herophilus: The Art of Medicine in Early Alexandria*. Cambridge: Cambridge University Press, 1989.

I note in this article the significance of media. For Greek practices of reading and writing, the best guide now is

Johnson, William A. *Readers and Reading Culture in the High Roman Empire: A Study of Elite Communities*. Oxford: Oxford University Press, 2010.

For the much more specific media of counter-calculation, see

Schärlig, Alain. *Compter avec des cailloux: Le calcul élémentaire sur l'abaque chez les anciens Grecs.* Lausanne: Presses polytechniques et universitaires romandes, 2001.

I emphasize throughout the Greek contribution. Recently, more light has been shed on Roman science:

Lehoux, Daryn. *What Did the Romans Know? An Inquiry into Science and Worldmaking.* Chicago: University of Chicago Press, 2012.

I also emphasize the theoretical sciences, and a useful corrective is

Cuomo, Serafina. *Technology and Culture in Greek and Roman Antiquity.* Cambridge: Cambridge University Press, 2007.

Indeed, one of the most promising recent works in the literary study of science involves, precisely, the study of technical literature is

Roby, Courtney A. *Technical Ekphrasis in Greek and Roman Science and Literature: The Written Machine between Alexandria and Rome.* Cambridge: Cambridge University Press, 2016.

Futures Past and Present: Literature and Science in an Age of Whitehead

Bais, Sander. *The Equations: Icons of Knowledge.* Cambridge: Harvard University Press, 2005.

Epperson, Michael. *Quantum Mechanics and the Philosophy of Alfred North Whitehead.* New York: Fordham University Press, 2004.

Fletcher, Angus. *A New Theory for American Poetry: Democracy, the Environment, and the Future of Imagination.* Cambridge: Harvard University Press, 2006.

Ford, Lewis S. *The Emergence of Whitehead's Metaphysics, 1925–1929.* Albany: State University of New York Press, 1984.

Green, Herb. *Painting the Mental Continuum: Perception and Meaning in the Making.* Berkeley: Berkeley Hills Books, 2003.

Haraway, Donna J. *Modest_Witness@Second_Millennium.FemaleMan©_Meets_Onco Mouse™.* New York: Routledge, 1997.

James, William. *A Pluralistic Universe: Hibbert Lectures at Manchester College on the Present Situation in Philosophy.* Lincoln: University of Nebraska Press, 1996.

Langer, Susanne K. *Mind: An Essay on Human Feeling.* Abridged edition. Baltimore: Johns Hopkins Press, 1988.

Latour, Bruno. *An Inquiry into Modes of Existence: An Anthropology of the Moderns.* Cambridge: Harvard University Press, 2013; modesofexistence.org.

Pesic, Peter. *Music and the Making of Modern Science.* Cambridge: MIT Press, 2014.

Robbin, Tony. *Shadows of Reality: The Fourth Dimension in Relativity, Cubism, and Modern Thought.* New Haven: Yale University Press, 2006.

Waddington, Conrad H. *Behind Appearance: A Study of the Relations between Painting and the Natural Sciences in this Century.* Cambridge: MIT Press, 1970.

Wilson, Mark. *Wandering Significance: An Essay on Conceptual Behavior.* Oxford: Oxford University Press, 2006.

Wimsatt, William C. *Re-Engineering Philosophy for Limited Beings: Piecewise Approximations to Reality*. Cambridge: Harvard University Press, 2007.

Wright, Jay. *Music's Mask and Measure* ["Equations One to Five"]. Chicago: Flood Editions, 2007.

Zammito, John. *A Nice Derangement of Epistemes: Post-Positivism in the Study of Science from Quine to Latour*. Chicago: University of Chicago Press, 2004.

Wilde, Oscar, 235
Williams, William Carlos, 45, 49, 224,
    236, 237
Wilson, E. O., 8, 220n8, 259
    and biodiversity, 198
    See also consilience
Wilson, Edmund, 4
Winnicott, D. W., 178, 182–4
wisdom, 130n27
    contrasted with demonstration, 48, 50
Wolfe, Cary, 127
Wolfram, Stephen, 139, 140
wolves, 200, 201–2
    gray wolf, 201
Wonders and the Order of Nature (Daston
    and Park), 58
Woolgar, Steve, 8–9, 121, 136, 150n2, 158
Wordsworth, William, 3, 216, 258–9, 263–4,
    267, 271
world, 60n26, 98, 151n19, 173n32, 231
    actual, 51, 262, 263–4
    another, or different, 31, 32
    Darwinian, 68, 271
    destructive, 64, 128
    enchantment of, 31, 64
    free from opposition between "sound"
        science and fiction (or speculation), 29
    immaterial, 137
    material, 50–1, 82, 123–6, 127, 142,
        253
    Mediterranean, 243, 251
    messy, 31, 36, 37
    of experience, 34, 158–60, 163, 165,
        170, 271
    of fluxes and flows, 76, 165, 166, 271
    of objects and events, 161, 169

    our contrasted with "the," 29, 30, 31–2,
        158, 260, 271
    real, 51, 123, 171n6, 262
    sensible, or sensory, 49, 51–2, 106, 270
    social, 70, 71, 160
    without humans, 128
    See also disenchantment; Earth; Gaia;
        nature; New World; rarefaction;
        universe
world literature, 76, 195
World of Warcraft, 140
"World's End" (Empson), 99
worlding, 31, *See also* Haraway
world-planning, 228, 229–30, 231, 232, *See
    also* control
Wright, Jay, v, 269–70
writing, 132–3, 134, 136–8, 228, 242–54
    and performance, 242–3, 245, 253–4
    science and, 64–5, 121, 137, 144–5, 243–54
    technologies of, 8, 15, 137
    See also consciousness; discourse;
        inscription
Writing Science, 132, 135, 136–7, 138,
    142–3, 149
    contrasted with structural linguistics,
        132–4

x-rays, 135

Yeats, W. B., 226, 229, 232, 233

Zammito, John H., 18n17
zero, 50, 137
zoology, 81, *See also* ethology; *names of
    individual species*
Zunshine, Lisa, 208, 212, 217–18

Cambridge Companions to...

AUTHORS

Edward Albee edited by Stephen J. Bottoms

Margaret Atwood edited by Coral Ann Howells

W. H. Auden edited by Stan Smith

Jane Austen edited by Edward Copeland and Juliet McMaster (second edition)

Balzac edited by Owen Heathcote and Andrew Watts

Beckett edited by John Pilling

Bede edited by Scott DeGregorio

Aphra Behn edited by Derek Hughes and Janet Todd

Walter Benjamin edited by David S. Ferris

William Blake edited by Morris Eaves

Boccaccio edited by Guyda Armstrong, Rhiannon Daniels, and Stephen J. Milner

Jorge Luis Borges edited by Edwin Williamson

Brecht edited by Peter Thomson and Glendyr Sacks (second edition)

The Brontës edited by Heather Glen

Bunyan edited by Anne Dunan-Page

Frances Burney edited by Peter Sabor

Byron edited by Drummond Bone

Albert Camus edited by Edward J. Hughes

Willa Cather edited by Marilee Lindemann

Cervantes edited by Anthony J. Cascardi

Chaucer edited by Piero Boitani and Jill Mann (second edition)

Chekhov edited by Vera Gottlieb and Paul Allain

Kate Chopin edited by Janet Beer

Caryl Churchill edited by Elaine Aston and Elin Diamond

Cicero edited by Catherine Steel

Coleridge edited by Lucy Newlyn

Wilkie Collins edited by Jenny Bourne Taylor

Joseph Conrad edited by J. H. Stape

H. D. edited by Nephie J. Christodoulides and Polina Mackay

Dante edited by Rachel Jacoff (second edition)

Daniel Defoe edited by John Richetti

Don DeLillo edited by John N. Duvall

Charles Dickens edited by John O. Jordan

Emily Dickinson edited by Wendy Martin

John Donne edited by Achsah Guibbory

Dostoevskii edited by W. J. Leatherbarrow

Theodore Dreiser edited by Leonard Cassuto and Claire Virginia Eby

John Dryden edited by Steven N. Zwicker

W. E. B. Du Bois edited by Shamoon Zamir

George Eliot edited by George Levine

T. S. Eliot edited by A. David Moody

Ralph Ellison edited by Ross Posnock

Ralph Waldo Emerson edited by Joel Porte and Saundra Morris

William Faulkner edited by Philip M. Weinstein

Henry Fielding edited by Claude Rawson

F. Scott Fitzgerald edited by Ruth Prigozy

Flaubert edited by Timothy Unwin

E. M. Forster edited by David Bradshaw

Benjamin Franklin edited by Carla Mulford

Brian Friel edited by Anthony Roche

Robert Frost edited by Robert Faggen

Gabriel García Márquez edited by Philip Swanson

Elizabeth Gaskell edited by Jill L. Matus

Goethe edited by Lesley Sharpe

Günter Grass edited by Stuart Taberner

Thomas Hardy edited by Dale Kramer

David Hare edited by Richard Boon

Nathaniel Hawthorne edited by Richard Millington

Seamus Heaney edited by Bernard O'Donoghue

Ernest Hemingway edited by Scott Donaldson

Homer edited by Robert Fowler

Horace edited by Stephen Harrison

Ted Hughes edited by Terry Gifford

Ibsen edited by James McFarlane

Henry James edited by Jonathan Freedman

Samuel Johnson edited by Greg Clingham

Ben Jonson edited by Richard Harp and Stanley Stewart

James Joyce edited by Derek Attridge (second edition)

Kafka edited by Julian Preece

Mary Wollstonecraft edited by Claudia L. Johnson

Virginia Woolf edited by Susan Sellers (second edition)

Wordsworth edited by Stephen Gill

W. B. Yeats edited by Marjorie Howes and John Kelly

Xenophon edited by Michael A. Flower

Zola edited by Brian Nelson

TOPICS

The Actress edited by Maggie B. Gale and John Stokes

The African American Novel edited by Maryemma Graham

The African American Slave Narrative edited by Audrey A. Fisch

Theatre History by David Wiles and Christine Dymkowski

African American Theatre by Harvey Young

Allegory edited by Rita Copeland and Peter Struck

American Crime Fiction edited by Catherine Ross Nickerson

American Gothic edited by Jeffrey Andrew Weinstock

American Modernism edited by Walter Kalaidjian

American Poetry Since 1945 edited by Jennifer Ashton

American Realism and Naturalism edited by Donald Pizer

American Travel Writing edited by Alfred Bendixen and Judith Hamera

American Women Playwrights edited by Brenda Murphy

Ancient Rhetoric edited by Erik Gunderson

Arthurian Legend edited by Elizabeth Archibald and Ad Putter

Australian Literature edited by Elizabeth Webby

The Beats edited by Stephen Belletto

British Black and Asian Literature (1945-2010) edited by Deirdre Osborne

British Literature of the French Revolution edited by Pamela Clemit

British Romanticism edited by Stuart Curran (second edition)

British Romantic Poetry edited by James Chandler and Maureen N. McLane

British Theatre, 1730–1830, edited by Jane Moody and Daniel O'Quinn

Canadian Literature edited by Eva-Marie Kröller (second edition)

Children's Literature edited by M. O. Grenby and Andrea Immel

The Classic Russian Novel edited by Malcolm V. Jones and Robin Feuer Miller

Contemporary Irish Poetry edited by Matthew Campbell

Creative Writing edited by David Morley and Philip Neilsen

Crime Fiction edited by Martin Priestman

Dracula edited by Roger Luckhurst

Early Modern Women's Writing edited by Laura Lunger Knoppers

The Eighteenth-Century Novel edited by John Richetti

Eighteenth-Century Poetry edited by John Sitter

Emma edited by Peter Sabor

English Literature, 1500–1600 edited by Arthur F. Kinney

English Literature, 1650–1740 edited by Steven N. Zwicker

English Literature, 1740-1830 edited by Thomas Keymer and Jon Mee

English Literature, 1830-1914 edited by Joanne Shattock

English Novelists edited by Adrian Poole

English Poetry, Donne to Marvell edited by Thomas N. Corns

English Poets edited by Claude Rawson

English Renaissance Drama, second edition edited by A. R. Braunmuller and Michael Hattaway

English Renaissance Tragedy edited by Emma Smith and Garrett A. Sullivan Jr.

English Restoration Theatre edited by Deborah C. Payne Fisk

The Epic edited by Catherine Bates

Erotic Literature edited by Bradford Mudge

European Modernism edited by Pericles Lewis

European Novelists edited by Michael Bell

Fairy Tales edited by Maria Tatar